# Evolution and Procedures in Central Banking

This volume collects the proceedings from a conference on the evolution and practice of central banking sponsored by the Central Bank Institute of the Federal Reserve Bank of Cleveland. The articles and discussants' comments in this volume largely focus on two questions: the need for central banks, and how to maintain price stability once they are established. The questions addressed include whether large banks (or coalitions of small banks) can substitute for government regulation and central bank liquidity provision; whether the future will have fewer central banks or more; the possibility of private means to deliver a uniform currency; if competition across sovereign currencies can ensure global price stability; the role of learning (and unlearning) the lessons of past inflationary episodes in understanding central bank behavior; and an analysis of the most recent experiment in central banking, the European Central Bank.

**David E. Altig** is the Vice President and Director of Research for the Federal Reserve Bank of Cleveland. He manages the department's money/macroeconomics division and specializes in monetary and fiscal policy research. His current work focuses on tax policy, business cycle issues, and monetary policy analysis. Dr. Altig has served on the faculties of Case Western Reserve University, Cleveland State University, John Carroll University, Indiana University, and the University of Chicago. He holds a doctoral degree in economics from Brown University.

**Bruce D. Smith** was the Hofheinz Regent's Professor of Economics at the University of Texas–Austin and was the author of more than 90 articles on the topics of monetary economics, banking, and monetary history. He served on the editorial boards of the *Journal of Economic Theory, Economic Theory, Journal of Financial Intermediation*, and *Macroeconomic Dynamics*. In addition, Dr. Smith was a Central Bank Institute scholar at the Federal Reserve Bank of Cleveland and a consultant to the Federal Reserve Banks of Atlanta, Kansas City, Minneapolis, New York, and St. Louis, as well as the Board of Governors of the Federal Reserve System. Dr. Smith passed away in July 2002.

# Evolution and Procedures in Central Banking

Edited by
**DAVID E. ALTIG**
*Federal Reserve Bank of Cleveland*

**BRUCE D. SMITH**
*University of Texas*

HG
1811
E94
2003
WEB

![CAMBRIDGE UNIVERSITY PRESS]

PUBLISHED BY THE PRESS SYNDICATE OF THE UNIVERSITY OF CAMBRIDGE
The Pitt Building, Trumpington Street, Cambridge, United Kingdom

CAMBRIDGE UNIVERSITY PRESS
The Edinburgh Building, Cambridge CB2 2RU, UK
40 West 20th Street, New York, NY 10011-4211, USA
477 Williamstown Road, Port Melbourne, VIC 3207, Australia
Ruiz de Alarcón 13, 28014 Madrid, Spain
Dock House, The Waterfront, Cape Town 8001, South Africa

http://www.cambridge.org

First published 2003

Printed in the United Kingdom at the University Press, Cambridge

*Typeface* Times Roman 10/12          *System* Quark Express [AU]

*A catalog record for this book is available from the British Library.*

*Library of Congress Cataloging in Publication data available*

ISBN 0 521 81427 8 hardback

# Contents

# Contents

# Contributors

**Jasmina Arifovic**
Simon Fraser University

**John H. Boyd**
University of Minnesota

**Matthias Brückner**
Center for European Integration Studies

**James Bullard**
Federal Reserve Bank of St. Louis

**Stephen G. Cecchetti**
The Ohio State University

**Bruce Champ**
Federal Reserve Bank of Cleveland

**Vitor Gaspar**
European Central Bank

**Mark Gertler**
New York University

**Charles Goodhart**
London School of Economics

**Gary Gorton**
University of Pennsylvania

**Edward J. Green**
Federal Reserve Bank of Chicago

**Lixin Huang**
University of Pennsylvania

Contributors

**Donald L. Kohn**
Board of Governors of the Federal Reserve System

**Randall S. Kroszner**
University of Chicago

**Jeffrey M. Lacker**
Federal Reserve Bank of Richmond

**Ross Levine**
University of Minnesota

**Arthur J. Rolnick**
Federal Reserve Bank of Minneapolis

**Thomas J. Sargent**
Stanford University

**Klaus Schmidt-Hebbel**
Central Bank of Chile

**Christopher A. Sims**
Princeton University

**Bruce D. Smith**
University of Texas–Austin

**Jeremy C. Stein**
Harvard University

**Alberto Trejos**
Instituto Centroamericano de Administración de Empresas

**Jürgen von Hagen**
Center for European Integration Studies

**Neil Wallace**
Pennsylvania State University

**Warren E. Weber**
Federal Reserve Bank of Minneapolis

# Acknowledgments

The essays in this volume represent the collected contributions from a conference originally titled "The Origins and Evolution of Central Banking," sponsored on May 21–22 by the Central Bank Institute of the Federal Reserve Bank of Cleveland. The product is the result of much hard work by many industrious and committed people. Beyond those who are acknowledged elsewhere in this volume, special mention goes to Kathy Popovich, Mary Mackay, and, especially, Connie Jones for her patient and tireless administrative assistance; Darlene Craven, Patricia DeMaioribus, and Deborah Zorska for shepherding our end of the production process; Scott Parris for being our advocate at Cambridge University Press; and Monica Crabtree-Ruesser for making sure that whatever else needed to get done got done.

And, oh yes—the views expressed herein do not necessarily reflect those of the Federal Reserve Bank of Cleveland, the Board of Governors, or anyone else in the Federal Reserve System.

# In Memoriam

On July 9, 2002, as the final touches were being prepared to bring this conference volume to the public, Bruce Smith, the Hofheinz Regent's Professor of Economics at the University of Texas–Austin and Central Bank Institute scholar for the Federal Reserve Bank of Cleveland, passed away. It is no exaggeration to say that this volume likely would not have seen the light of day without Bruce. The effort here reflects Bruce's vision and hard work from conception, through organization of the program, to all but the smallest details in preparation of the volume.

The articles collected here represent the first formal conference of the Federal Reserve Bank of Cleveland's Central Bank Institute. The Institute was founded to promote research and education on central banks as institutions. Specifically, with the Institute we hope to stimulate thinking on all aspects of central banking, from payments to supervision and regulation to monetary policy, and the connections (or lack thereof) across these varied activities.

In late 1999, when the Bank decided to create the Central Bank Institute, our first course of action was to enlist the support of a small number of eminent scholars to assist us in the endeavor. We established three criteria for our choice: First, the individuals would need to be widely published and recognized as intellectual leaders in the profession. Second, we were interested in individuals whose research interests had been, and would be, at the frontier of questions relevant to understanding the past, present, and future of central banking. Third, we were looking for scholars who had a demonstrated commitment to the future of the Federal Reserve Bank of Cleveland and the Federal Reserve System.

The mere recitation of these criteria brings Bruce to mind. The volume and influence of his work placed him among the elite of monetary economists of his generation. His research covered virtually all areas of interest to central bankers, from payments mechanisms to supervision and regulation to monetary policy. To the very end, he was an unfailing mentor and advocate for the Research Department, the Central Bank Institute, the Cleveland Fed, and, indeed, the Federal Reserve System.

Bruce's influence can be found everywhere in the Central Bank Institute's activities and programs. In fact, it was to Bruce that we turned to produce the "white paper" that would, and still does, provide the vision that underlies the Institute's core research mission. (That article can still be found at *www.clev.frb.org/CentralBankInstitute/ cbi.pdf.*)

It was only natural that we would ask Bruce to organize the Institute's inaugural conference. In fact, there really could have been no other choice. In his amazingly prolific—if all too short—career, Bruce's work practically defined the nexus between payments, banking, and monetary research. Any doubt about this can be quickly dispelled by perusing the list of his published work provided in the fall 2002 issue of the Federal Reserve Bank of Minneapolis' *Quarterly Review*.

Besides the breadth and volume of his work, one thing that stands out about his record was the large number of coauthors who had the privilege to work with him. This is not just a testament to his intellectual capacity, but to his generosity as well. Bruce's death was an enormous loss to the academic community, to the Federal Reserve System, and to us at the Federal Reserve Bank of Cleveland. His professional contributions will be difficult to replace. His friendship will be impossible to replace.

# Introduction

In his book *The Cash Nexus*, historian Niall Ferguson felt it necessary to argue against the view that it is entirely economic forces that have shaped the history and current state of societies around the world. While we would not take the extreme view that only economic factors are important in understanding history, it is certainly true that economic forces have had a huge impact on many aspects of society. Central banks are, and have been, a major economic force, influencing a wide range of other economic events and, as a consequence, the course of history. But a tantalizing and important question remains: Are central banks an inevitable historical outcome, or just one of many possible institutions that can (and will) arise in the course of economic development?

As we enter the twenty-first century, it seems natural to reevaluate the appropriate roles—if not, in fact, the need—for central banks. To foster this reevaluation, in the spring of 2001 the Federal Reserve Bank of Cleveland held a conference on "The Origins and Evolution of Central Banking." The purpose of the conference was to shed light on how central banks have come to be what they are, what their objectives ought to be, how central banks should operate to best achieve these objectives, and what kinds of challenges such institutions might face in the twenty-first century.

There have been few times in history when so many fundamental questions about the role of central banks have been on the table simultaneously. We have recently witnessed major revolutions in the technology of transacting, and undoubtedly we will witness many more. These fundamental changes raise many questions that central banks must confront. What role should central banks play in the payments system? Can central banks promote useful innovations in the technology for making payments, or does their presence in the payments system inhibit innovations that would occur otherwise? As payments system innovations have continued, the need for base money in transactions has declined and will continue to decline dramatically—at least within the United States. What

challenges does this pose for central banks? With a decline in the use of central
bank liabilities in transactions, can central banks conduct monetary policy in traditional ways, or will their operating procedures need to be dramatically revised?
Does a declining role for central bank liabilities in transactions pose a challenge to
the maintenance of a stable price level?

Spurred in part by technological advances, the legal environment in which central banks operate has experienced rapid and dramatic change as well. Recent
changes in banking legislation in the United States have made it possible for banks
and nonbanks to play many new roles. This fact raises questions about the regulation of banks and of entities that provide payments services but do not operate
under bank charters. What regulation is needed, and is the regulation of payments
service providers optimally coupled with other central banking functions, such as
the conduct of monetary policy? Should the "safety net" provided to banks be
extended as they take on new functions and as nonbanks begin to perform many of
the functions traditionally associated with banking? Some studies[1] suggest the provision of banking system safety nets, such as deposit insurance, actually increases
the likelihood of a banking crisis, and that the existence of such safety nets raises
the social costs of banking crises when they do occur. In the end, is the existence
of a banking system safety net socially optimal?

These questions, of course, evoke other long-standing economic issues. To what
extent do banks—or other payments service providers—need to be regulated at all?
Why isn't market discipline sufficient for banks, as we often take it to be for other
industries? Can coalitions of banks perform what amounts to "peer monitoring,"
thereby rendering government regulation unnecessary? And can organizations such
as clearinghouses effectively provide liquidity as needed, as they have tried to do at
various times in U.S. history before the advent of the Federal Reserve System?

The last question is an illustration of a historically important issue that has
recently reemerged. Another example is the private provision of money. Hayek
(1976) and others have argued that "the market" can provide currency as effectively—if not more so—than the government. The real bills doctrine, while not necessarily asserting Hayek's claim, certainly suggests that appropriately backed provision of currency and currency substitutes by private entities poses no threat to price
stability or to the general functioning of the economy. This contrasts starkly with
the sentiments of Friedman (1960) (and others), who argues that lending should be
strictly segregated from currency issue.[2] In Friedman's view, the comingling of
lending activity and the provision of payments instruments is a formula for creating "excessive economic volatility"—leading him to advocate that providers of
payments instruments face 100 percent reserve requirements.[3] This, of course, is

---

[1]  For instance, Demirguc-Kunt and Detragiache (2000) or Boyd, Kwak, and Smith (2002).
[2]  See Sargent and Wallace (1982) for a modern interpretation of these issues.
[3]  Some revisions of this viewpoint can, however, be found in Friedman (1960).

an extreme version of other calls for "narrow banking," reflecting historical arguments that when private agents can create substitutes for base money, optimism or pessimism can cause the money stock to expand and contract, thereby creating multiplicities of equilibria. Many of these equilibria will display economic volatility that is a result of self-fulfilling prophecies.[4]

The history of banking and private currency provision is indeed marred by a long sequence of banking panics, some of which were accompanied by huge fluctuations in the value of privately issued currencies. The driving force behind the creation of the Federal Reserve System was the search for a way to prevent these events, or at least to mitigate their severity. But is it clear that modern economies need central banks to respond to extreme events, such as banking crises or stock market crashes? If so, how should central banks respond? Even today, thinking on this issue seems to have advanced little since Bagehot (1873), who argued that in a crisis, central banks should lend liberally on collateral that "would be good" under normal circumstances, but should charge a high rate of interest. How well does this advice apply today?

The set of questions confronting central banks—or the governments that create them—are even more complex in an international context. What kinds of exchange rate regimes contribute (or not) to banking and financial crises? Is the choice of an exchange rate regime just a way of determining whether a crisis manifests itself as a currency or a banking crisis, as Chang and Velasco (2000) suggest? When events such as the Asian financial crisis of 1997 occur, who should be the lender of last resort or the provider of the safety net? Should it be the national central bank, an international organization like the International Monetary Fund, or some combination of both?

Even if there is a need for central banks in their modern variations, does every country need one? The number of national currencies in the world is shrinking. Ecuador and El Salvador, for example, have formally adopted the dollar as their national currency, [5] and this kind of complete, or near complete, dollarization has been debated in many Latin American countries. In Europe, 13 national currencies already have been abandoned in favor of the euro, and more will certainly follow.

These observations raise some obvious questions: Which countries are good candidates for dollarization?[6] Which countries are good candidates for a new common currency, such as the euro? In monetary unions characterized by limited political unification, such as the European Monetary Union, how should monetary policy be formulated and implemented?

---

4 See Smith (1988) for a formalization of this idea.
5 Cohen (2001) classifies Ecuador and El Salvador as "near-dollarized": "Independent states that rely primarily on one or more foreign currencies but also issue a token local currency" (22).
6 See the May 2001 *Journal of Money, Credit, and Banking*—Federal Reserve Bank of Cleveland conference symposium issue for several different perspectives on dollarization.

Dollarization or currency unions raise questions as well for countries only peripherally involved in the adoption decision. For instance, what are the implications for the United States if many countries, or some large country like Mexico, unilaterally dollarize? Does this alter how United States monetary policy should be conducted? Does dollarization create channels through which volatility elsewhere can be transmitted to the U.S. economy? And, if the answer is yes, how should the Federal Reserve System respond to this possibility?[7]

Alternatively, one could ask how the formation of third-party monetary unions affects the policymaking of other nations. Will the European Monetary Union and the formation of the European Central Bank affect the way monetary policy will be—or ought to be—conducted in the United States or elsewhere? When one set of countries forms a common currency area, how should other countries respond? Does the formation of a common currency area make other areas more or less attractive?

All of these issues are inherently linked to questions about what central bank objectives should be and how they can or should be best achieved. There seems to be a consensus that the obvious objective of a central bank should be price stability: the maintenance of low and relatively stable rates of inflation. It may be surprising that such a consensus could have been achieved despite the academic literature, which so far has identified few major consequences for social welfare, even under sustained and relatively high rates of inflation. Nonetheless, such a consensus does seem to exist. Thus, it is natural to ask what kinds of challenges central banks face in maintaining price stability, and what mechanisms can best maintain stable price levels. Inflation targeting is now commonly advocated.[8] The maintenance of strong versions of fixed exchange rate regimes, such as currency boards or outright dollarization, is often suggested for places like Latin America.[9] Are these obvious, natural institutional choices, even if we agree the maintenance of price stability is an appropriate objective for a central bank?[10]

Moreover, ever-evolving environmental factors may threaten the maintenance of low inflation rates even among those institutions that have thus far proven capable of delivering on that objective. One is the need for seigniorage revenue, and the other is the (possibly misguided) view that central banks face an exploitable Phillip's curve trade-off. But less traditional problems also exist. For instance, in the United States, the use of central bank liabilities in domestic transactions is declining; this trend is expected to continue, and perhaps to accelerate.[11] Furthermore, traditional sources of demand for central bank liabilities, such as reserve requirements, have less and less significance in advanced economies such

---

[7]   See Altig (2002) or Altig or Nosal (forthcoming) for informal discussions of these issues.
[8]   See, for instance, Leiderman and Svensson (1995) or Bernanke et al. (1999).
[9]   See, for instance, Calvo (2001).
[10]  See Bencivenga, Huybens, and Smith (2000) for an argument that inflation targeting and fixed exchange rate regimes create more scope for the indeterminacy of equilibrium and for endogenously arising volatility than does a regime of flexible exchange rates with a low and relatively constant rate of money growth.
[11]  See Schreft and Smith (2000) for a discussion.

as the United States. Does the decline in the demand for central bank liabilities threaten price stability? How does it affect the feasibility of various methods of conducting monetary policy?

Similarly, the potential for private agents to create currency substitutes—which is now legally and technologically feasible in the United States, for example—raises all of the questions we have already touched on: about the central bank's ability to guarantee price stability, about the feasibility of different policy operating procedures, and about the central bank's ability to maintain a uniform currency. Relatively little modern research has been done on the determination of the price level or rates of interest when private agents can issue liabilities that compete with currency. When many private entities can create currency substitutes, the following questions immediately arise: Will we observe several currencies that coexist but circulate against each other, or against outside money, at discounts or premiums that potentially fluctuate? If so, what are the economic consequences? Will privately issued currencies create a "race to the bottom" (the Gresham's law implication that poorly backed currencies will drive out better backed and more stable private currencies)? Or will the outcome be a Hayekian "race to the top" (in which the market disciplines the issuers of private currencies and guarantees that only adequately backed currencies will circulate)?[12] And how does the answer to these questions affect what the central bank can and should do when private agents compete with it in the provision of currency?

Clearly, we have laid out a dauntingly large, diverse, and difficult set of questions. No single conference or volume could reasonably be expected to address all of them. The chapters in this volume largely focus on two questions: The need for central banks, and the maintenance of price stability by central banking institutions as we know them today.

## DO WE NEED CENTRAL BANKS?

Three papers in this volume—by Gary Gorton and Lixin Huang, Art Rolnick, Bruce Smith, and Warren Weber, and Alberto Trejos—explore the extent to which central banks are necessary to improve the functioning of an economy's banking and payments system.

Gorton and Huang explore whether large private banks or coalitions of small banks can effectively eliminate the need for government regulation of banking and the need for an outside entity—like a central bank—to provide liquidity in the event of a banking crisis. The authors proceed from the observation that central banks emerged as a response to systemic banking crises, but that some banking systems—such as that in the United States—seem to have been particularly prone to such problems. Others—the Canadian banking system, for instance—seem to

---

[12] See Schreft (1997) for a presentation of alternative points of view on this topic.

have been relatively immune. Gorton and Huang relate these differences in susceptibility to panics to the industrial organization of the banking system.

The analysis of Gorton and Huang's paper is based on the idea, familiar from Diamond and Dybvig (1983), that banking panics can emerge as part of the mechanism by which market participants effectively discipline and monitor banks. In particular, threats of large-scale withdrawals of deposits can be a means of deterring the moral hazard problems confronted in banking.[13] In Gorton and Huang's framework, however, the formation of bank coalitions, such as clearinghouses, also can serve as a device for resolving moral hazard. In addition, these coalitions can create liquidity in the event of a panic, in effect becoming their own lender of last resort.

The setup is relatively straightforward. Banks are imperfectly diversified and better informed than depositors about the return on their assets. Moral hazard problems arise in banking because banks may liquidate funds to their own advantage when they know the return on their assets is going to be low. To confront the resulting agency problem, depositors require banks to hold reserves. When reserve levels are high, banks are less likely to liquidate projects early in response to low returns. But to force banks to hold high levels of reserves, there must be some probability that withdrawal demand will be high. Thus, some potential for "panics" is required to induce banks to hold the necessary level of reserves.

In this context, Gorton and Huang consider three alternative structures for the banking system. One is a system of small unit banks, meant to approximate the situation that prevailed in the United States before the Federal Reserve System was created. Under unit banking, banks hold inefficiently high levels of reserves to reduce the potential for panics and to control the moral hazard problem. An alternative organizational structure allows unit banks to form bank coalitions. When banks enter a coalition, they agree to an asset-sharing rule in the event of a panic, and they agree to hold a certain level of reserves. The coalition becomes active only in the event of a panic. Because asset-sharing rules can create an "externality" in the event of a panic, banks have incentives to monitor each other. This, along with the potential for sharing reserves, mitigates the moral hazard and permits banks to economize on reserve holdings. Hence, the resulting allocation under the coalition structure is more efficient than that attained by a system of strictly independent unit banks.

Gorton and Huang also consider the possibility of a single large bank, which internalizes the externality that exists under a coalition of unit banks. Moreover, because a large bank is better diversified than many small banks, depositors are not disadvantaged by their lack of knowledge about the idiosyncratic component of returns on bank assets. Hence, the agency problem between banks and depositors is mitigated, again resulting in an efficiency gain. Indeed, in Gorton and Huang's

---

[13] See Calomiris and Kahn (1991) for an early formalization of this idea in the context of banking. The idea that the threat of funds withdrawals can discipline management in settings with agency conflicts was articulated earlier by Jensen and Meckling (1976) and Mayers and Smith (1981).

model, removing depositor concern about the idiosyncratic component of the return on bank assets eliminates the informational asymmetry in the economy altogether, thereby eliminating the disciplinary role of bank panics.

The Gorton–Huang analysis suggests that it is by no means clear that the creation of a central bank can improve upon the allocation of resources that can be achieved by an appropriately organized banking system. Furthermore, as the authors note, clearinghouses issued 2.5 percent of the money supply (in the form of clearinghouse loan certificates) in the U.S. banking panic of 1893 and 4.5 percent in the panic of 1907. The authors thus pose an interesting challenge to the purported need for a central bank to confront the problem of liquidity provision during bank panics.

There are, however, some natural questions raised by Gorton and Huang's analysis. For instance, was it difficult as a practical matter for depositors to infer information about the return on bank assets? In a world without deposit insurance, and without regulation of rates of interest on deposits, might depositor funds have been priced (that is, rates of interest on deposits been set) in a way that revealed information about bank asset returns? When bank shares were publicly traded, couldn't equity values have revealed similar information?

Perhaps more importantly, the Gorton–Huang analysis abstracts from monopoly distortions that might be expected to emerge in the case of a single large bank or multiple banks with the potential to collude through coalitions. John Boyd raises this point in his discussion and effectively asks whether the welfare losses from creating bank monopolies might not outweigh other welfare gains that result from moving away from strict unit banking. Boyd's point has broader generality in view of another common argument: that giving banks monopoly profits provides them with incentives to avoid taking excessively risky positions, which might lead to the loss of their "charter value." Granting banks monopoly power, whether by explicit design or mere acquiescence to monopolistic banking structures, may create welfare losses that more than offset the potential gains from reduced risk taking.

Boyd's discussion of Gorton and Huang raises another important consideration. In practice, large banks are not necessarily better diversified than small banks. Until we understand why this might be the case, we may want to exercise caution in considering arguments that proceed from the idea that a small number of large banks is necessarily preferable to a large number of small banks.

Rolnick, Smith, and Weber's contribution to this volume considers another problem—currency uniformity—which has, at some points in history, led to the creation of a central bank. In antebellum United States, the bulk of the money supply consisted of notes issued by private banks.[14] Almost all of these banks

---

[14] Temin (1969), for instance, estimates that privately issued notes constituted nearly 90 percent of the money supply in the late 1820s.

operated under state charters or state-created free banking laws. The state bank-notes often circulated against each other, and against government-issued coins, at market-determined exchange rates. In other words, discounts and, in some cases, premiums were observed on the notes of different banks. These discounts and premiums could and did vary over time and across locations. The result was that a variety of "dollars" with different market values were being issued by different entities—the currency was not uniform.

The lack of currency uniformity was viewed as an important economic problem throughout the history of the antebellum United States, at least by the federal government, and various attempts were made to produce a superior monetary payments system. Indeed, the Second Bank of the United States—the sole federally chartered bank in the country—was created with the explicit objective of creating a uniform currency. In 1832, Andrew Jackson vetoed the renewal of the Second Bank's charter, citing among his reasons the Bank's failure to produce a uniform currency. Rolnick, Smith, and Weber identify reasons why the Second Bank of the United States was unsuccessful in creating a uniform currency. But central to their paper is a private arrangement for creating a uniform currency that prevailed in New England from the mid-1820s until nearly the Civil War, the Suffolk Banking System.

The Suffolk Banking System was a private arrangement, operated by the Suffolk Bank of Boston, for clearing notes issued by various banks.[15] New England banks could join the Suffolk system and, if they did, the Suffolk Bank would clear their notes at par (face value). Moreover, the costs of note clearing were largely born by note issuers, a condition that Rolnick, Smith, and Weber identify as an important feature in creating an environment in which banknotes would circulate at par.[16] In fact, the Suffolk system succeeded in creating a uniform currency throughout New England. Indeed, Bruce Champ's discussion alludes to yet other private arrangements that came close to achieving currency uniformity within restricted geographical regions. As with the Gorton–Huang essay, Rolnick, Smith, and Weber challenge the need for central banks to guarantee currency uniformity or the existence of an efficient payments system.

Open questions do, of course, remain. In his remarks, Neil Wallace asks whether it is necessarily optimal for all privately issued notes to circulate at par.[17] In addition, the Suffolk system gave the Suffolk Bank monopoly power in certain areas, raising the same issues that John Boyd emphasizes in his comments on Gorton and Huang. Indeed, consistent with Boyd's criticism of market arrangements that work by giving some banks monopoly power, other work by Rolnick,

---

[15] See Rolnick, Smith, and Weber (1998) for a concise overview of the Suffolk Banking System and its activities.

[16] The costs of note clearing and presentation were born by the issuers of notes under the National Banking System in the United States as well.

[17] See also Smith and Weber (1999), who show that the resource allocation achieved through a private arrangement like the Suffolk system need not have dominated that achieved with private note issue, and with notes sometimes circulating at discounts.

Smith, and Weber (1998) suggests that most of the welfare gains generated by the Suffolk system accrued to the owners of the Suffolk Bank.

It may be premature to conclude that market arrangements can completely supplant central banks. At the very least, however, Rolnick, Smith, and Weber suggest that private market arrangements for issuing currency can work well in providing a uniform currency, calling into question the necessity of central banks regarding this particular function.

Alberto Trejos also contemplates the need for central banks (or lack thereof), although in a much different context. Trejos' contribution, in particular, is about "dollarization." Rooted in the modern context of almost universal governmental monopoly control of fiat money creation, discussions of dollarization proceed on the assumption that some large countries will issue currency—presumably, through a central bank. But dollarization is at least partly the international extension of the quest for a uniform currency. The impulse for a national central bank that Rolnick, Smith, and Weber take up echoes in the arguments for a single or small number of dominant central banks discussed by Trejos and other proponents of dollarization. But then, so may the private-market challenge posed by the Suffolk experiment. It seems useful to separate the question of the optimality of a uniform currency (or effectively uniform, in the case of different currencies that always trade at parity) from the question of whether the sources of money should be the institutions of government. The dollarization debate typically deals with the former question, letting stand an implicit affirmative answer to the latter. In this, Trejos' analysis is no exception.

Because of its international context, dollarization introduces elements that are absent when the questions are posed within the confines of individual sovereign nations. In particular, even if we conclude that a uniform currency is desirable, and even if we further conclude that currencies should be government liabilities, dollarization raises the question of whether every country needs a central bank. In effect, dollarization adds the optimal number of central banks to the list of unknowns.

As Trejos notes, de facto dollarization is well under way in many parts of Latin America. In Costa Rica, for instance, 61 percent of bank credit is dollar denominated. In Peru, the analogous number is 82 percent. There have been strong trends toward unofficial dollarization. In Peru, only 50 percent of bank credit was dollar denominated in 1990. Observations such as this lead Trejos to describe a vision of the future in which there will be many small countries with no national currency and no meaningful central bank. The potential benefit, according to Trejos, would be a reduction of the currency premium associated with international borrowing for the countries involved in dollarizing. Ross Levine, in his discussion, also notes the potential for reduced inflation and a resulting increase in long-term rates of real economic growth.[18]

This vision seems to stand in stark contrast to the one proposed in Randall Kroszner's paper. Kroszner envisions a world in which rapid advances in information technology make possible a system of "sophisticated barter" in which media of exchange take the form of multiple private mutual-fund-like assets. The few dominant central banks predicted by Trejos' framework vanish, replaced by (potentially many) providers of asset bundles bearing little resemblance to government-created fiat currency. Where dollarization feeds on the presumed benefits of eliminating exchange rate variation, such variation is intrinsic to sophisticated barter.

Trejos and Kroszner pose interesting yet opposing views on whether having a small number of central banks in the world will produce "good" economic outcomes. Kroszner focuses on the possibility that currency competition and, in particular, the ability of economic actors to use the currencies of other countries in transactions imposes discipline on national central banks. Indeed, Kroszner argues that currency competition has imposed significant discipline on national central banks and that this was an important factor in the large reductions observed in many national inflation rates during the 1990s. If there were a small number of national central banks, as Trejos envisions, would currency competition cease to discipline the remaining central banks? More specifically, would widespread dollarization tempt the United States, for example, to raise resources from the rest of the world by levying the inflation tax on those who use dollars in other countries? Wouldn't such use of the inflation tax be particularly tempting as the use of base money in the domestic economy declines? Or are a few dominant central banks sufficient to ensure contestability, and hence the discipline that Kroszner proposes?

## WHY HAS THE INFLATION RATE FALLEN?

Kroszner bridges the two general issues considered in this volume, as he also focuses on both the attainment of price stability and the necessity of government-created central banks and government-dominated monetary and payments systems. On the former, Kroszner begins with an account of what almost everyone acknowledges: The performance of central banks over the past 20 or so years has been vastly superior to the 20 or so years before. But why and how did this improvement come to pass? On this point, there is remarkably little consensus. One need look no

---

[18] Fischer (1993), Barro (1995), Bullard and Keating (1995), and Khan and Senhadji (2000) all provide empirical evidence that inflation is detrimental to long-run growth, at least if the rate of inflation is sufficiently high. King and Levine (1993a,b), Levine and Zervos (1998), Benhabib and Spiegel (2000), and Levine, Loyaza, and Beck (2000) all argue that the degree of financial development is strongly linked to real growth performance. Boyd, Levine, and Smith (2001) show that inflation can be highly detrimental to the performance of the financial system.

further than the papers at this conference—in particular, those by Randall Kroszner, Alberto Trejos, Charles Goodhart, Jasmina Arifovic and Thomas Sargent, and Matthias Brückner and Jürgen von Hagen—to appreciate that this is so.

Goodhart adheres to what Sargent has elsewhere calls "the triumph of the natural rate theory."[19] In Goodhart's view, "the most crucial change that has occurred in our way of thinking about the working of the macroeconomic system was the shift from a belief that the Phillips curve remained downward sloping, even in the longer term, to a belief that it would become vertical" (65).

The belief that there is no long-run output–inflation trade-off is not, of course, sufficient to banish inflation bias from the fiat currency landscape. After all, the archetypal Barro–Gordon (1983) (by way of Kydland and Prescott [1977]) time-consistency problem requires only that potential short-run trade-offs exist. Still, Goodhart finds little plausibility in the notion that today's policymakers hold to a view that short-run Phillips curves are exploitable for practical purposes. Absent this view, all that is left is the vertical long-run Phillips curve—inflation costs without the benefits. (A variant of this argument is proposed by Jeffrey Lacker in his comments on Kroszner's essay. Following an argument made by Marvin Goodfriend [1997], Lacker offers up the idea of "spontaneous enlightenment," whereby policymakers and the public come to appreciate—perhaps by way of hard experience—the costs of inflation, and consequently develop preferences for lower inflation outcomes.)

Despite this, Goodhart strikes a relatively pessimistic note about the capacity of modern central banks to consistently deliver price stability. The really crucial problem, as he sees it, is forecast uncertainty coupled with political pressures that inhibit preemptive strikes against inflation. Echoing the concerns about activist monetary policy articulated by Friedman years ago,[20] Goodhart fears that "[b]ecause of the same lags in the transmission mechanism, by the time [monetary authorities] are prepared to act, it will be too late. With political control of monetary policy, 'too little and too late' is likely to be the order of the day" (67).

One way to think about the evolution of monetary policy as Goodhart formulates it is that it has been reduced to the unlearnable. Although a better understanding of the costs of inflation and the futility of pursuing long-run objectives other than price stability may represent progress, there are limits to policymakers' capacity to filter the very noisy information about complex economic dynamics in real time. (Jürgen von Hagen and Matthias Brückner, in fact, suggest this may be one reason the European Central Bank has been reluctant to specifically articulate the time horizon relevant to maintaining its inflation targets.)

---

[19] See Sargent (1999).
[20] See Friedman (1966).

Goodhart implies that the imperfect (and, to a degree, imperfectable) nature of information, coupled with reasonable degrees of accountability to larger political preferences, lends an inevitable precariousness to the consistent maintenance of stable inflation. Such precariousness also appears in Arifovic and Sargent's essay. But where Goodhart's pessimism is about things that cannot be learned, Arifovic and Sargent's is about things that can be learned but are periodically unlearned.

In an experimental setting—quite literally, a laboratory—Arifovic and Sargent address an alternative to the triumph-of-the-natural-rate theory that Sargent (1999) labeled "the vindication of econometric policy evaluation":

> Recurrently [policymakers re-estimated a distributed lag Phillips curve and used it to reset a target inflation-unemployment pair...Decisions emerged from econometric policy evaluation. The method revealed an adversely shifting Phillips curve, which when interpreted mechanically, led policy makers to pursue lower inflation.

The pessimistic element of the vindication story is that the adaptive nature of policy learning means that monetary authorities may unlearn the lesson that long-run trade-offs between inflation and unemployment are nonexistent. The characteristics of the world Sargent describes are such that the economy will, in the long run, spend time in both low-inflation and high-inflation regimes.

Arifovic and Sargent's strategy in this volume is to determine whether the predictions of the vindication theory are confirmed in an experiment where the participants live (during the experiment) in the stylized Barro–Gordon/Kydland–Prescott environment. In particular, the private agents in the laboratory game lose by having their expectations violated, but policymakers in the game can gain by fooling them.

Some of the intrinsic uncertainty that Goodhart refers to is introduced into Arifovic and Sargent's experiments in a limited way: Inflation outcomes are random, and therefore not wholly controllable by the monetary authority. Whether this really captures the flavor of significant "lags in the transmission mechanism," however, is debatable. Furthermore, the experimental environment does not incorporate some key elements of the models that are proposed in other variants of the natural-rate-triumph story. Ireland (1999), for example, argues that the natural rate of unemployment itself is stochastic and that the inflation of the 1970s and subsequent disinflation can be understood in terms of the optimized choices of a central bank faced with the actual (exogenous) natural-rate realizations.

In most of Arifovic and Sargent's trials, the experimental outcomes converge to the fully time-consistent Ramsey solution (which is zero inflation given the structure of the payoffs). This appears to be broadly consistent with (again in Sargent's lexicon) the 1950s version of an adaptive expectations model, in which policymakers know the model, but private agents do not. Contrary to this variant of adaptive expectations, however, the rate of convergence in the experiments is slower than would be predicted when the public's adaptive rules are known by the monetary authority. There is, furthermore, evidence of backsliding, or reversion to the non-zero-inflation Nash equilibrium. This outcome is consistent with an environment in which policymakers do not know the structure of the economy, which Sargent refers to as the 1990s version of adaptive expectations.

It is a bit difficult, however, to know exactly how to interpret the backsliding result. As James Bullard notes in his commentary, model uncertainty by the central bank story is not a feature of Arifovic and Sargent's experiments (because the policymaker players do know the model structure). Bullard points to yet another problem in invoking the 1990s adaptive expectations theory as an explanation for the experimental results. Sargent shows in his book that the theory predicts dynamics that "spike" to the Ramsey outcomes and then converge slowly to the Nash equilibrium. The pattern is one in which Nash is the norm, with periodic escapes to Ramsey. This is difficult to reconcile with the predominant experimental observation of slow convergence to the Ramsey zero-inflation equilibria. The fact of multiple-equilibrium outcomes—Ramsey, Nash, and even other focal points—is consistent with a model with subgame perfect equilibria (essentially the generalization of reputational equilibria, such as in Barro [1986]), but perhaps this is more a statement about the inability of that framework to theoretically narrow the possibilities.

Christopher Sims' position is that we probably shouldn't try to put too fine a point on the experimental outcomes, and in fact we should view the collection of results as relatively good news:

> Arifovic and Sargent show that college students acting as policymakers and forecasters… with no special coaching, for the most part manage to achieve outcomes close to the Ramsey, full-commitment equilibrium…

> This outcome is not surprising, except perhaps to economists who take game theory too seriously. Policymakers believe that by persistently choosing a long-run, optimal, low-inflation policy, they can convince the public they are likely to continue doing so, and it seems both in reality and in these experiments that they are right." (62)

In other words, despite lingering doubts by the authors, Arifovic and Sargent's results look like evidence in support of the position that the "just do it" approach to eliminating inflation bias works. If this interpretation of the experiments is correct, they lend support to Goodhart's view that the potential time inconsistency of optimal monetary policy is of little practical moment.

But what would lead a central bank to "just do it"? The triumph of the natural-rate theory is obviously one answer. The aforementioned thesis proposed by Kroszner is another, perhaps quite different, explanation: Competition from alternative payments media has increasingly disciplined (and will increasingly discipline) the production of government fiat money, and it has promoted (and will further promote) price stability.

In Kroszner's view, central bank independence is probably not sufficient to explain the dramatic reduction in worldwide inflation, to guarantee that it emerges when high inflation is a problem, or to sustain price stability where it currently exists. In fact, the independence of Russia's central bank is offered as a counter-example: "In Russia…the central bank and its employees enjoyed direct benefits from inflation because it was able to keep some of the profits from high inflation for its management and staff (Shleifer and Treisman 2000). During part of the 1990s, the Russian central bank's independence from political control was an obstacle to inflation control" (281).

Independence, according to Kroszner, is insufficient because "in order for central bank independence to lead to lower inflation, the independent central banker must have a preference for lower inflation…" (281). This claim, and the Russian example offered to support it, is problematic in that it comingles independence and accountability. Goodhart, for example, takes pains to argue that it is only "proper" to endow a central bank with a large degree of independence when it is accountable for a clearly articulated objective, such as price stability. This more refined notion of independence does not pertain to the setting of objectives, but to the operational capacity to pursue those objectives with some distance from short-term political exigencies. The problem with Russia's central bank was not independence, but rather the lack of accountability.

Still, making the distinction between accountability and independence just begs the question of how low-inflation preferences can emerge and be sustained in the larger political infrastructure. Kroszner alludes to this when he comments on the empirical observation that greater central bank independence seems to be correlated with lower average inflation: "[T]he inverse correlation between independence and inflation does not necessarily imply causation…[C]entral bank independence may be the result of a coalition of anti-inflation interests or a deeper political consensus against inflation…" (282). Once we broaden the scope of the inquiry to include the entire sociopolitical context in which central banks operate, Kroszner's main argument—that low-inflation outcomes relying solely on preferences for price stability are likely to be unstable—retains its force.

This leads Kroszner to propose the aforementioned Hayekian competition as a central part of the story in the decline in worldwide inflation. Once again, Russia is offered as a case in point, this time along with Brazil. The observation is that inflation performance did not change appreciably after Russia and Brazil abandoned their fixed exchange rate regimes in 1998 and 1999, respectively. Here, it appears that an extreme form of commitment to price stability (or to the inflation rates of the countries to which the currencies were pegged) was not a necessary condition for realizing low inflation rates. Instead, Kroszner emphasizes the role of currency competition and expanded opportunities for choosing alternative payments vehicles made possible by technology-led reductions in transaction costs.

It may be premature to draw too-confident conclusions about the Russian and Brazilian case studies, and there are certainly caveats to the general argument. In developing his argument, Kroszner relies heavily on seigniorage motives as a source of inflationary bias. Essentially, currency competition works to lower sovereign inflation rates because greater competition increases the elasticity of demand for domestic currencies, which in turn lowers revenue-maximizing rates of inflation. But, as Jeremy Stein argues in his commentary on the essay, the seigniorage motive can be a double-edged sword. Stein invites us to contemplate a government that has a fixed target for revenues to be collected through the inflation tax. In such a case, as demand elasticity rises and seigniorage declines for any given rate of inflation, the affected government may actually raise the inflation rate to maintain the revenue target.

Stein's example apparently requires the hypothetical government to operate below the revenue-maximizing rate of inflation—it does for certain if we consider standard Cagan-like money demand functions—but this is not a hard case to contemplate. Furthermore, there are other reasons that competition combined with seigniorage motives might yield a result that is opposite to the one Kroszner suggests. For example, Jeffrey Lacker notes that it is not immediately obvious how advances in technology will, on net, affect the elasticity of money demand.

Once again, the chapter by Alberto Trejos provides an interesting counterpoint to Kroszner. Trejos proposes a two-country environment in which "inflation" is higher (and seigniorage lower) in noncooperative equilibria with currency competition (in the sense that both currencies circulate in both countries) relative to what can be achieved by cooperative behavior in which seigniorage is jointly maximized.[21] In fact, in Trejos' view of the evolution of monetary systems, seigniorage revenues eventually fade into the background. Ultimately, according to Trejos, the cost of maintaining a local currency in light of expanding trade will outweigh whatever seigniorage role can be claimed for a sovereign domestic currency.

The skepticism that seigniorage is ultimately a key part of the story about current and prospective central bank behavior was shared by others—see, for example, Jeffrey Lacker's comments on Kroszner—although one contrary opinion was

---

[21] Inflation in the Trejos model takes the form of an exogenous tax on money.

provided by Klaus Schmidt-Hebbel. Commenting on Trejos' article, Schmidt-Hebbel argues that in "countries with little de facto dollarization, renouncing seigniorage unilaterally, without a sharing arrangement, may cause huge annual revenue losses (about 0.5 percent of GDP)" (171). "Huge," however, appears to be in the eye of the beholder. Ross Levine interprets earlier work by Easterly and Schmidt-Hebbel (1994) as showing that "seigniorage is not huge—perhaps a maximum of 1 percent–2 percent of GDP per year in the long run." (177).

But the debate about the importance of seigniorage may, in the bigger picture, be little more than a diversion from Kroszner's main thesis. Presumably, the basic logic of the currency-competition hypothesis extends to a broader class of sources of "inflation bias." Consider, for example, the time-inconsistency problem. If the costs of currency substitution became so low that even short-run Phillips curve trade-offs ceased to exist, then the too-high equilibrium inflation rates wrung out of the Kydland–Prescott/Barro–Gordon framework would cease to exist as well. Kroszner's central argument would seem to apply without essential modification.

In the end, there may be less conflict between Trejos and Kroszner in their views of the evolution of central banks than meets the eye. Kroszner's story is essentially about the emergence of contestable markets. The emergence of a few dominant currencies is a sensible equilibrium in a contestable-markets environment, and, indeed, Kroszner suggests that such an outcome might very well develop as a result of historical progression. In fact, the argument does not preclude the emergence of a single, dominant central bank if potential competition from other private or governmental alternatives is present. Given the stakes, it would be comforting to believe that this is so.

## AND SO, ON TO THE FUTURE

There are, to be sure, many questions about the evolution and practice of central banking that this volume barely touches upon. Several of these are raised by Charles Goodhart, including optimal governance structures, potential conflicts (or not) between exchange rate stabilization and inflation stabilization, and the role of asset prices, money, and other indicators in the formulation and communication of monetary policy. The reader can obtain no better appreciation of the unsettled nature of these issues than by reading von Hagen and Brückner's comprehensive review of the first years of the European Central Bank, along with the very different views of Stephen Cecchetti and Vitor Gaspar in their commentaries. And we can think of no better blueprint for the work of the Federal Reserve Bank of Cleveland's Central Bank Institute than the works collected in this volume.

## References

Altig, David. 2002. Dollarization: What's in It for US? Federal Reserve Bank of Cleveland, *Economic Commentary*, October 15.

Altig, David, and Ed Nosal. Forthcoming. Dollarization: What's in It (or Not) for the Issuing Country? *Current Developments in Monetary and Financial Law*. Vol. 3. Washington, D.C.: International Monetary Fund.

Bagehot, Walter. 1873. *Lombard Street: A Description of the Money Market*. London: William Clowes and Sons.

Barro, Robert J. 1986. Reputation in a Model of Monetary Policy with Incomplete Information. *Journal of Monetary Economics* 17: 3–20.

———. 1995. Inflation and Economic Growth. *Bank of England Quarterly Bulletin* 35: 166–76.

Barro, Robert J., and David B. Gordon. 1983. A Positive Theory of Monetary Policy in a Natural Rate Model. *Journal of Political Economy* 91: 589–610.

Bencivenga, Valerie, Elisabeth Huybens, and Bruce Smith. Forthcoming. What to Stabilize in the Open Economy? *International Economic Review*.

Benhabib, Jess, and Mark Spiegel. 2000. The Role of Financial Development in Growth and Development. *Journal of Economic Growth* 5: 341–60.

Bernanke, Ben, Thomas Laubach, Frederic Mishkin, and Adam Posen. 1999. *Inflation Targeting: Lessons from the International Experience*. Princeton, NJ: Princeton University Press.

Boyd, John, Sungkyu Kwak, and Bruce Smith. 2002. The Real Output Losses Associated with Modern Banking Crises, or "The Good, The Bad, and the Ugly." University of Texas at Austin, unpublished manuscript.

Boyd, John, Ross Levine, and Bruce Smith. 2001. The Impact of Inflation on Financial Market Performance. *Journal of Monetary Economics* 47: 221–48.

Bullard, James, and John Keating. 1995. The Long-Run Relation Between Inflation and Output in Postwar Economies. *Journal of Monetary Economics* 36: 477–96.

Calomiris, Charles, and Charles Kahn. 1991. The Role of Demandable Debt in Structuring Optimal Banking Arrangements. *American Economic Review* 81: 487–513.

Chang, Roberto, and Andres Velasco. 2000. Financial Fragility and the Exchange Rate Regime. *Journal of Economic Theory* 92: 1–34.

Cohen, Benjamin J. 2001. Monetary Governance in a World of Regional Currencies. University of California–Santa Barbara, unpublished manuscript.

Demırgüç-Kunt, Asli, and Enrica Detragiache. 2000. Monitoring Banking Sector Fragility: a Multivariate Logit Approach. *World Bank Economic Review* 14: 287–307.

Diamond, Douglas, and Philip Dybvig. 1983. Bank Runs, Deposit Insurance, and Liquidity. *Journal of Political Economy* 91: 401–19.

Easterly, William, Carlos A. Rodriguez, and Klaus Schmidt-Hebbel. 1994. *Public-Sector Deficits and Macroeconomic Performance*. New York: Oxford University Press.

Ferguson, Niall. 2001. *The Cash Nexus: Money and Power in the Modern World, 1700–2000*. New York: Basic Books.

Fischer, Stanley. 1993. The Role of Macroeconomic Factors in Growth. *Journal of Monetary Economics* 32: 485–511.

Friedman, Milton. 1960. *A Program for Monetary Stability*. New York: Fordham University Press.

———. 1966. The Effects of a Full-Employment Policy on Economic Stability: A Formal Analysis. In *Essays in Positive Economics*, by Milton Friedman. Chicago, Ill.: University of Chicago Press.

Friedman, Milton, and Anna Schwartz. 1963. *A Monetary History of the United States, 1867–1960*. Princeton, NJ: Princeton University of Press.

Hayek, Friedrich. 1976. *The Denationalization of Money*. London: Institute of Economic Affairs.

Goodfriend, Marvin S. 1997. Monetary Policy Comes of Age: A 20th Century Odyssey. *Federal Reserve Bank of Richmond Economic Quarterly* 83: 1–22.

Ireland, Peter. 1999. Does the Time-Consistency Problem Explain the Behavior of Inflation in the United States? *Journal of Monetary Economics* 44: 279–91.

Jensen, Michael C., and William H. Meckling. 1976. Theory of the Firm: Managerial Behavior, Equity Costs, and Ownership Structure. *Journal of Financial Economics* 3: 305–60.

Khan, Mohsin, and Abdelhak Senhadji. 2001. Threshold Effects in the Relationship between Inflation and Growth. *IMF Staff Papers* 48: 1–21.

King, Robert, and Ross Levine. 1993a. Finance and Growth: Schumpeter Might Be Right. *Quarterly Journal of Economics* 108: 717–38.

———. 1993b. Finance, Entrepreneurship, and Growth: Theory and Evidence. *Journal of Monetary Economics* 32: 513–42.

Kiyotaki, Nobuhiro, and Randall Wright. 1989. On Money as a Medium of Exchange. *Journal of Political Economy* 97: 927–54.

———. 1993. A Search Theoretic Approach to Monetary Economics. *American Economic Review* 83: 63–77.

Kydland, Finn E., and Edward C. Prescott. 1977. Rules Rather Thank Discretion: The Inconsistency of Optimal Plans. *Journal of Political Economy* 87: 473–92.

Leiderman, Leonardo, and Lars Svensson. 1995. *Inflation Targets*. London: Centre for Economic Policy Research.

Levine, Ross, and Sara Zervos. 1998. Stock Markets, Banks, and Economic Growth. *American Economic Review* 88: 537–58.

Levine, Ross, Norman Loyaza, and Thorsten Beck. 2000. Financial Intermediation and Growth: Causality and Causes. *Journal of Monetary Economics* 46: 31–77.

Mayers, David, and Clifford Smith. 1981. Contractual Provisions, Organizational Structure, and Conflict Control in Insurance Markets. *Journal of Business* 54: 407–34.

Rolnick, Arthur, Bruce Smith, and Warren Weber. 1998. Lessons from a Laissez-Faire Payments System: the Suffolk Banking System (1825–1858). *Federal Reserve Bank of St. Louis Review* 80: 105–16.

Sargent, Thomas, and Neil Wallace. 1982. The Real-Bills Doctrine versus the Quantity Theory: a Reconsideration. *Journal of Political Economy* 90: 1212–36.

Schreft, Stacey. 1997. Looking Forward: the Role for the Government in Regulating Electronic Cash. *Federal Reserve Bank of Kansas City Economic Review* 82: 59–84.

Schreft, Stacey, and Bruce Smith. 2000. The Evolution of Cash Transactions: Some Implications for Monetary Policy. *Journal of Monetary Economics* 46: 97–120.

Shleifer, Andrei and Daniel Treisman. 2000. *Without a Map: Political Tactics and Economic Performance in Russia*. Cambridge, Mass.: MIT Press.

Smith, Bruce D. 1988. Legal Restrictions, "Sunspots," and Peel's Bank Act: The Real Bills Doctrine versus the Quantity Theory Reconsidered. *Journal of Political Economy* 96: 3–19.

Smith, Bruce, and Warren Weber. 1999. Private Money Creation and the Suffolk Banking System. *Journal of Money, Credit, and Banking* 31: 624–59.

Temin, Peter. 1969. *The Jacksonian Economy*. New York: W.W. Norton.

# PART I

## OPERATIONAL ISSUES IN MODERN CENTRAL BANKING

# 1

# Laboratory Experiments with an Expectational Phillips Curve

*Jasmina Arifovic and Thomas J. Sargent*

## 1. INTRODUCTION

This paper describes experiments with human subjects in an environment that provokes the time-consistency problem of Kydland and Prescott (1977). There is an expectational Phillips curve, a single policymaker, who sets inflation up to a random error term, and members of the public, who forecast the inflation rate. The policymaker knows the model. Kydland and Prescott consider a one-period model and describe how the inability to commit to an inflation policy causes the policymaker to set inflation to a Nash (that is, time-consistent) level that is higher than it would be if it could commit. With repetition (see Barro and Gordon 1983), the availability of history-dependent strategies multiplies the range of equilibrium outcomes. Some are better than the one-period, time-consistent one; others are worse.

Some commentators, including Blinder (1998) and McCallum (1995), assert that in practice, the time-consistency problem can be solved through an unspecified process that lets the monetary authority "just do it," in the terminology of an American sports shoe advertisement. Here, "it" is to choose the optimal or Ramsey target inflation rate. Although reputational macroeconomics provides no support for "just do it" as a piece of policy advice,[1] the range of outcomes predicted by that theory is big enough to rationalize such behavior. The large set of outcomes motivated us to put human subjects inside a Kydland–Prescott environment.

We paid undergraduate students to perform as policymakers and private forecasters in a repeated version of the Kydland–Prescott economy. A single policymaker repeatedly faced $N$ forecasters, whose average forecast of inflation positioned an expectational Phillips curve.

Inspired by the theoretical literature, we ask the following questions: (1) *Emergence of Ramsey*: Is there a tendency for the optimal but time-inconsistent (Ramsey), one-period outcome to emerge as time passes within an experiment? (2) *Backsliding*: After a policymaker has nearly achieved Ramsey inflation, does inflation ever drift back toward Nash inflation? (3) *Focal points*: Are there other

---

[1] The theory identifies multiple systems of expectations to which the policymaker wants to conform. It provides no guidance about how to switch from one system of expectations to another.

"focal points" besides the Nash and Ramsey inflation rates? (4) *History depend-ence*: Is there evidence of carryover across sessions in agents' forecasts of infla-tion? (5) *Inferior forecasting*: Are there sometimes systematic average errors in forecasting inflation? We answer yes to the first four questions and no to the last one. The positive answer to the first question supports the "just do it" position, but it is qualified by the positive answer to the second question.

The first two questions are inspired by Barro and Gordon (1983) and Sargent (1999). Barro and Gordon describe a reputational equilibrium that can sustain repetition of the Ramsey outcome. Sargent points out that Phelps's (1967) control problem for the monetary authority under adaptive expectations for the public even-tually leads the monetary authority close to Ramsey outcomes. However, Sargent also shows that repetition of the Nash equilibrium outcome is self-confirming,[2] and the "mean dynamics" of least-squares learning on the part of the government drive the system toward the self-confirming Nash equilibrium. The mean dynamics are essentially a differential version of "best response dynamics." They summarize and formalize the forces alluded to in Kydland and Prescott's heuristic sketch of an adaptive learning process that causes the government to depart from the Ramsey outcome and gradually approach the self-confirming Nash equilibrium outcome. We call this process of moving away from a Ramsey outcome, however attained, toward a Nash equilibrium "backsliding."[3]

**Figure 2.1: The Nash Equilibrium and
Ramsey Outcome for the Kydland–Prescott Model**

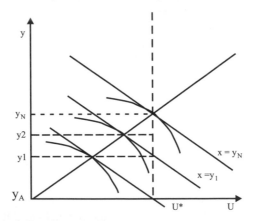

---

2   A self-confirming equilibrium is a regression of unemployment on inflation that reproduces itself under a government-decision problem that takes the regression as invariant under intervention and trades inflation for unemployment. The statement in the text that the Nash equilibrium outcome is the unique, self-confirming equilibrium must be qualified because it depends on a Phillips curve that regresses unemployment on infla-tion. If its direction is reversed, the self-confirming equilibrium has an inflation outcome that is higher than the Nash outcome. See Sargent (1999) for details.

3   John B. Taylor (see Solow and Taylor 1999) warns against backsliding because he believes standard time-series tests of the natural-rate hypothesis will reject it if the persistence of inflation continues to decrease, as it seems to have done in recent years in the United States.

## 2. THE ENVIRONMENT

Our basic model is Kydland and Prescott's. Let $(U_t, y_t, x_t, \hat{x}_t)$ denote the unemployment rate, the inflation rate, the systematic part of the inflation rate, and the public's expected rate of inflation, respectively. The policymaker sets $x_t$, the public sets $\hat{x}_t$, and the economy determines outcomes $(y_t, U_t)$.

The data are generated by the natural unemployment rate model

(2.1a)   $U_t = U^* - \theta (y_t - \hat{x}_t) + v_{1t}$

(2.1b)   $y_t = x_t + v_{2t}$

(2.1c)   $x_t = \hat{x}_t,$

where $\theta > 0$, $U^* > 0$, and $v_t$ is a (2 x 1) i.i.d. Gaussian random vector with $EV_t = 0$, diagonal contemporaneous covariance matrix, and $Ev_{jt}^2 = \sigma_{vj}^2$. Here $U^*$ is the natural rate of unemployment and $-\theta$ is the slope of an expectations-augmented Phillips curve. According to (2.1a), there is a family of Phillips curves indexed by $\hat{x}_t$. Condition (2.1b) states that the government sets inflation up to a random term, $v_{2t}$. Condition (2.1c) imposes rational expectations for the public and embodies the idea that private agents face a pure forecasting problem: Their payoffs vary inversely with their squared forecasting error. System (2.1) embodies the natural unemployment rate hypothesis: Surprise inflation lowers the unemployment rate, but anticipated inflation does not.

### 2.1. Nash and Ramsey Equilibria and Outcomes

The literature focuses on two equilibria of the one-period model. Both equilibria assume that the government knows the correct model. Called the Nash and the Ramsey equilibria, they come from different timing protocols. The Ramsey outcome is better than the Nash outcome, symptomatic of a time-inconsistency problem.

To define a Nash equilibrium, we need

**DEFINITION 2.1:** A government's *best response* map, $x_t = B(\hat{x}_t)$, solves the problem

(2.2)     $\min_{x_t} E (U_t^2 + y_t^2)$

subject to (2.1a) and (2.1b), taking $\hat{x}_t$ as given. The best response map is

$$x_t = \frac{\theta}{\theta^2 + 1} U^* + \frac{\theta^2}{\theta^2 + 1} \hat{x}_t.$$

A Nash equilibrium incorporates a government's best response and rational expectations for the public.

**DEFINITION 2.2:** A *Nash equilibrium* is a pair $(x, \hat{x})$ satisfying $x = B(\hat{x})$ and $\hat{x} = x$. A *Nash outcome* is the associated $(U_t, y_t)$.

**DEFINITION 2.3:** The *Ramsey plan* $x_t$ solves the problem of minimizing (2.2) subject to (2.1a), (2.1b), and (2.1c). The Ramsey outcome is the associated $(U_t, y_t)$.

A Ramsey outcome dominates a Nash outcome. The Ramsey plan is $\hat{x}_t = x_t = 0$, and the Ramsey outcome is $U_t = U^* - \theta v_{2t} + v_{1t}$, $y_t = v_{2t}$. The Nash equilibrium is $\hat{x}_t = x_t = \theta U_t^*$ and the Nash outcome is $U_t = U^* - \theta v_{2t} + v_{1t} = \theta U^* + v_{2t}$. The addition of constraint (2.1c) on the government in the Ramsey problem makes the government achieve better outcomes by taking into account how its actions affect the public's expectations. The superiority of the Ramsey outcome reflects the value to the government of committing to a policy before the public sets expectations.

### 3. REPETITION

We design our experiments to implement an infinitely repeated version of the Kydland–Prescott economy. The objective of the monetary authority is to maximize

$$(3.1) \quad J = -E_0 (1 - \delta) \sum_{t=0}^{\infty} \delta^t (U_t^2 + y_t^2), \delta \in (0,1).$$

The objective of private agents continues to be to minimize the error variance in forecasting inflation one period ahead.

Three types of theories apply to this setting.

(i) *Subgame perfection.* Reputational macroeconomics, also called the theory of credible or sustainable plans,[4] studies subgame perfect equilibria with history-dependent strategies. The theory discovers a set of equilibrium outcomes. For a large enough discount factor $\delta$, this set includes one that repeats the Ramsey outcome forever and others that sustain worse than the one-period Nash outcome. One sensible reaction is that because it contains so many possible equilibria, the theory says little empirically.

(ii) *Adaptive expectations (1950s).* Suppose the government believes that the public forms expectations by Cagan–Friedman adaptive expectations:

$$(3.2) \quad \hat{x}_t = (1 - \lambda) y_t + \lambda x_t$$

or $\hat{x}_t = (1 - \lambda) \sum_{j=0}^{\infty} \lambda^j y_{t-j-1}$, where $\lambda \in (0,1)$.

A version of Phelps's (1967) control problem is to maximize (3.1) subject to (2.1a), (2.1b), and (3.2).

---

[4]   See Stokey (1989) for a brief survey and Sargent (1999) for an application to the current problem.

The solution to this problem is a feedback rule,

$$(3.3) \qquad x_t = f_1 + f_2 \hat{x}_t.$$

With a high enough discount factor, the coefficients in (3.3) take values that make the government eventually push inflation toward the Ramsey outcome. Cho and Matsui (1995) refine this idea in the context of a broad class of expectations-formation mechanisms for the public that satisfy the same "induction hypothesis" that adaptive expectations exhibit: If sustained long enough, a constant inflation rate will eventually come to be expected by the public.[5]

(iii) *Adaptive expectations (1990s).* Sargent (1999) shows that a self-confirming equilibrium (see Fudenberg and Levine 1993) of the Kydland–Prescott model yields the pessimistic Nash equilibrium outcome. Sims (1988), Sargent (1999), and Cho, Williams, and Sargent (2001) perturb the behavior rules of that self-confirming equilibrium by imputing to the policymaker doubts about model specification, which cause him to use a constant-gain learning algorithm. Those papers show the resulting model has both "mean dynamics," usually propelling it toward the self-confirming equilibrium, and "escape dynamics," occasionally expelling it toward the Ramsey outcome. Sample paths display recurrent, abrupt stabilizations prompted by the monetary authority's experimentation-induced discovery of an approximate natural-rate-hypothesis government, followed by gradual backsliding toward the (inferior) self-confirming equilibrium.

## 4. EXPERIMENTS

### 4.1. Design

A group of $N + 1$ students composes the economy; we set $N$ equal to 3, 4, or 5. The first $N$ students form the public. Their decision is to forecast the inflation rate for each period of the experiment. Call agent $i$'s forecast $x_{it}$ and let $x_t$ be the average of the citizens' forecasts. Citizens receive payoffs that rise as their session-average squared forecast errors fall. Agent $i$'s payoff at the end of time period $t$ is given by

$$-.5 (y_t - x_{i,t})^2.$$

Student $N + 1$, chosen at random at the beginning of an experiment, is the policymaker. Each period, student $N + 1$ sets a target inflation rate, $x_t$. A random number generator sets $v_{2t}$ and the actual inflation rate equals $y_t = x_t + v_{2t}$.

---

[5]  Cho and Matsui (1999) study a version of the repeated model with alternating choices by the government and the public. They find that, depending on relative discount factors, the one-period Nash outcome is excluded in an equilibrium outcome, and a narrow range of outcomes near Ramsey can be expected under some parameter settings.

Unemployment is then generated by the Phillips curve (2.1a). Student $N + 1$'s payoff varies inversely with the session average of $U_t^2 + y_t^2$ and is given by

$$-.5 (U_t^2 + y_t^2).$$

The same student remains the policymaker throughout all sessions within a single experiment. Sessions within an experiment are separated by a stopping time.

### 4.2. Knowledge

The policymaker knows the true Phillips curve (2.1); the existence of private agents who are trying to forecast its action; and the histories of outcomes $(y_t, U_t)$ in the current experiment up to the current time. The private forecasters know the history of inflation and unemployment, including prior sessions of the current experiment. At the beginning of the economy, there is no history. The private forecasters do not know the structure of the economy. They know that a policymaker sets inflation up to a random term.[6]

### 4.3. Physical Details

Subjects sat at computer terminals and were isolated from one another. They received written instructions at the beginning of each experiment. Appendixes A and B reproduce the instructions. All experiments were conducted at the microcomputer lab of Simon Fraser University, in Burnaby, Canada. Subjects were undergraduate economics majors at Simon Fraser University. They were recruited for two-hour experiments but were not told in advance how many sessions would be played during each experiment. No subject was used in more than one experiment.

We conducted a total of 12 experiments, three in April 1998 and nine between February and April 1999.

### 4.4. Stopping Rule

We followed Duffy and Ochs (1999) and Marimon, McGrattan, and Sargent (1990) in using a random stopping rule to implement an infinite horizon and to discount future payoffs with the discount factor $\delta \in (0,1)$. At the end of each period, the computer program drew a random number from a uniform distribution over [0, 1]. If this random number was less than $\delta$, the experimental session would continue for one more period. If the number was greater than $\delta$, the session was terminated. An upper bound on the duration of an individual session was set at 100 time periods.

---

[6]  The experiments implement the environment described by Kydland and Prescott (1977), in which the government knows the model. Our assumptions about what the government and private forecasters know differ from those in Sargent (1999) and Cho, Williams, and Sargent (2002), where the private agents know the government's rule for setting the predictable part of inflation, and the government does not know the true Phillips curve model but estimates a nonexpectational Phillips curve.

## 4.5. Earnings

Subjects received a $10 payment (Canadian funds) for completing a two-hour experiment. They also could earn an additional $10 prize,[7] determined in the following way: At the end of each experimental time period, the number of *period points* was calculated by adding 100 points to the subject's payoff. If this number was less than 0, it was truncated to 0. Then the number of *total points* was calculated by adding all period points earned in a session. Finally, the number of *maximum points* was calculated as the product of 100 and the number of session periods. At the end of a session, a probability of winning the prize, $\pi_{win}$, was computed as the ratio between the total points and the maximum points.

Once an experiment was over, the computer program chose one of the sessions at random and chose a number, *rand*, from a uniform distribution over [0, 1]. If $\pi_{win}$ of the selected session was greater than *rand*, the subject earned an additional $10. The parameter values used in the experiments were $U^* = 5$, $\theta = 1$, and the discount parameter was $\delta = 0.98$. Two sets of values of the noise standard deviation $\sigma$ were used, $\sigma \equiv \sigma_1 = \sigma_2 = 0.3$. In addition to the setting of $\sigma$, an information variable (yes or no) recorded whether the policymaker had been told the value of $\hat{x}_t$ from the previous period.[8]

Each experiment was labeled an "economy" and consisted of a set of sessions with the same policymaker and group of forecasters. Each economy had several sessions. Table 4.1 summarizes the treatment variables across economies.[9]

### Table 4.1: Design of Experiments

| Experiment | Sessions | Information | $\sigma$ | N |
|:---:|:---:|:---:|:---:|:---:|
| 1 | 3 | * | .03 | 4 |
| 2 | 2 | ** | .03 | 4 |
| 3 | 3 | *** | .3 | 5 |
| 4 | 2 | yes | .3 | 3 |
| 5 | 2 | yes | .3 | 4 |
| 6 | 9 | yes | .3 | 4 |
| 7 | 6 | yes | .3 | 4 |
| 8 | 9 | yes | .3 | 4 |
| 9 | 4 | yes | .3 | 4 |
| 10 | 2 | yes | .3 | 4 |
| 11 | 9 | yes | .3 | 4 |
| 12 | 9 | yes | .3 | 4 |

[7]  We used a version of the Roth–Malouf (1979) binary lottery to determine actual cash payments with the intention to control for subjects' differing attitudes toward risk.

[8]  We used two alternative scales for the payoffs for the forecasters. For experiments 1–8, we used $-.5(y_t - \hat{x}_{it})^2$, while for experiments 9–12, we used $-5(y_t - x_{it})^2$. The second scale was introduced to increase the weight of poor forecasts in the calculation of $\pi_{win}$.

[9]  In table 4.1, (*) denotes (no, yes, yes), (**) denotes (no, yes), and (***) denotes (no, yes, yes) in successive sessions.

## 5. OUTCOMES

Tables 5.1, 5.2, and 5.3 and figures C1–17 describe the outcomes. Each economy corresponds to one set of $N+1$ students. Figures C14–17 contain evidence about the heterogeneity of the citizens' expectations of inflation. Each economy contains several sessions, determined by the realization of a random variable that terminated the session. The panels in figures C1–12 correspond to different sessions with the same group of students.

Table 5.1 reports the means and standard deviations of $\hat{x}_t$, $x_t$, $y_t$, $U_t$, $-.5\,(U_t^2 + y_t^2)$ across all sessions for each group. For the parameter values $U^* = 5$ and $\theta = 1$, the population values for these variables at the Nash equilibrium are 5, 5, 5, 5, and –25. For the Ramsey outcome, the values are 0, 0, 0, 5, and –12.5.

### 5.1. Patterns

Table 5.2 summarizes the patterns in figures C1–17. The column labels represent the following: "Ramsey" indicates the policymaker pushes the system to Ramsey at least for a substantial length of time (see figures C1 and C2 for economies 1 and 2). "Backsliding" indicates a resurgence of inflation after having attained Ramsey (see figures C3 and C6). "Other focal" indicates sustained inflation at values distinct from the Ramsey or Nash inflation (see figure C9). "Experimentation" indicates the presence of episodes in which the monetary authority seems to be engaging in purposeful experimentation. "Rank" denotes the rank order of the experiments in terms of the economywide average payoff for the monetary authority. An "x" signifies strong evidence for the pattern in question, a "y" signifies weaker evidence, and a blank signifies no evidence. Table 5.3 reports the results of regressions of inflation and the government payoff, respectively, on a constant and a dummy that takes value 0 in the first half of an experiment and 1 in the second half, where the second half is defined as the last $N/2$ sessions if $N$ is even and $N-1/2$ sessions if $N$ is odd. The table reports regression coefficients with standard errors in parenthesis; an asterisk denotes statistical significance at the 5 percent level. We summarize the main features of the results as follows.

- Figures C1–12 indicate that, on average, the public's forecasts of inflation are good and do not contain systematic forecast errors.
- In 9 of the 12 experiments, the policymaker pushes inflation near the Ramsey value for many periods.
- Backsliding occurs in 4 of 12 economies.
- Table 5.3 indicates that inflation falls and government payoffs rise during the second half of 10 of the 12 experiments; the decrease in inflation is statistically significant in 9 of the 12 experiments.
- The policymaker experiments in 3 of 12 economies.

### Table 5.1: Means and Standard Deviations of Outcomes

| Economy | $x$ | $\hat{x}$ | $y$ | $U$ | Gov. payoff |
|---------|-----|-----------|-----|-----|-------------|
| Nash | 5 | 5 | 5 | 5 | −25 |
| Ramsey | 0 | 0 | 0 | 5 | −12.5 |
| 1 | 4.1173 | 4.1497 | 4.1125 | 5.0381 | −22.4196 |
| | (1.5267) | (1.4923) | (1.5298) | (.4671) | (5.2823) |
| 2 | 1.4937 | 1.5047 | 1.4888 | 5.0183 | −16.5486 |
| | (2.2521) | (2.2286) | (2.2522) | (0.8135) | (7.2296) |
| 3 | 1.1266 | 1.1455 | 1.1162 | 5.0263 | −14.0370 |
| | (1.1115) | (1.0726) | (1.1347) | (0.5334) | (3.1575) |
| 4 | 1.3326 | 1.4218 | 1.2930 | 5.1438 | −14.5550 |
| | (0.7794) | (0.8094) | (0.8360) | (0.5383) | (2.8898) |
| 5 | 2.0143 | 2.2536 | 1.9998 | 5.2495 | −18.0040 |
| | (1.7884) | (1.7682) | (1.8025) | (1.1115) | (7.5711) |
| 6 | 1.9196 | 2.0600 | 1.9086 | 5.1636 | −21.4142 |
| | (2.8144) | (2.3279) | (2.8319) | (2.1278) | (26.5034) |
| 7 | 1.3561 | 1.4444 | 1.3080 | 5.0956 | −14.7334 |
| | (1.1482) | (1.1892) | (1.1962) | (0.6071) | (3.8102) |
| 8 | 0.7879 | 0.8354 | 0.7582 | 5.0545 | −13.5492 |
| | (0.7897) | (0.9031) | (0.8551) | (0.4979) | (3.0613) |
| 9 | 5.8802 | 5.8129 | 5.8274 | 4.9490 | −31.8680 |
| | (1.9699) | (1.7939) | (1.9725) | (1.1919) | (8.7549) |
| 10 | 2.4640 | 2.5443 | 2.4158 | 5.1006 | −20.8438 |
| | (2.4087) | (2.0490) | (2.4543) | (1.9718) | (11.6304) |
| 11 | 3.6396 | 3.6664 | 3.6158 | 5.0216 | −19.7498 |
| | (0.7379) | (0.7217) | (0.7873) | (0.7706) | (4.6579) |
| 12 | 2.6957 | 2.7048 | 2.6659 | 5.0161 | −18.8765 |
| | (1.7212) | (1.1878) | (1.7263) | (1.5879) | (15.8123) |

### Table 5.2: Patterns of Results

| Economy | Ramsey | Backsliding | Other focal | Experimentation | Rank |
|---------|--------|-------------|-------------|-----------------|------|
| 1 | x | | | | 11 |
| 2 | x | | | | 5 |
| 3 | x | x | | | 2 |
| 4 | x | | | | 3 |
| 5 | x | x | | x | 6 |
| 6 | x | x | y | x | 9 |
| 7 | x | | | | 4 |
| 8 | x | | | | 1 |
| 9 | | | y | | 12 |
| 10 | x | x | | x | 10 |
| 11 | | | x | | 8 |
| 12 | | | x | | 7 |

*Jasmina Arifovic and Thomas J. Sargent*

**Table 5.3: Inflation and Government Payoff on Second-Half Dummy**

| Economy | Inf. incpt | Inf. dummy | Gov. incpt | Gov. dummy |
|---|---|---|---|---|
| 1 | 4.5637 | −2.8665* | −23.7411 | 8.4138* |
| | (0.0882) | (0.2226) | (0.3396) | (0.8571) |
| 2 | 3.8583 | −3.8385* | −22.3969 | 9.4744* |
| | (0.1596) | (0.2031) | (0.7084) | (0.9017) |
| 3 | 1.3255 | −1.0571* | −14.1841 | 0.7430 |
| | (0.0829) | (0.8164) | (0.7084) | (0.9017) |
| 4 | 1.6127 | −0.9593* | −15.1001 | 1.6353* |
| | (0.0819) | (0.1419) | (0.3251) | (0.5631) |
| 5 | 3.1016 | −1.9891* | −21.4088 | 6.1463* |
| | (0.1917) | (0.2576) | (0.8823) | (1.1854) |
| 6 | 1.9549 | −0.2388 | −21.9732 | 2.8805 |
| | (0.1356) | (0.3079) | (1.2692) | (2.8811) |
| 7 | 1.6024 | −0.9722* | −15.0774 | 1.1365* |
| | (0.0840) | (0.0931) | (0.2088) | (0.3323) |
| 8 | 0.8524 | −0.2388* | −13.9437 | 0.9993* |
| | (0.0585) | (0.0931) | (0.2088) | (0.5195) |
| 9 | 5.4664 | 1.0468 | −30.7858 | −3.1381 |
| | (0.1658) | (0.2824) | (0.7498) | (1.2769) |
| 10 | 2.8456 | −1.2428* | −21.8264 | 2.8410 |
| | (0.2562) | (0.4357) | (1.2431) | (2.1137) |
| 11 | 3.4265 | 0.3872 | −18.8962 | −1.7463 |
| | (0.0533) | (0.0763) | (0.3199) | (0.4576) |
| 12 | 3.1043 | −1.1103* | −19.0925 | 0.5472 |
| | (0.1132) | (0.1802) | (1.0925) | (1.7388) |

- Economy 9 has a bad or indifferent policymaker. He attains an average payoff level worse than that associated with the Nash outcome—the only policymaker to fall short of the Nash outcome.
- Most of the transitions from Nash to Ramsey are smooth. Few (if any) have the drama of the Volcker-like rapid disinflations produced by the escape-route dynamics of Cho, Williams, and Sargent (2002) and Sargent (1999). Depending on parameter values, they could resemble a pattern predicted by Phelps (1967) and Cho and Matsui (1995). However, the stabilizations are too slow to be explained in this way, at least if policy-makers are assumed to know the rate at which the public is adapting its expectations.
- Heterogeneity of expectations across citizens is largest at the beginning of an experiment. It also tends to grow at the start of a new session within an experiment.

## 6. ADAPTIVE EXPECTATIONS

To check whether the results confirm the predictions of the Phelps (1967) problem, we estimated the parameter $\lambda$ in the adaptive-expectations model (3.2). We estimated the model for each individual within an experiment, pooling across sessions,[10] and for the average of households within an experiment, pooling across sessions.[11] For econometric reasons, we wrote the model in the form

$$(6.1) \qquad \hat{x}_t = (1 - \lambda_i) \sum_{j=0}^{t-1} \lambda^j_i \, y_{t-j} + \eta_i \, \lambda^t_i + u_{it},$$

where $u_{it}$ is a random disturbance with mean zero that is orthogonal to $y_{t-1-j}$ for $j = 0, \ldots, t - 1$, and $\eta$ is the systematic part of the initial condition (see Klein 1958). We estimated (6.1) by maximum likelihood, assuming a Gaussian distribution for $u_{it}$. For each individual, we pooled across sessions, estimating a common $\lambda_i$ but a different, session-specific $\eta_i$ for each session. For the average of forecasts across individuals, $x_t$, we proceeded in a similar way, estimating a common $\lambda$ across sessions as well as session-specific $\eta$'s.

Table 6.1 shows the estimates of $\lambda$,[12] most of which are below .5, indicating that most citizens formed forecasts by heavily overweighting the recent past. In the next section, we will study whether policymakers can be viewed as solving a Phelps problem in light of this rapid adjustment.

### 6.1. Adaptive Expectations with Heteroskedasticity

Tables 6.2 and 6.3 summarize some of the results of re-estimating the adaptive-expectations model (6.1) by maximum likelihood while allowing the variance of the disturbance $u_{it}$ to vary across the two halves of an experiment, defined the same way as table 5.3.[13] Table 6.3 reports estimates of the variances across the two halves, denoted $\sigma^1_2$, $\sigma^2_2$, respectively, as well as an estimate $\sigma^2_2$ that imposed homoskedasticity across the two halves. An asterisk by $\sigma^2_2$ denotes the difference across the two halves is statistically significant at the 5 percent level, according to a Chi-square test. In most experiments and for most of the private agents, the variance of $u_{it}$ fell across the two halves of an experiment.

### 6.2. Phelps Problem

In the row labeled L.S., table 6.4 records least-squares estimates of the government's rule (3.3). In the row labeled Phelps, the table also reports the rule that solves the Phelps problem for $\delta = .98$ and the value of $\lambda$ from table 6.1 for the

---

[10] Thus, there is one $\lambda_i$ for each subject.
[11] Here there is one $\lambda$ for each experiment for each individual.
[12] In experiment 3, there is a fifth private agent. His/her estimate of $\lambda_i$ is .2303 (.0314) with an $R^2$ of .9938.
[13] There is a fifth agent in experiment 3, with estimated $\lambda = .2310$ (.0276). For the fifth agent, we estimated $\sigma_2 = .0168$, $\sigma^2_1 = .0199$, $\sigma^2_2 = .0097$. The difference in disturbance variances across halves is not statistically significant at the .05 level.

*Jasmina Arifovic and Thomas J. Sargent*

**Table 6.1: Estimates of $\lambda_i$ in (6.1)**

| Exp. | | Agent 1 | Agent 2 | Agent 3 | Agent 4 | Average |
|---|---|---|---|---|---|---|
| 1 | $\lambda$ | 0.1395 | 0.0942 | 0.3136 | 0.1618 | 0.1896 |
| | s.e. | (0.0350) | (0.0828) | (0.0549) | (0.0436) | (0.0322) |
| | $R^2$ | 0.9983 | 0.9919 | 0.9952 | 0.9972 | 0.9986 |
| 2 | $\lambda$ | 0.1698 | 0.1366 | 0.2501 | 0.0007 | 0.1950 |
| | s.e. | (0.0915) | (0.0885) | (0.0506) | (0.0015) | (0.0382) |
| | $R^2$ | 0.9475 | 0.9736 | 0.9656 | 0.9692 | 0.9912 |
| 3 | $\lambda$ | 0.3278 | 0.4007 | 0.3363 | 0.4627 | 0.3556 |
| | s.e. | (0.0649) | (0.0452) | (0.0381) | (.0359) | (0.0278) |
| | $R^2$ | 0.9737 | 0.9809 | 0.9897 | 0.9862 | 0.9938 |
| 4 | $\lambda$ | 0.7345 | 0.3849 | 0.2635 | | 0.4126 |
| | s.e. | (0.0805) | (0.0641) | (0.0638) | | (0.0547) |
| | $R^2$ | 0.9755 | 0.9852 | 0.9820 | | 0.9893 |
| 5 | $\lambda$ | 0.5059 | 0.3644 | 0.2605 | 0.7918 | 0.5006 |
| | s.e. | (0.0493) | (0.0609) | (0.0605) | (0.0343) | (0.0360) |
| | $R^2$ | 0.9569 | 0.9498 | 0.9539 | 0.9092 | 0.9846 |
| 6 | $\lambda$ | 0.8413 | 0.7829 | 0.7059 | 0.6335 | 0.7452 |
| | s.e. | (0.0232) | (0.0635) | (0.0147) | (0.0292) | (0.0137) |
| | $R^2$ | 0.7844 | 0.5853 | 0.8761 | 0.8569 | 0.9461 |
| 7 | $\lambda$ | 0.2585 | 0.3362 | 0.7562 | 0.3124 | 0.4160 |
| | s.e. | (0.0409) | (0.0295) | (0.0368) | (0.0505) | (0.0746) |
| | $R^2$ | 0.9840 | 0.9929 | 0.6209 | 0.9801 | 0.9692 |
| 8 | $\lambda$ | 0.4893 | 0.4200 | 0.2788 | 0.3632 | 0.3935 |
| | s.e. | (0.0370) | (0.0329) | (0.0014) | (0.0048) | (0.0236) |
| | $R^2$ | 0.9544 | 0.9691 | 0.9696 | 0.9769 | 0.9872 |
| 9 | $\lambda$ | 0.5649 | 0.1233 | 0.2662 | 0.2073 | 0.3392 |
| | s.e. | (0.0214) | (0.0730) | (0.0405) | (0.0503) | (0.0201) |
| | $R^2$ | 0.9960 | 0.9907 | 0.9940 | 0.9875 | 0.9983 |
| 10 | $\lambda$ | 0.1300 | 0.2877 | 0.4176 | 0.6609 | 0.3800 |
| | s.e. | (0.0476) | (0.1145) | (0.0322) | (0.0438) | (0.0442) |
| | $R^2$ | 0.9368 | 0.4668 | 0.9667 | 0.9151 | 0.9393 |
| 11 | $\lambda$ | 0.4796 | 0.4856 | 0.5322 | 0.4378 | 0.5109 |
| | s.e. | (0.0244) | (0.0422) | (0.1162) | (0.0356) | (0.0367) |
| | $R^2$ | 0.9966 | 0.9861 | 0.8596 | 0.9915 | 0.9888 |
| 12 | $\lambda$ | 0.7083 | 0.0663 | 0.7136 | 0.4836 | 0.4776 |
| | s.e. | (0.0366) | (0.0222) | (0.0476) | (0.0410) | (0.0264) |
| | $R^2$ | 0.8338 | 0.9533 | 0.9249 | 0.9255 | 0.9708 |

**Table 6.2: Estimates of $\lambda_i$ with Heteroskedasticity**

| Economy | | Agent 1 | Agent 2 | Agent 3 | Agent 4 | Average |
|---|---|---|---|---|---|---|
| 1 | $\lambda$ | 0.1107 | 0.0100 | 0.3409 | 0.0698 | 0.1374 |
| | *s.e.* | (0.0229) | (0.0073) | (0.0473) | (0.0433) | (0.0203) |
| 2 | $\lambda$ | 0.1842 | 0.1645 | 0.3222 | 0.0364 | 0.2176 |
| | *s.e.* | (0.0522) | (0.0454) | (0.0573) | (0.0602) | (0.0373) |
| 3 | $\lambda$ | 0.2675 | 0.4102 | 0.3312 | 0.4499 | 0.3616 |
| | *s.e.* | (0.0508) | (0.0444) | (0.0408) | (0.0344) | (0.0277) |
| 4 | $\lambda$ | 0.5592 | 0.3642 | 0.2519 | | 0.3727 |
| | *s.e.* | (0.1141) | (0.0564) | (0.0586) | | (0.0548) |
| 5 | $\lambda$ | 0.5582 | 0.3690 | 0.2750 | 0.6021 | 0.5030 |
| | *s.e.* | (0.0436) | (0.0598) | (0.0671) | (0.0657) | (0.0307) |
| 6 | $\lambda$ | 0.8220 | 0.0009 | 0.7153 | 0.7187 | 0.7571 |
| | *s.e.* | (0.0183) | (0.0815) | (0.0156) | (0.0347) | (0.0154) |
| 7 | $\lambda$ | 0.2075 | 0.3321 | 0.3259 | 0.3076 | 0.3288 |
| | *s.e.* | (0.0288) | (0.0274) | (0.0728) | (0.0468) | (0.0397) |
| 8 | $\lambda$ | 0.5618 | 0.4133 | 0.2981 | 0.3466 | 0.4087 |
| | *s.e.* | (0.0264) | (0.0327) | (0.0347) | (0.0317) | (0.0207) |
| 9 | $\lambda$ | 0.5625 | 0.2461 | 0.3094 | 0.2021 | 0.3574 |
| | *s.e.* | (0.0224) | (0.0509) | (0.0425) | (0.0369) | (0.0210) |
| 10 | $\lambda$ | 0.1639 | 0.3319 | 0.3958 | 0.6542 | 0.3866 |
| | *s.e.* | (0.0478) | (0.0744) | (0.0327) | (0.0438) | (0.0458) |
| 11 | $\lambda$ | 0.4917 | 0.5969 | 0.4790 | 0.3748 | 0.5323 |
| | *s.e.* | (0.0234) | (0.0242) | (0.0307) | (0.0367) | (0.0203 |
| 12 | $\lambda$ | 0.8196 | 0.0169 | 0.7855 | 0.4647 | 0.4696 |
| | *s.e.* | (0.0175) | (0.0160) | (0.0307) | (0.0391) | (0.0253) |

averaged-across-individuals values of $\hat{x}_t$. The least-squares estimates of (3.3) show the policymakers seem to have adjusted inflation downward too slowly relative to the solution to the Phelps problem. In particular, the least-squares values of $f_2$ are always substantially larger than those associated with the optimal rule from the Phelps problem. If policymakers are to be interpreted as solving a Phelps problem, then they must be regarded as acting as though they think members of the public adjust much more slowly (have higher $\lambda$) than they apparently do.

**Table 6.3: Restricted vs. Unrestricted MLE**

| Economy | | Agent 1 | Agent 2 | Agent 3 | Agent 4 | Average |
|---|---|---|---|---|---|---|
| 1 | $\sigma^2$ | 0.0321 | 0.1544 | 0.0906 | 0.0541 | 0.0265 |
| | $\sigma_1^2$ | 0.0367 | 0.1816 | 0.1015 | 0.0622 | 0.0312 |
| | $\sigma_2^2$ | 0.0085* | 0.0165* | 0.0330* | 0.0182* | 0.0043* |
| 2 | $\sigma^2$ | 0.3784 | 0.1903 | 0.2476 | 0.2208 | 0.0635 |
| | $\sigma_1^2$ | 1.1004 | 0.5318 | 0.6957 | 0.6105 | 0.2080 |
| | $\sigma_2^2$ | 0.0034* | 0.0042* | 0.0057* | 0.0043* | 0.0017* |
| 3 | $\sigma^2$ | 0.0659 | 0.0477 | 0.0257 | 0.0345 | 0.0154 |
| | $\sigma_1^2$ | 0.0791 | 0.0499 | 0.0252 | 0.0303 | 0.0161 |
| | $\sigma_2^2$ | 0.0141* | 0.0389 | 0.0278 | 0.0515 | 0.0129 |
| 4 | $\sigma^2$ | 0.0574 | 0.0348 | 0.0421 | | 0.0250 |
| | $\sigma_1^2$ | 0.0713 | 0.0410 | 0.0492 | | 0.0298 |
| | $\sigma_2^2$ | 0.0343 | 0.0226 | 0.0283 | | 0.0160 |
| 5 | $\sigma^2$ | 0.3089 | 0.3603 | 0.3304 | 0.6516 | 0.1102 |
| | $\sigma_1^2$ | 0.4310 | 0.4824 | 0.3543 | 1.3211 | 0.1674 |
| | $\sigma_2^2$ | 0.2168* | 0.2635 | 0.3118 | 0.2209* | 0.0649* |
| 6 | $\sigma^2$ | 2.4741 | 4.7589 | 1.4214 | 1.6426 | 0.6182 |
| | $\sigma_1^2$ | 2.6390 | 5.8032 | 1.6929 | 1.9862 | 0.7254 |
| | $\sigma_2^2$ | 1.8053 | 0.4827* | 0.3028* | 0.3424* | 0.1787* |
| 7 | $\sigma^2$ | 0.0492 | 0.0198 | 1.1652 | 0.0613 | 0.0945 |
| | $\sigma_1^2$ | 0.0666 | 0.0220 | 0.18567 | 0.0577 | 0.1396 |
| | $\sigma_2^2$ | 0.0106* | 0.0269 | 0.0238 | 0.0693 | 0.0135* |
| 8 | $\sigma^2$ | 0.0574 | 0.0384 | 0.0380 | 0.0278 | 0.0153 |
| | $\sigma_1^2$ | 0.0879 | 0.0440 | 0.0482 | 0.0332 | 0.0209 |
| | $\sigma_2^2$ | 0.0131* | 0.0298 | 0.0228* | 0.0195* | 0.0070* |
| 9 | $\sigma^2$ | 0.1474 | 0.3448 | 0.2236 | 0.4676 | 0.0641 |
| | $\sigma_1^2$ | 0.1823 | 0.5061 | 0.3063 | 0.6947 | 0.0901 |
| | $\sigma_2^2$ | 0.0816* | 0.0534* | 0.0710* | 0.0395* | 0.0157* |
| 10 | $\sigma^2$ | 0.7407 | 6.2520 | 0.3909 | 0.9958 | 0.7112 |
| | $\sigma_1^2$ | 0.5203 | 8.9559 | 0.2525 | 0.8240 | 0.8237 |
| | $\sigma_2^2$ | 1.1613 | 1.2152* | 0.6536 | 1.3176 | 0.5013 |
| 11 | $\sigma^2$ | 0.0441 | 0.1870 | 1.8837 | 0.1137 | 0.1499 |
| | $\sigma_1^2$ | 0.0377 | 0.3194 | 3.6244 | 0.0818 | 0.2655 |
| | $\sigma_2^2$ | 0.0509 | 0.0567* | 0.0740* | 0.1487 | 0.0298* |
| 12 | $\sigma^2$ | 1.6382 | 0.4612 | 0.7400 | 0.7296 | 0.2879 |
| | $\sigma_1^2$ | 2.5643 | 0.6409 | 0.9146 | 0.5356 | 0.2661 |
| | $\sigma_2^2$ | 0.3454* | 0.2042* | 0.4928* | 1.0261 | 0.3213 |

**Table 6.4: Estimates of Phelps Rule (3.3)**

| Experiment | | $f_1$ | $f_2$ | $n$ | $R^2$ | $\lambda$ |
|---|---|---|---|---|---|---|
| 1 | L.S. | 0.0515 | 0.9798 | 191 | 0.9172 | 0.1896 |
| | s.e. | (0.0944) | (0.0214) | | | |
| | Phelps | 0.0779 | 0.3655 | | | |
| 2 | L.S. | 0.0672 | 0.9480 | 162 | 0.8800 | 0.1950 |
| | s.e. | (0.0743) | (0.0277) | | | |
| | Phelps | 0.0785 | 0.3649 | | | |
| 3 | L.S. | 0.0238 | 0.9627 | 202 | 0.8630 | 0.3556 |
| | s.e. | (0.0425) | (0.0271) | | | |
| | Phelps | 0.0997 | 0.3504 | | | |
| 4 | L.S. | 0.0349 | 0.9127 | 111 | 0.8984 | 0.4126 |
| | s.e. | (0.0480) | (0.0294) | | | |
| | Phelps | 0.1099 | 0.3456 | | | |
| 5 | L.S. | 0.1190 | 0.8410 | 139 | 0.6914 | 0.5006 |
| | s.e. | (0.1373) | (0.0480) | | | |
| | Phelps | 0.1298 | 0.3386 | | | |
| 6 | L.S. | 0.2215 | 0.8243 | 541 | 0.4649 | 0.7452 |
| | s.e. | (0.1183) | (0.0381) | | | |
| | Phelps | 0.2509 | 0.3233 | | | |
| 7 | L.S. | 0.0488 | 0.9051 | 251 | 0.8787 | 0.4160 |
| | s.e. | (0.0398) | (0.0213) | | | |
| | Phelps | 0.1105 | 0.3453 | | | |
| 8 | L.S. | 0.0771 | 0.8508 | 347 | 0.9467 | 0.3935 |
| | s.e. | (0.0134) | (0.0109) | | | |
| | Phelps | 0.1063 | 0.3472 | | | |
| 9 | L.S. | 0.5250 | 0.9213 | 203 | 0.7038 | 0.3392 |
| | s.e. | (0.2564) | (0.0422) | | | |
| | Phelps | 0.0971 | 0.3519 | | | |
| 10 | L.S. | 0.5248 | 0.7622 | 133 | 0.4204 | 0.3800 |
| | s.e. | (0.2551) | (0.0782) | | | |
| | Phelps | 0.1038 | 0.3484 | | | |
| 11 | L.S. | 1.1289 | 0.6848 | 401 | 0.4486 | 0.5109 |
| | s.e. | (0.1420) | (0.0380) | | | |
| | Phelps | 0.1326 | 0.3378 | | | |
| 12 | L.S. | 0.8612 | 0.6782 | 347 | 0.2191 | 0.4776 |
| | s.e. | (0.2036) | (0.0689) | | | |
| | Phelps | 0.1240 | 0.3404 | | | |

## 7. SESSION DEPENDENCE

Figures C1–12 display visual evidence of what we call "session dependence," a tendency of the monetary authority to set the systematic part of inflation equal to its value at the end of the preceding session within an experiment. A regression of the beginning-of-session setting of $x$ against the previous session's last setting of $x$, pooled across sessions and experiments, shows there is some such tendency, but it is weak:

$$x_{1(j)} = 1.71 + .67x_{T(j-1)},$$
$$(.70) \ (.25)$$

where standard errors are in parentheses, $R^2 = .14$, $x_{1(j)}$ is the first-period setting of $x$ within session $j \geq 2$, and $x_{T(j-1)}$ is the last-period setting of $x$ within session $j - 1$.

## 8. DISPERSION

Figure C13 displays sample variances of individual forecasts of inflation, $\hat{x}_{it}$, around average forecasts $\hat{x}_t$ across sessions for each experiment. If there is a pattern, it is for inflation diversity to fall, at least in early sessions of an experiment. Figures C14–17 display time series of $\max_i \hat{x}_{it} - \min_i \hat{x}_{it}$ for each experiment. Vertical lines denote inaugurations of new sessions. Generally, diversity of forecasts is highest at the beginning of an experiment, and there is some tendency for increased dispersion at the inauguration of a new session within an experiment. Only occasionally is there a within-session increase in dispersion.

## 9. CONCLUDING DISCUSSION

Before our experiments, we were skeptical that chanting "just do it" would solve the time-consistency problem posed by an expectational Phillips curve. Our experiments have softened but not fully arrested our skepticism. A supermajority of experimental sample paths show the monetary authority gradually reaching for the Ramsey value. This might reflect the "just do it" spirit. We think it probably reflects a Phelps–Cho–Matsui monetary authority that imputes an "induction hypothesis" (that is, adaptive expectations) to the private forecasters and that sets out to manipulate private forecasts by its actions. However, there is a big gap between estimated feedback rules and those that would have been chosen by the optimal Phelps planner, who knows the value of citizens' adaptive expectations coefficient. Our policymakers exploit the "induction hypothesis" too slowly, when they exploit it at all. There are more than enough deviations from Ramsey for us not to take the solution of the time-consistency problem for granted. In addition to occasional backsliding, our experimental economy can be stuck with an incompetent policymaker.

### APPENDIX A: INSTRUCTIONS FOR POLICYMAKERS

Today you will participate in an experiment in economic decisionmaking. Various research foundations have provided funds for the conduct of this research. The instructions are simple, and if you follow them carefully and make good decisions, you can earn up to $20, which will be paid to you in cash at the end of this experiment.

You will be assigned the role of a policymaker. In each period of the experimental economy, your job will be to choose the target inflation rate. As a policymaker, you are concerned about the values of inflation and unemployment. However, you can directly affect only the inflation rate.

You will play a series of experimental sessions. An experimental session will consist of a number of experimental periods. At the beginning of each period of an experimental session, you will be asked to choose the target inflation rate. The actual inflation rate will then be determined by adding a stochastic shock to the target inflation rate. This reflects the fact that you, as the policymaker, do not have complete control over the inflation rate.

The stochastic shock is normally distributed and has the mean value equal to 0 and the standard deviation equal to 0.3. This means that approximately 68 percent of the values of the shock will be between –0.3 and 0.3. In addition, approximately 95 percent of the values will be between –0.6 and 0.6. Almost all the values, 99.7 percent, will be between –0.9 and 0.9

At the beginning of each time period, private agents will forecast the inflation rate for that time period. At the end of each experimental period, you will see the average forecasted inflation rate (averaged over the forecasts of all private agents) on your computer screen. You will also see the actual rate of inflation and the rate of unemployment for that experimental time period.

The actual inflation rate and the average forecasted inflation rate (averaged over the expectations of private agents) play a role in determining the rate of unemployment in the economy. The rate of unemployment is calculated in the following way:

$$\text{unemployment} = u^* - (\text{inflation} - \text{average forecasted inflation}) + \text{shock},$$

where $u^*$ is the *natural rate of unemployment*, which prevails in the economy if the actual rate of inflation is equal to average forecasted inflation rate; *average expected inflation* is the rate computed as the average of private agents' expected rates;

and shock is a stochastic *shock* normally distributed, with mean value 0 and the standard deviation equal to 0.3.

At the end of every experimental period, you will also see the payoff that you earned in that period. The payoff is calculated in the following way:

payoff $= -0.5$ (inflation$^2$ + unemployment$^2$).

Thus, your payoff decreases with increases in both the inflation and unemployment rates.

At any given experimental period, the probability that the current session will continue for one more period is equal to 0.98. Whether the session is played for one more period is determined in the following way: A random number between 0 and 1 is drawn from a uniform distribution. If the number is less than or equal to 0.98, the current session continues into the next period. If the number is greater than 0.98, the session is over. This number will appear in the last column of your screen at the end of each experimental time period. Once the randomly drawn number is greater than 0.98, the session will automatically be terminated.

You will start every experimental session by running a computer program. The experimenter will give you the name of the program. Once you start the program, you will be prompted to enter the session number. You will enter these numbers in the consecutive order, starting with 1 for the first session, 2 for the second, etc. After entering the session number, you will be prompted to enter the probability that a particular session will end at any given experimental time period. Enter the number 0.98 for this question. Once you have answered these two questions, an experimental session will begin.

### Earnings

The experiment will last two hours. If you complete this two-hour experiment, you are guaranteed to receive a $10 payment. Moreover, you can earn an additional $10, for a total of $20.

At the end of each session, the probability of winning a prize of an additional $10 will be computed in the following way.

1. For every time period of the session, the number of period points is calculated by adding 100 points to the payoff you obtained in that time period.
2. The number of total points is calculated by adding the period points earned in all time periods of a given experimental session. If this number is less than 0, it is set equal to 0.
3. The number of maximum points is calculated by multiplying the total number of periods of the session by 100. This number is the number of total points that you would earn in an experimental session if your payoff were equal to 0 in every experimental period.

4.  The probability of winning the prize is then calculated in the following way:

1 – (*maxpoints* – *total points*) / *maxpoints*.

Table A1 presents an example of how the total points, maxpoints, and the probability are calculated in a hypothetical experimental session. The length of the session is five experimental periods.

**Table A1**

| Period | Payoff | Period points |
|--------|--------|---------------|
| 1 | –20.25 | 79.75 |
| 2 | –115.25 | –15.25 |
| 3 | –5.16 | 94.84 |
| 4 | –10.37 | 89.63 |
| 5 | –30.25 | 69.75 |
| Total points | | 318.72 |

*maxpoints* = 100 x 5 periods = 500

Thus, the probability of winning the prize in this session is

1 – (500 – 318.72)\500 = 0.64.

Higher values of your payoff in each time period (lower in absolute terms) result in higher period and total points. Higher values of total points result, in turn, in higher probability of winning the prize.

5.  If your total points happen to be less than zero, then your probability of winning the prize in that session is set equal to zero.

At the end of the experiment, one of the sessions that you played will be randomly selected. Each session will have an equal chance of being selected. The session will be selected by running the program draw.exe at the DOS prompt.

Once you type draw and press enter, you will be asked to enter your ID number. Your ID number as the policymaker is 5. Once you have entered it, you will be prompted to enter the total number of sessions played in the experiment. When you enter this number, the computer will randomly choose a number between 1 and the number of sessions played. This number will appear on your computer screen and will indicate the number of the selected session.

The second number that will appear will be a number between 0 and 1, *rand*, drawn from the uniform distribution. You will take that number and compare it to the probability of winning the prize for the selected session. If *rand* is less than or equal to the probability of winning a lottery, you win an additional $10. If *rand* is greater than the probability, you do not win the additional $10 prize. Thus, the higher the probability of winning the prize, the higher your chances that *rand* will be less or equal to the probability. Are there any questions?

### APPENDIX B: INSTRUCTIONS FOR FORECASTERS

Today you will participate in an experiment in economic decisionmaking. Various research foundations have provided funds for the conduct of this research. The instructions are simple, and if you follow them carefully and make good decisions, you can earn up to $20, which will be paid to you in cash at the end of this experiment.

You are assigned the role of a private agent whose task is to forecast the rate of inflation in the economy in each experimental time period. The target inflation rate in the economy is set by a policymaker.

The actual rate of inflation is determined by adding a stochastic shock to the target inflation rate, which reflects the fact that the policymaker does not have total control over the inflation rate. The shock is normally distributed and has the mean value equal to 0 and the standard deviation equal to 0.3. This means that approximately 68 percent of the values of the shock will be between –0.3 and 0.3. In addition, approximately 95 percent of the values will be between –0.6 and 0.6. Almost all the values, 99.7 percent, will be between –0.9 and 0.9. Your payoff will depend on how close your forecast is to the actual rate of inflation.

You will play a series of experimental sessions. An experimental session will consist of a number of experimental periods. At the beginning of each experimental time period, you will be prompted to forecast the inflation rate. At the end of each experimental period, you will see the actual rate of inflation and the rate of unemployment for that time period on your computer screen.

At the end of every experimental period, you will also see your payoff for that period. The payoff is given by:

$$\text{payoff} = -5\,(\text{inflation} - \text{forecast})^2.$$

Thus, the higher the squared difference between the actual rate of inflation and your forecast, the lower your payoff.

At any given experimental period, the probability that the session will continue for another period is equal to 0.98. This will be determined in the following way: A random number between 0 and 1 will be drawn from a uniform distribution. If the number is less than or equal to 0.98, the current session will continue into the next period. If the number is greater than 0.98, the session is over. This number will appear in the last column of your screen at the end of each experimental time period. Once the randomly drawn number is greater than 0.98, the session will automatically be terminated.

You will start every experimental session by running a computer program. The experimenter will give you the name of the program. At the beginning of the experiment you will be assigned your identification number. You will keep the same identification number in all experimental sessions and will be prompted to type it at the start of each session. You will also be prompted to enter the probability that the session will end. Enter 0.98 for this question.

### Earnings

The experiment will last two hours. If you complete this two-hour experiment, you are guaranteed to receive a $10 payment. Moreover, you can earn an additional $10, for a total of $20.

At the end of each session, the *probability of winning a prize* of an additional $10 will be computed in the following way:

1. For every time period of the session, the number of period points is calculated by adding 100 points to the payoff that you obtained in that time period.
2. The number of *total points* is calculated by adding the period points earned in all time periods of a given experimental session. If this number is less than 0, it is set equal to 0.
3. The number of maximum points is calculated by multiplying the total number of periods of the session by 100. This number is the number of total points that you would earn in an experimental session if your payoff were equal to 0 in every experimental period.
4. The probability of winning the prize is then calculated in the following way:

   $1 - (maxpoints - total points) / max points$.

   Table B1 presents an example of how the total points, maxpoints, and the probability are calculated in a hypothetical experimental session. The length of the session is five experimental periods.

**Table B1**

| Period | Payoff | Period points |
|--------|--------|---------------|
| 1 | −20.25 | 79.75 |
| 2 | −115.25 | −15.25 |
| 3 | −5.16 | 94.84 |
| 4 | −10.37 | 89.63 |
| 5 | −30.25 | 69.75 |
| Total points | | 318.72 |

*maxpoints* = 100 x 5 periods = 500

Thus, the probability of winning the prize in this session is

$1 - [(500 - 318.72) / 500] = 0.64.$

Higher values of your payoff in each time period (lower in absolute terms) result in higher period and total points. Higher values of total points result, in turn, in higher probability of winning the prize.

5.  If your total points happen to be less than zero, then your probability of winning the prize in that session is set equal to zero.

At the end of the experiment, one of the sessions that you played will be randomly selected. Each session will have an equal chance of being selected. The session will be selected by running the program draw.exe at the DOS prompt. Once you type draw and press enter, you will be asked to enter your ID number. Once you have entered it, you will be prompted to enter the total number of sessions played in the experiment. When you enter this number, the computer will randomly choose a number between 1 and the number of sessions played. This number will appear on your computer screen and will indicate the number of the selected session.

The second number that will appear will be a number between 0 and 1, *rand*, drawn from the uniform distribution. You will take that number and compare it to the probability of winning the prize for the selected session. If *rand* is less or equal to the probability of winning a lottery, you win an additional $10. If *rand* is greater than the probability, you will not win the additional $10 prize. Thus, the higher the probability of winning the prize, the higher your chances that *rand* will be less than or equal to the probability.

## ACKNOWLEDGMENTS

The authors thank Yong-Seok Shin for excellent help with the calculations. They thank James Bullard, Colin Camerer, Timothy Cogley, John Duffy, Tom Palfrey, Christopher Sims, and seminar participants at the University of Amsterdam, California Institute of Technology, the University of California at Los Angeles, and the Federal Reserve Bank of Cleveland for helpful comments. Dr. Arifovic thanks the Social Sciences and Humanities Research Council of Canada for support of her part of the research. Dr. Sargent thanks the National Science Foundation for support of his part of the research.

REFERENCES

Barro, Robert J., and David B. Gordon. 1983. A Positive Theory of Monetary Policy in a Natural Rate Model. *Journal of Political Economy* 12: 101–21.

Blinder, Alan. 1998. *Central Banking in Theory and Practice.* Cambridge: MIT Press.

Cho, In-Koo, and A. Matsui. 1995. Induction and the Ramsey Policy. *Journal of Economic Dynamics and Control* 19: 1113–40.

———, and ———. 1999. Time Consistency in Alternating Move Policy Games. University of Illinois, Urbana–Champaign. Mimeo.

Cho, In-Koo, Noah Williams, and Thomas Sargent. 2002. Escaping Nash Inflation. *Review of Economic Studies*, 1:40, January.

Duffy, J., and J. Ochs. 1999. Emergence of Money as a Medium of Exchange: An Experimental Study. *American Economic Review* 89: 847–77.

Fudenberg, Drew, and David K. Levine. 1993. Self-Confirming Equilibrium. *Econometrica* 61: 523–45.

Klein, Lawrence R. 1958. The Estimation of Distributed Lags. *Econometrica* 26: 553–65.

Kydland, Finn E., and Edward C. Prescott. 1997. Rules Rather than Discretion: The Inconsistency of Optimal Plans. *Journal of Political Economy* 85: 473–91.

Marimon, Ramon, Ellen McGrattan, and Thomas Sargent. 1990. Money as a Medium of Exchange in an Economy with Artificially Intelligent Agents. *Journal of Economic Dynamics and Control* 14: 329–74.

McCallum, Bennett T. 1995. Two Fallacies Concerning Central Bank Independence. *American Economic Review* 85: 207–11.

Phelps, Edmund S. 1967. Phillips Curves, Expectations of Inflation and Optimal Unemployment over Time. *Economica* 2: 22–44.

Roth, Alvin, and M. Malouf. 1979. Game-Theoretic Models and the Role of Information in Bargaining. *Psychological Review* 86: 574–94.

Sargent, Thomas. 1999. *The Conquest of American Inflation.* Princeton, N.J.: Princeton University Press.

Sims, Christopher A. 1988. Projecting Policy Effects with Statistical Models. *Revista de Analisis* Economico 3: 3–20.

Solow, Robert M., and John B. Taylor. 1999. *Inflation, Unemployment, and Monetary Policy.* Cambridge: MIT Press.

Stokey, Nancy L. 1989. Reputation and Time Consistency. *American Economic Review* 79: 134–39.

Williams, Noah. 1999. Analysis of the Convergence and Escape of a Constant Gain Learning Algorithm. University of Chicago. Mimeo.

## APPENDIX C

### Figure C1:  Economy 1. The $\hat{x}_t$ (gray) and $x_t$ (black)

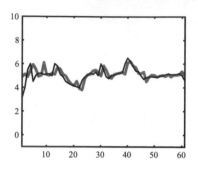
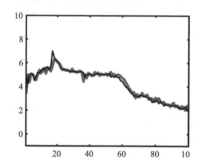

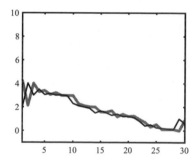

**Figure C2:  Economy 2. The $\hat{x}_t$ (gray) and $x_t$ (black)**

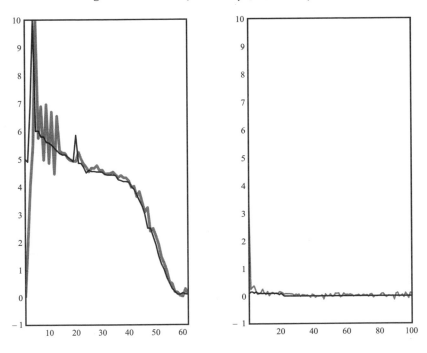

**Figure C3:  Economy 3. The $\hat{x}_t$ (gray) and $x_t$ (black)**

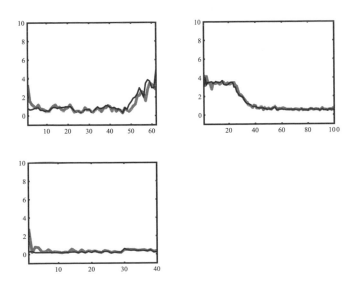

**Figure C4: Economy 4. The $\hat{x}_t$ (gray) and $x_t$ (black)**

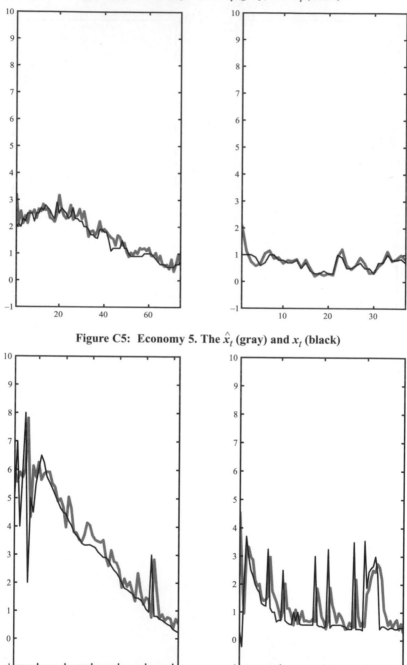

**Figure C5: Economy 5. The $\hat{x}_t$ (gray) and $x_t$ (black)**

**Figure C6: Economy 6. The $\hat{x}_t$ (gray) and $x_t$ (black)**

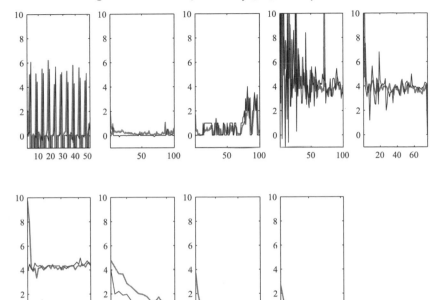

**Figure C7: Economy 7. The $\hat{x}_t$ (gray) and $x_t$ (black)**

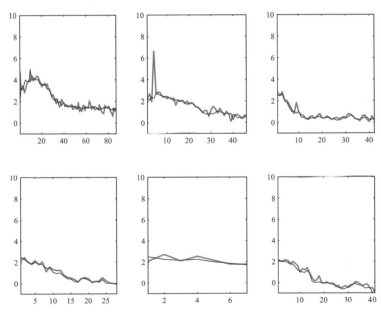

*Jasmina Arifovic and Thomas J. Sargent*

**Figure C8: Economy 8. The $\hat{x}_t$ (gray) and $x_t$ (black)**

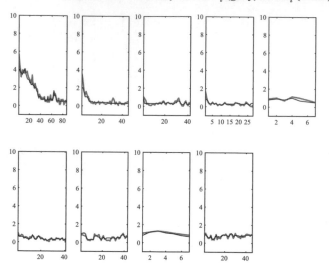

**Figure C9: Economy 9. The $\hat{x}_t$ (gray) and $x_t$ (black)**

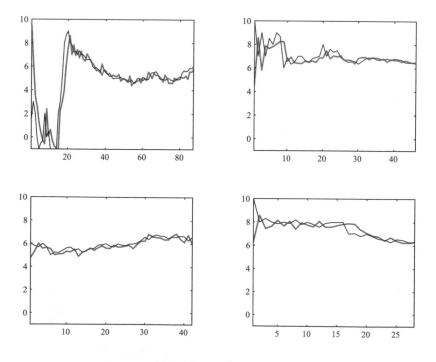

**Figure C10: Economy 10. The $\hat{x}_t$ (gray) and $x_t$ (black)**

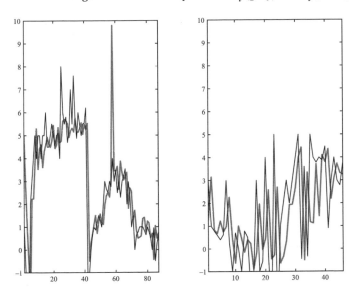

**Figure C11: Economy 11. The $\hat{x}_t$ (gray) and $x_t$ (black)**

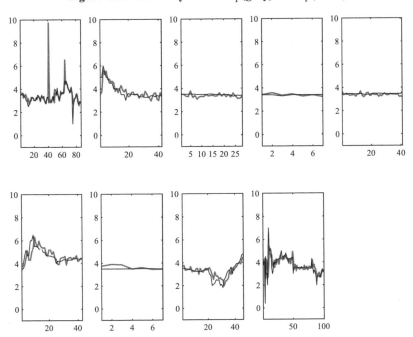

*Jasmina Arifovic and Thomas J. Sargent*

**Figure C12:   Economy 12. The $\hat{x}_t$ (gray) and $x_t$ (black)**

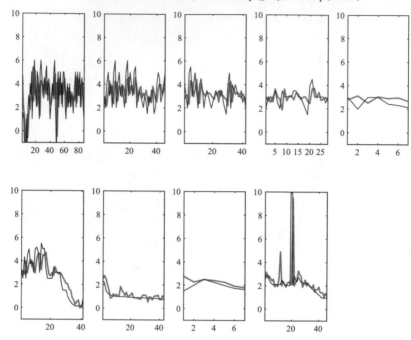

**Figure C13: Dispersion of inflation forecasts across agents ($\frac{1}{T} \sum_t \sum_i (\hat{x}_{it} - \hat{x}_t)^2$, for twelve experiments; experiments 1–12 appear from top to bottom, left to right.**

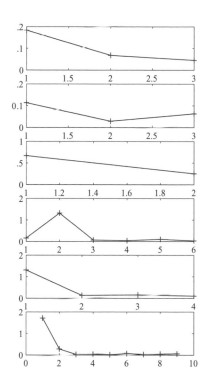
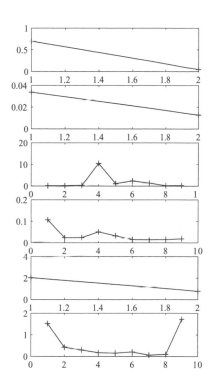

**Figure C14:** $\max_i \hat{x}_{it} - \min_i \hat{x}_{it.}$

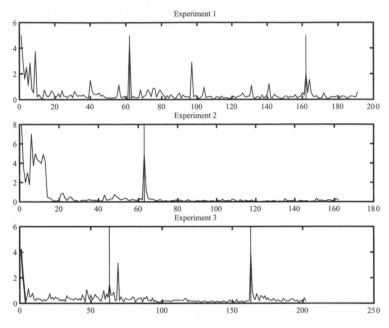

**Figure C15:** $\max_i \hat{x}_{it} - \min_i \hat{x}_{it.}$

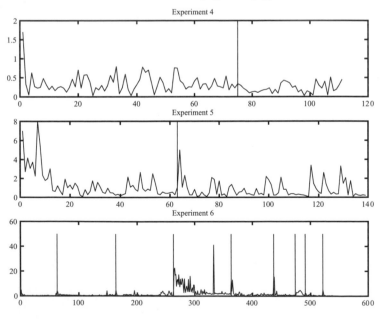

**Figure C16:** $\max_i \hat{x}_{it} - \min_i \hat{x}_{it.}$

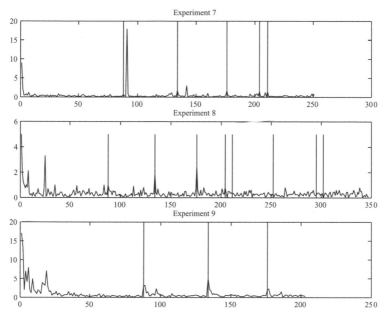

**Figure C17:** $\max_i \hat{x}_{it} - \min_i \hat{x}_{it.}$

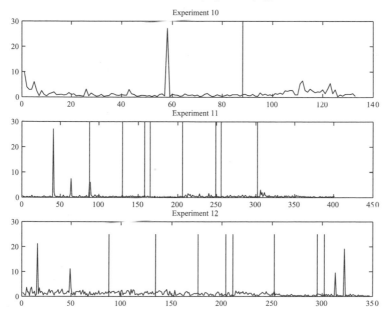

# Commentary

*James Bullard*

## 1. LABORATORY EXPERIMENTS
### IN MACROECONOMIC ENVIRONMENTS

Experiments such as the ones undertaken in Arifovic and Sargent's paper are rare. The conventional wisdom has been that controlled laboratory environments are infeasible for macroeconomic questions because we are attempting to understand how a very large number of individual households and firms interact to produce the prices and quantities we observe in the data. While this conventional wisdom is, of course, true at some level, there is more to the story. There are good reasons to take experimental macroeconomics very seriously. Mainly, we need to obtain laboratory confirmation of predictions from *simple* models before we can hope to correctly infer what forces are at work in large, industrialized economies.

We economists often write down simple models in an effort to get some core economic intuition concerning topics of interest. The literature begun by Kydland and Prescott (1977) and continued by Barro and Gordon (1983), Rogoff (1985), Walsh (1995), and many others is one outstanding example. In these simple models, we presume to know how human beings would act when confronted with the environments we construct. Laboratory experiments can help us to understand whether such presumptions are warranted. In fact, the current paper calls those presumptions into question.

The literature begun by Kydland and Prescott (1977) has been perhaps the most influential for central bankers during the last 25 years. It provides the leading explanation of why there is so much inflation among the industrialized countries of the world today. The word "credibility" rolls off of the tongues of seemingly every-one connected with monetary policymaking. In this literature, the presumption that the economy's participants would coordinate on the time-consistent, high-inflation, Nash equilibrium of the model has been almost axiomatic. Only the recent chal-lenges of Cho and Matsui (1995, 1999), Sargent (1999), and, less formally, McCallum (1995) and Blinder (1998), have seriously questioned this assumption. That is why the current paper provides such an important service: The main finding is that the Nash equilibrium is not consistently sustained in the laboratory. What is sustainable, and how to interpret it, presents us with a challenge.

## 2. THREE THEORIES

The environment considered in this paper can be viewed as encompassing three theories. The most natural one is a basic version of the Kydland and Prescott economy, in which time-inconsistency problems lead to a Nash equilibrium characterized by an inflation bias. I want to caricature this theory as simply predicting that the Nash equilibrium will be sustained in the laboratory implementation, perhaps after some transition dynamics that are not in the neighborhood of the Nash outcome.

The existence of a Ramsey outcome characterized by distinctly lower inflation facilitates interpretations of the experiments in terms of Cho and Matsui (1995, 1999) or, perhaps closer to the intent of the authors, Blinder (1998) and McCallum (1995). These theories suggest the Ramsey outcome could be sustained, but the details either do not exist or are not implemented here. Thus, the link between these theories and the actual laboratory results is somewhat tenuous. According to McCallum (1995, 208–9), "the central bank [could]...recognize that its objectives would be more fully achieved on average if it were to abstain from attempts to exploit...temporarily given expectations." Possibly, the human subjects playing the central bank in the laboratory could make such a leap of faith and simply play Ramsey. I want to caricature this group of theories as predicting sustained Ramsey outcomes in the laboratory, possibly in conjunction with some initial transition dynamics.

Finally, the environment here has many of the ingredients of Sargent (1999), where the policymaker's use of a misspecified model and an approach to learning characterized by the discounting of past data leads to a system in which both the Nash equilibrium and the Ramsey outcome are visited on a recurrent basis. Sargent's (1999) dynamics involve a relatively long time spent in transition from the Ramsey outcome to the Nash equilibrium, while the time spent in transition from Nash to Ramsey is relatively short. The details of these dynamics are sensitive to parameter choices. In addition, the assumptions concerning the knowledge available to the government and to the private sector differ in the laboratory experiments relative to Sargent. Thus, it not that clear what Sargent's predictions actually are and whether they map clearly into the experimental design examined here. Nevertheless, I want to caricature the Sargent prediction as one in which the laboratory systems display considerable time—beyond initialization time—in transition between Nash and Ramsey, and more so from Ramsey to Nash than from Nash to Ramsey.

## 3. RESULTS

The main results that I want to focus on are as follows: The laboratory systems tend to spend a good deal of time in the neighborhood of the Ramsey outcome. There is evidence that systems sometimes achieve the Ramsey outcome, but then "backslide" or creep toward a Nash equilibrium. In general, the Nash equilibrium is not often observed in these experiments. Based on these results, which theory is best supported by the laboratory data?

The most striking finding is simply that the Nash equilibrium is not observed on a sustained basis. Thus, Kydland and Prescott's basic prediction is disconfirmed in the laboratory. If such results hold up in future experiments, it will be a crushing blow to the leading theory of why we have observed so much inflation in industrialized economies during the post–World War II era. How many papers have been written assuming, in similar environments, that the Nash equilibrium could be sustained? Those assumptions are simply not supported by the laboratory data assembled here.

It is not as clear as the authors suggest that we can effectively distinguish between the two remaining theories based on these data. Sargent's theory has wide-ranging predictions. A relatively long, sustained period at the Ramsey outcome could be consistent with this theory; not observing much time at a Nash equilibrium could also be consistent. The slow transitions toward a Ramsey outcome are not consistent. As for Blinder's and McCallum's positions, it is not clear how they can account for the non-Ramsey outcomes observed in these data.

It seems clear that to frame these questions more appropriately, one needs to obtain more detailed predictions from a specific version of Sargent's model and implement that version of the model in the laboratory. The rapid escapes from the Nash equilibrium, for instance, are relatively rare events in Sargent, and I am not sure we should expect to observe them in experiments of this length. With a more specific implementation of the Sargent model, one could calculate an expected time to escape and use that to interpret the data. Similarly, backsliding from Ramsey also takes a good deal of time. But, again, one could obtain a more detailed prediction from a specific implementation of Sargent and then compare that prediction with the data.

Experiments 9 through 12 involved a better compensation scheme for the policymaker, and these systems spent much less time in the neighborhood of the Ramsey outcome. This seems to be a significant finding, and the authors should discuss it in more detail.

## 4. SOME ALTERNATIVE EXPERIMENTS

Experiments beget experiments. Many more laboratory implementations of the Kydland–Prescott model need to be executed before we can be fully convinced that the Nash equilibrium is not the right prediction. To get a better approximation to the point of view emphasized by Blinder and McCallum, the authors may want to consider experimental designs in which subjects playing the policymaker role are familiar with ideas from the monetary policy games literature. This seems to be part of McCallum's critique. To more closely match the spirit of the Sargent model, in which policymaker learning is crucial, experimental designs that involve pitting a policymaker against a robotic "rational expectations" private sector might be interesting, instead of letting both sides learn, as in the current implementation. Such experiments would also have the benefit of being cheaper and easier to run.

## 5. CONCLUSION

This is a problematic paper from the perspective of the monetary policy games literature. It brings empirical evidence to bear on the predictions from simple, widely used models, evidence that does not square well with traditional interpretations of the theory. I do not think the results here are definitive. On the other hand, we economists are not so successful that we can afford to ignore evidence from controlled experiments.

### REFERENCES

Barro, Robert J., and David B. Gordon. 1983. A Positive Theory of Monetary Policy in a Natural Rate Model. *Journal of Political Economy* 12: 101–21.

Blinder, Alan. 1998. *Central Banking in Theory and Practice*. Cambridge, Mass.: MIT Press.

Cho, In-Koo, and A. Matsui. 1995. Induction and the Ramsey Policy. *Journal of Economic Dynamics and Control* 19: 1113–40.

Cho, In-Koo, and A. Matsui. 1999. Time Consistency in Alternating Move Policy Games. University of Illinois, unpublished manuscript.

Kydland, Finn E., and Edward C. Prescott. 1977. Rules Rather Than Discretion: The Inconsistency of Optimal Plans. *Journal of Political Economy* 85: 473–91.

McCallum, Bennett T. 1995. Two Fallacies Concerning Central Bank Independence. *American Economic Review* 85: 207–11.

Rogoff, Kenneth. 1985. The Optimal Degree of Commitment to an Intermediate Monetary Target. *Quarterly Journal of Economics* 100: 1169–90.

Sargent, Thomas. 1999. *The Conquest of American Inflation*. Princeton, N.J.: Princeton University Press.

Walsh, C. 1995. Optimal Contracts for Central Bankers. *American Economic Review* 85: 150–67.

# Commentary

*Christopher A. Sims*

## 1. INTRODUCTION

This is a thought-provoking paper. It should contribute to a reassessment of the way we teach and think about monetary policy and the design of monetary institutions. I urge readers to take the time to examine the plots of the experimental outcomes in detail, as they show interesting patterns that are not easily summarized in words and tables.

My comments first discuss the broader implications of this and related work on time inconsistency in monetary policy; I then give an example of the kind of speculation that can be set off by detailed examination of the plots.

## 2. IS TIME INCONSISTENCY UNIMPORTANT?

The Kydland–Prescott rational expectations Phillips curve model is an appealing teaching device, as it gets across the idea of the time-inconsistency problem in a simple model. But it is becoming increasingly clear that it should not be thought of as a good metaphor for actual monetary policymaking behavior. Here are some of the reasons, starting with those given least attention in this paper.

### 2.1. Commitment Technology

The assumption that policymakers cannot make a commitment that lasts even one period is unrealistic. Individuals regularly make promises and threats and often carry them out, even when there is apparently an incentive not to do so. Central bank presidents and chairmen are individuals. It is true in most cases that their terms do not last a lifetime, but they live on after their terms are over and carry reputations with them. A recent paper (Schaumburg and Tambalotti 2001) shows that even a monetary authority that can make commitments only over a random span of a few periods will arrive at policies that are not far from the Ramsey solution.

### 2.2. Learning by Policymakers

As Arifovic and Sargent point out, the Kydland–Prescott Nash (KPN) equilibrium is a self-confirming equilibrium if policymakers assume a static, linear Phillips curve and regularly re-estimate it. However, I pointed out in 1988 that convergence to the steady state in this setup is extremely slow with realistic parameter values, with unemployment rates taking centuries to rise by even a percentage point or two. That paper also points out that if policymakers believe the parameters of the Phillips curve can drift over time—and therefore estimate it with a Kalman filter— they can, without ever learning the true, natural-rate Phillips curve theory, arrive permanently at nearly the Ramsey policy. This outcome occurs if they expect drift in the slope as well as the intercept of the Phillips curve. If they expect drift main- ly in the intercept, then the unemployment rate tends to drift slowly upward toward the KPN rate, except during brief episodes of rapid return to near-Ramsey behav- ior. Labeling this latter pattern "backsliding" and "escape dynamics," Sargent (1999) confirms that it occurs in a slightly different modeling setup and elucidates the underlying mathematical structure. However, his less flexible model of policy behavior apparently cannot reproduce the pattern of a permanent shift to near- Ramsey behavior.

### 2.3. Private-Sector Learning

As Arifovic and Sargent point out, Cho and Matsui (1995) show that if private agents have adaptive expectations, an optimizing policy authority that understands this and also understands the correct rational expectations Phillips curve model is likely to converge to near-Ramsey behavior.

### 2.4. Dynamic Game Theory with Reputation

Starting even before the advent of rational expectations theory, monetary policy- makers have long been concerned with reputation, credibility, the "acceleration" dynamics of inflationary expectations, and concepts such as the "sacrifice ratio," which describes how much output loss or unemployment must be endured to attain a given reduction in inflation. Therefore, it is clear that realistic modeling of policy behavior must take into account the fact that the policy game is repeated, and policy can depend on lagged realized values of itself and other "nonfundamental" components of history.

Suppose we ignore learning and use a model that assumes there is a rational expectations Phillips curve in which only surprise inflation has real effects, that the policy authorities understand this, and that the public understands policy behavior. As Arifovic and Sargent point out, the KPN equilibrium is then a topologically tiny component of the space of possible equilibrium outcomes, many of which yield higher welfare. Since the KPN equilibrium concept has no room for the reputa- tional notions that form such a large part of actual policy discussion, there seems to be no reason to focus on it in a positive analysis.

### 2.5. Observed Behavior

Arifovic and Sargent show that college students acting as policymakers and forecasters in the presence of an artificial, natural-rate Phillips curve, with no special coaching, for the most part manage to achieve outcomes close to the Ramsey, full-commitment equilibrium. To the extent that the results show deviations from this pattern, they do not look like the observed behavior of any monetary authority. The deviations tend to involve isolated, short, sharp inflationary episodes, or they display very erratic oscillations in inflation.

This outcome is not surprising, except perhaps to economists who take game theory too seriously. Policymakers believe that by persistently choosing a long-run, optimal, low-inflation policy, they can convince the public they are likely to continue doing so, and it seems both in reality and in these experiments that they are right. Of course, it is a logical possibility that the public, seeing that the gains from surprise inflation increase as the level of expected inflation drops, will never be convinced, in which case the policy authority might never attempt to hold inflation low. But this seems not to be the way people behave, at least most of the time, in most countries.

### 3. DESCRIPTIVE REALISM OF LEAST SQUARES LEARNING

Arifovic and Sargent make the point that the pattern of experimental results is not what would be expected if the forecasters had adaptive expectations and policymakers knew the coefficients of the expectational rule. Expectations seem to adapt so fast that policymakers should have reduced inflation much quicker. While it is true that this pattern does not fit the simple, linear, adaptive expectations model, it is perhaps not very mysterious. Observe the actual distribution of policy behavior in the experiments: Most policymakers, most of the time, keep inflation fairly low and change it smoothly. One policymaker keeps inflation persistently high. A few "experiment," jumping inflation around or creating brief "surprises." The forecasters probably see such patterns, and maybe others as well, as possibilities. That is, they see the stochastic process they are forecasting as quite nonlinear, probably even non-ergodic. They are hoping they are dealing with a Ramsey policymaker, but they are aware there is an incentive to be erratic or to create high inflation. Under these circumstances it is quite plausible that in order to move to a Ramsey equilibrium, it is important to make policy changes smooth, slow, and predictable.

One can see this possibility most clearly in the plots for economy 6, where it appears that in the seventh frame, when the policymaker finally decided for low and stable inflation, as a legacy of his or her earlier drastic experiments with erratic inflation rates, expected inflation stays well above actual for a long time even while actual inflation drops smoothly.

This type of nonlinear policy behavior and expectation formation is likely to show up in the real world as well, and it raises a note of caution for empirical application of least squares learning models. If the public perceives the possibility of persistently "responsible" and "irresponsible" or "erratic" policymakers or institutions, then its expectations may be much more sensitive to brief episodes of high inflation than least squares learning theory would suggest.

#### REFERENCES

Cho, In-Koo, and A. Matsui. 1995. Introduction and the Ramsey Policy. *Journal of Economic Dynamics and Control* 19: 1113–40.

Sargent, Thomas J. 1999. *The Conquest of American Inflation*. Princeton, N.J.: Princeton University Press.

Schaumburg, Ernst, and Andrea Tambalotti. 2001. An Investigation of the Gains from Commitment in Monetary Policy. Princeton University, Discussion Paper, September. Available at *www.princeton.edu/~tamba/quasi.pdf* [24 January 2002].

Sims, Christopher A. 1988. Projecting Policy Effects with Statistical Models. *Revista de Analisis Economico*: 3–20. Available at *www.princeton.edu/~sims* [24 January 2002].

# 2

# Whither Central Banking?

*Charles Goodhart*

## 1. INTRODUCTION

The success of delegating the achievement of price stability to an operationally independent central bank has been regarded as so manifest in the OECD countries where
this regime has been adopted, the question is now often posed, why not also dele-
gate fiscal policy to an independent fiscal authority (see Blinder 1998, 59)? My
answer is that almost every fiscal decision involves *choices* between priorities and
objectives, among them macro stability, micro efficiency, and distributional effects,
to name but three. The essence of politics is to make such difficult choices, and that
should not, in my view, be delegated to an unelected, primarily technical body.

In my lifetime, the most crucial change that has occurred in our way of thinking about the working of the macroeconomic system was the shift from a belief that
the Phillips curve remained downward sloping, even in the longer term, to a belief
that it would become vertical (Friedman 1968; Phelps 1970). Given the former
downward-sloping Phillips curve, there remained choices to be made, essentially
political choices, about the "best" combination of inflation and output. With a vertical Phillips curve, all that monetary policy *could* deliver in the medium and long
term was price stability. Moreover, periods of severe price instability, whether of
high and variable inflation or of deflation, were inimical to growth. So the best the
monetary authorities could do in the medium and long term for real growth was to
achieve such stability; for the rest, issues relating to growth were not primarily in
their province.

Such a single objective—price stability—meant that its achievement could properly be delegated to an independent central bank that could use its single instrument,
control over the short-term interest rate, to achieve that objective. There remain some
second-order questions as to whether the political authorities, having mandated the
achievement of price stability to the central bank, should go further and quantify in
numerical terms what exactly they mean by that: for example, to hold the headline
consumer price index between 0 percent and 3 percent annual growth. My own belief
is that reserving the exact definition of the inflation target to the political authorities
is desirable; it enhances the democratic legitimacy and the accountability and transparency of the exercise. It has the side effect of committing the political authorities

to supporting the process and helps to protect a monetary policy committee from political (as contrasted with technical) attack. That said, I doubt that this question—which constitutional body should quantify the generally agreed objective of price stability—makes a critical difference between outcomes in countries with such politically set targets (such as the United Kingdom) and in countries without them (such as the European Central Bank and Japan).

This one objective/one instrument context simplifies and clarifies the conduct of monetary policy enormously, but it does not, of course, remove *all* the remaining difficult choices and problems. In particular, there do remain *short-run* problems of choice, between stabilizing inflation around its target following shocks and stabilizing output around its sustainable growth path; in an open economy, the choice is between stabilizing the internal and external value of the currency and deciding what weight to give to the path of asset prices, as well as to those of goods and services, in the achievement of the inflation target. I shall turn to these issues in due course. First, I want to discuss at greater length the delegation of operational independence to a central bank.

## 2. WHY DELEGATE?

The one objective/one instrument context of monetary policy allows for the delegation of monetary policy without any major infringement upon democratic sovereignty. But equally it does not require it. Ministers of finance and chancellors of the exchequer are (in most cases) fully aware of the doctrine of the vertical Phillips curve. Why can they not *themselves* just continue to fix interest rates so as to achieve price stability?

The answer is that delegating the achievement of price stability to an independent central bank—with that objective specified in public and preferably in quantitative terms—is, as I shall argue, a commitment device. Why might we need a commitment mechanism? The standard answer to this is time inconsistency. A politician will promise to achieve price stability when she first comes into office, but as the next elections come near, she will be tempted to renege and generate a pre-election boom. It is a clever story, and it appeals to the cynicism with which most people view politicians. But I am doubtful whether it is a true story. First, lags in the transmission mechanism of monetary policy are so long, and the conduct of monetary policy—that is, cutting interest rates—is so obvious and transparent that few would be fooled. People would see the forthcoming inflation, and so the exercise would be largely futile for the government. Second, the evidence collected by Alesina (1989) and others does not confirm the existence of systematic, monetarily driven pre-election booms.

My own view is that the cause of politicians' inflation bias is much more mundane. Because of the long lags in the monetary-transmission process, today's interest rates should be set in light of the *forecast* balance of inflationary pressures some six (or more) quarters hence, when the effect of interest rates on inflation will be greatest. But future forecasts of inflation, output, and the like, one or two years ahead, are horribly uncertain and imprecise. No one knows with any certainty what should be done today to have an optimal effect on the economy a year or two in the future.

Meanwhile, interest rate increases and reductions in credit availability are currently painful. Asset prices fall. Exchange rates (usually) appreciate. The pain is felt most by certain concentrated, politically powerful groups, such as manufacturers, construction and property companies, and home buyers who have taken out mortgages. With uncertain forecasts—and the known political unpopularity of monetary tightening—politicians are likely to wait until there is incontrovertible evidence of worsening inflation before they act. Because of the same lags in the transmission mechanism, by the time they are prepared to act, it will be too late. With political control of monetary policy, "too little and too late" is likely to be the order of the day.

Central bankers are likely to be subject to many of the same problems and pressures, notably uncertain forecasts. Why, then, should delegation be a good commitment device? There are several reasons: First, a minister can commit more credibly to sacking a central banker for failing than to disciplining himself. Second, the resulting single focus on achieving the inflation target will concentrate the mind of the monetary authority. Third, the central bank is likely to be most technically proficient in forecasting and judging the effects of monetary measures, especially if it is operationally independent. Fourth, a monetary policy authority is likely to be more removed from direct lobbying than politicians. I have advocated paying central bankers by results[1]—known as a Walsh-type contract—but thus far, this has been rejected on public relations grounds.

In some countries (such as New Zealand and Canada), responsibility for the interest rate decision is delegated to an individual central bank governor, whereas in others (United Kingdom, Japan, the United States, and the European Central

---

[1] I did so in my capacity as an external adviser to the Reserve Bank of New Zealand in the run-up to the Reserve Bank of New Zealand Act of 1989. Then I had proposed (prior to the publication of Walsh's (1995a,b) articles in that vein, that the governor receive a bonus, calibrated according to how closely the target was achieved. That proposal was eventually scuppered on presentational grounds, the New Zealand Treasury fearing that it might be claimed that the governor was personally and financially benefiting from interest rate increases that would throw workers out of jobs. That objection could have been deflected by making proper use of the lags in the transmission process, that is, any bonus to be earned by a decisionmaker today should be calibrated on the inflation outcome two years hence, and any bonus payment deferred to that later date. Hence, an interest rate increase now would not benefit the governor until it had had its full subsequent effect on inflation and could be shown ex post facto to have been appropriate. In any event, I know of no case in which any pecuniary incentive scheme has been applied to the monetary authorities.

Bank), it is vested in a committee. In view of the importance of getting the technical issues right—that is, the significance of the forecast, the assessment of future risks, and the need to protect those making the decision from lobbying and outside pressures—there is, I believe, a strong case for the policy committee approach. In practice, most governors would surround themselves with an advisory committee anyhow, so the question is not, perhaps, of the first importance.

Let me now turn to the main part of this paper, concerning issues where decisions and trade-offs remain to be taken despite the vertical, medium-term Phillips curve.

## 3. CHOICES AND TRADE-OFFS

### 3.1. The Short-Run Balance between Inflation and Output

At any time, nominal magnitudes are anchored by existing (wage/price) contracts, the cost of revising prices, current expectations, etc., and such rigidities provide both the real leverage that monetary policy can exert in the short run and a downward-sloping, short-run Phillips curve. Initially, this means that the effects of monetary policy will be mediated mainly through changes to real output before coming to affect inflation. If inflation is perceived as likely to go off course, an attempt to return it to target *quickly* will tend to cause marked deviations in output from its sustainable trend, especially because of the lags in the transmission mechanism. On the other hand, attempts to smooth the course of output—depending on the stochastic shocks hitting the economy—will likely limit the extent to which monetary policy is aggressively used, so that inflation will not be driven back to its target for rather a long time.

There are several alternative ways of expressing and resolving this trade-off. One is to decide the time horizons (the length of time) for returning inflation to target after some digression. Another is to determine the optimal trade-off between the deviation of output from its natural rate and the deviation of inflation from target. The relationship between these two approaches is shown diagrammatically in Batini and Haldane (1999). The most common and most popular expression of this trade-off, however, is encapsulated in the Taylor rule, where an interest-rate-reaction function is presented as a combination of deviations of inflation from target and deviations of output from its sustainable rate:

$$R_t = a + b_1(\pi_t - \pi^*) + b_2(y - y^*) + b_3R_{t-1}.$$

So long as the coefficient $b_1$ is high enough to ensure the target will eventually be met, then the coefficients in this equation (and in the IS curve) will determine how long it takes for inflation to return to target and the relative variance of output and inflation along the way.

In theory, if one could identify the shocks hitting the economy, had confidence in one's model and forecast of the economy, and could specify a clear loss function, then the optimal-control theory could be used to minimize losses.[2] The problem is that, except on rare occasions, the current shocks are not easily identifiable. Few people who actually have had to make decisions based on model forecasts are confident about such models and forecasts; for a variety of good, practical reasons, neither politicians nor central bankers are keen on pinning themselves down by offering, even introspectively, to set a formal loss function for themselves. "It all depends on circumstances."

As a result, optimal-control methods have not been used much, if at all. In particular, they seem to be very sensitive to the structure of the model and the precise form of the shock, neither of which is generally obvious (Batini and Nelson 2000).

One important element in (the model of) the economy is whether (inflation) expectations are forward or backward looking. If expectations are forward looking and the monetary authorities are credible, then a price-level target is better than an inflation target because the forward-looking expectations help with stabilization (Gaspar and Smets 2000). My own judgment is that, under normal circumstances, most ordinary people base their expectations on developments in the (recent) past. If so, with backward-looking expectations, it is safer to stick with inflation targets, as central banks have all chosen to do.[3]

There are several approaches to balancing the (short-run) volatility of output against deviations of inflation from its target, but, on examination, they all amount to much the same thing.

### 3.2. Open Economy Issues

Most of the time, a floating exchange rate works with the grain of monetary policy to support the work of the monetary authorities. When the economy is growing above trend and incipient inflationary pressures are mounting, investors see an enticing combination of rising profitability and rising relative interest rates. Capital flows in and the exchange rate rises. That increase in exchange rates helps to limit the boom and the inflationary upsurge, thus reducing the rise in domestic interest rates that is necessary to restore price stability. The case is the reverse, of course, when the economy weakens. Those who seek to peg their exchange rates close off a highly desirable safety valve and introduce a serious danger that the needs of domestic stabilization and the aim of maintaining the external peg will run counter to each other.

---

[2] This ignores some remaining abstruse concerns about manipulating expectations in a time-consistent fashion (Woodford 1999), but I am happy to do just that.

[3] The choice of price-level (inflation) targets is largely, but not entirely, independent of whether the inflation target should incorporate a margin above zero. A price-level target can also be rising over time.

If the exchange rate had varied as proponents of floating had imagined and expected, then movements in nominal exchange rates would have offset, virtually one for one, movements in relative inflation rates. This would mean that real exchange rates would and should have responded only to relative real shocks, such as changes in productivity. The academic expectation (at least in the 1960s, before generalized floating was adopted) was that such movements in real rates would be relatively modest. So the achievement of comparable low inflation rates in two currency zones with floating exchange rates between them should, according to such theories, have left nominal and real exchange rates unaffected. If that had been the case in practice, as it was in theory, arguments for combining the objective of domestic price stability at home with externally floating nominal exchange rates would have been even stronger, indeed usually overwhelming.

It is well known, however, that movements of nominal and real exchange rates have not corresponded well with the initial, hopeful theory. The reason is still not clear; in my own view, one reason is the virtual absence of long-term speculators who were prepared to take a bet on the exchange rate reverting over time to some (fundamental) equilibrium. Just as there are good bacteria and bad bacteria, there also can be good speculators and bad speculators—and one has to worry whether measures that prevent speculation may worsen rather than improve market volatility.

In reality, both nominal and real exchange rates have been disturbingly and unpredictably volatile. Let me give an example: Between the beginning of 1999 and April 2001, inflation in the euro zone was marginally higher than in the United Kingdom and lower than in the United States. But the euro lost approximately 25 percent of its value against both currencies, with equivalent changes (more or less) in real exchange rates. Alas, this is not an isolated example. During the 1980s, the U.S. dollar first appreciated and then declined by even more in real terms. Fluctuations of the yen have been equally dramatic. Movements in real exchange rates among all countries, at all stages of development, have been much larger than economic fundamentals could account for.

This causes a problem for countries that focus on domestic price stabilization while maintaining a floating exchange rate. If real exchange rates massively overshoot their equilibrium, then concentrating on domestic price stability *in aggregate* may result, for instance, in a price deflation in the tradable-goods sector that is balanced by (excessive) inflation in the nontradable (service) sector if the real exchange rate has appreciated too much, and vice versa if the opposite occurs. In large, relatively closed economies, such as the United States or the euro zone, external trade is so small relative to internal trade that the complications and problems arising from volatile real exchange rates can be largely ignored. Even in the case of the euro, however, the political desiderata of wanting the new currency to appear reasonably strong to the public means that concern about its depreciation transcends simple calculations about its effect on the Harmonized Index of Consumer Prices. But in smaller, more open economies, can one afford to concentrate just on the aggregate domestic price level and ignore the potentially wrenching effects of movements in (real) exchange rates on exposed parts of the economy?

Just as many of the adverse effects of domestic inflation arise from deterioration in the allocative efficiency of the price mechanism, as Richard Cooper (1984) has argued, disturbances to nominal and real exchange rates can reduce the efficiency of the price mechanism in an open economy. But unless most of one's trade is done with a single partner country, then linking one's currency to *one* other single currency will not resolve the problem, because of the risk of variations in the real value of that currency. In the United Kingdom, however, more than 50 percent of that country's trade is now done with the euro zone, which is one reason why most of the tradable-goods sector is keen on euro entry. If that proportion were below 30 percent, for instance, then opposition to euro entry would be even more widespread.

There is still the possibility of pegging or linking one's own currency to a trade-weighted basket of currencies, as Australia attempted to do for a time. But one problem with this approach is that it does not have the simplicity or transparency that a good nominal anchor should possess. People will be cynical about the weighting process and will find it difficult to predict or understand the reasons for interest rate changes or other monetary policy measures. It will hardly serve to anchor expectations or to allow a simple, straightforward explanation of monetary policy measures.

The next problem that currency linking poses is that the country with the pegged currency must accept whatever interest rates are set at the center; depending on constitutional circumstances, it may or may not play any part in setting such rates. As the saying goes, "one size has to fit all," but of course it rarely does. Asymmetric shocks occur almost as often within countries as they do between countries. What is the glue that holds a within-country monetary union together, while making between-country monetary unions somewhat fragile? My own answer is that countries normally enjoy both an internal political union and comity, augmented by a fiscal or other burden-sharing mechanism, which is traditionally absent between countries (but is in the process of construction, somewhat slowly and painfully, in Europe).

If the maintenance of a pegged or linked currency causes domestic economic and political pain that is greater than the will of the people and of the politicians who represent them can bear, then the link will snap. Such a break point depends on a host of political, historical, and economic circumstances, including the extent of domestic wage/price flexibility and the other options for monetary policy regimes that are available. If the pain barrier, or break point, is perceived as low, then a currency peg will not be credible. Moreover, standard measures to protect a currency, such as raising interest rates or raising taxes, may be counterproductive beyond some unknown level, because they will only make outside observers feel the political break point is much closer.

Circumstances—often political and historical as much as economic—lead to currency pegs and links of various kinds (ranging from complete unification, through currency boards, down to pegged but adjustable exchange rates), facing differing intensities of pain with varying break points. In my own career, I have strongly advocated fixed currency links in a few cases.[4] In other cases, I have doubted whether the necessary political and economic infrastructure has been in place, as with the euro. And in other cases, it is patently obvious that such infrastructure is *not* in place, as with relationships across the Atlantic between the euro and the dollar. It all depends, of course, on political, historical, and economic circumstances.

Assuming that a country has adopted an internal inflation target, what should be done, if anything, about overshooting the exchange rate? There is a range of options: The first, and minimalist, approach is to take account of the exchange rate insofar as it is expected to affect domestic inflation. The second is to give a somewhat larger weight to the exchange rate in the implicit central bank reaction (or loss) function. This could be formalized in a monetary-conditions index that weights the exchange rate more heavily than its (normal) effect on domestic inflation would justify. But with such an index, there is an inherent difficulty that the exchange rate can vary for a range of reasons, caused by home or foreign shocks, portfolio or real shifts. Because of such diversity, the directly measured (reduced-form) effects of exchange rate changes on domestic variables such as inflation, output, and exports, are heterogeneous. Any formalization of response to exchange rate fluctuations, as Canada and New Zealand have attempted, is likely to—and did—go awry. There is no substitute for (discretionary) judgment in an open economy.

The next option, then, is to make a judgment as to when (real) exchange rates have overshot, and then adjust interest rates in response, at least temporarily. Given the tendency of real exchange rates to revert to equilibrium, this can be interpreted as fully consistent with longer-run inflation (price-level) targeting (Cecchetti et al. 2000). Problems lie in assessing the extent to which the target has been overshot, the appearance of some favoritism toward one sector of the economy (tradable goods), and a perception of some willingness to compromise with domestic targets. At least one member of the United Kingdom's Monetary Policy Committee has argued for such an approach.

---

[4] As in Hong Kong, where I advised on the link in 1983 and have remained involved much of the time since then.

If central banks have two separate objectives—that is, domestic price stability and stable real exchange rates (I have argued this should not be the case in theory, though it often is in practice)—that naturally leads to a hunt for a second instrument. Two come to mind in this field, sterilized intervention and exchange controls. Sterilized intervention is a relatively weak mechanism. The signal is obscure at best (often indicating a desire for a different exchange rate but an unwillingness to take real actions to achieve it—that is, it signals weakness, not strength), and the scale of portfolio adjustment is usually tiny relative to the market. Even so, if the scale of exchange rate disequilibrium is large enough to convince the central bank that it can reap medium-term profits, why shouldn't the authorities act as profit-making, long-term, stabilizing speculators? Too few other such speculators exist, and I cannot see why a central bank should sign a self-denying ordinance to abjure potentially profitable and stabilizing opportunities. Rather, the danger comes when a central bank is required to defend a (probably indefensible) pegged rate—not when it intervenes as a well-informed, long-term speculator on an essentially floating rate.

That leaves exchange controls. Some kinds of capital flows have exhibited great volatility, especially short-term flows between developed and developing countries. Volatility can place great pressures on the stability of the internal financial structure of an emerging country. There is now widespread agreement that countries that are sheltered behind exchange controls (such as China) should *not* be pressured to remove these barriers until their banking structures are reformed, until commercial bank balance sheet strength has been regained, and until the banking regulation and supervision system has really become efficient. In the sequential program for financial liberalization and reform, exchange-control removal comes right toward the end.

The issues are different when the question is not long-term structural change, but the intermittent use of time-varying exchange controls as an instrument to stabilize the exchange rate, while monetary policy is used for internal, domestic stabilization. It is well known that the (Washington) consensus was violently opposed to the use of exchange controls. Recently, attitudes have softened somewhat, and there has been a willingness to contemplate controls on certain capital *inflows,* with the aim of lessening the otherwise unpalatable alternatives (for more successful emerging countries) of rapidly appreciating exchange rates or an unduly lax domestic monetary policy. But, as I said at the outset of this section, some appreciation in such circumstances supports the aims of monetary policy. Trying to hold exchange rates below their fundamental equilibrium will not only be ultimately unavailing, it also will distort the economy in the meantime. But how does one assess what that equilibrium may be?—a good, but largely unanswerable, question.

How about reintroducing outward exchange controls in a crisis? If they can be effectively administered without corruption (sometimes a big if), they may prove successful in certain circumstances—for example, where further capital *inflows* are not necessary to sustain the exchange rate. This may have been the case in Malaysia during the Asian crisis. But the more such an exercise is perceived as successful, the more others may be tempted to emulate it; and the more widespread exchange controls become as a last resort, especially if they are used at the first whiff of trouble, the greater the disintegration of the international capital market. There is a global time-inconsistency problem, especially if the reintroduction of exchange controls in the initial countries is perceived as successful.

On the other hand, it could be argued that Malaysia's example during the Asian crisis had no apparent effect on other countries' policies, perhaps because of the International Monetary Fund's role. Moreover, historical experience suggests that memories in international capital markets are (blessedly) short, so the adverse effects on such markets of previous waves of controls, defaults, etc., have been quite limited in time.

### 3.3. Other Asset Prices

Just as there may be structural and other reasons for giving more weight (in monetary decisions) to exchange rate movements than their direct measured effect on future inflation can justify, the same argument can be used for a variety of other asset prices. Two sets of assets are commonly considered in this respect: housing and property assets, and equity assets.

Several arguments can be used in this respect. First, the standard, sticky-price, extended Keynesian model may underestimate the effect of asset prices on future output and inflation. For example, simpler, reduced-form VARs often give a higher weight to housing than the larger Keynesian models (Goodhart and Hofmann 2000). But this is a weak argument, because the correct response to such a discrepancy is to analyze why the two approaches give different answers and to try to improve the models themselves.

The second argument is that asset prices *should* be included in a correct measurement of inflation. For example, Japan's consumer price index has remained steady since 1985. By this measure, Japan's monetary policy has been one of the most successful in the world over the last two decades—but few believe that! Alchian and Klein (1973) give theoretical reasons for including asset prices in any cost of living index. If it is taken literally, the preferred measure overweights asset prices, making the resulting index too volatile to use. In an economy in which people use a significant share of their income to buy housing, and in economies in which people are now using much of their income to buy equities (to provide for their retirement, for example), excluding these purchases from the price index (relevant for the measurement of inflation) seems misguided. Because the question of the best way to measure housing inflation is contentious is not a satisfactory excuse for not doing so at all.

The third argument, and perhaps the strongest, is that the extension of credit by financial intermediaries—and the profitability and stability of those same intermediaries—is intimately linked (for example, by collateralization) with the valuation of property and, to a *much* lesser extent, equities. The credit channel, analyzed by Kiyotaki and Moore (1997), Bernanke and Gertler (1999), Minsky (1986), and many others, depends largely on property valuation. A rise (fall) in property prices will affect expenditures, output, and inflation in ways that may not be exactly correlated with or well measured by the pure interest rate channel. However, if the argument is that the workings of the credit channel are not adequately measured in standard forecasting models, then the best solution is to improve the models.

Even if the models are improved to appropriately account for the credit channel (*not* an easy exercise), fluctuations in housing and property prices may cause similar fluctuations in financial conditions, notably the stability of the banking system. One of the objectives/functions of a central bank is to maintain the systemic stability of the banking system. This is partly because of linkages between financial development and output and growth (Levine, Loayza, and Beck 2000), and partly for its own sake. Volatility in asset prices, especially property, endangers that stability. Examples are numerous and obvious.

The question is how to respond, especially when an asset-price boom coincides with stable current goods and services prices. Bernanke and Gertler (1999) advocate doing so only insofar as asset-price movements affect future forecasts of goods and services prices; Cecchetti et al. (2000) would have monetary policy aim off by more. We already rehearsed this when discussing exchange rates.

One point that needs further consideration in this context is the availability of other instruments—here I am thinking of prudential requirements. In practice, however, prudential requirements usually have the effect of amplifying, rather than restraining, macroeconomic cycles. Capital adequacy is rarely a problem when an asset boom expands profitability and balance sheet values, while limiting bad debts. Declines in asset values weaken (bank) balance sheets, so prudential requirements tend to reinforce banks' reluctance to lend during deflationary downturns.

Can anything be done about this, especially during the preceding asset boom? One problem (as with exchange rates) is identifying the (unsustainable) deviation from the fundamental equilibrium. Given the difficulty of doing so and the strength of special-interest lobbying, it is hard to raise the level of prudential requirements—capital adequacy ratios, minimum loan margins, etc.—when asset prices

are high. One proposal, which I think has some merit, is to tie changes in prudential requirements to the *change* in (some index of) asset prices over the preceding
period. For example, suppose that housing and property prices normally grow
2 percent more than retail prices; in that case, in each quarter the required margin
on housing loans could change by $X$,

$$X = 1.2 \, [Y - (2 + \pi)],$$

where $Y$ is the annualized growth in housing prices and $\pi$ is the rate of growth of
the retail price index. That brings me, rather neatly, toward the putative role of the
central bank in supervision and regulation.

## 4. THE CENTRAL BANK'S ROLE IN REGULATION AND SUPERVISION

It is not possible to maintain macro stability if the financial system becomes seriously unstable; nor is it possible to maintain financial stability with any confidence
if macro stability is lost, especially if (asset) prices become unstable and go through
a boom/bust sequence. Accordingly, the objectives of macro/price stability and
financial stability have always been seen as complementary. The history of central
banks reveals how such objectives have been jointly pursued. The earliest great texts
on central banking, Thornton (1802) and Bagehot (1873), describe how authorities
should respond when a liquidity crisis threatens. Even though such domestic crises
typically have arisen when there was also an external currency drain (which, by
itself, seems to require more restrictive monetary policies), the proposed remedy
was liberal domestic lending (lender of last resort) with safeguards (collateral, high
interest rates, and concern with reputation).

Given the complementarity of objectives and information—for instance, supervisory information on banks can influence macro policies, and the central bank's
role in running payments systems and operating in markets can inform the supervisors—there seems to be a strong case for undertaking the supervision of commercial banks within the same institution (the central bank) that is charged with
maintaining macro/price stability. To some extent, this is what has been done
historically. But over the period 1930–70, a combination of direct controls on
commercial bank credit extensions and their freedom to compete in pricing, and
controls on new entry, led to a cartel structure. In this system, there was a largely
guaranteed oligopolistic profit margin and a sizeable franchise value. Little supervision was required, and it was often self-regulation.

In all countries, liberalization of the financial system has led to competition, the
removal of automatic franchise values, and greater risk. The need for banking
supervision has increased sharply. Despite historical precedents and the complementarity of financial and macro/price stability, the trend in many developed

OECD countries has been toward separating bank supervision from the central bank and vesting it in a separate, unified, financial supervisory authority.

The main reason for this trend may be that liberalization, allied with technological innovation (notably in information technology and now in e-finance), has broken down the dividing lines between financial intermediaries. The old separations between commercial banking, investment banking, insurance companies, fund management, etc., have become irreversibly blurred. Developments in e-finance will complicate the picture further.

In a financial system without clear boundaries, the maintenance of institutionally organized separate supervisors is not efficient, involving overlaps and/or gaps. There is a clear argument that a single, though amorphous, financial system must be matched by a single, comprehensive regulator—meanwhile, the argument that competition in regulation is desirable can be answered by noting that the effective competition in most cases is international. But if supervision needs to be undertaken in a unified authority across the whole financial spectrum, it would take central banks beyond their normal area of expertise. Much, probably most, supervision in several of these other areas—for example, fund management, mortgages, and pensions—is essentially concerned with customer protection, not with systemic stability. Is this a field a central bank would want to enter?

Moreover, if a central bank were responsible for supervision of the whole financial system, it could become a huge power center—even more so if it were also given more operational independence for determining the conduct of macro monetary policy. There are questions as to whether an (unelected) body, such as a central bank, should be delegated quite so much power within a democratic system.

There are the perennial issues of conflicts of interest between the functions of supervision and regulation on one hand and macro monetary management on the other. At the most mundane level, there is competition for senior managerial attention. Management time is limited, and handling financial crises can be extremely time consuming. The purpose of supervision and regulation is to prevent bad things from happening; therefore, it is usually only noticed when disasters occur. To be blunt, financial supervisors are either largely invisible to the wider public (no disaster) or get very bad press (disaster). Does a central bank that seeks credibility and a good reputation for its macro monetary policy really want to face the opprobrium of also being responsible for financial supervision?

The main plank of the conflict-of-interest argument is that responsibility for supervision may adversely influence monetary policy. I believe the main concern in this case is that the monetary authorities will, on occasion, make monetary policy too lax to support fragile financial institutions. There have been cases in which central banks have argued against pushing interest rates sky-high in order to maintain a pegged exchange rate, partly (but not only) out of concern for domestic financial stability. But was this necessarily wrong in itself? For the rest, evidence of conflicts of interest of this genre adversely affecting macro monetary policy seems sparse.

To counter such arguments, there is the point that separation would likely weaken the flow of information, primarily from supervisor to central bank, but also in the reverse direction, given the bank's involvement in the payments system and financial markets. The focus and professional skills of a separate, unified supervisor are likely to diverge from those of a central bank (tending toward lawyers and customer protection and away from economists and systemic stability). One can pose this point in terms of the question, can a financial crisis be run as well by a committee as it can by the central bank on its own? Because the trend toward establishing a unified, specialist financial supervisor is quite recent, we are unlikely to learn the answer to this question until many years have passed.

I doubt that the pressures to establish a unified, specialist supervisory agency are quite so strong in most developing countries. Their financial systems are less complex, and dividing lines are less blurred. Commercial banks remain the key players. Moreover, the central bank in most developing countries is relatively well placed for funding, is a center of technical excellence, and can maintain greater independence from the lobbying of commercial and political interests on behalf of certain favored institutions. If the supervisory agency is placed under the aegis of the central bank, it should share these benefits of better funding, technical skills, and independence. There are too many cases of supervisory bodies that are outside central banks failing in such respects. For such reasons, I do not believe the case for separation, which has become stronger in developed countries, should be transposed to developing countries.

## 5. CONCLUSION: WHERE WILL CENTRAL BANKS BE IN 10 YEARS' TIME?

*Can monetary authorities control domestic inflation and maintain price stability?* Here I am cautiously optimistic. As long as politicians allow or require the central bank to focus on this objective, then, with operational independence, we know enough to stop any inflationary bias. The danger, as always, will come from a breakdown of good governance—such as war or civil unrest—especially if it involves an escalating fiscal deficit.

Because of lags in the transmission mechanism, the appropriate target is an inflation *forecast*. Because forecasts are always uncertain and subject to unforeseen shocks, inflation can never be controlled perfectly, but it can be held at the desired rate on average.

*Can the central bank, consistent with its role of stabilizing goods and services prices, also tame large fluctuations in asset prices?* This seems much more doubtful. Asset-price fluctuations, whether of exchange rates, property prices, or equities, do not seem to have diminished in recent years (although there is no evidence of them getting worse, especially in comparison with the turbulent 1970s). There is rarely agreement on where the fundamental equilibrium may be, and little evidence of much longer-term speculation to drive asset prices back to their equilibrium. Given this uncertainty, central banks are always liable to attract criticism for intervening to affect asset prices. Although it is agreed that central banks *should* respond, in that asset-price fluctuations are assessed in the forecasting models as affecting future inflation, such effects are not confidently modeled. More important, there is disagreement on whether and how much a central bank should shade policy to account for the important connections between the housing/property market and financial stability, and between the exchange rate and the health of the tradable-goods sector.

*Can we simultaneously achieve and maintain internal and external price stability?* The extraordinary volatility of real exchange rates has been one of the greatest macroeconomic puzzles of our age. There are no good theoretical reasons, nor empirical explanations, for its occurrence. So long as it continues, it will present a problem to all but the largest economies. Whatever the argument for capital controls in times of crisis, they would be neither feasible nor desirable as a long-run solution to this problem. I have argued that a major cause of such volatility is an unfortunate absence of stabilizing speculators; therefore, any measure that further penalizes speculators could just as easily worsen volatility.

Continuing volatility in real exchange rates, combined with a growing ease of undertaking e-commerce in any currency at any time with any counterparty, could lead to growing pressure for the greater use of a regional currency. South America, as well as North America, may become even more explicitly a dollar area, while Europe and Africa adopt the euro. Asia presents more of a problem in this respect. One superpower temporarily fallen on hard times, and two emerging giants, can neither fall in behind a single hegemony, as in the Americas, nor benefit from a rapprochement, as France and Germany have achieved. The future of international monetary policy in Asia looks, at least from a distance, particularly opaque.

REFERENCES

Alchian, Armen A., and Benjamin Klein. 1973. On a Correct Measure of Inflation. *Journal of Money, Credit, and Banking* 5: 173–91.

Alesina, Alberto. 1989. Politics and Business Cycles in Industrial Economies. *Economic Policy: A European Forum* 8: 55–98.

Bagehot, Walter. 1873. *Lombard Street: A Description of the Money Market.* London: Kegan, Paul and Co.

Batini, Nicoletta, and Andrew G. Haldane. 1999. Forward-Looking Rules for Monetary Policy. Bank of England, Working Paper no. 91, January.

Batini, Nicoletta, and Edward Nelson. 2000. Optimal Horizons for Inflation Targeting. Bank of England, Working Paper no. 119, July.

Bernanke, Ben, and Mark Gertler. 1999. Monetary Policy and Asset Price Volatility. *Federal Reserve Bank of Kansas City Economic Review* 84: 17–51.

Blinder, Alan S. 1998. *Central Banking in Theory and Practice.* Cambridge, Mass.: MIT Press.

Cecchetti, Stephen G., Hans Genburg, John Lipsky, and Sushil B. Wadhwani. 2000. *Asset Prices and Central Bank Policy.* Geneva Reports on the World Economy 2. London: Centre for Economic Policy Research.

Cooper, Richard. 1984. A Monetary System for the Future. *Foreign Affairs* 63: 166–84.

Friedman, Milton. 1968. The Role of Monetary Policy. *American Economic Review* 58: 1--17.

Gaspar, Vitor, and Frank Smets. 2000. Price Level Stability: Some Issues. *National Institute Economic Review* 174: 68–79.

Goodhart, Charles, and Boris Hofmann. 2000. Do Asset Prices Help to Predict Consumer Price Inflation? *The Manchester School Supplement* 68: 122–40.

Kiyotaki, Nobuhiro, and John Moore. 1997. Credit Cycles. *Journal of Political Economy* 105: 211–48.

Levine, Ross, Norman Loayza, and Thorsten Beck. 2000. Financial Intermediation and Growth: Causality and Causes. *Journal of Monetary Economics* 46: 31–77.

Minsky, Hyman P. 1986. *Stabilizing an Unstable Economy.* New Haven, Conn.: Yale University Press.

Phelps, Edmund S. 1970. *Microeconomic Foundations of Employment and Inflation Theory.* New York: W.W. Norton.

Thornton, Henry. 1802. *An Enquiry into the Nature and Effects of the Paper Credit of Great Britain.* London: J. Hatchard.

Walsh, Carl E. 1995a. Optimal Contracts for Independent Central Bankers. *American Economic Review* 85: 150–67.

————. 1995b. Is New Zealand's Reserve Bank Act of 1989 an Optimal Central Bank Contract? *Journal of Money, Credit, and Banking* 27: 1179–91.

Woodford, Michael. 1999. Optimal Monetary Policy Inertia. Princeton University, unpublished paper, January.

# Commentary

*Donald L. Kohn*

## 1. INTRODUCTION

It's always a pleasure to read a paper by Charles Goodhart, who brings a unique blend of academic rigor and originality, frontline experience, and plain common sense to his musings on central banking. Goodhart points out that the controlling consensus for monetary policy is that it should be focused on achieving and maintaining price stability over time. Both economic theory and experience indicate that prolonged deviations from reasonable price stability—in either direction—can have serious negative implications for economic performance.

Goodhart highlights a number of issues that arise in implementing policy within this framework. I'm not going to comment directly on Goodhart's paper. Rather, reading the paper sparked my own musings on some areas that might benefit from further research, and I thought that with the Federal Reserve Bank of Cleveland launching its Central Bank Institute, this might be an opportune moment for such a discussion. There is considerable overlap between Goodhart's topics and my own; in large measure he was my inspiration, though in some cases we come at the same subject from different angles. I call this comment "Whither Central Banking Research?" Obviously, my list is not a complete research agenda; rather, it covers four topics that have caught my attention in my work with the Federal Reserve, reinforced in some cases by my experience at the Bank of England.

## 2. THE IMPLICATIONS OF NUMERICAL INFLATION TARGETS

As Goodhart notes, a logical extension of the recognition of the importance—indeed, the primacy—of controlling inflation is an explicit numerical inflation target. Many countries have adopted such targets in recent years, but two of the world's largest economies—the United States and Japan—have yet to take them up, and a third, the euro area, has a regime that is often criticized by the more doctrinaire inflation targeters. This suggests that questions remain about the costs and benefits of such numerical targets, as opposed to more vague goals such as "price stability," especially where the latter (as in the United States) is coupled with a legislated objective related to output or employment.

The point of numerical targets is to constrain central bank flexibility in the pursuit of other objectives. That is both their benefit and their potential cost, as targeting central banks might feel limited in leaning against deviations of output from potential. One senses that as central banks with less precisely stated objectives, such as the Federal Reserve, emphasize long-run price-stability objectives, and as inflation-targeting central banks emphasize the flexible nature of their inflation targets, the differences in practice between the regimes may be narrowing. Still, many are advocating that the United States and Japan adopt explicit inflation targets. My hope is that with the passage of time and the spread of explicit inflation targets, it may be possible to examine more rigorously the questions that arise in evaluating such targets compared to less precise regimes.

Those questions are related most importantly to whether and how numerical targets affect economic performance. Do numerical inflation targets affect where central banks end up on the inflation- and output-variability frontiers? That is, is output more variable when central banks have numerical inflation goals? If so, does this matter for economic performance over time? Inflation and inflation variability are problems, in part, because they complicate planning and shorten horizons, but output variability may have similar effects. Which regime tends to offer the mix that maximizes growth? Does inflation targeting enhance credibility and reduce sacrifice ratios, over and above the credibility gained from simply delivering low inflation? It is often asserted that explicit inflation targets reduce uncertainty. Is this demonstrable? What is the evidence on this from, say, financial markets as they react to incoming information on prices and output under both vague and explicit regimes? Do we have enough evidence across countries and policymakers to test the often-stated proposition that explicit inflation targets help to guard against bad outcomes when the quality of decisionmakers slips?

## 3. POLICYMAKING UNDER UNCERTAINTY

Whatever the exact regime, among the more difficult and troubling questions that policymakers face is how to deal with uncertainty. Thanks to Thomas Sargent and others, the profession has made some progress beyond the Brainard (1967) paradigm of additive and multiplicative uncertainty. But policymakers constantly struggle with this issue as they confront everyday situations.

Policymakers try to blend their sense of the degree of uncertainty and the costs and benefits of being wrong about important elements in the economic situation as they contemplate forecasts and implied actions. In some uncertain situations, they are willing to act on forecasts; in others, they are less willing to be pre-emptive. For example, in the United States, policymakers tended to be forward looking in tightening policy to restrain the growth of output down to the growth of potential in 1999 and early 2000, despite inflation remaining relatively well behaved. They were confident that the unemployment rate could not go much lower without causing problems. However, they did not think they were tightening enough to relieve pressures on labor markets; they had much less confidence that the NAIRU was above prevailing levels and would not have acted on a forecast based on that presumption. In effect, their reactions to uncertainty were much more nuanced than would be suggested by the traditional Brainard model. Were they right? Is there further guidance we, as economists, can give them to balance their discomfort with uncertainty with their desire to act pre-emptively to stabilize inflation and output?

A related set of issues under uncertainty involves the treatment of possible asymmetries in the distribution of possible outcomes—the "forecast skews," in U.K. parlance. Central banks seem mostly to act on modal forecasts, adjusting their policies to make the most likely outcome consistent with their objectives. What role should the possibility of important one-sided risks to the forecast play, which might drive the mean expectation away from the mode? Most often, we know little enough about the possible outcomes that this distinction is without meaning. But on occasion, when there is a significant risk of a very bad outcome, central banks may aim off from keeping the most likely forecast on target to take account of this possibility, sometimes using terminology such as "buying insurance." When is this appropriate? Is the nature and size of the contingency important?

In the fall of 1998, the Federal Reserve acted on the contingency that major disruptions to financial markets might continue and impede the performance of the economy. But we have not acted on the financial market contingency of adverse consequences from possible future asset-price movements in, say, the dollar or equity prices when those appeared to be misaligned. The Bank of England has drawn a distinction between one-sided risks arising from possibly different economic relationships—such as a higher or lower NAIRU or growth rate of potential—and those arising from possible movements in asset prices that haven't occurred yet. Is this appropriate? It is perhaps a tribute to the success of monetary policy that its focus can shift from time to time away from the middle of the distribution of possible outcomes to its tails. But shift it has, and, from my perspective, more systematic thinking about the possibilities would be beneficial.

## 4. THE ROLE OF ASSET PRICES IN POLICY

This naturally brings me to my next topic—the role of asset prices in monetary policy. Much of Goodhart's paper deals with this topic, and he does a good job of laying out the relevant issues. Research by Bernanke and Gertler (1999) and Cecchetti et al. (2000) has helped us to focus on the important parameters.

Debate about whether policy formulation should pay special attention to asset prices seems to have intensified in recent years, owing, no doubt, to perceptions that both real exchange rates and equity prices have been persistently misaligned. Conceptual arguments may support giving some special attention to asset prices. Doing so can smooth longer-term variations in prices and output, though at the expense of shortfalls from the best possible outcomes in the short and intermediate term. As the embodiment of the prices of future consumption, some types of asset-price inflation can distort resource allocation, just as inflation in the prices of currently produced goods and services can. Central banks cannot escape making some judgments about asset prices, which play a prominent role in any projections that influence policy.

Central banks have resisted giving special prominence to such prices beyond their role in the forecast. To do so would require a firm view of when assets were or were not likely to become misaligned, and, as someone once asked, "But how do we know when irrational exuberance has unduly escalated asset values?" It also requires some estimate of the trade-offs of near-term economic performance for better-priced assets—how much would rates need to be raised or lowered to affect asset prices, and how would that affect economic performance? At least for tightening, to lean against a potential equity-price bubble would require a very thick hide to stand up to the inevitable questions about why you are opposed to constituents becoming wealthier and are trying as well to limit their job opportunities to keep their net worth from increasing more rapidly. And weight on asset prices in policy would muddy the message and the accountability of central banks, especially under explicit inflation targets.

Nonetheless, I suspect this issue is not going away, and its prominence in Goodhart's paper is only one indicator I have used to make this projection. A number of observers, including some in sister central banks, were urging the Federal Reserve to act against a perceived stock market bubble, in some cases beginning in 1997. The Bank of England has been wrestling with how to factor into its policy a perceived overvalued pound over the last several years. The rise and fall of high-tech stock prices, with the aid of perfect hindsight, does appear to have played a role in misallocating capital in recent years, and perhaps it has also accentuated, if not caused, significant variations in overall economic activity. The questions about asset prices are well defined, but the answers are not. Recent developments are providing another data point that economists should be using to further the research and discussion.

## 5. THE IMPLICATIONS OF POLICYMAKING BY COMMITTEE

The final topic I want to raise is one that Goodhart has heard me ruminate on before, and one that was highlighted for me by my time at the Bank of England: the implications of the fact that, most of the time, policy is made by a committee, not by an individual.

As central banks have been granted instrument independence, decisionmaking often has been restructured to reside in a group rather than an individual governor. It is partly a form of accountability, since rolling appointments give the political process more frequent chances to shape monetary policy. As Goodhart notes, a committee affords the opportunity to bring greater expertise to bear on this difficult task, so it should result in better decisions and provide some protection against the potential for very bad decisions from an unchecked individual. Who makes the decisions remains an issue in New Zealand and in Canada, where authority still rests in individual governors.

Except for Blinder and Morgan (2000), very few economists seem to have given much thought to the implications of group policymaking. For example, it would have been interesting to see whether group versus individual policymaking would have made any difference in the Arifovic/Sargent paper presented at this conference. We tend to assume one utility function, one model of the world, one forecast, and one response function for the monetary authority, when in fact there are usually many of each. How the committee functions can have important implications for the conduct of policy, its explanation to the pubic, and the accountability of policymakers.

As I already have remarked, one suspects that committees, by allowing multiple voices to be registered, result in better decisions, on average, over time. But other than Blinder and Morgan (2000), has anyone tried to test this hypothesis? Group decisionmaking can be sluggish as consensus is built, a particular concern when the situation is changing rapidly or is turning out much different than had been anticipated—for example, around interest rate turning points. Are there procedures that can be followed to enhance the positive and reduce the negative aspects of committee decisionmaking?

Committees definitely complicate transparency. Any given decision may be compatible with a number of rationales and diverse views of the outlook. How can a committee state a clear set of reasons for its decisions and, even more difficult, a sense of its strategy going forward? In the context of the Monetary Policy Committee at the Bank of England, both Goodhart and I have wrestled with how a committee of nine individually accountable members can come up with a forecast that represents the center of the committee, is consistent and coherent, and is reliably related to its decisions. Neither of us was particularly successful, I would judge.

Committees also are difficult to hold accountable. Whom does the political process blame for a failure to achieve objectives? How does one discipline a committee—for example, who does not get reappointed? In the United Kingdom, Parliament demands considerable individual accountability from members of the Monetary Policy Committee. I wonder whether the increasing emphasis in this direction may hinder decisionmaking by the committee itself. Sometimes the most effective strategy by a participant will involve compromise to move the group in the appropriate direction, which might produce votes that an individual could find difficult to explain. And the skills that allow an individual to do well in the parliamentary give-and-take that largely implements individual accountability may not be the same skills that enhance the performance of the committee.

In the United States, we have tended to deal with the ambiguities of group transparency and accountability by emphasizing consensus and strong chairmen who shape and speak for the consensus. But will this organization tend to produce the best possible monetary policy over time?

Taking account of these complications, what should be the size and composition of the committee? How large should it be to obtain a sufficient diversity of views while keeping decisionmaking flexible and facilitating exchanges of views? Who should be included? Should it be largely limited to experts in macroeconomics, as in the United Kingdom, or will decisionmaking benefit from including more diverse backgrounds in business, economics, and finance, as in the United States?

These are some of the issues that confront designers and participants in monetary policy decision frameworks, which, in my view, have gotten too little attention from economists.

## REFERENCES

Arifovic, Jasmina, and Thomas J. Sargent. 2001. Laboratory Experiments with an Expectational Phillips Curve. Paper presented at the Federal Reserve Bank of Cleveland's Conference on The Origins and Evolution of Central Banking, May 21–22.

Bernanke, Ben, and Mark Gertler. 1999. Monetary Policy and Asset Price Volatility. In *New Challenges for Monetary Policy*, 77–128. Kansas City, Mo.: Federal Reserve Bank of Kansas City.

Blinder, Alan S., and John Morgan. 2000. Are Two Heads Better Than One? An Experimental Analysis of Group vs. Individual Decisionmaking. National Bureau of Economic Research, Working Paper no. 7909.

Brainard, William. 1967. Uncertainty and the Effectiveness of Policy. *American Economic Review* 57: 411–25.

Cecchetti, Stephen G., Hans Genberg, John Lipsky, and Sushil Wadhwani. 2000. *Asset Prices and Central Bank Policy*. Geneva Reports on the World Economy 2. London: Centre for Economic Policy Research.

Kohn, Donald L. 2000. The Kohn Report on MPC Procedures: Report to the Non-Executive Directors of the Court of the Bank of England on Monetary Policy Processes and the Work of Monetary Analysis. *Bank of England Quarterly Bulletin* 41: 35–49.

# Commentary

## *Mark Gertler*

Not surprisingly, Charles Goodhart has provided us with a masterful description of how central banking has evolved over the postwar period. The paper contains an assessment of both the progress that has been made and the major unresolved issues that remain.

I mostly agree with what Goodhart has to say. My only significant complaint is that he sometimes fails to fully exploit the valuable insights obtained from "Goodhart's Law," particularly in his discussion of how central banks should react to real exchange rate movements and other financial variables. As he observed long ago, it is dangerous for central banks to try to exploit reduced-form relationships—particularly those involving financial variables—as these relationships depend on the historical policy rule intact at the time. (In this respect, Goodhart's Law may seem to be a precursor to the Lucas critique.)

The failure of monetary conditions indices (MCIs) in Canada and elsewhere provides a recent example of Goodhart's Law in action. Roughly speaking, MCIs are weighted averages of various combinations of various financial indicators of the stance of monetary policy, such as the exchange rate, the money supply, and so on. Attempts by central banks to target these indicators have invariably led to changes in the relation of these indicators to the real economy and inflation.

History is replete with other examples of Goodhart's Law. Perhaps the best known involved the attempts of a number of central banks to control money aggregates during the 1970s and early 1980s. The breakdown of Bretton Woods during the early 1970s led to the loss of a nominal anchor for monetary policy for most of the industrialized world. As a result, a number of major central banks, including the Bundesbank, the Federal Reserve, and the Bank of England, turned to monetary targeting. By and large, attempts to stabilize the growth of monetary aggregates were largely unsuccessful, inducing not only unpredictable movements in money but also the breakdown of historical comovements of money with output and inflation. The Federal Reserve Board quickly abandoned monetary targeting, and other central banks soon followed suit. While the Bundesbank never formally renounced money targeting, my work with Richard Clarida (Clarida and Gertler 1997) suggests that it often let money grow outside the target range and, in practice, operated as if these targets were not significant constraints.

In this regard, the only other notable omission in the paper is a description of the shift in emphasis by central banks away from money-growth targets and toward inflation targets as nominal anchors. In a similar vein, many central banks now think in terms of adjusting short-term interest rates to control inflation, as opposed to money aggregates. That is, across the industrialized countries, central banks treat short-term interest rates as the operating instrument as opposed to a money aggregate. Again, Goodhart's Law is highly germane to these developments.

Let me now turn to the central point of Goodhart's paper: namely, that the most significant development in central banking over the years has been the shift toward price stability as the central medium-term objective of monetary policy, coupled with the broad acceptance of the importance of central bank independence. Here I completely agree. In particular, I share Goodhart's view that this development has been central to the improved performance of monetary policy over the years and gives some reason to be optimistic about the future, though, of course, there may exist a danger of overoptimism.

In particular, the case for optimism rests on the view that monetary policy has played a nontrivial role in the strong macroeconomic performance across the OECD countries (except Japan) over the past 25 years or so. Indeed, evidence from the United States and a number of European countries suggests a decline in output volatility since the mid-1980s, relative to the late 1960s and 1970s. Differences in the pattern of exogenous shocks could, in principle, account for the phenomenon. However, associated with the decline in output volatility has been a significant decline in both the mean and variance of inflation.[1] Hence, any story of improved macroeconomic performance should take into account the favorable shift in the dynamics of both inflation and output.

Why should inflation matter to output dynamics? There is compelling evidence that a strong factor in each of the postwar recessions through the early 1980s was the Federal Reserve's tightening of monetary policy in response to inflationary pressures. By maintaining relative price stability over the past 15 years, central banks have largely avoided the need for draconian tightening of monetary policy, which occurred in the early 1980s. Maintaining relative price stability, further, has not been simply a matter of luck. A number of papers (Clarida, Gali, and Gertler 2000; Judd and Rudebusch 2000; Boivin 2000; Taylor 2000; Cogley and Sargent 2001) have presented evidence of a shift in the monetary policy rule in favor of a more aggressive approach toward fighting inflation. Specifically, these papers estimate interest rate feedback rules for monetary policy in the United States and show the estimated coefficient on inflation in the feedback rule rose significantly after 1979.

---

[1]  In addition, Barsky and Killian (2001) present evidence suggesting that the oil shocks actually had a minimal role in creating the economic turmoil of the 1970s.

Put differently, the Federal Reserve appears to have adjusted short-term rates in response to inflationary pressures far more aggressively after 1979 than it did before 1979. Clarida, Gali, and Gertler (1998) show this increased focus on curtailing inflation also applies to the other major central banks across the globe. In sum, the lengthy period of relative price stability appears not to have been simply an accident, but rather the product of the deliberate course of monetary policy.

The question remains, however, why did central banks adopt what appears to have been—with the great benefit of hindsight—a decidedly inferior accommodative monetary policy during the 1970s? Here I think there are two main factors. First, as DeLong (1997) argues, for the postwar period up to the early 1970s, policymakers were largely guided by the experience of the Great Depression, which led them to underestimate the costs of sustained inflation. Second, as Cogley and Sargent (2001) emphasize, policymakers' state of knowledge was rather different than it is today. During the late 1960s and early 1970s, the notion of a long-run trade-off was still prevalent. Some support for this view is that both private-sector forecasts and Federal Reserve *Green Book* forecasts indicate significant underforecasting of the rise in inflation during the late 1960s and early 1970s.

To the extent there has been a tangible improvement in monetary policy management, we should expect that the gains in macroeconomics performance over the past 15 years are unlikely to dissipate entirely. This is not to suggest that good luck is an insignificant factor. It is also true, as I have suggested, that there is some likelihood of a danger of overconfidence. The public has come to expect good policy management. No doubt, however, the high productivity growth over the last half of the previous decade has lent the Federal Reserve a significant hand. Being in a position to accommodate high productivity growth is every central banker's dream. If it becomes apparent, however, that these recent productivity gains are unlikely to persist, the Fed is likely to face some pressures that it has not seen in recent years. The experience of the 1970s suggests that how well it handles these pressures may be critical. I think Goodhart would agree.

## REFERENCES

Barsky, Robert, and Lutz Kilian. 2001. Do We Really Know that Oil Caused the Great Stagflation? A Monetary Alternative. In *NBER Macroeconomics Annual*, vol. 16, edited by Ben S. Bernanke and Kenneth Rogoff. Cambridge, Mass.: MIT Press.

Boivin, Jean. 2001. The Fed's Conduct of Monetary Policy: Has It Changed and Does It Matter? Columbia University, mimeo.

Clarida, Richard, and Mark Gertler. 1997. How the Bundesbank Conducts Monetary Policy. In *Reducing Inflation: Motivation and Strategy,* edited by Christina and David Romer, 363–406. Chicago: University of Chicago Press.

Clarida, Richard, Mark Gertler, and Jordi Gali. 1998. Monetary Policy Rules in Practice: Some International Evidence. *European Economics Review* 42: 1033–67.

Clarida, Richard, Mark Gertler, and Jordi Gali. 2000. Monetary Policy Rules and Macroeconomic Stability: Evidence and Some Theory. *Quarterly Journal of Economics* 115: 147–80.

Cogley, Timothy, and Thomas J. Sargent. 2001. Evolving Postwar U.S. Inflation Dynamics. In *NBER Macroeconomics Annual*, vol. 16, edited by Ben S. Bernanke and Kenneth Rogoff. Cambridge, Mass.: MIT Press.

Judd, John, and Glenn Rudebusch. 1998. Taylor's Rule and the Fed: 1970–1997. *Federal Reserve Bank of San Francisco Economic Review* 0: 3–16.

Taylor, John. 1999. A Historical Analysis of Monetary Policy Rules. In *Monetary Policy Rules*, edited by John Taylor, 319–41. Chicago: University of Chicago Press.

# PART II

## MONETARY UNION

# 3

# Monetary Policy in Unknown Territory:
# The European Central Bank in the Early Years

*Jürgen von Hagen and Matthias Brückner*

## 1. INTRODUCTION

The creation of a monetary union in Europe on January 1, 1999, was undoubtedly one of the largest macro- and politico-economic experiments in modern history. It was the capstone of the so-called Maastricht Process, designed to achieve macroeconomic convergence, which shaped monetary and fiscal policies in the countries striving for membership in the European Monetary Union (EMU) over much of the 1990s.[1] The start of the EMU was marked by the conversion of member states' national currencies into euros and the beginning of the operations of the new Eurosystem, the new European Central Bank (ECB), and the national central banks of the participating states (national central banks).[2] While euro cash rested in the form of the previous national currencies for the first three years, interbank and most noncash payments were denominated in euros from the start, and European financial markets quickly adopted the euro as their common unit of account. The replacement of the national currency signs by euro cash at the start of 2002 will complete the introduction of the EMU.

The new EMU has a combined population 11 percent larger than that of the United States and a combined GDP of 61 percent of U.S. GDP.[3] Like the United States—and in sharp contrast to the individual member states—it is a fairly closed economy whose trade with third countries is about 20 percent of GDP. The EMU has created a large financial area with a combined initial stock market capitalization of 28 percent of that of the United States and a securities market with an initial value of about 60 percent of the U.S. market.[4] By 2000, the combined stock market valuation of the euro economy had risen to about 37 percent of that of the United States, and its securities market value to about 69 percent of the U.S. market, suggesting that the EMU has stimulated financial market growth. Because

---

[1] For a review of fiscal policies in the EMU member states during the 1990s, see Hughes-Hallett, Strauch, and von Hagen (2001).

[2] In addition to the Eurosystem, there is also the European System of Central Banks (ESCB), which consists of the ECB and the national central banks of the European Union member states.

[3] The following data are from the European Commission, *European Economy Statistical Appendix*, Fall 2000. The EMU started with Austria, Belgium, the Netherlands, Germany, Finland, France, Ireland, Italy, Luxembourg, Portugal, and Spain. Greece joined on January 1, 2001.

[4] These data are for 1998 and taken from von Hagen (1999a).

of institutional and regulatory differences, financial market integration is still less than perfect, but market-driven integration proceeds rapidly.[5]

Despite the large degree of nominal convergence achieved at the end of the 1990s, the start of the EMU was surrounded by many uncertainties. Little was (and is) known about the properties and stability of basic macroeconomic relations in the new monetary area, such as its money-demand function.[6] Aggregate data for the euro area were not readily available and had to be constructed from national sources on the basis of newly developed common definitions. Reconstructed time series data span only one or two decades, which makes the estimation of empirical models difficult, and even the data now available leave open serious questions of aggregation.[7] The first empirical macro models of the euro economy are only starting to appear now, more than two years after the start of the common monetary policy.[8] Thus, in 1999, monetary policy was entering unknown territory.

The institutional environment of the common monetary policy constituted further unknown territory. By delegating the common monetary policy to the European System of Central Banks (ESCB) and giving the ECB the task of executing the monetary policy determined by the ESCB, the Maastricht Treaty (Articles 3 and 5 of the Statutes of the ESCB) suggests that the ECB is subordinated to the national central banks. However, Article 14.3 of those Statutes holds that the national central banks are an integral part of the ESCB and act according to the directives of the ECB, suggesting the latter is superior to the former. According to the ECB, the national central bank presidents sit in the ECB Council as individuals rather than as representatives of their respective institutions (Gaspar, Masuch, and Pill 2001), implying that the national central bank presidents would not take account of any country-specific circumstances when making their decisions. But this reading of the Treaty is not uncontested; legal scholars point out that the national central bank presidents' membership in the Council results only from their positions, not from personal appointment (Herdegen 1998). In view of this, how the ECB Council members, coming from very different countries and traditions, could agree on a common monetary policy, to what extent that policy would be affected by national circumstances and preferences, and how it could be

---

[5]  See, for example, European Commission (1997), International Monetary Fund (2001a,b), and Danthine, Giavazzi, and von Thadden (2000).

[6]  A number of empirical studies in the 1990s point to the existence of a conventional money-demand function at the EU and show that its stability exceeded that of national money-demand functions. See Kremers and Lane (1992), Fagan and Henry (1999), and Browne, Fagan, and Henry (1997). However, these studies are plagued with aggregation problems that make the interpretation of these results difficult; see Wesche (1997) and Arnold and de Vries (2000), who argue that the stability of the aggregate function is a statistical artifact.

[7]  See Gaspar (2000). In public statements, the ECB's chief economist, Otmar Issing, has pointed to the difficulties created by the lack of euro-area macroeconomic data and their history, which implies that, compared to his experience at the Bundesbank, his staff finds it much more difficult to explain data irregularities on the basis of historical analogies and experience.

[8]  See Fagan, Henry, and Mestre (2001) and Coenen and Wieland (2000).

communicated effectively to a very heterogeneous European public have attracted a lot of interest in the public and academic debates preceding the start of the EMU.[9]

This paper reviews the experiences of the new central bank and its monetary policy in the EMU's early years. Section 2 provides some institutional background. Section 3 discusses the ECB's strategy and its monetary policy so far. Section 4 looks at the evolution of monetary conditions in the euro economy and assesses the central bank's policy on that basis. Section 5 concludes.

## 2. THE ECB AND THE EURO SYSTEM: INSTITUTIONAL BACKGROUND

The Maastricht Treaty provides the institutional framework for the ECB. The Treaty requires that the national central banks of all participating states must be politically independent. The ECB is similarly independent from the governments of the member states and the political bodies of the European Union. The ECB is owned by the national central banks.

Monetary policy decisions are made by the Governing Council (the ECB Council), whose members are the national central bank presidents and the six members of the ECB Board.[10] Formally, Council decisions are taken by majority vote, with each member having one vote and the ECB president a second one in case of a tie. The ECB Board is responsible for preparing the ECB Council's meetings. In doing so, it relies on its own staff, but it also uses the input of a number of Eurosystem committees, which include staff members of the national central banks, of which the Monetary Policy Committee is the most important. The established practice now is that ECB Council members meet informally on the eve of ECB Council meetings to discuss monetary policy developments in the euro economy. The monetary policy discussion at the official meeting opens with a statement by the chief economist, which gives the Board (and the chief economist in particular) considerable agenda-setting power.[11] Numerous statements by the ECB president, Wim Duisenberg, indicate that the Council takes its decision by consensus or near-consensus rather than simple majority. In most instances, the debate seems to continue until a broad consensus is reached about the monetary policy proposal presented to the Council. In both aspects, the ECB Council seems to follow the practice of the Bundesbank Council in earlier years (von Hagen 1999c).

This procedural practice is important because it diminishes the role in ECB Council decisions of the median voter and his preferences. The chief economist's role as agenda setter in monetary policy debates implies that a national central bank president proposing an alternative policy would thus have to justify any

---

9   See von Hagen and Süppel (1994), de Grauwe, Dewachter, and Aksoy (1999), Dornbusch, Favero, and
     Giavazzi (1998), Cecchetti, McConnell, and Perez-Quiros (1999), and Brückner (1997), among others.
10  The president of the European Council and a member of the European Commission have the right to participate in
     ECB Council meetings.
11  There are also other indications that the ECB Board operates very much as a collegiate body. See Marshall (1999).

deviation from the chief economist's proposal and find convincing arguments why this would serve the euro economy better. Formal voting models show that consensus voting protects the chief economist's proposal against alternatives. Assuming that the chief economist always argues from an aggregate, euro-area perspective, the established procedure thus assures that country-specific preferences and asymmetrical shocks hitting individual member countries, which might be reflected in proposals submitted by individual national central banks, do not significantly affect the common monetary policy (von Hagen 1999b).[12]

A significant feature of the Treaty is that it mandates the ECB regard price stability as monetary policy's principal objective, the heritage of a similar mandate in Germany's Bundesbank Act. But the Treaty does not define price stability in operational terms. The independence of the central bank, as defined in the Treaty, implies that such a definition can only be supplied by the ECB itself, a point we will return to later. The principal mandate is qualified (Article 105(1)) by the call to support the general economic policy in the European Community and contribute to the policy goals defined in Article 2, as long as this does not compromise the goal of price stability. As in the case of the Bundesbank, where a similar qualification exists, this can be expected to remain inconsequential to the ECB for two reasons. First, it relates to general policies rather than specific actions of the governments; second, it relates to economic policies "in" rather than "of" the Community, and there are at least 15 different policies. The view presented in Issing et al. (2001), that the ECB does not regard output stabilization as a secondary goal for monetary policy, is consistent with this.[13] The European Parliament, through its Committee on Monetary and Financial Affairs, has repeatedly called upon the ECB to explain its goals and intentions under Article 105(1). So far, the ECB has declined to give such explanations, a refusal that could be indicative of commitments to other monetary policy goals in addition to price stability.

While monetary policy decisionmaking is centralized in the ECB Council, the implementation of monetary policy is largely decentralized. Key features of ECB monetary policy operations are the imposition of an interest-bearing reserve requirement on bank deposits; the provision of automatic-access lending and deposit facilities for banks at the Eurosystem at fixed interest rates, which establish a floor and a ceiling for overnight money market rates; and repurchase operations (repos), that is, reversible open market operations in eligible securities, as the main tool for creating central bank money. So far, the ECB has almost completely

---

[12] Note that given this procedure, the chief economist's power to shape Council decisions increases as the number of national central bank presidents on the Council increases. This is because, in a larger Council, any deviation from the chief economist's proposal must win more votes to be adopted. In contrast to Alesina et al. (2001), who simply assume that the ECB Council decides by majority vote, we conclude that the actual procedure implies that future enlargements of EMU will strengthen the power of the ECB Board in monetary policy decisions.

[13] Specifically, Issing et al. (2001) express doubts about the power of monetary policy to systematically stabilize output and argue that low inflation is the ECB's best contribution to real growth.

refrained from outright open market purchases or sales or foreign exchange market interventions. The provision that reserves averaged over a month are counted against the reserve requirement assures that money market rates' daily volatility remains low, even without frequent central bank interventions.

This design reflects the desire to involve the national central banks as much as possible in the implementation of the common monetary policy, which is mandated by the ESCB statutes. Apart from the institutional interest in keeping staff numbers high (Marshall 1999), there is probably a strategic motivation for this. Frequent money market interventions among the national central banks would be difficult to coordinate, and therefore would create a tendency for centralized operations. An ECB permanently active in the market would be in a much stronger position relative to the national central banks in determining the course of monetary policy. Being active in the market between meetings of the ECB's Governing Council would allow the ECB's Executive Board to confront the Council with interest rate developments that would be difficult to reverse without upsetting the markets. The national central banks probably resisted such a design, fearing loss of influence over the common monetary policy.[14]

### 3. MONETARY POLICY STRATEGY

#### 3.1. The ECB's Monetary Policy Strategy

Monetary policy strategies can be regarded from different perspectives. Monetary economists typically focus on optimal-control arguments. Assuming that the central bank wishes to minimize a quadratic loss function defined over inflation (and, possibly, some other variables), the question is how to achieve the smallest control-error variance. From this perspective, a strategy serves primarily to deal with time lags and uncertainties in the link between the central bank's instruments and its objectives. A key issue, then, is the choice of an intermediate target, a variable that can be observed faster and more frequently than the ultimate target variables. Under an intermediate target strategy, keeping the intermediate target on some path over time helps the central bank to achieve its ultimate targets. The preparatory work of the ECB's institutional precursor, the European Monetary Institute (1997), had narrowed the ECB's strategy choices in this regard to the alternatives of monetary targeting or inflation forecast targeting.

A second perspective is the importance of a strategy for communicating with the public. A strategy provides a framework for publicly explaining current and defending past central bank actions (Gaspar, Masuch, and Pill 2001). The EMI's (1997) list of general principles for assessing a monetary policy strategy

---

14 It is interesting to observe that the Bundesbank Council in the 1970s rejected a Bundesbank Board proposal for a more active open market policy on exactly these grounds. See von Hagen (1998).

emphasized this aspect: A strategy must convey the impression that the central bank can and intends to pursue a well-defined medium-term objective; it must enhance *accountability* through the formulation and announcement of targets; it must be sufficiently *transparent* so that the public can understand why the central bank adopted a given policy; and it must be compatible with central bank independence. Issing et al. (2001, 34) argue that adopting a strategy is an attempt to characterize to the best possible extent, given the imperfect knowledge of the economy, how the central bank will respond to the arrival of new information. From this angle, the public announcement of a strategy is important for gaining credibility.

The third perspective considers the role of a monetary strategy for regulating the flow of information and structuring deliberations within the central bank. From this angle, a strategy shapes the decisionmaking processes, with important implications for the distribution of strategic powers in the central bank (see Tietmeyer 1996; von Hagen 1999c; Gaspar, Masuch, and Pill 2001). In this vein, the ECB (2001, 46) says that the purpose of strategy is to assure that monetary policy decisions are made in a consistent and coherent way.

In October 1998, the ECB (1998, 1999) presented its strategy, which is based on a definition of price stability, and the two pillars that form the basis for assessing current developments and interest rate decisions.

### 3.1.1. Price Stability

The ECB defines price stability as an annual increase of less than 2 percent in the Harmonized CPI, its main gauge of average inflation in the euro area. Initial doubts, expressed in public debate, that this implied a tolerance for deflation were soon rejected. The 2 percent limit on inflation is another heritage from former Bundesbank practices. Issing et al. (2001) point out that it is also consistent with the preferences of European governments, expressed several times in the European Council's *Broad Economic Guidelines*.

Like the Bundesbank in the past, the ECB regards price stability thus defined as a goal to be achieved only in the medium run, a period of unspecified length. This implies that it would tolerate temporary moves of inflation outside the target range. The lack of an operational definition of the medium term is a visible contrast to central banks' practice in recent years of pursuing explicit inflation targets. For example, the Bank of England's inflation target is for annual inflation two years ahead. The Bank of Sweden (1997, 27) writes that "[t]he Riksbank has formulated [its objective] as limiting the annual increase in the price level to 2 percent." The ECB's unwillingness to define a more precise time horizon for its goal of price stability has been criticized by several authors, who argue that the vagueness of the medium-run designation deflects accountability and reduces the public's ability to form expectations about future price and monetary developments (see Gali 2001).

Specifying the time horizon over which price stability is to be reached touches on two issues. The first is an optimal-control question: Given a shock causing a rise in inflation, how should the adjustment to this shock be distributed over time? The answer to this question depends on the central bank's preferences and the properties of the economy. Smets (2000) and the papers discussed there show that the optimal horizon is a function of the weight of price stability relative to output stability in the central bank's loss function. Given the ECB's unambiguous mandate for price stability, this suggests that it should aim at a rather short horizon. Smets also shows that the optimal time horizon becomes shorter if the economy is more forward looking, that is, if forward-looking expectations dominate backward-looking expectations embodied in wage contracts and price setting, and if the slope of the Phillips curve increases. One might argue that the ECB wanted to avoid a more specific definition of its time horizon because of uncertainty about the empirical characteristics of the euro economy in this regard.

The second issue is whether price stability is regarded as a (not necessarily constant) price-level target or a target only for the inflation rate, that is, whether or not it is compatible with base drift in the price level. Faced with a nonmonetary shock to the price level, a central bank targeting the inflation rate would allow base drift and merely aim at bringing inflation back to its target. In contrast, a central bank pursuing a price-level target would have to bring the price level back to its target path and, therefore, engage in a stronger and longer-lasting monetary contraction.[15] In view of this, price-level targets have traditionally been regarded as inappropriate because they would cause greater variability in output, inflation, and interest rates. Recent studies, however, suggest that they may have superior stabilization properties at low inflation and nominal interest rates.[16] Smets (2000) finds that the optimal time horizon for a price-level target is generally longer than that for an inflation target. Given that the total monetary response to an inflationary shock is larger under a price-level target, avoiding excessive output instability calls for distributing it over a longer time period.

The difference between targeting inflation and targeting the price level also matters for reasons of political economy. Price-level targeting provides those who are negatively affected by rising prices with better protection against the consequences of fiscal expansions and does so at some cost to those benefiting from

---

[15] As long as the target path of the price level is positively sloped, this does not imply that the central bank has to force a reduction in the price level. Instead, it can maintain a lower growth rate until the target path is met again.
[16] See Svensson (1999). An example would be a deflationary shock to the price level, which, given a price-level target, triggers an increase in inflation expectations and a decline in the real interest rate.

expansions in output. Therefore, the choice between targeting inflation or the price level requires a value judgment from the central bank (Fischer 1996). Unless it shares this value judgment, targeting the price level may lead to more intense conflicts between the government and the central bank.

From this perspective, the ECB's unwillingness to make its target horizon for price stability more precise may reflect an unwillingness to reveal its choice between targeting inflation and targeting the price level and a desire to leave room for a flexible choice of the distribution of monetary policy responses to fiscal and other shocks over time. A priori, aiming at annual headline inflation of less than 2 percent in the medium run is compatible with targeting the average inflation rate and allowing for base drift on one hand, and with targeting the price level along a path with a slope below 2 percent on the other. With no further explanation, the observer can discover only with hindsight, possibly over a long period, how the central bank reacted to nonmonetary shocks to the price level. Interestingly, the Bundesbank's past policies following bursts of inflation in the 1970s and early 1990s seemed consistent with a price-level objective, although the Bank never made this objective explicit (von Hagen 1995). In view of this, the ECB's unwillingness to clearly define a target horizon might be interpreted as indicating a hope that this imprecision would allow the bank to pursue a more ambitious target with less political resistance. The drawback is that the beneficial, stabilizing effects on inflation expectations will only come about once the public has fully understood the central bank's true intentions through experience.

### 3.1.2. The First Pillar

The key characteristic of the first pillar is the announcement of a reference value for the annual growth rate of a broad monetary aggregate, M3. Using the term "reference value" rather than the target indicates the ECB does not target M3 in a rigid, mechanical sense. Like the Bundesbank's earlier practice, assessment of monetary developments does not focus narrowly on M3 growth but includes other monetary and credit aggregates. A further similarity is the derivation of the reference value from a simple velocity equation. The reference value takes the growth rate of potential output less an assumed velocity trend as a starting point and adds the implicit target inflation rate. In October 1998, the assumed growth rate of potential output was 2.0 percent to 2.5 percent, while the assumed trend in velocity was a decline of –0.5 percent to –1.0 percent. The announced reference value was 4.5 percent (ECB 1999). Taking midpoints for the growth rate estimates implies a target inflation rate of 1.5 percent.

At first glance, the ECB's first pillar seems to resemble the flexible monetary targeting from the Bundesbank's past.[17] The Bundesbank repeatedly affirmed its willingness to tolerate temporary deviations from its monetary target (a 2 percent corridor for annual M3 growth), if this was deemed compatible with low inflation. Nevertheless, monetary targets were a good predictor of money growth in the medium run (Neumann and von Hagen 1993). However, the ECB has frequently emphasized that it does not regard M3 growth as an intermediate target at all. The ECB (2001, 48) states that it does not attempt to keep M3 growth at the reference value at any particular point in time by manipulating interest rates. The ECB has explained that it deems monetary targeting inappropriate because of potential instabilities in the demand for money as well as measurement problems with monetary aggregates (ECB 2001, 48). The repeated emphasis of the differences between the reference value and (even a flexible form of) monetary targeting reject the allegation of Alesina et al. (2001) that the first pillar simply pretends the ECB conducts its monetary policy as the Bundesbank did in the past. Instead, the reference value serves as a yardstick to assess risks of the central bank's ultimate target, inflation. This gives M3 growth and monetary developments the status of information variables in monetary policy decisions.

### 3.1.3. The Second Pillar

The second pillar consists of a broadly based assessment of the outlook for future price developments in parallel with the first pillar (ECB 1998). Initially, the second pillar represented an analysis of short-run price developments in the euro area, based on a large and unspecified number of economic and financial variables, including measures of real activity, wage costs, asset prices, fiscal policy indicators, and indicators of business and consumer confidence (ECB 1999). No framework was specified regarding how these variables would be used to assess price developments or what their relative weights in such assessments should be. The second pillar thus adds opacity to the ECB's strategy. Issing et al. (2001, 74) explain that the relative importance of these variables changes constantly and that there is no permanently valid way to organize the assessment in a logically consistent manner.

The second pillar's nature appears to have changed since its introduction. Angeloni, Gaspar, and Tristani (1999) and Issing et al. (2001) drop business and consumer confidence indicators and substitute inflation expectations derived from asset prices and market surveys to the elements of the second pillar. Gaspar, Masuch, and Pill (2001, 13) explain that analysis (under the second pillar) is typically centered on the effects of interactions between supply and demand and/or cost pressures on pricing behavior. In contrast to the explanation of Issing et al., this

---

[17] Marshall (1999, 278) quotes Tietmeyer proposing this view.

suggests the analysis is indeed organized according to some consistent framework. The ECB's (2000) explanation of the staff projections, which it started to publish in its *Monthly Bulletin* in December 2000, supports that view.[18]

One interpretation of this gradual development of a more consistent framework under the second pillar is that it is becoming equivalent to inflation forecast targeting. The benefit of such an interpretation is that it increases the transparency of this pillar. However, Gaspar, Masuch, and Pill (2001) reject this interpretation and the ECB (2001) explains that it does not regard inflation-forecast targeting as a sufficient framework for monetary policy. Like the first pillar, the second pillar is merely a collection of information variables used to assess risks to price stability. Thus, the ECB's strategy is best characterized as a direct-targeting approach.

### 3.1.4. Reconciling the Two Pillars

The presentation of two pillars has left ECB observers and commentators puzzled. Issing et al. (2001) acknowledge at least partially that the two-pillar structure makes the strategy hard to comprehend. Part of the confusion results from the commentator's own wish to read the two-pillar strategy as an intermediate-target strategy in disguise (either monetary or inflation-forecast targeting). Accepting that it is not still leaves two questions: Why are there two pillars rather than a unified framework for analyzing risks to price stability; and, given that there are two pillars, what is their relative weight in ECB monetary policy decisions?

According to the ECB, the two-pillar structure reflects the fundamental uncertainty about its macroeconomic environment and the transmission of monetary policy. The ECB (2001, 54) explains that it was chosen because of the multiplicity of models of the transmission process in the current literature, some of which emphasize the role of money for inflation, while other emphasize non-monetary factors. The first pillar thus stands for models reserving a prominent role for money in the central bank's analysis of threats to price stability. This role is justified by the claim that inflation is ultimately a monetary phenomenon (ECB 1999, 47). To support that claim, the ECB frequently points to the close correlation between money growth and inflation in the medium and long run (for example, see Issing et al. 2001 and ECB 2001). The second pillar, in contrast, makes room for models of inflation that focus on other aspects of the macroeconomy, such as output, demand, labor market conditions, and asset prices, and that have a more short-term orientation.

---

[18] These projections are conditional forecasts based on the assumption of no policy change. As noted by Gali (2001), the December projections have rather low precision. For example, the projected HICP inflation rate for 2001 is 1.8 percent to 2.8 percent. The ECB explains that this range corresponds to twice the average absolute error of previous forecasts. This translates into a confidence level of 57 percent (Gali 2001). Applying a more conventional 95 percent confidence band would correspond to a range of 0.7 percent to 3.9 percent. It may be, of course, that due to the shortage of data, the ECB just can't do better.

On closer scrutiny, however, this distinction between the first pillar and the second pillar seems more artificial than helpful. Taken literally, a first-pillar model would have to be one in which the link between money growth and inflation does not operate through the interaction of aggregate demand and supply. Not even a classical model with fully flexible prices would have that property. While for expository convenience, such models are often presented as saying that the price level clears the money market, this is just a shortcut through a transmission process in which monetary expansion works its way through the entire economy. Similarly, models of the new Keynesian and new neoclassical syntheses are often written in ways that hide the importance of monetary aggregates because these are not the focus of the analysis, but it is certainly true that monetary policy plays an essential role in them and that they embed correlations between money growth and inflation. Under any reasonable interpretation, such models would, therefore, fall under the first pillar as well. But then second-pillar models would have to give no role at all to money and monetary policy for inflation. It seems unlikely that this is what the ECB has in mind. If not, it is hard to see how expository differences between models commonly used in academic and policy debates in the past decade support a substantive distinction between the two pillars.

Some authors have taken this conclusion as a reason for arguing that the ECB should abolish its first pillar and disregard monetary aggregates altogether in its assessment of risks to price stability (Gali 2001 and Alesina et al. 2001). Two points are commonly made to support this claim. The first is that monetary variables have little or no information value for inflation over other variables in Granger causality tests. The fallacies of this argument are well known. Suppose the central bank manipulates interest rates to steer money growth in order to achieve price stability. Variations in the interest rate, then, carry most of the information about variations in monetary aggregates, and the marginal information value of such aggregates is unsurprisingly low. Furthermore, the closer to its target inflation is kept, the smaller the information value in the variables used to steer it, unless the target varies systematically with other variables. Thus, causality regressions have no relevance for the value of monetary variables in assessing inflation risks.

The second point commonly made is that recent macroeconomic models do not assign money a special role in the transmission process of monetary policy. The fallacy of this argument is that it confuses statements about the language of economists (that is, modeling conventions) with empirical hypotheses; the former are obviously not relevant to the policy issue. A related point, noted by Gali (2001), is that the long-run correlation between money growth and inflation, emphasized in the ECB's justification of the first pillar, does not prove any causality from money to prices. This is trivially true, since causality is a theoretical concept, not an empirical one (Cooley and Leroy 1985). Its theoretical strength cannot be decided from data and depends, among other things, on the central bank's own policy. In sum, only weak grounds are presented in the current debate for neglecting monetary variables in analyzing risks to price stability.[19]

In contrast to ECB reasoning, model uncertainty does not justify unwillingness to specify the relative weights of the two pillars, either, as Issing et al. (2001) argue. If the central bank has a probability distribution over all economic models considered, this distribution defines the relative weights of individual models in the decisionmaking process. These weights ought to be relatively stable or vary in systematic ways that can be communicated. Brunner and Meltzer (1969) discuss model uncertainty in the sense that several non-nested alternatives are available and the central bank has no prior probabilities for their validity. They argue that policymakers should adopt a mini-max strategy under such circumstances, that is, monetary policy should aim at minimizing the largest possible damage under all alternative models considered. This is nicely formalized in von zur Muehlen (2001).[20] If this is the type of uncertainty the ECB is concerned with, optimal decisionmaking results in rules that could be communicated in much clearer ways.

In sum, the recourse to model uncertainty does not yield a convincing justification of the two-pillar structure. The proper interpretation of the strategy, therefore, ought to lie elsewhere. Recall the ECB's explanation that the strategy serves to structure internal debates and communication with the public. From this perspective, assigning a prominent role to money under the first pillar is primarily a statement about what the ECB thinks it is—or should be—responsible for. Building on the proposition that inflation is ultimately a monetary phenomenon, the prominent role assigned to monetary aggregates and their analysis under the first pillar indicates a responsibility for avoiding situations in which large, lasting expansions or contractions of monetary aggregates would result in bouts of inflation or deflation. In other words, the first pillar signals a commitment to avoiding monetary policy errors resulting from uncontrolled monetary developments.

Viewed in this way, the first pillar is much less than monetary targeting. In particular, it does not constrain monetary policy much, as long as money growth rates remain in an acceptable range around the reference value. But the monetary reference value could still serve to structure the internal policy debate in the ECB Council. The ECB's monthly reports, which always begin with an analysis of monetary developments, reflect this point. Regular discussion of monetary developments and how they would be affected by current interest rate policy ensures that the

---

[19] A number of recent papers argue that the neglect of monetary aggregates in conducting monetary policy can result in rather unpleasant outcomes in precisely the type of models advocates of abolishing money from the set of variables the ECB should look at; see Christiano and Rostagno (2001) and the literature cited there.

[20] For a treatment of robust optimal control in forward-looking monetary policy models, see Hansen and Sargent (2000).

central bank's policymakers keep the medium-run consequences of their decisions in perspective. In the Bundesbank's earlier experience, monetary developments gained importance relative to other considerations in times of protracted monetary expansions, thus inducing the Bundesbank to tighten monetary policy before inflation accelerated (von Hagen 1999c). In our interpretation, the ECB's first pillar thus serves as a commitment device that disciplines the ECB Council against uncontrolled accelerations or decelerations of money growth; it is also a signal to the general public that the ECB will watch over monetary developments in this way. The second pillar, then, serves merely as an assurance that the ECB will not narrowmindedly neglect other relevant information in conducting monetary policy. Interestingly, such an interpretation comes close to Christiano and Rostagno's (2001) recent proposal of a money-growth constraint on a monetary policy characterized by a Taylor rule. These authors show that such a constraint anchors long-run inflation expectations and reduces the risk of indeterminacies and high-inflation equilibria that can arise from central bank policies that follow Taylor rules. It is equally interesting, however, that their analysis suggests the ECB should frame its first pillar in terms of a lower and an upper bound of money growth rates rather than a reference value.

Interpreting the two-pillar strategy as a device for structuring debates within the central bank also explains why the ECB does not specify the relative weights of the two pillars. First, the nature of the first pillar implies that its weight should be variable: small in normal times and gaining importance in times of runaway monetary expansions. Second, Issing et al. (2001, 89) explain that, from a procedural viewpoint, the synthesis between the two pillars begins to take place first and foremost at the moment at which the analyses and options are elaborated and presented to the ECB decisionmaking bodies. Because the chief economist makes this presentation, the chief economist also defines the weights. Using the same weights consistently would increase the strategy's transparency at this stage, but it would render the chief economist unable to use the information strategically in the ECB Council or to determine the relative importance of medium- and short-run considerations himself. Not committing to a priori weights strenghtens the chief economist's leadership over national central bank presidents at Council meetings.

In this interpretation, the first pillar of the strategy assures the public of the ECB's medium-term orientation of avoiding any contribution of monetary policy to inflation. The opacity of the second pillar and its relation to the first one, however, hardly makes this strategy an effective framework for communicating the ECB's shorter-run intentions to the public. This may be the price of achieving the strategic purposes of the internal decisionmaking processes.

## 3.2. The Strategy at Work: Monetary Policy Decisions, 1999–2001

Many observers expected the ESCB to start its monetary policy by pushing up interest rates, even if that was not justified by economic conditions, in order to prove that it was hard-nosed on inflation (see, for example, Dornbusch, Favero, and Giavazzi 1998). The opposite happened. In a concerted effort, generally considered the Eurosystem's first policy action, all national central banks reduced their interest rates to 3 percent on December 3, 1998.[21] While this could still be regarded as a reaction to the Russian financial crises, the rate cut on April 8, 1999, cannot, because all the economies of the euro area except Germany and Italy had recovered from the 1999 slowdown by then.[22] As table 1 shows, the April 1999 rate cut came in the presence of low but rising inflation rates and a money growth rate that was slightly too high. The ECB reversed its course in November 1999. It raised its rate, first by 50 basis points and then by another 100 basis points distributed over the following 12 months. The upward move over 2000 was accompanied first by increasing money growth rates, which started to fall only in the summer of that year. Inflation continued to increase until the fall of 2000 and remains significantly above the 2 percent ceiling set by the ECB. In a surprise move, the ECB cut rates again in May 2001.

Recent literature has shown that Taylor rules are useful for describing and interpreting central bank policies under very diverse circumstances. The simple Taylor rule (Taylor 1993) has received considerable attention as a benchmark rule for the ECB (see, for example, Peersman and Smets 1999; Taylor 1998), since it found empirical support for the euro area before the introduction of the euro (see, for example, Gerlach and Schnabel 2000). Moreover, Taylor rules are also explicitly employed as a benchmark by parts of the financial press, such as the *Financial Times Deutschland*.[23] We base our exercise on the following specification:

$$(1) \qquad i_t = 4.0 + 1.2 \, (\pi_t - \pi^{ob}) + 0.2 y_t,$$

where $i_t$, $\pi_t$, $\pi^{ob}$, and $y_t$ denote the nominal money market interest rate, the inflation rate, the inflation objective of the Central Bank, and the output gap. We set $\pi^{ob} = 1.5$ percent, the value implicitly used by the ECB for their calculation of the reference value for M3, and assume an equilibrium interest rate of 4.0 percent, the sum of the ECB's assumed long-run real GDP growth rate and the inflation objective. The coefficients of this Taylor rule are similar to empirical estimates for the Bundesbank prior to the EMU, a plausible starting point for the ECB (Faust,

---

[21] The Bank of Italy cut its rate to 3.5 percent and then to 3.0 percent later that month. See Gaspar (2000) for a review of this action.

[22] Gaspar (2000) explains that move as a protection against deflationary risks in the euro area, although there were already signs that inflation was creeping up.

[23] Alesina et al. (2001) and Faust, Rogers, and Wright (2001) present similar studies of ECB monetary policy based on Taylor rules.

**Table 1: Interest Rate Decisions**

| Date | Change in interest rate | Cumulated change in interest rate | Current money growth rate (M3) | Current inflation rate |
|------|------------------------|-----------------------------------|-------------------------------|------------------------|
| 12/08/98 | −30 | −30 | 5.84 | 0.8 |
| 04/08/99 | −50 | −80 | 5.26 | 1.1 |
| 11/05/99 | 50 | −30 | 6.06 | 1.5 |
| 02/03/00 | 25 | −05 | 6.11 | 2.0 |
| 06/08/00 | 50 | 45 | 5.37 | 2.4 |
| 10/05/00 | 25 | 70 | 5.11 | 2.7 |
| 05/10/01 | −25 | 45 | 4.51 (April) | 3.4 |

Rogers, and Wright 2001). One advantage of this parameterization is that it yields a value of the Taylor rule for the euro area of 3 percent in December 1998, which corresponds to the actual value. In contrast to Faust, Rogers, and Wright, we use the current rather than an expected future inflation rate in the Taylor rule. Using an expected rate would not change the results below significantly, but calculating expected inflation rates from the data would force us to shorten the sample. In sum, we regard the specification of equation (1) as a plausible benchmark.

A well-known problem in applying Taylor rules is the measurement of output gaps. In fact, the measurement problem is used to explain why the weight of output gaps is lower than that of inflation (Smets 1998). Measuring output gaps is even more of a problem in the euro area, where data concerning output are rather inaccurate and released rather late. Here, we use simple interpolations of several output gap estimates to increase the robustness of our measure. The estimates are from the OECD (2001), IMF (2001), and two series from the European Union (2000, and 2001).

In figure 1, we plot the Taylor rule from equation (1), labeled *euro,* together with the ECB's main financing rate (*main rate*). The benchmark Taylor rule is not good at describing ECB interest rate decisions from January 1999 onward; the actual rate during that period was continuously lower than the rate implied by the Taylor rule. Nor is the difference between the two rates well explained by interest rate smoothing, under which the actual rate would adjust to the rate implied by the Taylor rule gradually, that is,

$$(2) \qquad i_t = \lambda i_{t-1} + (1 - \lambda) [4.0 + 1.2\,(\pi_t - \pi^{ob}) + 0.2 y_t] \,,$$

where $\lambda > 0$. Figure 1, however, shows that the actual rate and the rate calculated from our Taylor rule move in opposite directions in at least two instances.

**Figure 1: Taylor Rules for the Euro Area I**

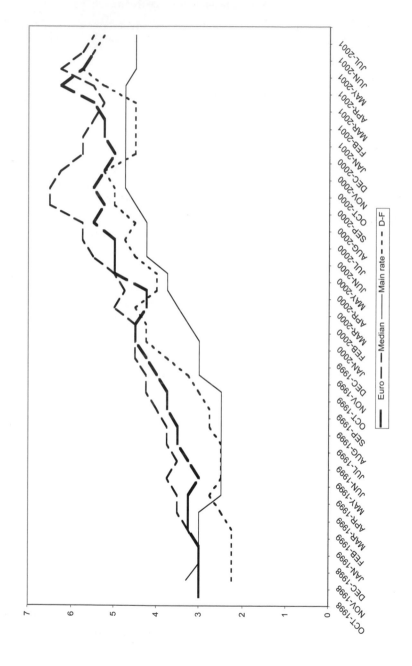

How can the difference between the actual rate and the plausible benchmark be explained? As noted above, pre-EMU literature has paid much attention to the voting behavior of the national central bank presidents on the ECB Board. If ECB Council decisions were made by simple majority, the median national central bank president would have considerable influence on them. Inflation rates in the EMU exhibited quite a large degree of cross-country variation during the period under consideration, as illustrated in figure 2. This could move the ECB's interest rate away from the benchmark. To evaluate this possibility, we calculate individual Taylor rules based on equation (1); using individual country data, we compute the median Taylor rate for each period. In figure 1, we plot this rate, labeled *median*. The actual rate set in December 1998 corresponded exactly to the choice of the median national central bank president. After that, however, the median rule would have implied a much faster and larger rise in interest rates, in response to the larger increase in the median inflation rate and the median output gap in the euro area. Thus, figure 1 confirms that the median national central bank president does not play a large role in shaping interest rate decisions.

Another possibility is that the Council gives particular weight to the circumstances of the two largest economies, Germany and France. To explore this, we average the rates calculated from equation (1) for these two countries. The two rates are quite similar during this period, since Germany had lower inflation rates than France but also a lower output gap. The resulting rate, labeled *D–F*, is shown in figure 1. It does more to explain the actual interest rate than the original Taylor rule (euro). Interestingly, the ECB's first interest rate move in April 1999 pushed the actual rate closer to the *D–F* rate. The subsequent movements in the actual rate seem quite consistent with a smooth adjustment of the actual rate to that implied by *D–F*. Thus, there is some suggestive evidence to support the idea that the ECB Council places more weight on economic developments in Germany and France than elsewhere.

Occasionally, it is argued that the ECB cares for core inflation instead of headline inflation. In figure 3, we show a Taylor rule with the Harmonized Index of Consumer Prices (HICP) replaced by core inflation, measured as HICP minus food and energy prices (*core 1*). Because core inflation's movements over this period are much flatter, the resulting Taylor rate is much flatter and misses the movements of the actual rate more than our first benchmark did. A variation of this alternative is to replace headline by core inflation in calculating the Taylor rule and increase the weight on the output gap. This follows the conjecture by Faust, Rogers, and Wright from a similar exercise, that the ECB places more weight on output stabilization than the Bundesbank formerly did. Assuming a weight of 0.8 for output yields the rate labeled *core 2* in figure 3. This rule tracks the observed rate quite well between

**Figure 2: Standard Deviation of Inflation Rates in the Euro Area**

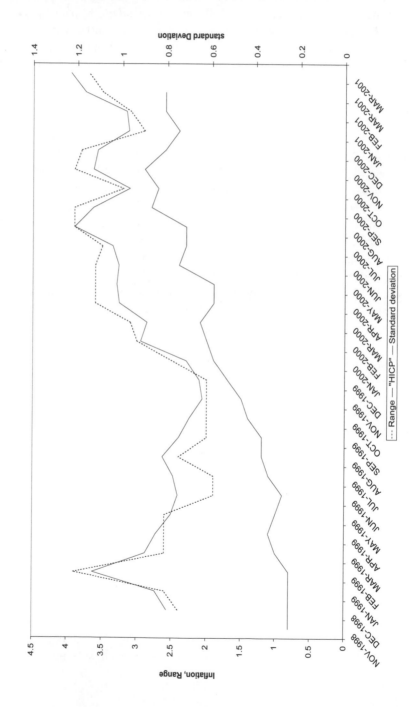

**Figure 3: Taylor Rules II**

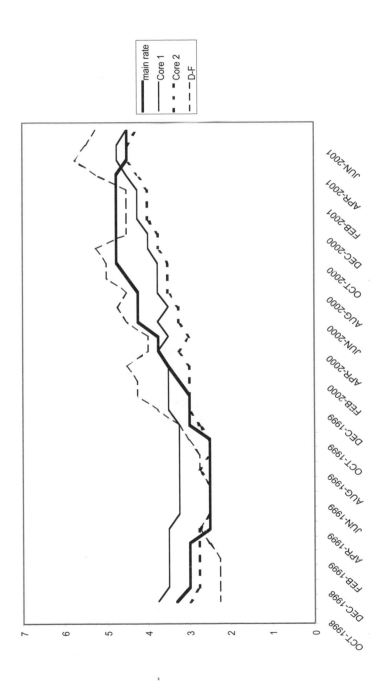

the start of the EMU and early 2000. For the remainder of 2000, however, the actual rate followed the *D–F* line more closely and moved away from the *core 2* line. Only the ECB's May 2001 interest rate move seemed to follow the *core 2* line more than the *D–F* line. Thus, there is also some preliminary evidence in the data that the ECB's interest rate policy gave more weight to output stabilization than does our original benchmark as suggested by Faust, Rogers, and Wright.

For a more formal test, we consider the regressions reported in table 2, where the dependent variable is the actual interest rate.

|                    | (1)            | (2)            |
| ------------------ | -------------- | -------------- |
| Constant           | −0.23 (−0.62)  | 0.03 (0.13)    |
| D–F                | 0.29 (2.73)    | 0.15 (2.67)    |
| Core 2             | 0.85 (4.04)    |                |
| Lagged main rate   |                | 0.84 (12.64)   |
| Standard deviation | 0.37           | 0.17           |
| ρ                  | 0.75           | 0.01           |
| $R^2$              | 0.86           | 0.96           |

Note: Number of observations = 32; dependent variable is the main rate; ρ is the first-order residual autocorrelation; and numbers in parentheses are *t* ratios.

The first regression suggests that the ECB's interest rate policy can be explained as a mix of a Taylor rule for Germany and France and a Taylor rule focusing on core inflation and giving relatively heavy weight to the euro area output gap. However, the residual autocorrelation is very high for this regression. The second regression model follows the interest-rate-smoothing model and has the actual rate depend on its own lag and the Taylor rule for Germany and France. The table shows that this model explains the actual rate very well and leads to a residual autocorrelation that is almost zero.[24] Adding *core 2* to this equation yields a negative, statistically insignificant coefficient for that variable. As a result, the ECB's policy is best described as following a Taylor rule focused on developments in Germany and France, augmented by a tendency for interest rate smoothing.

Our interpretation of these findings is that the ECB Board succeeded in emancipating itself quickly from the median country's perspective on monetary policy and that it did so by giving more weight to a policy responding to developments in France and Germany. The fact that the Taylor rules for Germany and France consistently called for lower rates than did the median country's Taylor rule may have helped the ECB Board, because the resulting policy was less proactive than a policy focusing on euro-area aggregates would have been. The relatively large

[24] The second-order autocorrelation is (−0.09).

weight Germany and France seem to receive in ECB interest rate decisions may reflect the other Council members' acknowledgment of these two countries' importance for European integration. Alternatively, it may reflect the ECB Council's shared view that these two economies, which together represent half of the euro economy, reflect the medium-run developments of the euro area better than the aggregate data used to compute the euro-area Taylor rule. Whether that is true is an empirical question that remains to be resolved.

## 4. MONETARY RELATIONS IN THE EURO AREA

In this section, we review the monetary developments in the euro area so far. We are mainly interested in two questions. First, is the link between money and prices empirically stable enough to support a monetary policy strategy focusing on money? Second, how did the ECB's monetary policy perform so far?

### 4.1. Money Demand

A number of empirical studies in the 1990s investigated the existence of a stable, long-run money-demand function for broad monetary aggregates at the EMU level (Browne, Fagan, and Henry 1997; Hayo 1999; Fagan and Henry 1999; Coenen and Vega 1999; Brand and Cassola 2000). Generally, they conclude that the stability of money demand at the level of the monetary union is greater than the stability of national money-demand functions. Broad money demand is found to have standard properties, that is, long-run real income and price-level elasticities of unity and a negative and significant elasticity with respect to the yield on alternative financial assets.

In Hayo, Neumann, and von Hagan (1998), we estimate a money-demand function for M3 based on a cointegrating framework using quarterly data from 1979–97. We use that estimate to derive the following long-run money-demand function for the euro area,

(3)  $m_t - p_t = y_t - 0.023i_t$ ,

where $m$, $p$, and $y$ are the logs of the money supply, the GDP deflator, and real GDP, respectively, and $i$ is the yield on 10-year government bonds in the euro area. Hayo (1999) finds a similar relationship using data from 1964 onward, pointing to the stability of the long-run relationship. Here, we use this function to evaluate the monetary relationships in the euro area since the start of the EMU. Note that, since our sample for estimation ends in 1997, all of the following exercises are true out-of-sample evaluations.

Equation (3) can be inverted to yield an equation for the velocity of M3. Figure 4 shows the actual velocity of M3 for the euro area from 1994 to 2000, together with the fitted values from equation (3). Comparing the estimated and the observed velocities confirms the considerable empirical stability of the money-demand function. The average forecast error of the out-of-sample forecasting exercise is 0.5 percent. Over this period, actual velocity fell almost 6.0 percent, consistent with the ECB's proposition of a trend decline in M3 velocity embedded in the calculation of the reference value for M3 growth. While the ECB interprets this decline as a fixed trend resulting from changes in portfolio habits and technological changes, our estimated model, which contains no trend, suggests that the gradual decline in velocity is a consequence of the decline in long-term interest rates since the 1980s.

Figure 4 also plots a log-linear trend velocity assuming, as the ESCB does, a trend rate of –0.75 percent. The estimated model outperforms the trend model clearly in the first part of the plot, where long-term rates are increasing slightly. In contrast, our long-run money-demand function overestimates velocity in 2000 somewhat, while the trend model underestimates it. Fitting a trend through the observed M3 velocity during the 1994–2000 period yields a slope parameter of –0.43 percent with a standard error of –0.038, which is significantly different from that assumed in the ECB's calculation of the monetary reference value. The implication is that the ECB's reference value is too large.

### 4.2. Money Growth

Apart from currency in circulation, M3 contains overnight deposits, deposits with fixed maturities of up to two years, deposits with statutory maturity of up to three months, repurchase agreements of financial institutions, money market fund shares and money market paper, and bank certificates of deposit and short-term obligations of maturities up to two years. Some of these elements of M3 are denominated in non-euro currencies; others are traded in secondary markets, which implies that these elements are subject to valuation changes as their market prices change. In calculating the monthly growth rate of M3, the ECB purges the monetary data from these valuation changes. The ECB's reasoning for this is that changes in monetary assets caused by valuation changes rather than transactions would not cause portfolio adjustments affecting private spending behavior (ECB 2001). The empirical strength of this conjecture, however, remains unclear.

Relative to balance sheet data, the adjusted money growth figures severely understate the monetary expansion from mid-1999 to early 2001. This results mainly from the euro's continuous depreciation during that period. At the peak of the monetary expansion in the spring of 2000, the difference between the two series was about 2 percent. Without a convincing justification for the adjustment, this

**Figure 4: M3 Velocity**

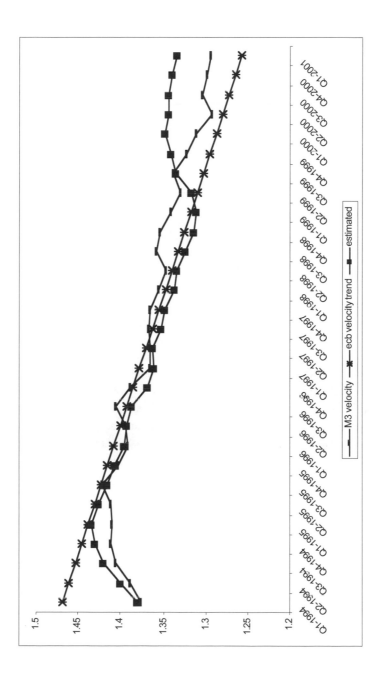

*Jürgen von Hagen and Matthias Brückner*

**Figure 5: Money Growth and Interest Rates**

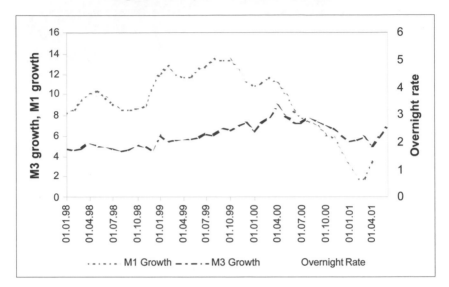

would imply that an inflation potential, building up in the euro area, was considerably higher than that which the ECB inferred from its indicator. In contrast, the adjusted growth rates indicate much less monetary tightening after September 2000. There is, therefore, a risk that the focus on adjusted money growth rates introduces a bias into the ECB's monetary policy, one that underestimates inflation risks in times when the external value of the euro is weakening and underestimates monetary tightening in times of external revaluation.

At the start of the EMU, money growth was already higher than the reference value. Figure 5 shows that it accelerated after April 2000, driven mainly by very rapid M1 expansion, which grew stronger after interest rates declined in the first months of 1999. Starting in the fall of that year, M1 growth came down quickly and substantially, responding to the rise in short-term rates. M3 growth peaked later than M1 and came down more gradually in the second half of 2000.

The difference between the two aggregates is caused by portfolio shifts from nonmonetary financial assets into the interest-bearing parts of M3. This is illustrated by the fact that the growth rates of money market funds and short-term obligations included in M3 fluctuated between 20 percent and 32 percent in the six months between October 2000 and March 2001. The ECB has argued recently that a large part of this increase results from foreign holdings of short-term, euro-denominated paper; these holdings do not create inflationary pressures and, therefore, should not be allowed to affect the ECB's monetary policy (Duisenberg 2001). Another likely reason for the rapid increase in these items is the turmoil in international stock markets in recent months. Excluding these items from M3 would reduce the annual growth rate to 3.3 percent in the first quarter of 2001. This suggests that the broad monetary aggregate tends to underestimate the extent of a monetary contraction, an observation that resembles the Bundesbank's earlier experiences (von Hagen 1993). The focus on a broad aggregate thus risks maintaining a tighter stance of monetary policy for longer than is necessary to maintain price stability.

### 4.3. Money Growth and Inflation in the Euro Area

In contrast, the first pillar of the ECB's strategy relies on the proposition that excess money growth is an indicator of future inflation. Figure 6 shows the growth rates of M3 together with the CPI inflation rate since 1998. Euro-area money growth started to accelerate in the fall of 1998, when inflation was still hovering around 1 percent. Inflation began to accelerate in the summer of 1999 and leveled out in the fall of 2000, a few months after M3 growth peaked. Eyeballing thus suggests a positive relation between the two variables.

**Figure 6: M3 Growth and Inflation**

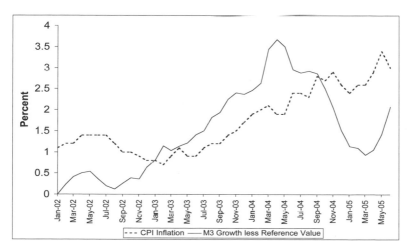

From this perspective, the most recent interest rate cut was justified, if the central bank is satisfied with lowering inflation to less than 2 percent after a period of higher rates. In contrast, an effort to bring inflation substantially lower in order to regain an average rate below 2 percent over time would have called for maintaining the tight stance of monetary policy. Thus, the most recent decision is interesting because it indicates that the ECB's definition of price stability allows for base drift in the price level.

For a more systematic analysis, we apply our long-run money-demand function to the concept of an equilibrium price level (von Hagen 1995) or P* model (Hallman et al. 1991) for the euro area. We solve the money-demand function for the price level that would result if all prices adjusted immediately to current output, money, and interest rates, that is, to the equilibrium price level:

(4)      $p_t^* = m_t - y_t^r + 0.023\ r_t.$

Next, we assume that the price level follows the equilibrium price level with a lag,

(5)      $\Delta p_t = a + b\,(p^*_{t-4} - p_{t-4}) + u_t.$

The left side of equation (5) is the annual inflation rate. With $b > 0$, the actual price level adjusts to the equilibrium price level over time. We estimate this equation using quarterly data for the GDP deflator for 1995–2000. This yields the following equation:

(6)      $\Delta p_t = 0.99 + 0.2\,(p^*_{t-4} - p_{t-4})$     $R^2 = 0.66,\ F(1, 24) = 42.0$
          $t$ values: (6.5) (6.5).

All parameters are statistically significant at the 1 percent level. Thus, there is a statistically significant relationship between the observed inflation rate and the lagged difference between the equilibrium and the actual price level. A rise in the equilibrium price level is followed by an increase in euro-area inflation a year later. Figure 7, which plots the actual and the fitted inflation rates against the price gap, shows that the fit of this model, simple and out-of-sample as it is, is quite high.[25] The implication is that the change in the equilibrium price level is an indicator of the future inflation potential caused by current monetary policy. A rising equilibrium price level shows that the money supply is growing faster than the long-run money demand at current income and interest rates and that this discrepancy creates inflationary pressures.

---

[25] There is some autocorrelation in the residuals of the regression, but the Durbin–Watson test is inconclusive. To address the problems resulting from the use of quarterly data of annual inflation rates, We also estimated this relationship based on quarter-to-quarter inflation rates and the price gap lagged one period. The results are very similar.

**Figure 7: Actual and Predicted Inflation Rates Based on Price-Gap Model**

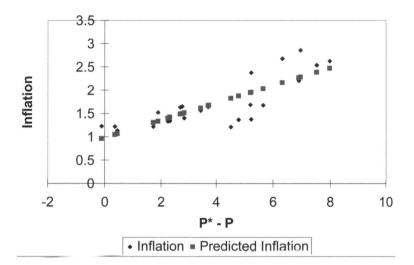

The ECB's main inflation gauge is Harmonized CPI inflation rather than the change in the GDP deflator. While consumer prices react faster to exchange rate movements and variations in individual prices such as energy, one would still expect the HICP to move in line with the GDP deflator in the longer run. To see whether this is true—and whether the equilibrium price level is a good indicator of the long-run development of the HICP—we regress the HICP inflation rate on our price gap. Following Gerlach and Svensson (2001), we include the change in oil prices lagged by four quarters in this regression. As before, we use data for 1995–2000. This yields the following regression model:

(7)     $\Delta p_t = 0.86 + 0.21 \, (p^*_{t-4} - p_{t-4}) + 0.05 \Delta p_{oil,t-1}$   $R^2 = 0.74$, F (2, 20) = 28.9,
        $t$ values:  (5.9)   (6.7)        (5.4)

Again, the relationship holds quite well. Equation (7) indicates that a rise in the equilibrium price level will result in higher HICP inflation rates after some time. These results are consistent with Gerlach and Svensson (2001), who estimate a similar relationship between inflation and the price gap but assume a constant velocity of money.

The empirical exercises in this section lead us to three conclusions. First, the out-of-sample properties of our simple velocity model suggest that money demand in the euro area is sufficiently stable to support a monetary policy strategy in which money plays a prominent role. Second, money is a leading indicator of inflation in the euro area. On the basis of these results, the ECB could revise its strategy and pay closer attention to M3 growth in the future. Finally, the ECB allowed M3 to grow too much during the EMU's early years. Monetary policy thus contributed to the resurgence of inflation. Our calculations show that the price gap contributed about 1 percent to HICP inflation in early 2001. With a more disciplined monetary policy in 1999 and 2000, the ECB could have held inflation below its 2 percent limit, even in the face of the oil price hike.

## 5. CONCLUSIONS

In this paper, we have presented a review of the ECB's institutional background, strategy, and monetary policy performance. This policy is characterized by a two-pillar strategy, which does not rely on any intermediate target. It serves to signal the ECB's intention of preventing large, lasting monetary contractions or expansions that would endanger price stability. It is also a strategic instrument to focus the deliberations of the ECB Council on monetary developments and give them a medium-run orientation. It does not, however, constrain ECB policy much in the shorter run or enable the public to make informed guesses about the central bank's policy in times when monetary aggregates show no signs of running away in either direction. In that sense, the strategy remains intransparent and leaves large room for discretionary manoeuvre. Empirical results based on Taylor rules suggest that ECB interest rate movements were dominated by considerations focusing on economic developments in Germany and France rather than the euro area as a whole.

The monetary and inflation developments of the early years are consistent with the conjecture of a stable money demand function and a significant relationship between monetary and price developments in the euro area. On the basis of these relations, the data suggest that the ECB allowed the money supply to expand too much in the EMU's first year, which caused inflation to rise later on. This illustrates the risk of a strategy that regards monetary aggregates merely as constraints in the sense described above rather than as intermediate targets guiding monetary policy in normal times as well. By revising its strategy and giving monetary developments more weight in guiding central bank decisions over a shorter time horizon, the ECB could improve its success in achieving price stability.

## ACKNOWLEDGMENTS

The authors thank their discussants, Vitor Gaspar and Stephen Cecchetti, David E. Altig, and an anonymous referee for helpful comments and suggestions.

## REFERENCES

Alesina, Alberto, Olivier Blanchard, Jordi Gali, Francesco Giavazzi, and Harald Uhlig. 2001. *Defining a Macroeconomic Framework for the Euro Area.* Monitoring the ECB 3. London: Centre for Economic Policy Research.

Angeloni, Ignazio, Vitor Gaspar, and Oreste Tristani. 1999. The Monetary Policy Strategy of the ECB. In *From EMS to EMU*, edited by David Cobham and George Zis, 3–42. London: Macmillan.

Arnold, Ivo, and Casper C.G. de Vries. 2000. Endogenous Financial Structure in the EMU. In *Regional Aspects of Monetary Policy in Europe*, edited by Jürgen von Hagen and Chris Waller. Boston: Kluwer.

Bank of Sweden. 1997. *Inflation Report.* Stockholm: Bank of Sweden.

Brand, Claus, and Nuno Cassola. 2000. A Money Demand System for Euro Area M3. European Central Bank, Working Paper no. 39, November.

Browne, F. X., Gabriel Fagan, and Jerome Henry. 1997. Money Demand in EU Countries: A Survey. European Monetary Institute, Staff Paper no. 7.

Brückner, Matthias. 1997. Voting and Decisions in the ECB. European Institute, Working Paper no. ECO 97/29.

Brunner, Karl, and Allan H. Meltzer. 1969. The Nature of the Policy Problem. In *Targets and Indicators of Monetary Policy*, edited by Karl Brunner. San Francisco: Chandler.

Cecchetti, Steven, Margaret M. McConnell, and Gabriel Perez-Quiros. 1999. Policy Makers' Revealed Preferences and the Output–Inflation Variability Trade-off: Implications for the European System of Central Banks. Unpublished manuscript.

Christiano, Lawrence J., and Massimo Rostagno. 2001. Money Growth Monitoring and the Taylor Rule. Unpublished manuscript.

Coenen, Günter, and Juan-Luis Vega. 1999. The Demand for M3 in the Euro Area. European Central Bank, Working Paper no. 6, September.

Coenen, Günter, and Volker Wieland. 2000. A Small, Estimated Euro-area Model with Rational Expectations and Nominal Rigidities. European Central Bank, Working Paper no. 30, September.

Coolcy, Thomas F., and Stephen F. LeRoy. 1985. Atheoretical Macroeconometrics: A Critique. *Journal of Monetary Economics* 16: 283–308.

Danthine, Jean-Pierre, Francesco Giavazzi, and Ernst-Ludwig von Thadden. 2000. European Financial Markets after EMU: A First Assessment. Centre for Economic Policy Research, Discussion Paper no. 2413.

de Grauwe, Paul, Hans Dewachter, and Yunus Aksoy. 1999. Effectiveness of Monetary Policy in Euroland. *Empirica* 26: 299–318.

Dornbusch, Rudiger, Carlo Favero, and Francesco Giavazzi. 1998. Immediate Challenges for the European Central Bank. *Economic Policy* 26: 17–64.

Duisenberg, Willem F. 2001. *Introductory Statement*. European Central Bank, press conference, May 10.

European Central Bank. 1998. A Stability Oriented Monetary Policy Strategy for the ESCB. Press release, October 13.

————. 1999. *Monthly Bulletin*, January.

————. 2001. *The Monetary Policy of the ECB*. Frankfurt: European Central Bank.

European Commission. 1997. *The Impact of the Introduction of the Euro on European Capital Markets* (Giovannini Report). Euro Papers 3. Brussels: European Commission.

European Monetary Institute. 1997. *The Single Monetary Policy in Stage Three*. Frankfurt: EMI.

European Union. 2000. European Economy. *Economic Trends*, supplement A, no. 1/2.

————. 2001. European Economy. *Economic Trends*, supplement A, no. 3/4.

Fagan, Gabriel, and Jerome Henry. 1999. Long-Run Money Demand in the EU: Evidence for Area-Wide Aggregates. In *Money Demand in Europe*, edited by Helmut Lütkepohl and Jürgen Wolters. Heidelberg: Physica-Verlag.

Fagan, Gabriel, Jerome Henry, and Ricardo Mestre. 2001. An Area-wide Model for the Euro Area. European Central Bank, Working Paper no. 42, January.

Faust, Jon, John H. Rogers, and Jonathan H. Wright. 2001. An Empirical Comparison of Bundesbank and ECB Monetary Policy Rules. Board of Governors of the Federal Reserve System, International Finance Discussion Paper no. 705, August.

Fischer, Stanley. 1996. Why Are Central Banks Pursuing Long-Run Price Stability? In *Achieving Price Stability: Symposium Proceedings*, 7–34. Kansas City, Mo.: Federal Reserve Bank of Kansas City.

Gali, Jordi. 2001. Monetary Policy in the Early Years of EMU. Paper presented at the European Commission Workshop on the Functioning of EMU: Challenges of the Early Years.

Gaspar, Vitor. 2000. The Role of Monetary Policy under Low Inflation. Paper presented at the IMES/Bank of Japan International Conference, July 3–4.

Gaspar, Vitor, Klaus Masuch, and Huw Pill. 2001. The ECB's Monetary Policy Strategy: Responding to the Challenges of the Early Years of EMU. In *The Functioning of EMU: The Challenge of The Early Years*, edited by M. Buti and A. Sapir. Oxford: Oxford University Press.

Gerlach, Stefan, and Gert Schnabel. 2000. The Taylor Rule and Interest Rates in the EMU Area. *Economics Letters* 67: 165–71.

Gerlach, Stefan, and Lars E.O. Svensson. 2001. Money and Inflation in the Euro Area: A Case for Monetary Indicators? Bank for International Settlements, Working Paper no. 98.

Hallman, Jeffrey J., Richard D. Porter, and David H. Small. 1991. Is the Price Level Tied to the M2 Monetary Aggregate in the Long Run? *American Economic Review* 81: 841–58.

Hansen, Lars, and Thomas Sargent. 2000. Robust Control and Filtering of Forward Looking Models. Unpublished manuscript.

Hayo, Bernd. 1999. Estimating a European Demand for Money. *Scottish Journal of Political Economy* 46: 221–244.

Hayo, Bernd, Manfred J.M. Neumann, and Jürgen von Hagen. 1998. A Monetary Target for the ECB. EMU Monitor Background Paper. Press conference, December 17, 1998. Available at *www.zei.de*.

Herdegen, Matthias. 1998. Kommentar zu Art 88 Grundgesetz. University of Bonn, unpublished manuscript.

Hughes-Hallett, Andrew, Rolf R. Strauch, and Jürgen von Hagen. 2001. Budgetary Consolidations in EMU. European Commission, Economic Paper no. 148, March.

International Monetary Fund. 2001a. *World Economic Outlook Database*.

———. 2001b. Monetary and Exchange Rate Policies of the Euro Area. Country Report no. 01/60.

Issing, Otmar, Vitor Gaspar, Ignazio Angeloni, and Oreste Tristani. 2001. *Monetary Policy in the Euro Area: Strategy and Decision-making at the European Central Bank*. Cambridge: Cambridge University Press.

Kremers, Jereon, and Timothy Lane. 1992. The Demand for Money in Europe. *IMF Staff Papers* 39: 730–37.

Marshall, Matt. 1999. *The Bank*. London: Random House.

Neumann, Manfred J.M., and Jürgen von Hagen. 1993. Germany. In *Monetary Policy in Industrialized Countries*, edited by Michele Fratianni and Dominik Salvatore. Westport, Conn.: Greenwood Press.

Organisation for Economic Co-operation and Development. 2001. *Economic Outlook*. Paris: OECD.

Peersman, Geert, and Frank Smets. 1999. The Taylor Rule: A Useful Monetary Policy Benchmark for the Euro Area? *International Finance* 2: 85–116.

Smets, Frank. 1998. Output Gap Uncertainty: Does It Matter for the Taylor Rule? Bank for International Settlements, Working Paper no. 60.

———. 2000. What Horizon for Price Stability? European Central Bank, Working Paper no. 24.

Svensson, Lars E.O. 1999. How Should Monetary Policy Be Conducted in an Era of Price Stability? Unpublished manuscript.

Taylor, John B. 1993. Discretion versus Policy Rules in Practice. *Carnegie–Rochester Conference Series on Public Policy* 39: 195–214.

———. 1998. The Robustness and Efficiency of Monetary Policy Rules as Guidelines for Interest Rate Setting by the European Central Bank. Sveriges Riksbank, Working Paper no. 58.

Tietmeyer, Hans. 1996. The Importance of Monetary Policy Strategy in Achieving Price Stability. In *Monetary Strategies in Europe*, edited by the Deutsche Bundesbank. Munich: Vahlen.

von Hagen, Jürgen. 1993. Money Demand, Money Supply, and Monetary Union—A Review of the German Monetary Union. *European Economic Review* 37: 803–36.

————. 1995. Monetary and Inflation Targeting in Germany. In *Inflation Targeting*, edited by Leonardo Leiderman and Lars E.O. Svensson. London: Centre for Economic Policy Research.

————. 1998. A New Approach to Monetary Policy, 1971–78. In *Fifty Years of the Deutsche Mark*, edited by the Deutsche Bundesbank. Oxford: Oxford University Press.

————. 1999a. Macroeconomic Consequences of the EMU. *Empirica* 26: 359–74.

————. 1999b. La Union Económina y Monetario: cuestiones y desafios de economía política. *Moneda y Crédito* 208: 25–58.

————. 1999c. Money Growth Targeting by the Bundesbank. *Journal of Monetary Economics* 43: 681–701.

————, and Ralph Süppel. 1994. Central Bank Constitutions for Federal Monetary Unions. *European Economic Review* 38: 774–82.

von zur Muehlen, Peter. 2001. Activist vs. Non-Activist Monetary Policy: Optimal Rules under Extreme Uncertainty. Board of Governors of the Federal Reserve System, Finance and Economics Discussion Series no. 2001–02.

Wesche, Katrin. 1997. The Stability of European Money Demand:  An Investigation of M3H. *Open Economies Review* 8: 371–91.

# Commentary

*Stephen G. Cecchetti*

## 1. INTRODUCTION

Jürgen von Hagen and Matthias Brückner have written a comprehensive and engaging summary of the European Central Bank's (ECB) first few years. They survey all of the ECB's salient institutional features and discuss its policy outcomes. In this comment, I will summarize much of the same material, but from a different vantage point; therefore, this comment is more a complement to the excellent von Hagen and Brückner paper than a critical evaluation.

Let me preface my remarks about the ECB by saying that all of my criticisms are made in an effort to improve what is already an extraordinary product. I sit in awe of the job that has been done in Frankfurt by the ECB's Executive Board and staff and by the governors and staffs of the 12 national central banks that have joined the European Monetary Union. The real measure of success of the European System of Central Banks (ESCB) is how truly minor our criticisms are. As I write this, the ECB has been in existence for three years and making policy for two and a half. Could any of us have done better?

That said, I will now discuss the relationship of the national central banks to the ECB, the policy strategy, issues of communication and transparency, policy performance, and future challenges.

## 2. INSTITUTIONAL STRUCTURE

On the surface, the European System of Central Banks resembles the Federal Reserve System—there are 12 regional banks with a central board—but appearances can be deceiving. In the Federal Reserve System, the Board of Governors controls budgeting and information flows. At the ECB, casual observation suggests the reverse is true: While the Board of Governors supervises the regional Federal Reserve Banks, approving their budgets and overall management decisions, in the European System of Central Banks, it is the national central bank governors who supervise the ECB.

The Governing Council of the ECB resembles the Federal Open Market Committee (FOMC). In both cases, membership includes the heads of the national or regional banks and the board from the center. But again, appearances may deceive. The most important difference is that information provided to the FOMC comes from the staff of the Board of Governors; virtually no relevant information from the staffs of the regional Federal Reserve Banks finds its way into the hands of all of the FOMC participants. In my experience, the only information that is universally distributed is generated by the Board of Governors in Washington, D.C. In contrast, the European System of Central Banks appears to have an elaborate committee structure that was created to ensure that information from the national central banks has a natural and straightforward way to enter the policymaking process.

There is one more important difference between the Federal Reserve System and the ESCB: The ECB is a bank, while the Board of Governors of the Federal Reserve System is not.[1] As a consequence, the ECB itself is capable of operating in financial markets—and it has done so. Surely, the European structure is set up to ensure that the bulk of operations take place at the national central banks. In many ways, this is the raison d'être of these satellites of the European System of Central Banks. But how long can a system be maintained that has (currently) 13 separate operating locations, each with nearly the same capability?

The logic of having national central banks maintain regular financial operations is that they have special knowledge of the mechanisms and participants in their local national markets. But because one of the major goals of monetary union is to accelerate the development of a pan-European financial system, it is just a matter of time before things are centralized. There will be an inexorable pull toward the center, draining resources and power from the periphery.

Von Hagen and Brückner comment on the potential problems created by the fact that each country has one vote on the Governing Council. As they note, this creates an inexorable pull toward the median country, compromising the objective of stabilizing euro-area prices. But these authors, as well as Alesina et al. (2001), suggest that if this were the outcome, the Executive Board would not be doing its job. It is heartening to read here and elsewhere of evidence that the Governing Council is following its mandate and not behaving in a nationalistic way.

### 3. POLICY STRATEGY

Turning to the policy strategy, von Hagen and Brückner provide a detailed description of the problem faced by the ECB and its approach to solving it. Briefly, the primary objective of the ESCB, mandated by the Maastricht Treaty, is the maintenance of price stability. An October 18, 1998, press release, "A Stability-Oriented Monetary Policy Strategy for the ESCB," provided important operational details about how this objective would be addressed. That press release (available on the ECB's Web site at *www.ecb.int*) stated the policy strategy would have three components:

---

[1] Importantly, the regional Federal Reserve Banks are private, nonprofit corporations and chartered banks, while the Board of Governors is technically a part of the U.S. federal government.

1.  The operational definition of price stability would be inflation, measured by the Harmonized Index of Consumer Prices (HICP), of less than 2 percent per year in the medium term.[2]
2.  Money would be assigned a prominent role in the evaluation of financial market conditions, and this role would be signaled by the announcement of a quantitative reference value for the growth rate of a broad monetary aggregate—they have chosen euro-area M3.
3.  A broadly based assessment of the outlook for future price developments and the risks to price stability in the euro area would play a major role.

Let us take a look at each of these in turn. First, defining price stability in a clear, quantitative manner is extremely difficult. Every inflation measure that we have available to us has its defects. All are distorted by problems with weighting, with quality changes, with the introduction of new goods, with changes in expenditure patterns, and the like. The HICP has a particular deficiency in that it does not (as of June 2001) include owner-occupied housing. Given the high ownership rate in Europe, it is unfortunate this is still not included in the index.

In looking at central bank strategies for achieving price-stability objectives, the time horizon is often the subject of heated debate. Here, again, the ESCB has been criticized for its vague use of the terminology "medium term." Von Hagen and Brückner suggest that central banks with fixed time horizons over which price stability is to be achieved might face serious difficulties in responding to various types of shocks. The overriding issue is that longer time horizons give somewhat more flexibility in responding to real short-run factors. Here, I believe the ESCB has done the right thing.

In the end, though, I agree with Mervyn King (1999), who argues that central banks with inflation objectives will be held accountable in a way that makes the time horizon irrelevant. As King notes, if a central bank has a 2 percent target, then after 10 years, the question will be whether inflation averaged less than 2 percent over the entire period.

We now move on to what are often referred to as "the two pillars of the monetary policy strategy": the prominent role for money, and the use of a range of indicators for future price developments. The first of these, which von Hagen and Brückner note pursued the strategy followed by the Bundesbank for many years, has come under substantial attack, and I will now join the chorus. As Alesina et al. (2001) write, the ESCB's ultimate goal is to keep inflation low. In fact, it has been doing something that closely resembles inflation-forecast targeting. In this context, it is difficult to see why M3 is special.

---

2   The ESCB was criticized from various quarters for not stating that the operational definition was HICP inflation between zero and 2 percent. The suggestion was that somehow the current formulation left open the possibility of deflation. I view this criticism as inaccurate and generally unfair, as the term *inflation* clearly implies a range of 0–2 percent.

What is the logic of this first pillar? I think the best explanation is based on politics and sociology, not economics. In creating the new institution, constructive ambiguity was useful. No one really knew what was going to work, and so the Governing Council hedged by saying it would look at money on the one hand, and everything else on the other. Beyond this, reaching consensus in a large group that had not worked together before was surely difficult. Differences in the backgrounds of the Governing Council members could easily lead to political compromise.

But we are now three years on, and the same arguments no longer apply. Instead, we can think of the ECB as just another central bank that controls interest rates in an effort to meet an inflation objective. Money is surely helpful in doing this, but then so are many other things. I agree with those who have said the first pillar stands in the way of effective communication.

There is precedent for throwing central-bank-articulated ranges for money growth overboard. In the Federal Reserve Board's July 20, 2000, *Monetary Policy Report to Congress*, a footnote reads:[3]

> *At its June meeting, the FOMC did not establish ranges for growth of money and debt in 2000 and 2001. The legal requirement to establish and to announce such ranges had expired, and owing to uncertainties about the behavior of the velocities of debt and money, these ranges for many years have not provided useful benchmarks for the conduct of monetary policy. Nevertheless, the FOMC believes that the behavior of money and credit will continue to have value for gauging economic and financial conditions, and this report discusses recent developments in money and credit in some detail.*

This statement concisely summarizes my own view, and it leads me to conclude the first pillar of the ESCB's monetary policy strategy should be jettisoned.[4]

Turning briefly to the second pillar, who can argue with the strategy of using broadly based assessments of future price developments? Addressing uncertainties by bringing all possible information to bear is the obvious thing to do. Importantly, though, it leads to inflation-forecast targeting, and it would be helpful if the ESCB were clear that this is what it is doing.

## 4. COMMUNICATION AND TRANSPARENCY

This brings us to communication and transparency. Von Hagen and Bückner rightly point out that the lack of a tradition, together with the diverse communication cultures of the European regions, makes transparent communication a formidable problem for the new central bank.

---

[3] This is footnote 2 in section 1 of the report, which is available on the Federal Reserve Board's Web site at *www.federalreserve.gov/boarddocs/hh/2000/July/ReportSection1.htm.*

[4] I would go even further and argue the term "monetary policy" should be changed to "central bank policy," to change the impression that it has anything directly do to with money.

Nevertheless, I believe this is where the ESCB has been at its worst. Let me give just one example from the spring of 2001. During March and April 2001, there were numerous calls for policy easing from places such as the International Monetary Fund, the OECD, and the U.S. Treasury. Critics cited evidence of an impending slowdown in euro-area growth as the rationale for interest rate cuts. Initially, the ESCB responded that its objective was price stability, and inflation was in fact increasing. Its policy of maintaining relatively higher interest rates was consistent with this objective. As ECB president Wim Duisenberg famously said on April 11, 2001, "I hear but I do not listen."

On May 10, 2001, the Governing Council reduced the target refinancing rate by 25 basis points, claiming that its long-term price-stability objective was not in jeopardy. The stated reason for the policy reversal was that euro-area M3 had been mismeasured; when the correction was made and inflation forecasts were adjusted, the proper policy was to ease.

The ridicule was deafening. The *Financial Times* headline was the most mild: "European Central Bank Rate Cut Trips up Markets." Things only got worse: One week later, a sharp rise was reported in the euro-area inflation measure to a five-month high of 2.9 percent in April 2001, compared with 2.6 percent in March. The general reaction was that this surely wasn't consistent with HICP inflation of less than 2 percent.

What is it about the ESCB's communication strategy that has been such a failure? Blinder et al. (2001) argue that in creating transparent and clear communications, a central bank must reveal what it is trying to achieve; the methods, data, and models used for analysis; and the substance of the policy deliberations, including which arguments have carried the day, how convincing they were, and the degree of certainty surrounding current conditions.

I believe that on the first two of these, the ESCB has done well. It has been clear about what it is trying to do, and it has provided substantial insights into its data, models, and forecasts. It is the third point—transparency of the substance of policy deliberations—that is the problem. Here, the Governing Council speaks in many voices, and they are occasionally at odds.

There are several solutions to this communication problem. Blinder et al. (2001) suggest shrinking the size of the Governing Council to reduce the chance that disgruntled members will air their disagreements in public, but this is probably politically impossible. Why not take the straightforward step of issuing minutes of meetings when they still matter?

## 5. PERFORMANCE

Von Hagen and Brückner evaluate the performance of the ESCB's policy by comparing it with various Taylor rules. They conclude that interest rates were initially too low and, later, too high. I question whether it is possible to actually evaluate policy using such an exercise. If the rule had been followed at the beginning of the period, then inflation and growth would have been different later. This is obvious, and what it means is that you cannot look at the actual policy relative to a Taylor-style rule without embedding the rule in a fully articulated, dynamic structural model of the euro area.

Rather than build such a model (or borrow one), I will simply look at the ESCB's performance since its inception. Figures 1 and 2 plot GDP growth and inflation in the euro area. Growth data begin in 1992 and inflation data in 1996—this is what is available from Eurostat and the ECB. Surely, it is difficult to tell from

**Figure 1:  Real GDP Growth in the Euro Area**

**Figure 2:  Inflation in the Euro Area**

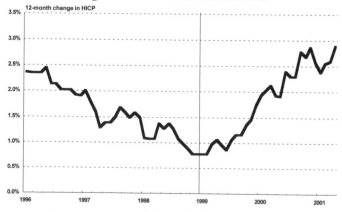

these data what the consequence of recent policy will be, but we can, nevertheless, make a preliminary evaluation. The results give the impression that policy has been more successful in fostering steady growth than in keeping inflation in check. The fact that HICP inflation has risen unabated since the ESCB was established on January 1, 1999, is somewhat troubling, and it supports von Hagen and Brückner's conclusion that policy was too loose early on. It is harder to argue that it became too contractionary, as inflation has continued its rise.

## 6. FUTURE CHALLENGES

In reviewing the European System of Central Banks' progress and performance, we see a new institution that has faced numerous challenges head on and come out only mildly bruised. It is difficult to see how things could have come out any better. But this is not the end of the story. The future challenges of the ESCB are nearly as daunting as those that have past.

The biggest problem facing the ESCB is dealing with what is likely to be a constant conflict among national interests in policy setting. Recent reports suggest the right policy for Germany is more stimulus, while France might be better off if policy were tighter.[5] Inflation and growth differentials across the euro area will continue, creating the need for a delicately balanced policy.[6]

The problem of national inflation differentials is compounded by the fact that, as Alesina et al. (2001) emphasize, not all inflation differentials are bad. During the early years of currency union and general economic harmonization, one can expect substantial relative price adjustments among the various regions of the euro area, which will show up as measured differences in national inflation indexes. But in many cases, these will be necessary real economic adjustments, not inflation differentials creating policy problems.

Let me say that I am impressed with von Hagen and Brückner's ability to write such a comprehensive survey of a new institution. They have really done an excellent job of a very difficult task. Nevertheless, I am reminded of a story that is told about a 1972 meeting between U.S. Secretary of State Henry Kissinger and Chinese Prime Minister Chou En Lai. According to the story, Kissinger asked Chou if he believed that when all its consequences were taken into account, the 1789 French Revolution had benefited humanity. Chou is reputed to have replied, "It is to early to tell."[7] So, too, for the early years of the European System of Central Banks—it is still too early to tell.

---

[5] See the *Wall Street Journal*, "The Right Rate for Europe?" May 17, 2001.
[6] See Cecchetti, Mark, and Sonora (forthcoming) for a discussion of how persistent inflation differentials are likely to be.
[7] I have not been able to find any reliable source for this quotation, and I do not believe that it is true. Nevertheless, it is a good story.

## REFERENCES

Alesina, Alberto, Olivier Blanchard, Jordi Galí, Francesco Giavazzi, and Harald Uhlig. 2001. *Defining a Macroeconomic Framework for the Euro Area*. Monitoring the European Central Bank 3. London: Centre for Economic Policy Research.

Blinder, Alan, Charles Goodhart, Philipp Hildebrand, David Lipton, and Charles Wyplosz. 2001. *How Do Central Banks Talk?* Geneva Reports on the World Economy 3. London: Centre for Economic Policy Research.

Cecchetti, Stephen G., Nelson C. Mark, and Robert Sonora. Forthcoming. Price Level Convergence Among United States Cities: Lessons for the European Central Bank. *International Economic Review.*

King, Mervyn. 1999. Challenges for Monetary Policy: New and Old. In *Challenges for Monetary Policy*, Federal Reserve Bank of Kansas City, Proceedings of the Symposium, 11–57.

# Commentary

## Vitor Gaspar

### 1. INTRODUCTION

Jürgen von Hagen and Matthias Brückner address the experience of the European Central Bank (ECB) in its early years as monetary policy in unknown territory. This is a perspective well worth taking. On January 1, 1999, the control of monetary policy was transferred from 11 of the member states of the European Union to a new, independent European institution—the European Central Bank. On Monday, January 4, 1999, the first open market operation under the single monetary policy was launched. This was an unprecedented, unique event and, given its relevance, historic. It is perfectly fair to highlight the challenges associated with the lack of knowledge and uncertainty.

Allan Meltzer (1993) defines a policy rule as "nothing more than a systematic decision process that uses information in a consistent and predictable way." The ECB aims at such systematic behavior through its monetary policy strategy, which aims precisely at inducing a systematic pattern of policy responses to ensure price stability over the medium term. The ECB's Governing Council presented the broad lines of the stability-oriented monetary policy strategy on October 13, 1998. Since then, the ECB strategy has been presented many times (ECB 1999, 2000; Angeloni, Gaspar, and Tristani 1999; Issing 2000; Issing et al. 2001; Gaspar, Masuch, and Pill 2001).

In a nutshell, the strategy includes three main elements: first and foremost, a precise definition of price stability; second, an analysis of current developments and prospects assigning a prominent role to money; and third, a broad assessment based on a multiplicity of models and indicators.[1]

Given the unique, unprecedented, and historic character of the transition to the single monetary policy, it is easy to accept that the initial challenges were manifold. These challenges seem to have been successfully overcome. First, in central banking, credibility is of paramount importance (Blinder 1999; Issing et al. 2001). This is a challenge for a new institution without reputation arising from its track record. Therefore, it is remarkable that since the announcement of the stability-oriented monetary policy strategy, long-term inflation expectations have consistently fallen inside the range the ECB has deemed compatible with price stability. Issing

---

[1] See Issing et al. (2001) for a comprehensive presentation.

(2001) makes this point, taking as an example the break-even inflation rates derived from French 10-year index-linked bonds. The stability of inflation expectations is particularly remarkable given the increase in headline inflation.[2] Of course, all countries participating in the euro area achieved low inflation during the 1990s. Some had long track records in maintaining price stability. The ECB seems to have been able to build on the reputation of the national central banks as guarantors of price stability.

Second, banks seem to have adapted quickly and easily to the new Eurosystem's operational framework. The transition does not seem to have had a major impact on the behavior of money market interest rates. For example, looking at the behavior of money market rates, Gaspar, Perez-Quiros, and Sicilia (2001) find the volatility of overnight interest rates was significantly smaller during the first days of 1999 when compared with the volatility associated with well-known recurring events such as the end of reserve maintenance periods. After just a few weeks, a single money market was already in place. More generally, the operational framework has worked successfully (Manna, Pill, and Quiros 2001; Perez-Quiros and Rodriguez-Mendizabal 2001). Third, markets seem to have been able to predict monetary policy actions announced by the ECB. Looking at the daily behavior of overnight interest rates, Gaspar, Perez-Quiros, and Sicilia (2001) show that monetary policy announcements do not affect mean interest rates in a statistically significant way. This, in turn, is consistent with markets not making systematic mistakes in anticipating policy decisions.

Jürgen von Hagen and Matthias Brückner's paper is very broad in its scope. In this comment, I will focus on an issue that I have not yet covered in print: the institutional setting of the ECB and the Eurosystem. Here the authors' findings are, in my view, based on an incorrect reading of the text of the Treaty and the Statute. They write: "The institutional environment of the common monetary policy constituted further unknown territory. Specifically, the Maastricht Treaty left the role of the ECB within the European System to be determined." In my view, the opposite is true: The Treaty and Statute are very clear about the allocation of responsibility for the conduct of monetary policy. The remainder of my comments will aim at making this point. The paper will be structured as follows: In section 2, I will refer to lessons from the early experience of the Federal Reserve and its bearing on the design of the Maastricht Treaty and the Statute of the European System of Central Banks (ESCB) and of the European Central Bank. In section 3, the main arguments concerning the allocation of responsibilities for governing the

---

[2]  Headline inflation has been above 2 percent since June 2000. This relates mainly to temporary disturbances in energy and food prices.

ESCB/Eurosystem will be made. Section 4 will illustrate how expertise available at the ECB and the national central banks on the *technical* aspects of monetary policy is channeled to the decisionmaking bodies. Section 5 will briefly conclude.

## 2. INDIVISIBILITY OF MONETARY POLICY AND THE EARLY EXPERIENCE OF THE FED

The early years of the Federal Reserve System after its creation in 1914 provide us with a fascinating episode in monetary history. The importance of institutional design is clear from Friedman and Schwartz (1963), who write: "The Federal Reserve Board and the Federal Reserve Banks were the bodies established to exercise jointly the functions both of controlling creation and retirement of Federal Reserve money and of handling the mechanical details. How the functions were initially divided between the two is complex and of no special interest for our purpose. The fact of division was, however, important and gave rise to numerous conflicts within the System" (190). Friedman and Schwartz go on, "The Federal Reserve System therefore began operations with no effective legislative criterion for determining the stock of money. The discretionary judgement of a group of men was inevitably substituted for the quasi-automatic discipline of the gold standard. Those men were not even guided by a legislative mandate of intent...Little wonder, perhaps, that the subsequent years saw so much backing and filling, so much confusion about purpose and power, and so erratic an exercise of power" (193). It took approximately 20 years for the conduct of U.S. monetary policy to be centralized in the Board of Governors and the Federal Open Market Committee. Many authors, including Miron (1989), Thygesen (1989, 1992), Gros and Thygesen (1992), and Eichengreen (1992), have examined the experience of the Fed in its early years and its relevance for European monetary unification. The magnitude of the consequences from the unclear assignment of responsibilities in this field may be perceived by quoting (again) from Friedman and Schwartz: "The dispute between the Board and the New York bank largely paralysed monetary policy during almost the whole of the important year 1929. In addition, it was probably the crucial engagement in the power struggle within the System" (255).

During the negotiations leading up to the Maastricht Treaty, the early history of the Fed and its relevance were clearly perceived (Thygesen 1989, 1992; Gros and Thygesen 1992). This helps to explain why the *principle of indivisibility of the responsibility for the conduct of monetary policy* was immediately consensual. From this principle derives the need for a clear allocation of power. More specifically, it was immediately accepted that issues of authority and control had to be addressed explicitly.

Therefore, the ESCB's organizational structure and the allocation of decision-making powers inside the system are addressed explicitly in the Treaty and the Statute. Specifically (following Zilioli and Selmayr 2001), it is clear that the ESCB may be regarded as a two-level organizational structure: The system is governed exclusively by the decisionmaking bodies of the ECB.

## 3. THE ESCB IS GOVERNED BY THE DECISIONMAKING BODIES OF THE ECB[3]

The title of this section reproduces Article 8 of the statute, labeled "General Principle." It provides suggestive evidence that the ESCB's organization and the allocation of responsibilities inside the system are explicitly addressed in the Statute.

The decisionmaking bodies of the ECB are the Governing Council and the Executive Board (Article 9.3). The Executive Board comprises a president, vice president, and four other members. The Governing Council comprises the members of the Executive Board plus the governors of the national central banks of the member states participating in the single monetary policy. For the sake of convenience, the ECB, together with the national central banks of the member states adopting the single currency, are grouped under the designation "Eurosystem."[4]

A number of provisions in the Statute make clear that the ECB's decisionmaking bodies govern the Eurosystem (in particular, Articles 9.2, 12.1, and 14.3). Article 9.2 states that the ECB is in charge of ensuring the tasks assigned by the Treaty to the system are carried out by the ECB itself or by the national central banks.

Article 12.1 defines the responsibilities of the Governing Council and the Executive Board. Concerning monetary policy, Article 12.1 states, "The Governing Council shall formulate the monetary policy of the Community including, as appropriate, decisions relating to intermediate monetary objectives, key interest rates and the supply of reserves in the ESCB, and shall establish the necessary guidelines for their implementation." Concerning the Executive Board, Article 12.1 states, "The Executive Board shall implement monetary policy in accordance with the guidelines and decisions of the Governing Council. In doing so the Executive Board will give the necessary instructions to national central banks." Article 14.3 states, "The national central banks are an integral part of the ESCB and shall act in accordance with the guidelines and instructions of the ECB. The Governing Council will take the necessary steps to ensure compliance with the guidelines and

---

[3] This section relies heavily on Zilioli and Selmayr (2001) and has benefited from extensive input from Chiara Zilioli.

[4] There is a complication in the institutional structure of the ESCB because of the distinction between central banks of member states that have adopted the single currency and other central banks. In 2001, 12 member states had adopted the single currency: Austria, Belgium, Finland, France, Germany, Greece, Ireland, Italy, Luxembourg, the Netherlands, Portugal, and Spain. Three member states were subject to derogation or had a special status: Denmark, Sweden, and the United Kingdom. In this paper, the issues associated with nonparticipating member states will be ignored. Therefore, the Eurosystem and the ESCB are regarded as identical.

instructions of the ECB, and shall require that any necessary information be given to it."

In addition, Article 35.6 assigns to the ECB a monitoring role over the national central banks' fulfillment of their obligations under the Statute and the Treaty. The ECB may even bring national central banks in front of the European Court of Justice in the event of dispute on these matters. Finally, it should be pointed out that the ECB has legal personality; this is not the case for the ESCB or the Eurosystem.

It is important to recall that the Treaty and the Statute define price stability as the primary goal of the ESCB (Article 2 of the Statute), while a plurality of objectives is set for the European Community (Article 2 of the Treaty). Moreover, the decisionmaking bodies of the ECB are independent from political interference, both nationally and from the European Community (Article 7 of the Statute). In this context, it is important to emphasize that, in line with the clear mandate and independence, national central bank governors are members of the Governing Council on their own personal capacity. They are not representing their country or their national central bank. This should be seen as immediately consistent with the rule "one member, one vote."[5] For monetary policy issues, each member of the Governing Council has one vote; formally, the Governing Council decides on the basis of simple majority.[6]

The members of the Governing Council are bound by the Treaty and the Statute to pursue the ECB's primary objective at the level of the euro area. The Governing Council made this very clear when it made the concept of price stability operational. To recall: The Governing Council of the ECB defined price stability as annual price increases of less than 2 percent, according to the Harmonized Index of Consumer Prices, for the euro area as a whole. The governors do not represent national interests or follow the objectives of national institutions.

The fact that the governors of national central banks are members of the Governing Council on their own capacity is a very important point, which, fortunately, can be demonstrated in a very clear way. One of the requirements of the Treaty is compatibility of the statutes of national central banks with the treaty and the statute. This has been labeled the "legal convergence exercise." In this context, the statutes of national central banks were changed, whenever necessary, to ensure that the decisionmaking bodies of the national central banks would not be in a position to impose any decision on their governor as a member of the ECB Governing Council. The idea is that the governor is completely free as a member of the

---

5  This contrasts with decisionmaking in the Council of Ministers of the European Union, where decisionmaking is subject to weighted voting.
6  There are a number of exceptions to this rule that are not related to monetary policy, including the capital of the ECB, the key for capital subscription, the transfer of foreign reserve assets to the ECB, the allocation of monetary income to the national central banks, the allocation of net profits and losses of the ECB, and the terms and conditions of employment of the members of the Executive Board.

Governing Council in Frankfurt. This is confirmed by the fact that, as a rule, members of the Governing Council cannot send a deputy to substitute for them; only members of the Governing Council who are present in person may vote. This means that in the event of an absence of a member of the Governing Council, his or her vote cannot be cast.[7]

The previous paragraphs make clear that the Eurosystem is governed by the ECB. This point is illustrated in figure 1, which depicts the centralization of decisionmaking in the ECB. The Eurosystem is governed by the decisionmaking bodies of the ECB, the Governing Council and the Executive Board. There is a clear allocation of responsibility following from the principle of indivisibility of monetary policy. It constitutes a very important factor of strength when exploring unknown territory.

**Figure 1: The ECB as Governor of the System**

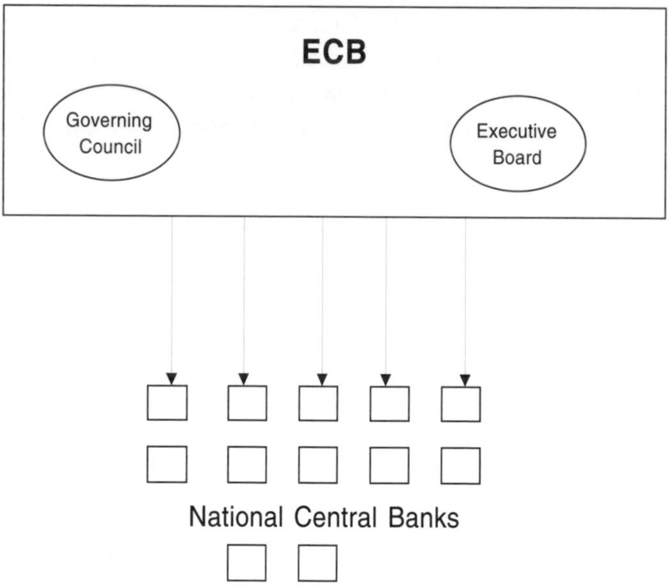

Source: Zilioli and Selmayr (2001).

---

[7] There are a number of exceptions to this rule. The possibility of a replacement is envisaged in the event that a member is prevented from voting for a prolonged period of time (Article 10.2 of the Statute); in addition, substitution is always possible for the issues listed in footnote 6.

## 4. PREPARING THE GOVERNING COUNCIL:[8]
## THE ECB AND THE NATIONAL CENTRAL BANKS

The way in which Governing Council meetings are prepared is illustrated schematically in figure 2. When preparing meetings of the Governing Council, the Executive Board relies on the work of the ECB staff. Moreover, expertise available throughout the Eurosystem is captured by a number of Eurosystem committees.[9]

**Figure 2: Preparing the Governing Council: The ECB and the NCB**

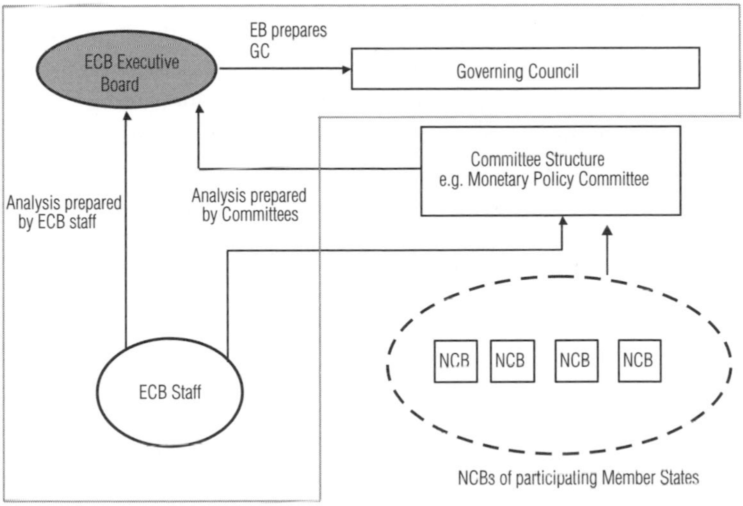

Source: Gaspar, Masuch, and Pill (2002).

These committees are advisory bodies that "assist in the work of the ESCB" (Article 9.1 of the ECB Rules of Procedure). They provide advice to the Executive Board and thereby to the Governing Council, and they comprise experts from the national central banks and the ECB.[10,11]

For the purpose of this paper, which focuses on monetary policy, the role of the Monetary Policy Committee should be highlighted. The composition of this committee significantly overlaps with the composition of the former Monetary Policy Subcommittee of the European Monetary Institute, which was intensely involved in the preparation of the instruments and procedures for the single monetary

---

[8] This section relies on Gaspar et al. (2001).

[9] To keep the presentation simple, I rely on the fiction that all member states have adopted the single currency. This simplifies the exposition significantly, as it makes the Eurosystem identical to the ESCB.

[10] The committees meet in various compositions. Specifically, experts from national central banks that do not belong to the Eurosystem are invited to participate in the discussions according to topic.

[11] There are 13 committees now set up by the System: accounting and monetary income, banking supervision, banknotes, budget, external communications, information technology, internal auditors, international relations, legal, market operations, monetary policy, payment and settlement systems, and statistics. The committees, in turn, may have substructures, including working groups and task forces.

policy (EMI 1997). The committees enable the ECB's decisionmaking bodies to benefit from the human capital and expertise scattered through the system. It also constitutes an important element of continuity. In this case, continuity applies at the senior-expert level.

The Governing Council defined the remit of the Monetary Policy Committee to include the design and implementation of the monetary policy strategy, the analytical tools and indicators for monetary policy, the operational framework, and so on. The committee is also active in producing forecasts and projections. Eurosystem staff macroeconomic projections are presented twice a year to the Governing Council as input into monetary policy deliberations. This illustrates a general feature of committee work: It inputs into the decisionmaking bodies' proceedings through the production of technical background documentation and analysis. The discussion of current monetary policy decisions is outside the scope of the Monetary Policy Committee's mandate. The Governing Council of the ECB has decided to publish the Eurosystem's staff macroeconomic projections. Since December 2000 (ECB 2001), they are published regularly in the June and December issues of the *ECB Monthly Bulletin*.

The Eurosystem's staff macroeconomic projections are obtained through a procedure that involves close interaction between the staff of the national central banks and the ECB.[12] These projections are conditional on a set of technical assumptions. The procedure makes use of both econometric models and experts' knowledge. The staff projections are fully consistent both across countries and for the whole of the euro area. The procedure has been designed so that the projections reflect all expertise available in the system. This helps in obtaining the best feasible input into the deliberations of the decisionmaking bodies.

## 5. CONCLUSIONS

Looking at the European Central Bank in the early years as monetary policy in unknown territory, as outlined by von Hagen and Brückner, is an interesting endeavor. It is also warranted by the unique and unprecedented character of the move to a single monetary policy in Europe. In these uncharted waters, the System relies *inter alia* on a clear assignment of decisionmaking powers to the ECB's Governing Council and Executive Board. It also relies on independence and a clear mandate: maintaining price stability in the euro area. Independence allows monetary policy to be conducted outside the realm of day-to-day politics. In maintaining price stability over the medium term, monetary policy facilitates economic growth and an efficient use of resources and contributes to the overall stability of the economy (see Garcia-Herrero et al. 2001 for an overview).[13]

[12] In this task, the Monetary Policy Committee is assisted by the Working Group on Forecasting.
[13] The costs associated with higher inflation may be associated with the role of money as a transaction mean and as a unit of account.

Another strength of the System is continuity relative to the experience of national central banks. The Eurosystem has organized itself in such a way that the wealth of experience and expertise available in the System can be channeled effectively into the deliberations of the decisionmaking bodies.

It is still too early for judgment. The ECB has built its reputation as a guardian of price stability over the medium term. As a result of steady and long-lasting efforts by the national central banks of the euro area, the ECB was established in a period of current and prospective price stability. This was a precious bequest.

## ACKNOWLEDGMENTS

The views expressed are the author's own and do not necessarily reflect those of the European Central Bank or the Eurosystem. The author thanks Klaus Masuch, Huw Pill, Oreste Tristani, and Chiara Zilioli for helpful comments. The remaining errors are his alone.

### REFERENCES

Angeloni, Ignazio, Vitor Gaspar, and Oreste Tristani. 1999. The Monetary Policy Strategy of the ECB. In *From the EMS to EMU*, edited by David Cobham and George Zis, 3–42. London: Macmillan.

Blinder, Alan. 1999. Central Bank Credibility: Why Do We Care? How Do We Build It? National Bureau of Economic Research, Working Paper no. 7161, June.

Eichengreen, Barry. 1992. Designing a Central Bank for Europe: A Cautionary Tale from the Early Years of the Federal Reserve System. In *Establishing a Central Bank: Issues in Europe and Lessons from the U.S.*, edited by Matthew B. Canzoneri, Vittorio Grilli, and Paul R. Masson, 13–40. Cambridge: Cambridge University Press.

European Central Bank. 1999. The Stability-Oriented Monetary Policy Strategy of the Eurosystem. *ECB Monthly Bulletin* January: 39–50.

———. 2000. The Two Pillars of the ECB Monetary Policy Strategy. *ECB Monthly Bulletin* November: 37–48.

———. 2001. A Guide to Eurosystem Staff Macroeconomic Projection Exercises. Frankfurt: European Central Bank. Available at *www.ecb.int* [10 September 2001].

European Monetary Institute. 1997. The Single Monetary Policy in Stage Three: Elements of the Monetary Policy Strategy of the ESCB. September. Available at *www.ecb.int/target/bt/tabt08tc.htm* [10 September 2001].

Friedman, Milton, and A. Schwartz. 1963. *A Monetary History of the United States 1867–1960*. Princeton, N.J.: Princeton University Press.

Garcia-Herrero, Alicia, Vitor Gaspar, Lex Hoogduin, Julian Morgan, and Bernhard Winkler, eds. 2001. *Why Price Stability?* Proceedings of the First ECB Central Banking Conference, European Central Bank, Frankfurt, Germany. Available at *www.ecb.int/pub/pdf/whypricestability.pdf* [10 September 2001].

Gaspar, Vitor, Klaus Masuch, and Huw Pill. 2002. The ECB's Monetary Policy Strategy: Responding to the Challenges of the Early Years of EMU. In *EMU and Economic Policy in Europe: The Challenge of the Early Years*, edited by Marco Buti and Andre Sapir. Northampton, Mass.: Edward Elgar.

Gaspar, Vitor, Gabriel Perez-Quiros, and Jorge Sicilia. 2001. The ECB Monetary Policy Strategy and the Money Market. European Central Bank, Working Paper no. 69, July.

Gros, D., and N. Thygesen. 1992. *European Monetary Integration: From the European Monetary System to European Monetary Union.* New York: St. Martin's Press.

Hartmann, P., M. Manna, and A. Manzanares. Forthcoming. The Microstructure of the Euro Money Market. European Central Bank, Working Paper.

Issing, Otmar. 2000. Monetary Policy in a New Environment. Speech delivered at the Bundesbank-BIS Conference on Recent Development in Financial Systems and Their Challenges for Economic Policy: An European Perspective, Frankfurt, Germany, September 29. Available at *www.ecb.int* [10 September 2001].

————. 2001. Why Price Stability? In *Why Price Stability?* Proceedings of the First ECB Central Banking Conference, European Central Bank, Frankfurt, Germany, edited by Alicia Garcia-Herrero, Vitor Gaspar, Lex Hoogduin, Julian Morgan, and Bernhard Winkler. Available at *www.ecb.int/pub/pdf/whypricestability.pdf* [10 September 2001].

————, Vitor Gaspar, Ignazio Angeloni, and Oreste Tristani. 2001. *Monetary Policy in the Euro Area: Strategy and Decision-Making at the European Central Bank.* Cambridge: Cambridge University Press.

Manna, M., Huw Pill, and G. Quiros. 2001. The Eurosystem's Operational Framework in the Context of the ECB's Monetary Policy Strategy. Mimeo.

Meltzer, Allen H. 1993. Commentary: The Role of Judgement and Discretion in the Conduct of Monetary Policy. In *Changing Capital Markets: Implications for Monetary Policy: Symposium Proceedings.* Kansas City, Mo.: Federal Reserve Bank of Kansas City.

Miron, J. 1989. The Founding of the Fed and the Destabilisation of the Post-1914 U.S. Economy. In *A European Central Bank? Perspectives on Monetary Unification after Ten Years of the EMS*, edited by M. de Cecco and A. Giovannini. Cambridge: Cambridge University Press.

Perez-Quiros, G., and H. Rodriguez-Mendizabal. 2001. The Daily Market for Funds in Europe: Has Something Changed with the EMU? European Central Bank, Working Paper no. 67, June.

Thygesen, N. 1989. Decentralisation and Accountability within the Central Bank: Any Lessons from the U.S. Experience for the Potential Organisation of European Central Banking Institution? In *The ECU and European Monetary Integration*, edited by P. de Grauwe and T. Peeters. London: Macmillan.

————. 1992. European Central Bank. In *The New Palgrave Dictionary of Money and Finance,* edited by John Eatwell, Murray Milgate, and Peter Newman. London: Macmillan.

Zilioli, Chiara, and M. Selmayr. 2001. *The Law of the ECB*. Oxford: Hart Publications.

# 4

# International Currencies and Dollarization

*Alberto Trejos*

## 1. INTRODUCTION

The dollar has become an international currency, used frequently in ordinary domestic transactions outside the United States. The extent to which the smaller Latin American countries have "dollarized" is fairly striking. For example, in Costa Rica's banking system, 61 percent of credit assets and 53 percent of interest-bearing liabilities are dollar denominated. Focusing on media of exchange rather than stores of value, 26 percent of checking account deposits and (less precisely) 30 percent of cash are in dollars. These numbers are biased downward, as they do not include the fairly extensive use by local businesses and consumers of foreign banks and the offshore subsidiaries of local banks. Many ads and contracts use dollars as the unit of account to post prices. The same phenomenon occurs in at least another dozen small Latin American countries. The process of dollarization has been relatively quick, and, although it started under high inflation, it has continued under price stability.

In some of these countries, there is debate about the possibility of eliminating their local monies entirely and using only the dollar as currency. In fact, in 2000 alone, two countries, El Salvador and Ecuador, formally made the decision to dollarize (joining Panama, which did so at the beginning of the century), and the discussion has been fairly intense in other places. If this trend continues, the question that this conference means to address—what is the future of central banking?—would be answered by a vision of many small countries that do not issue their own currency, a few mid-sized and large countries that do, and a handful of major central banks executing international monetary policy. This would add a series of new areas such as monetary policy cooperation, multinational banking supervision, international deposit insurance arrangements, seigniorage sharing, international logistics of money-supply management, international clearance and payment systems, and many others to the topics that the Federal Reserve–based Central Bank Institute should study.

The main hypothesis of this paper is that, given current trends toward increased openness, small economies will find it undesirable and even unfeasible in the long run to maintain a central bank and an independent currency. Section 2 shows a search-theoretic model of money that is helpful in illustrating this hypothesis and formalizing some of those long-run issues. Sections 3 and 4 are nontechnical, enumerating other pros and cons of prompt dollarization and matters of implementation.

Section 2 describes a two-country, two-currency search-theoretic model based on Trejos and Wright (2001). In that model, in which currency circulates where it is determined endogenously, and there are equilibria in which one money circulates only in the place where it is issued, while the other is used in both countries, as today's "pesos and dollars." Which regimes constitute equilibria under different parameters, and what is their purchasing power, is also determined endogenously. In this paper, we use a very simplified version of that model, solely to inquire as to what happens as a small economy becomes increasingly open (a strong trend the world over, due to the significant fall in communication and transportation costs and in self-imposed trade barriers). It turns out that as international trade becomes easier, small countries unavoidably absorb a large amount of international currency. Then, the value of the local money supply is reduced in real terms, as is the amount of seigniorage that can be collected by the local monetary authority. At some parameter values, issuing pesos carries a welfare loss and yields less seigniorage than sharing the revenue extracted locally by dollars. Also, there are inefficiencies associated with lack of policy coordination among monetary authorities if currencies overlap realms of circulation; here, it is shown that as the economy opens, those inefficiencies increase and there are larger potential gains (in welfare, seigniorage, and lower inflation) from coordinating policies and/or moving to a single, shared currency.

The smaller countries in Latin America have opened significantly to international trade and finance in the last few years, a trend that is likely to continue. Their use of U.S. dollars as international currency has also consistently expanded. To the extent that the theoretical ideas described in the previous paragraph apply in reality, one should not be surprised by this. One would be led to question whether, in the long run, these nations will be able to sustain their currencies and central banks.

Section 3 contains a nontechnical discussion about other pros and cons of dollarization that have emerged in the local debate, as well as some matters of implementation. Section 4 concludes.

## 2. THE MODEL

Time is continuous and never ends. The world is composed of two countries, labeled 1 and 2. There is a continuum of infinitely lived agents in each country, whose population grows at the same rate, $\gamma > 0$.

There are many varieties of consumption goods in this economy, all fully divisible but not storable. Each agent produces a specific variety. At any given time, a given agent will want to consume only one particular variety and derives no utility from consuming others. Agents discount the future, and the rate of time preference is denoted by $r$.

The utility from consuming $q$ units of the right variety is $u(q)$, where $u(0) = 0$, $u'(0) = \infty$, and $u'(q) > 0$, $u''(q) < 0$ $\forall q$; the disutility from producing them is $c(q) = q$. We will assume there is a value $q^\circ > 0$, such that $u(q^\circ) = q^\circ$. Given that one agent desires the variety that a second agent produces, the probability of a double coincidence of wants (the second also desires the variety produced by the first) is denoted by $y$. For simplicity, we assume here that $y = 0$.

Each country has a government, which is a monopolistic producer of a national fiat money. Each unit of currency is intrinsically useless and indivisible. The government of country $k$ issues money $k$ by spending one unit each on a fraction $M_k$ of its newborn citizens. This means that the number of units of currency $k$ in circulation, relative to the amount of agents that are citizens from that country, is also $M_k$. Agents holding money at any given time are referred to as *buyers*; those without money are called *sellers*. No buyer can carry more than one unit of money at a time. For buyers holding money $k$, there is the risk—which materializes with arrival rate $\mu_k$— that it will be confiscated by the government of country $k$, which will then spend it on a seller of the same nationality holding no money in exchange for the maximum amount he is willing to produce.[1]

Agents search for potential trading partners. Each agent posts the objects (which money, if he is a buyer, or which variety of consumption good, if he is a seller) he is able to offer, and what objects (monies, for a seller, or other varieties, for a buyer) he is willing to accept in return. The matching process brings together pairs of agents whose postings are compatible. There are infinitesimal but positive fixed

---

[1] Although $M_k$ relates to the amount of money in circulation, one should be careful not to interpret it too easily as the "money supply." The reason is that in this model, due to the assumptions that prevent agents from holding amounts of money other than 0 or 1, changes in $M_k$, along with different quantities of money in circulation, also imply different distributions of money holdings (different ratios of buyers to sellers), something that is not implied by changes in the money supply in other monetary models. The same assumptions make it impossible to introduce actual inflation in the model, so we must use $\mu_k$ (a tax on money holdings, in expected value proportional to the length of time the money is held) as an inflation proxy.

costs in matching and bargaining, and this means that no seller posts that he is willing to trade output for a given money if he believes he will not end up trading with anybody carrying that money.[2]

Once two agents are matched, they bargain over the terms of their exchange. In particular, if a seller meets a buyer wanting his production variety, they enter a bargaining game of alternating offers to determine the amount of output the seller is to produce in exchange for the buyer's cash. The bargaining power of the seller is denoted by $\theta$. For simplicity, we assume here that $\theta = 0$, so that buyers make take-it-or-leave-it offers. This implies that the amount of output a seller from country $k$ produces in exchange for a unit of money from country $j$ is independent of the nationality of the buyer. We denote it $Q_{kj}$, so prices are $P_{kj} \equiv 1/Q_{kj}$.

Search is time consuming, and, for a citizen from country $j$, the matching process generates suitable matches with agents from country $k$ at a Poisson rate of arrival $\alpha_{jk}$. We assume that $\alpha_{jj} > \alpha_{kj} \ \forall jk$, meaning that it is easier for a local to meet other locals than it is for a foreigner to do so. No other form of exchange aside from monetary trade is possible. Credit will not occur because contracts cannot be enforced, due to the lack of rematch; barter does not occur either because $y = 0$. The fraction of agents from country $i$ who carry currency $j$ will be denoted $m_{ij}$, and the fraction who are sellers carrying no currency will be denoted $m_{i0} = 1 - m_{i1} - m_{i2}$. Also, $V_{ij}$ denotes the expected discounted lifetime utility (the value function) for buyers from $i$ holding money $j$. The value function for a seller from country $i$ will be denoted $V_{i0}$. Because we have assumed that $c(q) = q$, $y = 0$, and $q = 0$, it is easy to show that $V_{ik} = q_{ik}$ and $V_{i0} = 0 \ \forall i,k$. This makes the model much simpler to solve.

We start with the case in which the policy variables $M_i$ and $\mu_i$ are exogenous and constant over time. We look only at steady-state equilibria in which prices don't change and the proportions $m_{ij}$ have converged to their stationary values, which depend on the policies $M_i$. We will call money $k$ a national currency if it is traded only between buyers and sellers from country $k$, but not in any other matches. We will call money $k$ an international currency if it is traded between all nationality combinations of buyers and sellers. In this model, a currency could be neither national nor international in this sense (for example, it could hold no value and thus never be traded). However, we study only three equilibrium regimes: one in which both currencies are national, one in which both are international, and one in which money 1 is national and money 2 is international.

---

2   This last assumption is needed if one desires all regimes studied here to be subgame perfect Nash equilibria under $y = \theta = 0$. This assumption is not necessary for other values of $y$ or $\theta$, but it makes the math unnecessarily complicated for the purposes of this paper. For the general model with arbitrary $y$ and $\theta$, and for the argument as to why this assumption is needed, see Trejos and Wright (2001).

A stationary equilibrium is a combination of values $(Q_{jk}, m_{jk})$ that satisfies the right Bellman equations, search conditions, and steady-state conditions. If money $j$ is a national currency, the Bellman equations associated with it are

(1)  $r\,Q_{kj} = \alpha_{kj}\,m_{j0}\,[u(Q_{jj}) - Q_{kj}] - \mu_j\,Q_{kj}$ for $k = 1, 2$;

the search condition is

(2)  $u(Q_{jj}) \geq Q_{jj} > u(Q_{kj})$  for $k \neq j$;

and the steady-state conditions are

(3)  $m_{jj} = M_j$,  $m_{kj} = 0$ for $k \neq j$.

If money $j$ is an international currency, its Bellman equations are

(1b)  $r\,Q_{kj} = \alpha_{k1}\,m_{10}\,[u(Q_{1j}) - Q_{kj}] + \alpha_{k2}\,m_{20}\,[u(Q_{2j}) - Q_{kj}] - \mu_j\,Q_{kj}$ for $k = 1, 2$;

the search condition is

(2b)  $\min\,[u(Q_{1j}), u(Q_{2j})] \geq \max\,[Q_{1j}, Q_{2j}]$;

and the steady-state conditions satisfy

(3b)  $\Delta m_{jj} = \alpha_{jk}\,m_{j0}\,m_{kj} - \alpha_{jk}\,m_{jj}\,m_{k0} + \gamma\,(M_j - m_{jj}) = 0$

$\Delta m_{kj} = \alpha_{jk}\,m_{k0}\,m_{jj} - \alpha_{kj}\,m_{kj}\,m_{j0} - \gamma\,m_{kj} = 0$ for $k \neq j$.

Before describing new results, I will summarize features of the equilibria derived in Trejos and Wright (2001):

- All three regimes mentioned above (the ones with no, one, or two international currencies) can be equilibria. For some parameter values, multiple equilibrium regimes exist. However, not all regimes can be equilibria for all parameter values. In particular, the regimes in which money $j$ is national cannot satisfy the equilibrium conditions if country $k \neq j$ is open enough (that is, if $\alpha_{kj}$ is high). Because the ratio of the populations of countries $j$ and $k$ can be shown to be $\alpha_{kj}/\alpha_{jk}$, this also means that international currencies tend to be issued by larger or more efficient economies. The regimes in which money $j$ is international cannot be equilibria if the two countries are very different (in particular, if $\alpha_{11}$ and $\alpha_{22}$ are very different). A high enough $m_j$ rules out equilibrium regimes in which money

$j$ is international, or in which money $k \neq j$ is not. Despite the multiplicity of equilibrium regimes, there is some degree of determinacy of prices: Within a given regime, for given parameter values, there is only one $(Q_{jk}, m_{jk})$ combination that satisfies the equilibrium conditions.

- $Q_{j1}$ is higher and $Q_{j2}$ is lower when money 1 is international than when it is not, all other things equal. More importantly, if the parameters are symmetric (fundamentals in both countries are the same) and the regime in which money 1 is national and money 2 is international exists, then $Q_{12} < Q_{22}$ in that regime. In other words, all else being equal, international currencies purchase more at home than abroad. This last result can be interpreted as an explanation of a well-known fact: The U.S. dollar is an outlier in the relationship between national income and deviations from purchasing power parity, as American prices are much lower than those regressions would predict, given what dollars can buy in the international market. In the equilibrium with two international currencies, it can be shown that $Q_{j1} = Q_{j2} = Q_j$ for $j = 1, 2$. In other words, if both monies circulate everywhere, they become perfect substitutes and, although prices vary across countries, they don't vary across currencies.

We now ask what happens in this model if a small economy is very open, which relates, as we shall see, to dollarization. Assume that country 1 is small relative to country 2 (that is, $\alpha_{12} > \alpha_{21}$), and compare equilibria with different values of $\alpha_{12}$. Openness relates to $\alpha_{12}$, as this parameter reflects the frequency with which agents from country 1 get an opportunity to trade with citizens from country 2. It is also associated (within a given regime) with the fraction of total purchases or sales by country 1 agents that are foreign transactions with country-2 agents. Because the number of cross-country matches is the same, whether measured in one country or the other, it follows that $\alpha_{12}/\alpha_{21}$ is also the ratio of country 2's population to that of country 1. Hence, a high value of $\alpha_{12}$, given $\alpha_{21}$, implies that country 1 is small.

Remember that for high enough $\alpha_{12}$, the regimes in which sellers from country 1 do not use money 2 as medium of exchange cannot be equilibria. It follows from equation (1) that, within those regimes, $Q_{12}$ is increasing in $\alpha_{12}$, and then, when the latter is high, condition (2) cannot be satisfied.

Now, within the regime in which money 2 is international and money 1 is national, one can show that

$$(4) \quad m_{12} = \frac{\alpha_{12}(1 - M_1)M_2}{\gamma + \alpha_{12} + \alpha_{21}(1 - M_1)} ,$$

which is increasing (and therefore $m_{10}$ and $Q_{11}$ are decreasing) in $\alpha_{12}$ (see figure 1). This implies that as the small, "dollarized" economy becomes more open, it will absorb more foreign money and its local money will become less and less valuable, especially relative to the foreign money (as $Q_{22}$ and $Q_{12}/Q_{11}$ increase in $\alpha_{12}$).[3]

Consider now the seigniorage extracted by issuing money $k$, which is given by

$$S_k = \gamma \, M_k \, Q_{kk} + \mu_k \, m_{1k} \, (1 - m_{10}) \, Q_{1k} + \mu_k \, m_{2k} \, (1 - m_{20}) \, Q_{2k}.$$

It can be shown that as $\alpha_{12}$ increases, $S_1$ falls. Figure 2 illustrates seigniorage collection as a function of $\alpha_{12}$ in the different regimes (the thicker line represents the regime in which money 1 is national and money 2 is international; the thinner line, the regime in which both monies are international and perfect substitutes). As the economy becomes more open, seigniorage collected in that country by issuing a national currency that lags behind what is collected—also in that country—in the regime in which both authorities are issuing the same international currency (or equivalently, two currencies that are perfect substitutes). We also find that $S_1$ is unambiguously higher in the regime in which both monies are international than in the regime in which money 1 is national and money 2 is international, every thing else given (see panel a in figure 2). For country 2 (panel b), seigniorage is higher in that regime unless the economy is very open. Welfare in country 2 (panel c) is unambiguously lower in that regime, meaning that a country benefits from issuing an international currency, and it benefits even more from that becoming the only currency.

**Figure 1: Dollarization in the Small Economy as a Function of Openness**

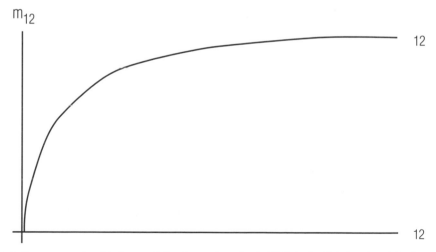

---

3  In the more general model where $y > 0$, there is a maximum level of "inflation," called $\mu^*_1 > 0$, such that if money 2 circulates and $\mu_1 > \mu^*_1$, there are no equilibria in which money 1 has value, even in country 1. It can be shown that $\mu^*1$ decreases with $\alpha_{12}$.

**Figure 2a: Seigniorage in a Dollarized Economy as a Function of Openness**

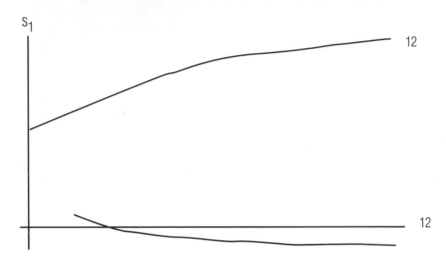

**Figure 2b: Seigniorage in Country 2 as a Factor of Openness**

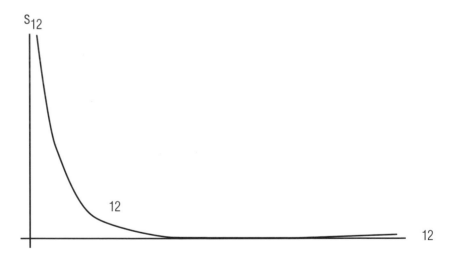

**Figure 2c: Welfare in Country 2 as it Varies with Openness Across Regimes**

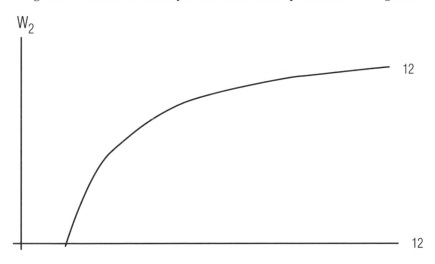

**Figure 3: Effectiveness of Changing $M_1$**

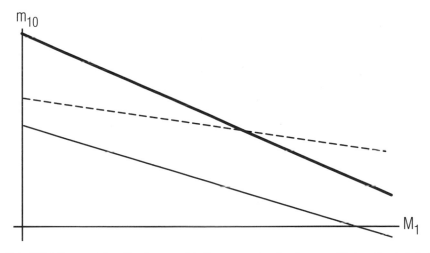

Note: Thick line: no international money, thin line: money 1 national, money 2 international; dashed line: both currencies international.

Notice also that $m_{12}$ increases in $M_2$ and decreases in $M_1$. In other words, in the regime in which one money is national and the other is international, higher amounts of the international currency spread through both countries, and higher amounts of the national currency crowd out the international currency from their own country. This is also true in the regime with two international currencies, where both values $m_{j0}$ fall when either $M_k$ increases. Furthermore, when a country absorbs foreign currency, it weakens the effects of local policy on the local money supply (figure 3).

So far, we have taken the policy parameters $M_k$ and $\mu_k$ to be exogenous. Allow them now to be the outcome of a game between the monetary authorities, which care about either their national welfare or their seigniorage extraction. To keep things tractable, we still assume that governments take the regime as given and restrict their choices to policies that allow for the existence of that regime as an equilibrium (that is, we ignore policies aimed precisely at changing a currency's realm of circulation). Neither will we look at policies in which $M$ changes over time and reduce to comparisons of steady states.

One thing to do is look for Nash equilibria in the interaction between governments, when each government chooses its policy unilaterally, taking as given the decisions of its counterpart and seeking to maximize the seigniorage it collects. We also consider the possibility of international policy coordination by letting governments choose the parameters jointly, assuming they care about seigniorage (which is freely transferable across countries), in which case they maximize $S_1 + S_2$. Alternatively, we can assume seigniorage is not transferable, in which case we use Nash's cooperative bargaining solution, with threat points given by the non-cooperative solution. Then the choice maximizes $(S_1 - S^*_1)(S_2 - S^*_2)$, where $S^*_j$ denotes the seigniorage that government $j$ would obtain in the non-cooperative Nash equilibrium. As a point of reference, we also derive the non-cooperative Nash equilibrium when each government's objective function is to maximize the welfare of its citizens, $W_j = m_{j1} Q_{j1} + m_{j2} Q_{j2}$.

One result that can be derived analytically is that the non-cooperative Nash solutions are inefficient, in the sense that each government does not take into account the effect it has on the other. Starting from the non-cooperative Nash solution, reducing both $M_1$ and $M_2$ marginally increases both $S_1$ and $S_2$. To understand the reason, take an increase in $M_1$. As a function of $M_2$, $S_2$ shifts down and to the right; in other words, not only does country 2 get fewer taxes, but also incentives to increase $M_2$. This leads to a subsequent increase in $M_1$, and so forth, and the process converges to an allocation where both $M$ are high and $S$ low, especially in the global regime where the relationship is strongest. In fact, more taxes may be collected when both governments are trying to maximize welfare (which leads to more restraint in money creation) than when their goal is seigniorage itself. This is true in the regimes with one or with two international currencies. A similar result holds for endogenous $\mu_k$. Solving numerically for the solution to the "policy game" for given parameter values, one finds the feasibility frontier in $(S_1, S_2)$ space for the regime with two international monies contains the one for the equilibrium with one international money; in other words, given parameters, one can obtain (much) more seigniorage in the regime in which both countries issue international currencies (which end up being perfect substitutes) than in the regime in which some agents carry a lesser national currency that is not useful for international transactions. However, although this is true for combinations of $(S_1, S_2)$ that are feasible, it is also the case that when both monies are international, inefficiency in the game is largest. Hence, the non-cooperative solution in the regime with two international monies is farther from the frontier, and it may be dominated by the non-cooperative solution in the regime with one international money.

With endogenous policies, there is a tendency toward excessive issuing of currency that is stronger when both currencies circulate everywhere. There is, then, a role for cooperation between governments, which increase their seigniorage by coordinating policies. More to the point for the purposes of this paper, as $\alpha_{12}$ grows and the small economy 1 becomes more open, the inefficiency of the non-cooperative outcomes increases because the cross-effect is stronger and it is easier to "export inflation." In other words, in very small open economies, partial dollarization makes policy coordination very important, and, in its absence, the inefficiencies of maintaining a national currency are very large.

The results so far in this section tell us some things about a very stylized theoretical model. Despite its shortcomings, the model seems appropriate to address the issues of interest in this paper, as it has two features that are rare and valuable in this context: Monies in this model are primarily media of exchange, not stores of value, and which currencies circulate where is determined endogenously. One hopes, then, that the model derives some lessons that can be translated to the actual topic of dollarization is Latin America. What are those lessons?

- As a small economy opens—in the sense that trade with foreigners increases as a fraction of total activity—it is unavoidable that foreign currency will circulate locally. The only reason that an agent would not take foreign currency in payment is that he expects it would be difficult or costly to spend it at fair prices (in the model, because you can only spend it on some people; in reality, because you have to trade it at currency markets, which involves transaction costs). If one trades often enough with foreigners that accept foreign money, one has incentives to accept and keep that money, and one must believe that one's compatriots have them as well. Hence, to the extent that communication and transportation costs in international trade keep falling, more countries will become "dollarized," in the sense that the roles of money in them will increasingly be played by foreign currency.

• The presence of foreign money in one country implies that the local money's ability to capture seigniorage is reduced. In the extreme, one can capture more seigniorage through monetary union and coordination (using solely an international currency and finding a way to share the proceeds with its issuer) than by keeping a local currency whose realm of circulation is becoming limited.

• Issuing an international currency enhances a country's welfare, the value of its money, and the seigniorage collected by the monetary authority. That country is also unambiguously better off if the other nation "dollarizes" completely—if there is a switch from a regime in which the other country also issues a national money to one with a single currency (or two perfect-substitute currencies).

• When international currency circulates in a country, monetary policy becomes less effective, at least in the sense that, as in the model, injections of local cash crowd out some foreign cash and lead to a smaller impact on total liquidity. Because this also implies that policy in one place tends to have effects on another place, and authorities are bound to disregard this cross-effect, there is room for policy coordination and for inefficiencies if monetary authorities do not coordinate. The more open a small economy, the more costly miscoordination will be for its welfare and seigniorage, and the bigger the enticement to shift to a regime with coordinated policies or with only one money.

## 3. PROS AND CONS OF DOLLARIZATION IN LATIN AMERICA

The debate about dollarization has been very intense in the smaller Latin American countries in recent years. The most frequent argument in favor of dollarization is that the U.S. dollar has lower inflation rates than most Latin currencies, and local citizens would be better off enjoying those lower rates of inflation. The simplicity of this argument makes it compelling. It also relates to an important problem: These nations have a history of very high inflation and even hyperinflation. Despite the stabilization efforts of the 1980s and 1990s, only Panama—the one dollarized nation—enjoyed continuous single-digit inflation in the period; the other nations kept significantly higher rates, some in excess of 50 percent per year.

While a dollarized economy would eventually achieve American inflation rates, early on there may be significant price increases if the local currency is very under-valued when it is retired. In Ecuador (figure 4), where dollarization was announced and the exchange rate frozen in January 2000, prices increased 110 percent in 2000 and 35 percent in 2001. It took nine months for the annualized three-month rate to fall under 50 percent.[4] This happened after the nominal value of all financial assets had been pegged to the U.S. dollar, and the resulting real demonetization worsened an already deep recession.

It is not obvious at first glance that dollarization should necessarily be a precon-dition for price stability. Dollarization requires a fiscal adjustment, enough to make the public deficit and debt manageable without the support of central bank financ-ing. If a country performs such fiscal adjustment, it will achieve price stability, regardless of whether it keeps its own currency. However, dollarization may just be the simplest form of ensuring political and institutional sustainability in fiscal pru-dence. Dollarization is politically more costly to reverse than fiscal discipline itself.[5]

**Figure 4: Inflation in Ecuador after Dollarization**

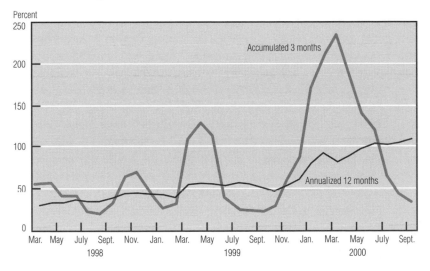

4   Ecuador had gone through a balance-of-payments crisis and a very strong real depreciation of the currency in the two years before dollarization was announced. When it was, central bank reserves were very low, so implementation required valuing the local currency in circulation very poorly. There had been a 425 percent nominal depreciation over two years, and a 100 percent real depreciation in the 12 months previous to enact-ment. Going through inflation this high after the nominal value of assets has been pegged to the dollar implies a sizeable fall in the real money supply and the real stock of financial assets.
5   The conservative Salvadorian government may have chosen to dollarize in late 2000, at least in part, to make expansionary fiscal policies in future administrations more difficult politically. At the moment of writing this paper, it seems that Argentina may fall again into high inflation after 11 years of avoiding it. The fixed-exchange-rate regime, by not being accompanied with fiscal discipline and an elimination of local currency, proved to be unsustainable.

The size of the fiscal adjustment necessary to achieve price stability may be affected by whether there is dollarization. Dollarization may be a cheaper way of fighting inflation in the few countries where a sizeable fraction of government debt is denominated in local currency, due to the resulting fall in domestic real interest rates (which shall be discussed below). On the other hand, low inflation may be more expensive fiscally in other countries where reserve seigniorage (that is, the portion of seigniorage that comes, not from issuing new currency, but from interest earned by the existing foreign reserves in the central bank) is a significant portion of public revenue.

Whether or not dollarization achieves price stability better than other alternatives that enact the necessary fiscal adjustment, there are other reasons for or against dollarization. The first has to do with interest rates: The financial systems of the small Latin American countries tend to have unusually short maturities for assets and liabilities and very high interest rates. For example, Central American countries have real interest rates that are 60 percent higher and eight times more volatile than in Panama, which has been dollarized for a long time.

Part of the reason for high interest rates is independent of the currency and relates instead to poor banking supervision, high levels of political risk and violence, uncertainties in the legal and logistical systems, etc. Hence, even in dollar-denominated contracts, rates tend to be higher in these nations than in the United States. But there is also high and variable inflation, as well as very variable nominal exchange rates, creating large, sustained differences between dollar- and peso-denominated assets, when we compare their ex post returns expressed on a common currency. In most of these countries, this spread is consistently above 1,000 basis points (especially on long-term paper and banking credit) and must be interpreted as the insurance premium that peso-denominated assets pay so that the lender will bear the risks associated with a very uncertain future value of the contract. It would be important to relieve agents of those risks and allow lower interest rates (which reflect the quantity of investment) and longer maturities (which reflect the kind of investment).[6]

Figure 5 shows the interest rate premium for three countries that are very different in terms of exchange rate stability and predictability. The top panel shows the spread between lending interest rates in colones and dollars in Costa Rica, a country that has a stable real exchange rate achieved by daily minidevaluations to compensate for inflation differentials. The premium for assuming the risks of colones, even in six-month maturity assets (shown in the figure), has averaged over 450 basis points for the decade. The middle panel shows the spreads between interest rates (both lending and borrowing) in soles and dollars in Peru, a country with

---

[6]  Relieving agents of currency risk is not simply a matter of borrowing and investing in dollars in an otherwise non-dollarized economy. As long as the local currency exists, the currency risk exists as well, and the money in which a financial contract is written simply determines which party bears it. Prudent banking supervision, furthermore, requires companies that primarily sell in the local market to borrow in local currency.

**Figure 5: Interest Rate Premiums on Local Currency and U.S. Dollars**

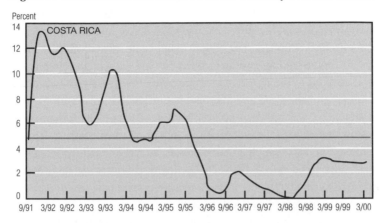

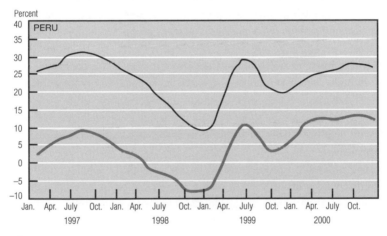

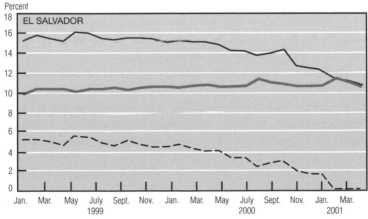

a less predictable flexible exchange rate. We can see that the punishment for borrowing in local currency can be as much as 2,500 basis points in high-uncertainty periods, and the difference between active and passive rates is much higher in soles than in dollars. The bottom panel is the most illustrative, as it shows the dollar and colon lending rates in El Salvador and the margin between them. For the period covered in the figure (and seven years before that), this country had a fixed nominal exchange rate and international inflation levels. Still, we find a significant premium (over 400 basis points) for most of the period. It is only when dollarization is announced (November 2000) that local rates begin to fall, and they merge with dollar rates (which do not increase) with the enactment of dollarization in January 2001. The spread between lending and borrowing rates also fell, by almost 300 basis points. Hence, this is a picture-perfect case to illustrate the interest rate reduction coming from dollarization.

It is surprising that the difference in peso and dollar interest rates is so high in some of these countries, where the data, ex post, seem to indicate that the currency "risk" is not big. This *other* premium puzzle lacks a good explanation. Figure 6 shows how the exchange rate policy in Costa Rica has been so predictable that swings in the bilateral real rate—off the charted path—of more than 2 percent a month, or more than 5 percent in a quarter, have not taken place at all in over a decade. El Salvador's fixed nominal rate is another example of predictable policy. Comparatively, there seems to be a disproportionate reward for taking risks associated with holding assets in those currencies, especially considering that the spread persists.

Another argument for dollarization has to do with the inherent inefficiency of issuing currencies with very small realms of circulation in very open economies. Like languages, monies pose a coordination game, so one currency plays the role of money much better than two. Unlike the model in section 2, in reality there are accessible financial services that trade currencies, so a peso holder would not have to miss an opportunity to buy from a foreigner just because he holds the wrong kind of cash. However, those financial services (and the other transactions that are necessary when one deals with multiple currencies) are costly to society; though they fulfill a need *within* a multicurrency world, the costs can be avoided by switching to a regime with fewer currencies. I know of no reliable measurements of the portion of the financial services sector that would be made redundant if peso-for-dollar transactions were no longer necessary. However, reliable estimates for the European Union (regarding the savings for switching from many currencies to one euro) reached as much as 0.6 percent of GDP. The small Latin American countries mentioned in this paper are significantly more open (according to World Bank figures, on average the trade-to-GDP ratio is 70 percent higher in these nations than in the European Union), and their financial services industry much less efficient, so the cost reductions from eliminating the need of currency-for-currency trades are probably larger than that figure.

**Figure 6: Costa Rican Real Exchange Rate**

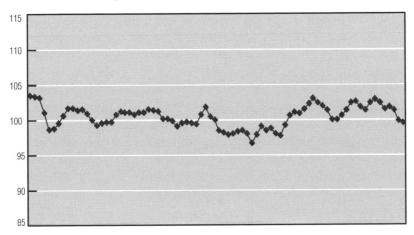

A third argument for dollarization is that in the absence of national currencies, it may be easier to maintain financial stability. The financial sector of these countries is particularly unstable and subject to crises. These come from different sources: institutional (bank-solvency problems and bank runs), fiscal (debt moratoria on the part of governments), or balance of payments. Dollarization makes these countries less susceptible to some of these sources of instability because a dollarized economy is not subject to speculation about the sustainability of the exchange rate or the currency regime, which is a frequent source of crises.[7]

The argument most often mentioned *against* dollarization is that after the local currency ceases to exist, the central bank is left without exchange rate policy instruments, and almost without monetary policy instruments; therefore, it shall be much less able to stabilize business cycles. This is certainly a valid point. Moreover, these instruments are going to be determined by the Federal Reserve, and American cycles are not perfectly correlated with local ones, so we may occasionally end up with procyclical policies and higher short-run volatility.

The loss of policy instruments may not be so painful after all. First, business cycles in the smaller Latin American economies are already fairly correlated to the ones in the United States (at least more so than the average euro economy is correlated to Germany), and presumably once they share currency, the correlation

---

7   Until early 2002, Argentina maintained a currency board that essentially commits it to the same stringencies (about monetary and fiscal policy and about fixed exchange rates) as dollarization for almost a decade now. One salient difference is that markets are prone to speculating about the sustainability of the board mechanism, and when they do, there are incentives to run on the peso. Under a dollarized system, even if there were doubt about the sustainability of it, there would not be incentives to run on the dollar.

would increase. In that sense (and also because of the sizeable integration in trade and migration), these nations and the United States constitute an optimal currency area; under dollarization, the tailored policy they need would still be implemented, and with more efficacy. Second, for various reasons, local policy is already pro-cyclical and has often been less than brilliant. Without the wealth of legal and political institutions that developed countries take for granted, it may be difficult for a small, poor economy to maintain reasonable monetary policy anyway. Third, and most importantly, dollars are already a large fraction of the money supply in these countries, which reduces local authorities' ability to exercise independent monetary and exchange rate policy. In some of these countries, very open and exposed to relatively large capital flows, the monetary authorities have no control over real exchange rates, interest rates, and liquidity. Public debt tends to be very high, and a big share of that debt is denominated in U.S. dollars, so there are fiscal implications that make it costly or impossible to use monetary policy or exchange rate policy at liberty. Unlike larger countries, small dollarized economies do not have autonomous policy to begin with.

**Figure 7: Seigniorage Revenue (percent of GDP)**

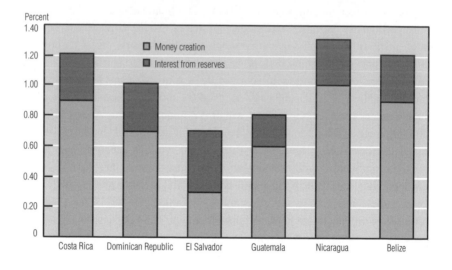

Another objection to dollarization is that without their own currency, these nations cease to receive seigniorage as government revenue and even "pay" seigniorage to the Federal Reserve. Figure 7 shows the total revenue from issuing local currency for the Central American countries in the 1990s, as estimated by Hausmann and Powell (1999). The fiscal sacrifice from dollarization can be sizeable. Direct seigniorage, the value of issuing new currency and extracting an inflationary tax, averages 0.7 percent of GDP for those nations (this number can be much higher in countries with more inflation, such as Ecuador). Reserve seigniorage (interest earned by foreign reserves) rounds it up to an even 1 percent. In some of those countries, past mistakes in managing foreign debt mean that central banks are insolvent, and, without seigniorage revenue, their losses need to be transferred back to the Treasury.

To the extent that dollarization in other countries benefits the United States, it may make sense to consider alternative formulas to share the additional seigniorage with them, to compensate for the loss of seigniorage as they cease to issue their own currency. There have been some proposals along these lines (most notably, the IMSA law considered in the Senate). This is not even costly, as the Fed seigniorage revenue expands, given the dollar inflation rate, as other countries dollarize.

Unmentioned so far are matters of implementation, both for the dollarizing small economy and for the Federal Reserve. If a country decides to eliminate its currency, what should the exchange rate be (or does it matter)? Are there sufficient reserves? What institutional arrangements need to be reformed for dollarization to function? What agreements with the issuer of international currency are necessary?

The exchange rate at which the old currency is retired truly matters. Downward rigidities in prices do exist in these countries, and it is difficult to overcome the consequences of overpricing the peso. Argentina and the experience of absorbing East Germany into West Germany are two examples of places that started out "too expensive" in a way that was difficult to correct and costly in terms of employment and output growth. Argentina's collapse after a seven-year recession is largely the consequence of a strong overvaluation of the peso, which rendered most firms uncompetitive in the international market and prevented export-led growth to fuel the economy during the 1990s.

Upward rigidities in prices are much rarer, so the consequences of retiring an underpriced peso can be more quickly overcome. However, when that happens, monetary aggregates shrink as a fraction of GDP, reducing output in the short run. Ecuador is a particularly eloquent example why the size of the central bank foreign reserves should not be what makes the choice of exchange rate, even if that means delaying the implementation.

Sufficiency of reserves at the "right" exchange rate is also relevant. Besides covering the peso supply and local-currency bank deposits in the central bank, it is healthy to leave a cushion of reserves to cover for other potential liabilities and problems (especially, to fund some kind of bank deposit insurance) and to generate a future source of seigniorage. How big that cushion should be is a matter that has not been studied seriously. The amount of reserves available is not easy to calculate: Some of the foreign assets held by the monetary authority may not be liquid enough to use them to retire currency. On the other hand, to the extent that the United States might give back some of the foregone seigniorage, one may be able to securitize that flow and add it to the available dollar supply when dollarization is enacted.

Other topics, which I shall not address here, also need resolution during the implementation of dollarization. For example, in many developing countries, banking deposit insurance does not exist formally, yet bank failures are often bailed out by the monetary authorities. This kind of limbo is not sustainable in a dollarized economy, where either a formal insurance scheme is established and funded, or the law must make explicit that depositors must bear all the risk; the central bank cannot take on the role of lender of last resort. As another example, some countries have debated whether to dollarize alone or as a group, or to pursue another form of monetary integration with their neighbors that does not involve the U.S. dollar. This matter returns us to considerations about what is the optimal currency area for these nations, although it seems obvious that, due to cyclical alignment, migration, trade and financial flows, the optimal currency area for these countries revolves around the U.S. dollar. One may wonder if dollarization should be imposed as a shock treatment (as in Ecuador), gradually, or even through the intermediate step of establishing a monetary board first (although this last alternative is probably politically unfeasible now, using the Argentinean crisis as a model). Other outstanding issues relate to agreements between the local monetary authorities and the Federal Reserve, and to the transitional adjustment to existing financial contracts denominated in a currency that disappears.

## 4. CONCLUSIONS

In small and very open economies, the presence and use of international currency is unavoidable. As the use of dollars increases with openness in the future, problems may emerge with the effectiveness of monetary policy and the ability of local authorities to collect seigniorage. There may also be a role for coordination of monetary policy among countries that are connected by a common international currency. The model's predictions in section 2 seem to be confirmed, at least, by the experiences of the smaller Latin American economies that are largely dollarized already.

In those nations, a debate has emerged as of late about whether they should do away with their currencies completely and use the U.S. dollar as their currency. Although there are arguments in both directions, the reasons in favor of that move seem to be compelling, and already a few countries have made the decision to dollarize completely in the short run. Some of those arguments are summarized in section 3.

If the trend continues, or if the forces moving these nations in this direction extend to larger countries, or to different latitudes, the vision about the future of central banking is very different from today. The world could be reduced to only a handful of monetary authorities, with some of them exercising monetary policy internationally, and with strong need for coordination.

Perhaps more relevant to the topic of this conference, this vision about the future of central banking and the dollarization phenomenon brings about questions for the issuers of the international currency. Should the United States encourage other countries to use the U.S. dollar as their official currency and, if so, what is a fair amount of seigniorage to return and a good mechanism to return them? Should the Federal Reserve's systems for payments, clearance, and currency logistics be redesigned to include those of dollarizing countries (whether they dollarize partially or completely), or should each country maintain an independent arrangement? How should further financial integration be pursued? Can bank supervision be performed across national borders? Does monetary integration enhance the need for other forms of integration? Should the macroeconomic conditions and performance of dollarized economies be a codeterminant of how monetary policy instruments are managed, or should the Federal Reserve concentrate solely on the American business cycle performance and let the chips fall where they may for the smaller dollarized countries? These are all issues that should be included in the research agenda of the new Central Banking Institute within the U.S. Federal Reserve.

## ACKNOWLEDGMENTS

Special gratitude is owed to Ross Levine and Klaus Schmidt-Hebbel.

### REFERENCES

Hausmann, Ricardo, and Andrew Powell. 1999. Dollarization: Issues of Implementation. Paper presented at for the Inter-American Development Bank, Alternative Exchange Rate Regimes for the Region, July 23–24, 1999, Panama City, Panama. Available *www.iadb.org/OCE/exchange_rate/implement.pdf* [24 January 2002].

Trejos, Alberto, and Randall Wright. 2001. International Currency. Advances in Macroeconomics. *Bell Economic Journals* 1(1).

# Commentary

*Klaus Schmidt-Hebbel*

## 1. INTRODUCTION

This is a very good paper on some theoretical issues and many empirical aspects of dollarization, and it is great fun to read. The first part of my comments will briefly describe the main features and findings of Trejos' model, as well as its major limitations. Next, I will refer to some recent work that covers issues not addressed by the model but identified in the second, empirical section of Trejos' paper. Then I will briefly discuss issues that relate to dollarization in Latin America, before ending with a brief note on optimal exchange rate regimes.

## 2. THE MODEL

This paper develops a welfare-based evaluation of monetary regimes in a search-theoretic model for transactions money, describing various monetary and real equilibria in a two-country world. The model, extending previous work by Trejos and Wright, is meant to assess current issues in the hot debate about dollarization in some Latin American countries, issues that are discussed in the second part of the paper.

The model provides a stylized framework in which national and international monies are demanded to overcome the mismatch between different goods demanded and supplied by agents that engage in a costly search for a domestic or foreign trading partner. Domestic and foreign currencies are issued by monopolistic governments abroad and at home, respectively, but they have the potential to circulate freely and are used for buying both domestic and imported goods.

The model is used to analyze possible monetary equilibria under three monetary regimes: both currencies are national; one is national and the other is international; or both are international. Extending previous findings by Trejos and Wright (2001), the paper derives three results. First, if a small economy increases its trade with a large economy, it will switch from the first to the second regime. The smaller economy will increasingly adopt its trading partner's currency because its own currency becomes less valuable as matches between domestic buyers and domestic sellers become less frequent. In other words, there is a one-to-one relationship between foreign trade and the use of the corresponding foreign currency.

Second, seigniorage collected by the home government declines with international trade, while a larger supply of foreign currency spreads through both countries.

Third, an increased supply of domestic currency crowds out foreign currency in the home country and therefore produces a smaller impact on total liquidity. Hence, monetary policy becomes less effective in a dollarized economy. There is room for policy coordination. Domestic governments could raise more seigniorage if they adopted the foreign currency under a seigniorage-sharing agreement.

## 3. LIMITATIONS OF THE MODEL

Some of the model's shortcomings are inherent in search-theoretic frameworks, in which agents are dichotomous and money itself is not divisible. Money has real effects: If per capita money supply is increased, the ratio of buyers to sellers rises and trade declines. Inflation is not a direct consequence of expansionary monetary policy (governments do not raise inflation when they maximize seigniorage). Instead, inflation is approximated by an exogenous tax on money holdings.

These features of money, inflation, and monetary policy make search-theoretic models somewhat cumbersome for analyzing monetary issues generally and dollarization particularly. In my view, these models are dominated by the use of mainstream, neoclassical, open-economy models that combine rational expectations, micro foundations, and short-term sticky prices to analyze alternative monetary regimes, including full dollarization. Examples of these models include Hamada (1998), Devereux and Engel (1999), and the models surveyed by McCallum (1999).

In Trejos' model, increased international trade unavoidably leads to a small open economy's wider adoption of its larger trading partner's currency. I am not sure if this is a general result obtained in the standard open-economy models mentioned above, even when introducing aggregate money (the aggregate of domestic and international currency) as a cash-in-advance constraint on aggregate spending. Aggregate demand will be a composite of domestic and foreign currency, with the relative demand for each currency determined by variables such as the difference in alternative costs (including expected depreciation and exchange rate risk premium) and currency-exchange transaction costs. Only under two separate cash-in-advance constraints—for domestic spending and money and for international spending and money (as in Altug and Labadie 1994)—does increased trade lead, all else being equal, to higher demand for international currency.

Most of this model's other limitations in analyzing the issues that inform the dollarization debate in the real world are identified in the paper's second section: The model lacks short-term price stickiness, so it has no role for a flexible exchange rate or an independent monetary policy. The model is deterministic, so it has no shocks and no optimal currency area (OCA) issues arise on the international correlation of shocks and economic cycles. It has no fiscal policy, so it has no problems of fiscal and monetary credibility leading to high inflation or balance-of-payments crises. In the model, the interest rate is exogenous, so there is no financial sector and, consequently, no fragile banking systems leading to high interest rates and possible financial crises. There are no assets in the model and hence no problems of currency and maturity mismatch in assets and liabilities that could lead to a twin crisis.

## 4. OTHER WORK ON DOLLARIZATION

No existing model can encompass all of the issues mentioned above. Certainly, it would be naïve to expect a general welfare-based model to include all traditional and new OCA and dollarization issues in order to provide a clear-cut answer on the net benefits of alternative exchange rate arrangements. Hence, the best we can do is to deal separately with each issue, which is the approach used in the recent work to which I next refer selectively.

One rather neglected means of distinguishing dollarization is by type: Dollars may be used as (1) a medium of exchange, (2) a unit of account, or (3) a store of value. Currency substitution refers to the first two types (as in Trejos), and asset substitution to the third. Larry Ball (2001), using a simple open-economy model for assessing monetary policy, argues that type 1 dollarization matters little for the effective conduct of monetary policy, while types 2 and 3 increase devaluation passthrough, destabilize money demand, weaken the transmission mechanism between domestic interest rates and spending, and threaten financial stability when depreciation hurts balance sheets through dollar-denominated liabilities.

In a three-country world of one small and two large economies that float, Hamada (1998) shows that pegging the smaller economy to one of the larger ones under wage and price rigidities is less advantageous than pegging it to a basket of the two larger economies (as proposed for Argentina by its economy minister Domingo Cavallo). But the basket is shown to be inferior to a free float.

Whether dollarization promotes fiscal discipline is very much an empirical question. Goldfajn and Olivares (2000) express doubt that the absence of seigniorage forces fiscal adjustment. Dollarization unavoidably lowers inflation to U.S. levels, corrected by the effect of Harrod–Balassa–Samuelson (HBS) differences between domestic and U.S. traded/nontraded productivity growth differentials. Hence, it helps countries with moderate or high inflation rates by getting rid of ineffective central banks. But it does not benefit countries with fiscal discipline and low inflation (say, Chile); indeed, it deprives them of the ability to determine their own "optimal" level of inflation (in Chile, for example, the optimal rate is 3 percent, which is higher than the U.S. rate; this reflects HBS in conjunction with significant domestic wage and price rigidities).

Dollarization eliminates exchange rate risk and, as Powell and Sturzenegger (2000) argue, it may reduce country risk premiums. By lowering domestic interest rates and boosting investment and growth, this could significantly benefit economies beset by high devaluation expectations and exchange risk premiums (Calvo 1999).

In an economy with large net short-term U.S. liabilities, high exchange rate risk, and fragile banks, dollarization could strengthen banks (Schuler 1999), extend maturities (Goldfajn and Olivares 2000), boost access to foreign credit (Savastano 1999), and reduce the consequences of international crises and contagion (Calvo 1999). However, dollarization alone will not suffice to turn around a financial system beset by implicit government bailout guarantees, ineffective deposit insurance, and inadequate regulation and supervision.

Against the benefits discussed above, dollarization has costs, particularly in economies with strong fiscal and financial fundamentals and an effective monetary policy. Giving up the nominal exchange rate means renouncing a useful instrument for making quick, real exchange rate corrections in economies affected by idiosyncratic shocks and short-term domestic price and wage rigidities. Giving up monetary policy typically entails forgoing use of the only effective instrument of domestic stabilization policy.

Dollarization eliminates central banks' traditional lender-of-last-resort role, which, as long as it is well played, contributes to bank strength, not bank fragility. Calvo (1999) argues that this loss could be offset by having a larger presence of foreign banks (such as Panama and Argentina) or by contracting contingent foreign credit lines (Argentina, for instance). However, as the ongoing Argentine drama suggests, these remedies seem insufficient to guarantee financial stability in a quasi-dollarized economy.

Finally, there is the issue of seigniorage. Abstracting from nationalistic arguments, the main issue here is sharing. As shown in Trejos' model, dollarization accompanied by a sharing agreement with the United States could allow the dollarized economy to collect more seigniorage revenue than it collected when it was de facto quasi-dollarized. Again, this issue is political as well as empirical. In countries with little de facto dollarization, renouncing seigniorage unilaterally, without a sharing agreement, may cause huge annual revenue losses (about 0.5 percent of GDP).

## 5. DOLLARIZATION IN LATIN AMERICA

Trejos' empirical section applies to a set of Latin American countries that show a conjunction of structural features and initial policy conditions characterized by "original sin" (Hausmann 1999). These countries' structural features include small size, a high degree of openness, large shares in goods and asset trade with the United States, and strong correlation with U.S. shocks and cycles. But these features are not enough to qualify a country for dollarization; it should also be beset by "original sin" in the form of ineffective monetary policy, fiscal profligacy, fragile financial systems, large short-term dollar liabilities, high exchange and sovereign risk premiums, high interest rates, and, therefore, large de facto dollarization. Ecuador, the paramount example, adopted dollarization as a last resort, with the added hope that this discipline would have positive spillovers into other realms of domestic policy.

Another set of countries, the medium and large Latin American economies, have much better policies and less trade and financial integration with the United States, as well as idiosyncratic shocks and cycles not closely related to that country's. A case in point is Chile, a medium-sized economy with highly diversified trade, effective domestic policies, and low correlation of shocks and cycles with the U.S. economy (see table 1).

Such countries shy away from dollarization, and not only for nationalistic reasons. Moreover, they increasingly tend to adopt a highly successful combination of floating exchange rates and explicit inflation targeting. Only a couple of countries were on the road to this regime in 1996; today, five countries (Brazil, Chile, Colombia, Mexico, and Peru), representing roughly 75 percent of Latin America's GDP and population, have adopted full-fledged or at least half-fledged inflation targets with free floats. The empirical evidence for both industrialized and developing countries shows that this regime can succeed in making monetary policy in open economies far more effective (Corbo, Landerretche, and Schmidt-Hebbel 2002; Mishkin and Schmidt-Hebbel 2001).

**Table 1: Macroeconomic Correlations between Chile and the United States**

| Terms of trade, 1980–95 | −0.49 | GDP growth rate, 1986:IIQ–1998:IVQ | −0.10 |
|---|---|---|---|
| Real interest rate, 1986:IQ–1999:IIIQ | 0.03 | GDP growth trend deviation, 1986:IQ–1998:IVQ | 0.03 |
| Stock market real return, 1990:IQ–1999:IIIQ | 0.15 | Consumption growth, 1980–98 | −0.22 |
| Unemployment rate, 1993:IQ–1999:IIQ | −0.07 | Consumption growth trend deviation, 1980–98 | −0.21 |

### 6. ON OPTIMAL EXCHANGE RATE SYSTEMS

Let me finish with a brief general discussion of optimal exchange rate regimes. The profession has come a long way in assessing the relationship between exchange rate flexibility and welfare (see figure 1). In the simple textbook case of full-price flexibility, fully credible policies, no financial system, and no idiosyncratic shocks, welfare is orthogonal to the choice of exchange rate regime (schedule A). However, consideration of the latter real-world features alters this assessment significantly. In the 1970s, 1980s, and early 1990s, a substantial part of the profession argued for intermediate arrangements like exchange rate bands, pegs, and even currency boards, which supposedly would bring the net benefits of limited flexibility and/or monetary policy without the costs of the extremes (schedule B). A non-monotonic relation of this kind is still advocated by some economists, including John Williamson (who argues that bliss is achieved by means of a crawling peg system) or the aforementioned Cavallo (with his euro- and dollar-based basket proposal for Argentina).

For small open economies that are either highly integrated with their prospective currency partners (such as Euroland members) or beset by problems of original sin, the relationship between exchange rate flexibility and welfare is negative (schedule C). In this case, monetary union or dollarization represents bliss. At the other extreme are countries with asynchronous shocks and cycles, sound policies and fundamentals, and short-run price rigidities, for which a floating regime represents bliss (schedule D).

What has happened in the real world? Since most intermediate exchange rate regimes either have shown substantial weakness or have simply collapsed in the wake of terminal attacks, there is a worldwide trend toward the two extremes. Not surprisingly, a critical mass of economists are following suit, embracing the two-corner hypothesis (schedule E). Intermediate regimes are out, and one recommends either full monetary integration or a full float. Time will tell if we all (except the United States) will end up on the left axis in Mundell's one-currency, dollarized world or if a sizeable number of currencies will compete, with some countries issuing currencies on the right axis and others issuing currencies on the left.

### Figure 1:  Exchange Rate Regimes and Welfare

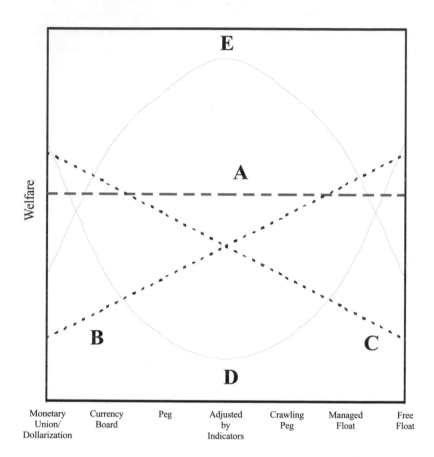

Source:  Corbo and Schmidt-Hebbel (2001).

## References

Altug, S., and P. Labadie. 1994. *Dynamic Choice and Asset Markets*. San Diego: Academic Press.

Ball, Larry. 2001. Policy Rules in Partially Dollarized Economies. Unpublished paper presented at the Central Bank of Peru/IMF Conference on Inflation Targeting. Lima Peru: Central Bank of Peru, March.

Calvo, G. 1999. Testimony on Full Dollarization, presented at a Joint Hearing of the Subcommittees on Economic Policy and International Trade and Finance, April.

Corbo, V., and Klaus Schmidt-Hebbel. 2000. Inflation Targeting in Latin America, presented at the Latin American Conference on Fiscal and Financial Reforms, Stanford University, November.

Corbo, V., Ó. Landerretche, and Klaus Schmidt-Hebbel. 2002. Does Inflation Targeting Make a Difference? In *Inflation Targeting in the World: Design, Performace, Challenges*, edited by N. Loayza and R. Soto. Santiago: Central Bank of Chile, forthcoming.

Devereux, Michael B., and Charles Engel. 1999. The Optimal Choice of Exchange-Rate Regime: Price Setting Rules and Internationalized Production. National Bureau of Economic Research, Working Paper 6992, March.

Goldfajn, I., and G. Olivares. 2000. Is Adopting Full Dollarization the Solution? A Look at the Evidence. Pontificia Universidade Católica, Discussion Paper no. 416.

Hamada, K. 1998. Economic Consequences of Pegging to the Dollar in a Multicurrency World. Yale University, unpublished manuscript.

Hausman, Ricardo. 1999. Should Thgere Be Five Currencies or One Hundred and Five? Foreign Policy 116: 65–79.

McCallum, Bennett T. 1999. Theoretical Issues Pertaining Monetary Unions. National Bureau of Economic Research, Working Paper no. 7393, October.

Mishkin, F., and Klaus Schmidt-Hebbel. 2001. One Decade of Inflation Targeting in the World. National Bureau of Economic Research, Working Paper no. 8397, July.

Morandé, F., and Klaus Schmidt-Hebbel. 2000. Chile's Peso: Better than (Just) Living with the Dollar? *Cuadernos de Economía* 110: 117–226.

Powell, A., and F. Sturzenegger. 2000. The Link between Devaluation and Default. Paper presented at the Meeting on Dollarization, Universidad Torcuato di Tella, Buenos Aires, May.

Trejos, Alberto, and R. Wright. 1995. Search, Bargaining, Money and Prices. *Journal of Political Economy* 103: 118–41.

———, and ———. 2001. International Currency. Advances in Macroeconomics. *Bell Economic Journal* 1 (1).

# Commentary

*Ross Levine*

## 1. INTRODUCTION

Dollarization is a complex policy issue with obviously dramatic implications for central banks in countries that choose to dollarize. In analyzing the future of central banking in small, open economies, Alberto Trejos makes at least three contributions to the dollarization literature. First, he provides an excellent review of the standard arguments surrounding dollarization, focusing on seigniorage. Second, the paper stresses that countries are already dollarizing as bank liabilities and assets become increasingly dollar denominated. The paper suggests that dollarization is an inevitable process of openness for many countries. Third, the paper develops a bargaining model between a small country and a big country over the seigniorage revenues lost by the small country to the large country. The paper suggests that coordination can improve welfare in both countries. This coordination involves the small country "dollarizing" more quickly than it would without a bargained outcome, and the large country sharing some of its seigniorage gain with the small country. In my comments, I will briefly discuss each of the three contributions.

## 2. REVIEW OF THE MAJOR THEMES IN DOLLARIZATION

Trejos does a nice job of reviewing many of the big issues in dollarization, some of which have potentially large macroeconomic implications. Trejos notes that high-inflation countries may dollarize to reap the growth dividends of lower inflation. Some work suggests that inflation has substantial long-run growth effects. In recent work, Levine and Carkovic (2001) find that a substantial reduction in inflation—from, say, 14 percent to 4 percent, would induce an increase in the long-run per capita growth rate of 0.3 percentage point to 0.4 percentage point per year. This is substantial and would increase the actual growth rates that many Latin American countries have experienced in the last 30 years by 50 percent to 100 percent. One may question these estimates. Some researchers suggest the growth effects of inflation are much smaller; others, however, find similarly large growth effects. The point I want to emphasize is that potential growth effects such as these could turn the heads of some policymakers toward dollarization.

Trejos further notes that the currency risk premium reflected in some countries reaches 10 percentage points. Even in Costa Rica, where the central bank has achieved relatively stable inflation rates, the currency risk premium is sometimes estimated to run around 5 percentage points. Because financial intermediary credit to GDP has averaged about 20 percent of GDP in Costa Rica, a 5 percentage point drop in the interest rate would save borrowers approximately 1 percent of GDP in interest payments. In Argentina, the potential savings are larger, perhaps reaching 2 percent of GDP. These numbers are not staggering. However, they might not simply represent a level drop in interest payments. The drop in the cost of capital to firms could stimulate long-run productivity growth increases. These numbers may also be dubious. Again, the point is that some back-of-the-envelope calculations suggest that by eliminating a very costly currency risk premium imbedded in interest rates, dollarization could have large growth effects.

Trejos discusses other major dollarization issues. Dollarization may induce a reduction in transaction costs that eases international integration. Dollarization would eliminate independent monetary policy and, under some circumstances, limit the ability of the government to act as a lender of last resort. Dollarization might also force fiscal austerity and better bank regulation by eliminating discretionary monetary policy. Again, the point is that there are some reasons for believing that inflation, currency risk premiums, and relinquishing control of monetary policy are very big issues.

This discussion, however, raises the following question: Given these important factors in the dollarization debate, is bargaining over seigniorage revenue a critical issue? For instance, in a book on fiscal policy, Easterly, Rodriguez, and Schmidt-Hebbel (1994) show that seigniorage is not huge—perhaps a maximum of 1 percent–2 percent of GDP per year in the long run. They also show that in many developing countries, revenues from the tax on cigarettes are greater than seigniorage revenues. I would really like the current paper to provide evidence—or rough calculations—that suggest that bargaining over seigniorage is a first-order issue. This is particularly important because the paper suggests that many countries are losing seigniorage revenue anyway as residents increasingly move into dollars.

### 3. THE INEVITABILITY OF DOLLARIZATION

Trejos' paper suggests that many countries are on an inevitable path toward dollarization and that this trend has been increasing and will continue to increase. Maybe.

If this is the case, then the paper has obviously enormous implications for the future shape of central banking. If international integration is a decisively attractive building block of economic success, and if international integration is leading inexorably to dollarization, then we will end up with the type of world discussed by Alberto Trejos: a world with few currencies. This is important and could change the nature of the discussion about dollarization. If dollarization were an inevitable product of lowering official taxes and limits on transacting with the rest of the world, then this would importantly alter the debate.

This still strikes me as an open question, however: How much confidence should we have in the claim that as countries become increasingly open, they will move persistently toward dollarization? I would like to see more convincing evidence that countries are moving toward dollarization because of openness and not because people have little confidence in the domestic policy regime. In a nice paper, Savastano (1992) shows that dollar-denominated deposits as a share of total deposits vary considerably over time in Latin American countries. How much confidence should we have that recent trends in Latin America are going to continue?

## 4. BARGAINING OVER SEIGNIORAGE

The paper develops a nice bargaining model based on joint work with Wright. I would simply like to pose a few questions about the focus of the model.

Is the United States really going to bargain over seigniorage revenue with a very small country, especially when (1) the country already holds a substantial portion of its medium of exchange in U.S. dollars; and (2) the model presumes an ongoing process of dollarization, so that the U.S. is going to get all of the seigniorage revenue in the end anyway? I would benefit from additional arguments that bargaining over seigniorage revenue will be a crucial element in shaping central banking over the next 20 years.

This paper made me think, and I urge others to read it. It gave a great review of major policy issues, and it forced me to reconsider where dollarization fits into the literature on international financial liberalization.

REFERENCES

Easterly, William, Carlos A. Rodriguez, and Klaus Schmidt-Hebbel. 1994. *Public Sector Deficits and Macroeconomic Performance*. New York: Oxford University Press.

Levine, Ross, and Maria Carkovic. 2001. How Much Bang for the Buck? Mexico and Dollarization. *Journal of Money, Credit, and Banking* 33(2): 339–63.

Savastano, Miguel. 1992. The Pattern of Currency Substitution in Latin America: An Overview. *Revista de Analysis Economico* 7: 29–72.

# PART III

## PRIVATE ALTERNATIVES
## TO CENTRAL BANKS

# 5

# Banking Panics and the Origin of Central Banking

*Gary Gorton and Lixin Huang*

## 1. INTRODUCTION

Central banking is a twentieth-century phenomenon. According to Capie (1997), there were only 18 central banks at the beginning of the twentieth century. By 1950, there were 59 central banks, and by 1990 there were 161. At the beginning of the twentieth century, the U.S. Federal Reserve System had not yet been established; this would occur in 1914. The Bank of Canada came into being *after* the Great Depression, in 1934. Prior to the twentieth century, central banks were established as institutions with monopoly rights over money issuance. But if a critical element of central banking is the function of lender of last resort, then these institutions generally did not become central banks until later, typically during the twentieth century. For example, although the Bank of England was established in 1694, it did not behave as a lender of last resort until much later (Lovell 1957).

Explicit government deposit insurance is an even later development than the lender-of-last-resort role of government central banks. In 1980, only 16 countries had explicit deposit insurance programs; by 1999, 68 countries had such programs (Garcia 1999; Demirgüç-Kunt and Sobaci 2000). Deposit insurance was adopted in the United States in 1934 and in Canada in 1967. In Germany, deposit insurance remains a private scheme, set up and run by the banks themselves. As with central banking generally, not only is deposit insurance late in developing, but also there is substantial cross-sectional variation as to whether it is private or public.

While the spread of central banks in the twentieth century is likely related to the growth of activist monetary policy, it has been difficult to explain the origin of central banking. According to Goodhart (1985), central banks evolved as a response to banks' inability to cope with panics. This was a natural evolution because some private banks assumed special roles in their capacity as the government's bank. These banks "evolved" into central banks.

West (1974) and Timberlake (1987) focus on the origin of the Federal Reserve System, relating it to the real bills doctrine. Livingston (1986) argues that the Federal Reserve System came into being as part of the rise of finance capital, a manifestation of class struggle. Smith (1936) argues that central banks came into being as a tool to raise revenue for the government, but he says little about the lender-of-last-resort role of central banks. In the case of Canada, Bordo and Redish (1987) argue that its central bank's origin was essentially political—there was no economic rationale. Indeed, it is not an oversimplification to say that political explanations predominate over economic explanations in the literature on central banking.

Why was central banking, by which we mean the lender-of-last-resort function, late in developing? Why did it develop in some countries first and not in others? Similarly, why is deposit insurance such a modern institution, when panics have occurred for some time in some economies? Gorton and Huang (2001) argue that the development of a central banking role as lender of last resort, as well as deposit insurance, is intimately connected to the industrial organization of the banking system. Central banking first developed as a private response to problems in banking systems with many small, undiversified banks. In such systems, uninformed depositors need to monitor their banks. Briefly, depositors know the state of the macroeconomy, but not the idiosyncratic state of their own bank. The way to check on a bank is to ask the bank to convert its demand deposits into currency. But banks, as a whole, cannot do this, and the banking system faces liquidation. In response, banks form coalitions that can turn illiquid loan portfolios into liquid claims, convincing depositors that the banks, as a group, are solvent, even if a depositor's particular bank may not be. This is the lender-of-last-resort function. But these problems do not arise in banking systems with a small number of well-diversified banks. Such banking systems do not experience panics or high bank failure rates. Notably, as in the case of Canada, they also do not develop central banks or adopt deposit insurance. These observations are important because they strongly suggest that banking panics are not a manifestation of an inherent problem with banks. We review the historical evidence further below.

The logic of Gorton and Huang's model closely follows the U.S. experience with panics. In the United States, private bank clearinghouses issued private money called "clearinghouse loan certificates" during panics. These certificates functioned as a form of deposit insurance from the depositors' point of view because they converted claims on a single bank into claims on a group of banks in a coalition. For depositors to accept these certificates, they must be convinced that banks will coinsure one another. The coinsurance system works only if there are banking panics; panics impose externalities on banks that are doing well, forcing them to subsidize and monitor the banks that are not doing well. Monitoring through the coalition is more efficient than it is without the coalition, because not all banks are closed in the panic. The coalition distinguishes banks doing well from those doing poorly, closing some of the latter banks and altering the incentives of other poorly performing banks. Banking panics play a critical economic function in enforcing the incentive compatibility of bank coalitions. Also, in order for the bank coalition to form during times of panic, the banks had to agree to mutually monitor each other to enforce reserve and capital requirements. This monitoring is the historical origin of bank examination and supervision.

To summarize, Gorton and Huang make three related points. First, banks are not inherently unstable institutions prone to panics. Rather, the likelihood of bank panics depends on the industrial organization of the banking system. A system with a few large, well-diversified banks is a very different system than one with many small, undiversified banks. In the latter system, panics occur. Second, banking panics serve an economic function because they correspond to depositors monitoring banks, which induces coalitions to engage in self-monitoring. Third, private bank coalitions are a more efficient way for monitoring to occur, but the coalitions function only if panics occur. Private bank coalitions have functioned as lenders of last resort and have provided a form of deposit insurance.

To assess these arguments, we begin by surveying some of the historical evidence on the incidence of panics and the industrial organization of the banking system. We also look briefly at private bank coalitions. Private bank coalitions seem to have been most formally developed in the United States, though other countries also had such coalitions, less formally or in combination with a government central bank. Gorton and Huang's argument suggests that government central banks develop first as lenders of last resort in countries where the banking system consists of many small, undiversified banks. These systems would experience panics and would form private bank coalitions. Economic historians have not looked explicitly at this rather complicated set of issues, but comparing Canada and the United States is informative, as these two systems contrast differing types of banking systems.

Next, we examine some of the costs of banking panics that contemporary observers of panics have highlighted. The costs concern disruptions of the transactions system during banking panics. It appears that during panics, when the value of bank liabilities comes into question, they stop functioning as a circulating medium. This evidence is reviewed as a prelude to our main theoretical argument as to why the government assumed the role of lender of last resort, supplanting private bank coalitions.

The theoretical argument we propose begins where Gorton and Huang leave off. In particular, Gorton and Huang do not explain why the government needs to take over the role of the private bank coalitions of clearinghouses. Indeed, they suggest that it is not obvious how the government can improve upon the private arrangements, lending credence to the view that political explanations are perhaps most persuasive in explaining why the government introduced central banks. In this paper, we extend Gorton and Huang's model to include a role for consumers using bank liabilities as a medium of exchange. This seems like a natural extension because bank liabilities do, indeed, serve this role. We show that, although panics can discipline banks by forcing coalitions to behave incentive compatibly, panics disrupt the use of bank liabilities as a medium of exchange. This is costly. Because, according to this argument, a panic itself is costly, the government may improve welfare if panics can be avoided. But panics are not just irrational runs on banks; they serve an economic function. So, if the government eliminates panics with deposit insurance, then the government must take over the function of monitoring banks. The government may not be as effective at monitoring as the private coalitions, resulting in a cost. Whether the government central bank is superior to the private arrangements depends on this trade-off.

The paper proceeds as follows: In Section 2, we briefly review some of the historical and cross-country evidence on the performance of banking systems and the history of panics. The goal of this review is to provide a context that a model should take into account. In particular, we summarize the experience of banking systems historically and internationally. In Section 3, we review Gorton and Huang's model and basic results. In Section 4, we extend the model to include a role for consumers/depositors to use bank liabilities (banknotes or demand deposits) as a circulating medium of exchange. We then introduce a government central banking scheme and analyze the welfare implications of the government's scheme in contrast to the private bank coalition system. We provide conditions under which welfare improves under the government's scheme. Section 5 concludes.

## 2. PANICS AND THE INDUSTRIAL ORGANIZATION OF BANKING: HISTORICAL AND CROSS-COUNTRY EVIDENCE

In this section, we briefly summarize research on banking history: in particular, the incidence and timing of banking panics in different countries, specifically in relation to the industrial organization of the banking industry. Then we compare the experiences of Canada and the United States to emphasize the differences. We briefly review the workings of bank coalitions, focusing on the American clearinghouse system. Finally, we discuss the disruption of the payments system during panics.

To begin, we need a definition of a "banking panic." Calomiris and Gorton (1991) define a panic as an event in which bank debt holders (depositors) at many or even all banks in the banking system suddenly demand that their banks convert their debt claims into cash (at par), to such an extent that banks cannot jointly honor these demands and suspend convertibility. This definition excludes events in which a single bank faces a run; a panic is a systemwide phenomenon. Also, cases in which depositors seek to withdraw large amounts from the banking system, but banks can honor these withdrawals, are not "panics," although the banking system may shrink significantly. This definition is specific enough to differentiate the event of interest from other events with nebulous names such as "financial crisis," "contagion," and so on. For a discussion of bank panic definitions in the literature, see Gorton and Winton (forthcoming).

Using the above definition, Calomiris and Gorton (1991) identify six panics in the United States prior to 1865, seven during the national banking era, and, finally, the panics of the Great Depression. In each case, the phenomenon of interest is complicated, appears to have special circumstances, and seems to vary in important respects from other episodes, making any definition and inference problematic. In fact, there are few observations of panics in any country, making hypothesis testing difficult. Nevertheless, some important empirical regularities have been found.

### 2.1. Some Empirical Regularities about Panics

Banking panics are more likely to occur in certain types of banking systems and at certain stages of the business cycle. Because the U.S. economy has had the most experience with panics (for reasons we discuss below), most of the research has focused on the United States. The banking panic regularities are documented in a fairly large literature on the historical and international experience of banking panics, and we review it only briefly here. Bordo (1985, 1986), Calomiris and Gorton (1991), Calomiris (1993), and Gorton and Winton (forthcoming) survey much of the literature and provide some new evidence on the causes of panics. Andrew (1908a, 1908b), Sprague (1910), Wicker (1980, 1996, 2000), Donaldson (1993), Moen and Tallman (1992, 2000), Calomiris and Schweikart (1991), McGrane (1924), and White (1984), among many others, study individual episodes of U.S. panic.

The most important empirical regularity is that the industrial organization of the banking industry is a critical determinant of an economy's propensity to experience panics. As Calomiris (1993) summarizes, "International comparisons of the incidence and costs of banking panics and bank failures, and comparisons across regulatory regimes within the United States, clearly document differences in banking instability associated with different regulatory regimes. The central lesson of these studies is that instability is associated with some historical examples of banking that had common institutional characteristics; it is not an intrinsic problem with banking per se ... the single most important factor in banking instability has been the organization of the banking industry" (21). Basically, banking panics are much less likely to occur in banking systems in which there are a few relatively large, well-branched, and well-diversified banks. Bordo (1986) studies the experiences of six countries (United States, United Kingdom, Canada, Sweden, Germany, and France) during 1870–1933; one of his conclusions is that most severe cyclical contractions in all the countries were associated with stock market crises, but not with banking panics, except for the United States. He notes, "In contrast with the U.S. experience, the five other countries in the same period developed nationwide branch banking systems consolidating into a very few large banks" (230). Bordo (1985) surveys banking and securities market panics in six countries from 1870 to 1933 and concludes "the United States experienced panics in a period when they were a historical curiosity in other countries" (73). Grossman (1994) examines the experience of Britain, Canada, and 10 other countries during the Great Depression to determine the causes of the "exceptional stability" exhibited by their banking systems. He considers three possible explanations: the structure of the banking system, macroeconomic policy and performance, and the behavior of the lender of last resort. He concludes that banking stability is the product of exchange rate policy and banking structure.

Cross-sectional variation within the United States is also interesting because some states allowed branch banking while other states did not. States that allowed branching experienced lower failure rates in the 1920s, and it was the smaller banks that were more prone to failure (see Bremer 1935; White 1983, 1984). Studying this cross-section of state experiences, Calomiris (1990) reaches the same conclusion about the importance of branching: "States that allowed branch banking saw much lower failure rates—reflecting the unusually high survivability of branching banks… From 1921 to 1929 only 37 branching banks failed in the United States, almost all of which operated only one or two branches. Branching failures were only 4 percent of branch-banking facilities, almost an order of magnitude less than the failure rate of unit banks for this period" (291). Calomiris (1993) reviews more evidence.

A second apparent regularity concerning banking panics is that there is an important business cycle and, possibly, a seasonal component to the timing of panics. Panics come at or near business cycle peaks. The interpretation is not that panics cause the downturns: There is not enough data to analyze that issue. Rather, the idea is that depositors receive information forecasting a recession and withdraw in anticipation of the recession, a time when bank failures are more likely (Bordo 1986; Gorton 1988; Calomiris and Gorton 1991; Donaldson 1993). While the relation of panics to the business cycle will be incorporated into the model below, the "regularity" is somewhat fragile, as there are few observations of panics. Some have argued that there is also a seasonal factor in panics; this factor is noted by Andrew (1907), Kemmerer (1910), Miron (1986), Donaldson (1993), and Calomiris and Gorton (1991), among others. But Wicker (2000), for example, disputes the evidence. The seasonal factor seems less clear than the business cycle component.

## 2.2. The Canadian and U.S. Banking Experiences

A comparison of the U.S. and Canadian banking experiences from the middle of the nineteenth century is an instructive example of the importance of industrial organization in banking and its relation to central banking. This comparison is interesting because Canada is a system that historically has consisted of a small number of highly branched banks, in contrast to the American system of many banks that were not, until recently, branched across state lines, and sometimes not even within the state. Canada's central bank came into existence in 1934, and deposit insurance was adopted in the late 1960s. The differences between the two systems are striking and have often been commented upon (see the citations below).

The United States set up the National Banking System in 1863–64. In this system, fairly high capital requirements were imposed on federally chartered banks, and there was a bond backing system for note issuance, reserve requirements, and other requirements, particularly the prohibition of branch banking across state lines. Canada followed a very different set of banking policies, allowing branch banking and imposing relatively fewer restrictions. The different national regulations led to very different banking systems. During 1870–1913, Canada had a branch banking system with about 40 chartered banks, each extensively branched. In 1890, the United States had more than 8,000 independent unit banks (Williamson 1989).

Haubrich (1990), Bordo, Rockoff, and Redish (1994, 1995), and White (1984), among others, study the different experiences of the two systems. In particular, there were high failure rates in the United States and low failure rates in Canada. Thirteen Canadian banks failed from 1868 to 1889. Depositors lost very little in these cases (zero in eight of the cases) (Vreeland, Weeks, and Bonynge 1910, 219). During the same period, there were hundreds of failures in the United States (OCC 1920). In contrast to the United States, there were no panics in Canada. Bordo, Rockoff, and Redish (1994) summarize the contrast in the experiences of the two systems: "There is an immediate and important difference between the Canadian and United States banking systems. The Canadian experience has been one of considerable stability. There has been only one major bank failure since World War I, and there were no failures during the Great Depression. In contrast, the American system has been characterized by a number of periods of instability. Rates of bank failures were high in the 1920s, and of course the entire system collapsed during the 1930s" (325).

The comparative experience of the Great Depression shows that while there were few bank failures in Canada, the Canadian banking system did shrink. According to White (1984), "In Canada, from 1920 to 1929, only one bank failed.

The contraction of the banking industry was carried out by the remaining banks reducing the number of their offices by 13.2 percent. This was very near the 9.8 percent decline in the United States...In spite of the many similarities with the United States, there were no bank failures in Canada during the years 1929–1933. The number of bank offices fell by another 10.4 percent, reflecting the shocked state of the economy; yet this was far fewer than the 34.5 percent of all bank offices permanently closed in the United States" (132). The Canadian banking system survived the Great Depression with few effects, while in the United States, which had enacted the Federal Reserve Act in 1914, the banking system collapsed. Canada's central bank came into being in 1935, well after the Great Depression. Furthermore, Bordo and Redish (1987) argue that the Bank of Canada was introduced for political rather than economic reasons.

### 2.3. Bank Coalitions in the United States and Other Countries

Until the last few years, there has been a very large number of rather small, undiversified banks in the United States. The United States also stands out as an outlier in the frequency of banking panics during its history. The research cited above strongly suggests that these two facts are linked. There is another, related fact: U.S. banking history has been intertwined with the development of the private clearinghouse system. Clearinghouses are private associations of banks that formed in major cities, spreading across the country during the nineteenth century. Originally having roots in the payments system, these organizations developed into important institutions for monitoring banks and creating liquidity in times of banking panic. We briefly describe the functioning of these U.S. clearinghouses and then briefly mention other bank coalitions in other countries and contexts. (On the U.S. clearinghouse system, see Andrew 1908b; Cannon 1910; Gorton 1984, 1985; Gorton and Mullineaux 1987; Timberlake 1984; Sprague 1910; Moen and Tallman 2000; Wicker 2000.)

The U.S. clearinghouse system developed over the course of the nineteenth century. For purposes here, the main point concerns the method that clearinghouses developed to turn illiquid loan portfolios into money—private money that could be handed out to depositors in exchange for their demand deposits during times of panic. Clearinghouse loan certificates originated in the interbank clearing system as a way to economize on cash during a panic. During a banking panic, member banks were allowed to apply to a clearinghouse committee, submitting assets as collateral in exchange for certificates. If the committee approved the submitted assets offered in exchange, then certificates would be issued, up to a percentage of the face value of the assets. The bank borrowing against its illiquid assets would have to pay interest on the certificates to the clearinghouse. The certificates could then be used to honor interbank obligations where they replaced cash, which instead could be used to pay depositors.

The clearinghouse loan certificate process is the origin of the discount window (it is described in detail in the above-cited sources) and serves the same function. One difference, however, is that under the private clearinghouse system, a member bank's application for loan certificates was secret. The identity of a weak member bank was not revealed. Notably, the loan certificates were the joint obligation of the clearinghouse member banks; the risk of member banks defaulting was shared by allocating member liabilities in proportion to member bank capital. Thus, the certificates were a risk-sharing device by which the members jointly assumed the risk that individual member banks would fail.

During the panics of 1873, 1893, and 1907, the clearinghouse loan certificate process was extended—in increasingly sophisticated ways—in a radical innovation. In particular, the clearinghouse loan certificates were issued directly to bank depositors in exchange for demand deposits, in denominations corresponding to currency. The amount of private money issued during times of panic was substantial. During the panic of 1893, about $100 million in clearinghouse hand-to-hand money was issued (2.5 percent of the money stock). During the panic of 1907, about $500 million was issued (4.5 percent of the money stock) (Gorton 1985). If the depositors accepted the certificates as money, then the banks' illiquid loan portfolios would be directly monetized. Like the interbank arrangement of loan certificates, the certificates issued directly to the public were the joint liability of the clearinghouse, not the individual bank. In this way, a depositor who feared his particular bank might fail was able to insure against this event by trading his claim on the individual bank for a claim on the portfolio of banks in the clearinghouse. This was the origin of deposit insurance.

Clearinghouses in the United States also developed bank examination and supervision methods, as well as reporting systems for information to be made public on a regular basis. (As previously mentioned, the revelation of information about individual banks was suspended during banking panics.)

The U.S. clearinghouse system was not the only private central bank–like institution. Before the U.S. Civil War, coincident with the beginnings of the clearinghouse system, the Suffolk Bank of Massachusetts was the focal point of a clearing system and acted as a lender of last resort during the panic of 1837 (see Mullineaux 1987; Calomiris and Kahn 1996; Rolnick, Smith, and Weber 1998a,b; Whitney 1878).

Bank coalitions are also not unique to the United States (see Cannon [1910] for information on the clearinghouses of England, Canada, and Japan). While most countries did not experience banking panics as frequently as the United States, there are many examples of bank coalitions forming on occasion in other countries as well. We mention a few examples. The Clearing House of Montreal was main-ained by the Canadian Bankers' Association and, according to Watts (1972), was officially recognized in 1901 "as an agency for the supervision and control of cer-tain activities of the banks" (18). According to Bordo and Redish (1987), "the Bank of Montreal (founded in 1817) emerged very early as the government's bank per-forming many central bank functions. However, the Bank of Montreal never evolved into a full-fledged central bank as did the Bank of England (or the gov-ernment's bank in other countries) perhaps because of the rivalry of other large Canadian banks (for example the Royal Bank)" (see Watts 1972; Haubrich 1990; Breckenridge 1910).

The pattern of the Bank of Montreal (and earlier precursors like the Suffolk Bank in the United States), in which the bank coalition is centered on one large bank, is quite common. Another common feature is the cooperation of a (perhaps informal) coalition of banks with the government to rescue a bank in trouble or to stem a panic. For example, major Canadian banks joined with the Canadian government to attempt to rescue the Canadian Commercial Bank in March 1985 (Jayanti, Whyte, and Do 1993). Similarly, in Germany, the Bankhaus Herstatt was closed on June 26, 1974. There was no statutory deposit insurance scheme in Germany, but the West German Federal Association of Banks used $7.8 million in insurance to cover the losses.

Germany is a particularly interesting case because it is a developed capitalist country where deposit insurance is completely private, provided by coalitions of private banks (there is a coalition for each of the three types of banking institutions) following the Herstatt crisis of 1974 (see Beck n.d.). It is not compulsory, and there is no public supervision. Germany is interesting in being so late in developing even a formal private coalition. But the German banking system is one dominated by a few very large banks. Gorton and Huang (2001) label such systems "big bank systems" and argue they have a much lower incidence of panic, hence little need for bank coalitions. In subsequent failures, the coalition of German banks worked in concert with public officials to resolve the situations (see Beck n.d.).

To summarize, private coalitions of banks have historically been important in functioning as lenders of last resort and in providing deposit insurance. Even today, private coalitions perform this function in many countries.

### 2.4. The "Currency Famine" during Panics

Banking panics may be costly because they disrupt the economy's transactions technology, which is based in large part on conducting trade with banknotes and bank deposits. Because agents in the economy doubt the value of bank-circulating liabilities during panics, and because banks suspend convertibility, trade can no longer be conducted with bank liabilities, but only with currency. As a result of this, scared agents begin to hoard currency, refusing to deposit it into banks. This causes currency to go to a premium. Companies cannot meet payrolls or conduct business; money substitutes begin to develop. The disruption of the transactions system has been described as a "currency famine." This description of a panic has not been formally studied by modern researchers, but it corresponds to the observations of contemporary observers and early-twentieth-century researchers. We briefly provide more detail.

Sprague (1910) describes the aftermath of a panic in this way: "A far more serious cause of disturbance from the suspension of payments is the dislocation of the domestic exchanges. In making payments at a distance local substitutes for money will not serve. When the banks in one locality refuse to remit to banks elsewhere upon drafts and checks sent to them for payment business must soon come to a standstill" (75). When bank liabilities are no longer acceptable as transactions media, agents in the economy start to hoard cash. Again, Sprague (1910) writes: "Uncertain whether the banks would provide the money they might shortly need, many persons began to discontinue paying into the banks cash received in the course of daily business" (68). Instead, people hoard currency (Sprague 1910; Andrew 1908a,b; Noyes 1909).

Such hoarding of currency has two effects. First, businesses cannot meet payrolls because there is not enough currency (Sprague 1910, 71). Sprague quotes the *Commercial and Financial Chronicle*, September 16, 1893:

> The month of August will remain memorable as one of the most remarkable in our industrial history. Never before has there been such a sudden and striking cessation of industrial activity. Nor was any section of the country exempt from the paralysis; mills, factories, furnaces, mines nearly everywhere shut down in large numbers, and commerce and enterprise were arrested in an extraordinary and unprecedented degree. The complete unsettlement of confidence and the derangement of our financial machinery, which made it impossible to obtain loans or sell domestic exchange and which put money to a premium over checks, had the effect of stopping the wheels of industry and of contracting production and consumption within the narrowest of limits, so that our internal trade was reduced to very small proportions—in fact, was brought almost to a standstill—and hundreds and thousands of men thrown out of employment. (202)

Second, currency goes to a premium, causing money substitutes to arise (Sprague 1910; Andrew 1908a,b; Noyes 1909). Andrew (1907a) and Sprague (1910) record the currency premiums during various panics. During the panic of 1907, the premium was as high as 4 percent. Again, Sprague writes: "While it is possible, though not probable, that the currency premium increased the domestic money supply, it is certain that it vastly increased the amount of money required for a given volume of transactions. Evidence for this conclusion is found in the apparent dearth of money which followed immediately the announcement that banks restricted payments" (195–96). Andrew (1907b) describes and estimates the volume of substitutes for cash that arose during the panic of 1907.

While the clearinghouse system developed over the course of the nineteenth century, clearinghouse money issued during panics was not sufficient to eliminate the hoarding of cash and the consequent currency premiums. The shock of the panic to the transactions system was sudden and uneven, affecting distant areas more dramatically. Because of withdrawals from banks just prior to suspension of convertibility, the money supply would drop by the money multiplier. Outstanding bank liabilities would no longer be acceptable. The extent of the consequent real effects on production and output has not been formally studied.

## 3. THE MODEL

The evidence in Section 2 suggests that banking systems are not inherently unstable, and panics are related to the industrial organization of the banking system. Gorton and Huang (2001) present a model consistent with this evidence. In this section, we review the details of their model and summarize their results as a prelude to extending their analysis. There are two core assumptions in the model. First, there is asymmetrical information: Banks are better informed than their depositors. Second, banks may engage in moral hazard if their equity falls below a critical value. These are fairly standard assumptions. Not surprisingly, these assumptions sometimes lead depositors to want to withdraw their bank deposits. Withdrawals may be inefficient because the bank may, in fact, be quite well off, but depositors do not know this.

### 3.1. The Gorton and Huang Model

The model economy has three dates, 0, 1, and 2, and two types of agents, consumers/depositors and bankers.

Bankers are unique in their ability to locate risky investment opportunities. Also, only banks can store endowments (that is, provide the service of safekeeping). There is a continuum of bankers. Each banker has capital $\beta$ and a measure 1 of potential depositors. Each bank has access to a riskless storage technology and to a risky investment technology. The share of the portfolio invested in the riskless storage technology is $\alpha$, subsequently referred to as "reserves." Investments in risky projects must be made at date 0, and the returns are realized at date 2. The date-2 return to a risky project depends on the state of the economy, which is a random variable realized at date 1. The return to a unit (of endowment good) invested in the risky project is $\tilde{\pi} + \tilde{r}$—that is, there is a systematic component, $\tilde{\pi}$, and an idiosyncratic component, $\tilde{r}$, to the return. The systematic component $\tilde{\pi}$ is uniformly distributed in the interval $[\pi_L, \pi_H]$. For future reference, the probability-density function of $\tilde{\pi}$ will be referred to as $A$, where $A \equiv \dfrac{1}{\pi_H - \pi_L}$. The idiosyncratic return for a risky project, $\tilde{r}$, is uniformly distributed in the interval $[0, 2M]$. For future reference, the mean of $\tilde{r}$ will be denoted by $M$, that is, $M = \dfrac{0 + 2M}{2}$.

At date 1, information about the date-2 return is realized, but there is asymmetrical information between bankers and depositors. Depositors observe the realized state of the macroeconomy ($\pi$), but they do not observe the realized state of their bank's idiosyncratic return, $r$. In addition to observing the macroeconomic state, each banker knows his own bank's state, $r$, and observes the realizations of other banks' idiosyncratic shocks at date 1. Idiosyncratic shock realizations at date 1 are not verifiable among banks, but realized cash flows at date 2 are verifiable. Therefore, banks cannot write contracts with other banks contingent on idiosyncratic shocks at date 1. At date 0, we assume the banks' choice of reserve level ($\alpha$) and the level of bank capital ($\beta$) are observable and verifiable.

There is a moral hazard problem, in that bankers have an opportunity to engage in fraud, which is socially wasteful, at date 1. If a banker engages in fraud, he gets a proportion $f$ of the return—that is, $f(\pi + r)$—where $f$ is between 0 and 1. The remaining amount, $(1 - f)(\pi + r)$, is wasted and depositors receive nothing. Projects can be liquidated at date 1, yielding a constant return of $Q$, regardless of the state of the project. A risky project is indivisible when liquidation occurs. Although a banker can choose how much to invest in a risky project at date 0, at date 1 all the assets in a risky project must be liquidated if liquidation occurs.

Each depositor/consumer is endowed with one (indivisible) unit of perishable endowment good at date 0. At date 0, depositors can choose to consume or deposit in the bank. If they deposit in the bank, they can choose to withdraw at date 1 or date 2 (see the discussion in Gorton and Huang 2001 concerning the optimality of the deposit contract). Depositors have a subsistence level of 1. Their utility function is

$$u(c_1, c_2) = \begin{cases} c_1(HE_1) + c_2(HE_2) & \text{if} \quad c_0 + c_1 + c_2 \geq 1 \\ -\infty & \text{if} \quad c_0 + c_1 + c_2 < 1 \end{cases}$$

where $c_i$ is consumption at date $i$ and for $E_2 > E_1 > 0$, $E_1$ and $E_2$ are arbitrarily small. In the analysis below, we ignore $E_1$ and $E_2$. Depositors will consume everything at a single date and will prefer to consume later if they can consume the same amount of consumption goods.

Depositors' utility function implies they will withdraw at date 1 if they anticipate any chance their bankers are going to engage in fraud. This is because they will receive less than one unit back if their banker engages in fraud, as explained below. Depositors deposit in a single bank.

Finally, bankers are risk neutral, and they get the entire surplus from investment. The promised payment to depositors is equal to one, regardless of when (date 1 or date 2) depositors withdraw.

To make the problem interesting, Gorton and Huang make the following assumptions:

**ASSUMPTION 1.** $(1 + \beta)(1 - f)(\pi_L + M) < 1$. This assumption assures there is a potential moral hazard problem. Suppose the economy turns out to be in the worst possible state $(\pi_L)$ at date 1. If a banker with the mean return $\pi_L + M$ engages in fraud, he will receive $f(1 + \beta)(\pi_L + M)$. If he does not engage in fraud, his payoff will be $(1 + \beta)(\pi_L + M) - 1$. The assumption that $(1 + \beta)(1 - f)(\pi_L + M) < 1$ ensures the banker has an incentive to engage in fraud.

**ASSUMPTION 2.** $\pi_L > Q > f(\pi_H + 2M)$. There is a deadweight loss if liquidation or fraud occurs.

**ASSUMPTION 3.** $\dfrac{\pi_L + \pi_H}{2} + M > 1 > Q$. In other words, a risky project is more efficient ex ante than riskless storage if there is no liquidation or fraud. However, if liquidation or fraud occurs, then the risky project is dominated by investment in riskless storage.

**ASSUMPTION 4.** $(1 + \beta)Q > 1$. If depositors withdraw from their bank at date 1, then their deposit contract can always be honored.

Depositors are rational in anticipating that their banker may have an incentive to engage in moral hazard in certain states of the world. If depositors anticipate that the banker is going to engage in fraud, they will withdraw their deposits to prevent it. This corresponds to monitoring. Bankers can commit to not engaging in moral hazard by holding reserves. The higher the level of reserves, the lower the probability that a bank run will occur. However, ex post, if the state of the economy is good at date 1, then it would have been better to invest in risky projects. The bankers' task at date 0 is to choose an optimal reserve level, $\alpha$ (the share of bank assets held in the riskless storage technology). This is the only choice variable.

Banks provide a way to transfer wealth from period to period because they are unique in being able to identify risky investment opportunities; consumers/ depositors cannot find these opportunities. In addition, banks can provide a claim—a demand deposit—which is consistent with the subsistence requirement of consumers. Because of their utility functions, consumers need to be assured that their claim will be worth one unit and that banks can satisfy this need. Implicitly, individual banks can diversify to this extent. The utility function is a reduced form of a consumer demand for a riskless trading claim (Gorton and Pennacchi 1990). The structure of preferences dictates the type of claim that banks will offer depositors: The bank must offer the right to withdraw deposits at face value at date 1, that is, a demand deposit contract. This is for simplicity.

### 3.2. Summary of the Results on Different Types of Banking Systems

Gorton and Huang analyze three types of banking systems. The first is a system of independent unit banks, which are undiversified. The second is a system of a few large, diversified banks. The system of small, independent "unit banks" and that of "big banks," as they are labeled, are essentially benchmark systems for comparison with the third system, one in which the banks form a coalition.

In the system of independent unit banks, the banks are small in the sense that a banker in charge of a unit bank can manage only one risky project. Such a banker cannot diversify risk by dividing his asset portfolio into many risky projects. In the unit banking system, at date 1 depositors observe the state of the macroeconomy, $\pi$, and can calculate whether, given that state, there is a chance that their banker will engage in moral hazard. Because their utility functions are kinked and they will get $-\infty$ if consumption is less than one, depositors do not care about the likelihood of moral hazard occurring, but whether there is *any chance* of moral hazard occurring. If depositors find there is a chance that bankers will engage in fraud (that is, $\pi < \dfrac{1-\alpha}{(1-f)(1+\beta-\alpha)}$), then they withdraw all their savings.[1]

Because all depositors receive the same macroeconomic information and all the banks are, from their viewpoint, homogeneous, if one bank suffers from a run, there will be runs on all the other banks. Therefore, a panic occurs. In terms of the model, a *banking panic* is a date-1 event in which depositors at all banks seek to withdraw their deposits and all banks are liquidated.

At date 0, anticipating what will happen in different states of the world at date 1, bankers choose the optimal reserve level to maximize their expected payoff. On one hand, bankers want to maximize investment in risky projects because it is more

---

[1] Suppose the banker has reserves of $\alpha$, and the realized idiosyncratic shock is $r = 0$. The realized state of the macroeconomy is $\pi$. If the banker does not engage in fraud, he earns $\pi(1 + \beta - \alpha) + \alpha - 1$. If he does engage in fraud, he earns $\pi f(1 + \beta - \alpha)$ because he cannot steal anything from the reserves. If $\pi f(1 + \beta - \alpha) > \pi(1 + \beta - \alpha) + \alpha - 1$, or $\pi < \dfrac{1-\alpha}{(1-f)(1+\beta-\alpha)}$, the banker engages in fraud. Otherwise, he has no incentive to engage in fraud.

profitable; on the other hand, they want to avoid being prematurely liquidated in a banking panic at date 1. When the reserve level is greater than or equal to

$$\bar{\alpha} \equiv \frac{1 - (1 + \beta)(1 - f)\pi_L}{1 - (1 - f)\pi_L},$$ banks have no incentive to engage in fraud, even if

the macroeconomy is in its lowest state, $\pi_L$. There is a unique, optimal level of reserves in the interval $[0, \bar{\alpha}]$ that solves unit banks' date-0 profit-maximization problem.

The big bank system is a different form of industrial organization. A big bank is a bank with a portfolio of assets that has a realized return of $\pi + M$ at date 1. In other words, its return is the systematic return plus the diversified idiosyncratic mean return, $M$. This is the essential point—the idiosyncratic risk is implicitly diversified away by virtue of the bank's size through branching. Consequently, at date 1, when the state of the economy is revealed, the return to a big bank's risky projects is also known. The state of the macroeconomy is sufficient information for assessing the state of a big bank. As a result, depositors know for sure whether a big bank is going to engage in moral hazard. If they anticipate that their big bank will engage in fraud, they run on the big bank. Otherwise, they wait until date 2 to withdraw.

Besides the fact there is no information asymmetry with big banks, there is another important difference: Big banks have the flexibility to partially liquidate their portfolios at date 1. In fact, a big bank only needs to liquidate some of the risky projects when a bank run occurs. It is assumed that liquidation (and fraud) can occur at the project level. In order to deal with depositors' withdrawals at date 1, a big bank only needs to liquidate a fraction $x$ of the risky projects, such that $\alpha + (1 + \beta - \alpha) xQ = 1$. Actually, however, a big bank can do even better if it can commit to not engaging in fraud by liquidating some of the projects and holding the proceeds as additional reserves. Although the risky projects have idiosyncratic returns, for simplicity we assume they have the same liquidation value, $Q$.

Suppose the big bank liquidates a fraction $x$ of the risky projects. It should liquidate optimally, as follows: It will liquidate projects that have realized idiosyncratic returns, $r$, in the interval $[0, x2M]$. The remaining $(1 - x)$ fraction of projects has higher realized idiosyncratic returns $r$ in the complementary interval $[x2M, 2M]$. The average return on the remaining—that is, nonliquidated—$(1 - x)$ fraction of projects is

$$\pi + \frac{x2M + 2M}{2} = \pi + (1 + x)M.$$

If the big bank allows the remaining projects to continue without engaging in fraud, its payoff is $\alpha + (1 + \beta - \alpha) xQ + (1 + \beta - \alpha)(1 - x)[\pi + (1 + x) M] - 1$. If the big bank engages in fraud on the remaining projects, its payoff will be $f(1 + \beta - \alpha)(1 - x)[\pi + (1 + x) M]$. Therefore, to convince depositors that moral hazard will not occur, the big bank has to liquidate a fraction $x$ of the risky projects such that $\alpha + (1 + \beta - \alpha) xQ + (1 + \beta - \alpha)(1 - x)(\pi + (1 + x) M) - 1 \geq f(1 + \beta - \alpha)(1 - x)[\pi + (1 + x) M]$. The optimal $x$ is the solution to the following problem:

$$\text{Max}_x \; \alpha + (1 + \beta - \alpha) xQ + (1 + \beta - \alpha)(1 - x)[\pi + (1 + x) M] - 1$$

$$\text{s.t. } (1 + \beta - \alpha)(1 - x)[\pi + (1 + x) M] - 1 \geq f(1 + \beta - \alpha)(1 - x)[\pi + (1 + x) M]$$

$$x \in [0, 1].$$

Gorton and Huang solve this problem and provide the unique optimal fraction to liquidate at date 1. Then the date-0 problem is solved for the choice of reserve level. For our purposes here, note that in the big bank system, banks may experience withdrawals at date 1, but they do not fail—that is, they are not liquidated. In the model, there is no difference between the bank liquidating projects and holding the proceeds as reserves and withdrawals. In other words, the big bank system can be viewed as experiencing deposit withdrawals, but there are no bank runs or failures. The big bank system does not experience banking panics. The independent unit banks have bank runs and failures because each unit bank's project is indivisible when liquidation occurs.

In broad outlines, the distinction between the big bank system and the system of small, independent unit banks corresponds to the difference between the Canadian and U.S. banking systems. As mentioned above, the Canadian system displayed fewer failures and no panics.

### 3.3. The Setting with Bank Coalitions

Finally, there is the case of bank coalitions. The basic idea for the coalition is as follows: Suppose there are small, independent unit banks at date 0. These small unit banks can decide to form a coalition at date 0, and the coalition can partially replicate the big bank in certain states of the world at date 1. The coalition is defined by rules concerning date-0 reserve and capital levels, as well as rules indicating that, if there is a panic at date 1, some banks will be liquidated and the remaining banks must follow a prespecified sharing rule (the details are in Gorton and Huang 2001). At date 0, unit banks can get together to form a coalition and reach an agreement about their individual capital and reserve levels. Because the idiosyncratic shocks are not verifiable—and thus not contractible—the coalition has no power to force its members to comply with the rules, and the member banks are free to quit at any time. The only requirement to become a member of the coalition at date 0 is to hold the required reserve (and capital) level. At date 1, depositors cannot observe whether the coalition rules have been carried out; they can only observe whether the coalition liquidates some of the member banks and combines the assets and liabilities of the remaining member banks.

The operation of the coalition intends to achieve two goals. First, by liquidating some of the member banks, the coalition tries to inform depositors that the nonliquidated banks are in relatively more sound states. This partially alleviates the panic caused by the asymmetrical information between the banks and depositors. Second, by pooling liabilities, the coalition tries to convince depositors that incentives to engage in fraud can be removed by monitoring and coinsurance among the remaining banks.

Gorton and Huang show that if there is no panic at date 1, then no bank coalition will operate. Banks will behave as unit banks. Because the rules of the coalition, adopted at date 0, are not binding, banks are free to deviate from those rules. They can, in principle, adopt any set of rules concerning transfers among members (as long as such rules satisfy the budget constraint for the coalition). Without a panic, banks will always deviate from the proposed coalition rules. The banking panic creates an externality for banks that would not engage in the moral hazard problem, the "good" banks. If good banks did not face a panic, they would have no incentive to monitor the banks that are going to engage in fraud, the "bad" banks. Because depositors cannot distinguish good banks from bad banks, all banks face the prospect of being liquidated. This creates the incentive for good banks to monitor bad banks.

Depositors anticipate that if they do not run on the banks, the coalition will not do anything to prevent member banks from engaging in fraud. Therefore, they run on all banks if and only if[2]

$$\pi < \frac{1 - \alpha}{(1 - f)(1 + \beta - \alpha)}.$$

Once depositors run on the banks, the coalition must operate to convince depositors that it can remove the incentives to engage in fraud from some of its member banks, and, therefore, there is no need to liquidate those banks.

Gorton and Huang prove the existence of a coalition equilibrium (see their definition). In this equilibrium, banks with idiosyncratic shocks $r \in [0, x^*(\alpha, \pi)2M]$

---

[2]  At date 1, each member bank in the coalition holds reserves of $\alpha$ when the state of the economy $\pi$ is realized.

If $\pi \geq \dfrac{1 - \alpha}{(1 - f)(1 + \beta - \alpha)}$, then even the bank with the lowest idiosyncratic shock ($r = 0$) has no incentive to

engage in fraud. Hence, there is no need for depositors to run on the banks. If $\pi < \dfrac{1 - \alpha}{(1 - f)(1 + \beta - \alpha)}$, then some banks have an incentive to engage in fraud.

are liquidated and these bankers are paid $\alpha + (1 + \beta - \alpha)(Q - 1)$, their outside option value of deviating from the coalition. The cut-off point $x^*(\alpha, \pi)$ is given by

$$x^*(\alpha, \pi) = \max\{0, \min\{1, \frac{1 - \alpha - \pi(1 - f)(1 + \beta - \alpha)}{M(1 - f)(1 + \beta - \alpha)} - 1\}\}.^3$$

No member bank quits the coalition, and no bank engages in fraud. For banks that are not liquidated, there is a specified set of transfers.

The coalition behaves as a lender of last resort by monitoring and by providing insurance. Monitoring corresponds to liquidating bad banks, that is, those with the worst idiosyncratic shock realizations. Member banks of type $r \in [0, x^*(\alpha, \pi)2M]$ are liquidated; these banks would have engaged in fraud. The insurance comes from the transfers implemented among the nonliquidated banks. Member banks of type $r \in [x^*(\alpha, \pi)2M, 2M]$ are not liquidated, but are assigned new debt obligations. Their original debt, that is, face value of the demand deposits, was one.

Banks with $r < \dfrac{1 - \alpha}{(1 - f)(1 + \beta - \alpha)}$ have their debt reduced, so these banks are subsidized to entice them not to engage in fraud. This is efficient because their projects are worth more if they are continued, so long as they do not engage in fraud. Member banks with $r < \dfrac{1 - \alpha}{(1 - f)(1 + \beta - \alpha)} - \pi$ have their debt increased,

so these banks are being taxed to pay the subsidy to the banks with low $r$. Banks with high idiosyncratic shock realizations cannot be taxed too much or they will engage in fraud. Transfers of the debt obligations must satisfy a budget constraint, which limits how much insurance the coalition can provide and, therefore, determines the point at which member banks are liquidated.

---

[3] To prevent a banker with idiosyncratic shock $r$ from engaging in fraud, the coalition must promise him a payoff of at least $f(1 + \beta - \alpha)(\pi + r)$. Therefore, to convince depositors that their deposits are safe if they accept clearinghouse loan certificates, the coalition must satisfy the condition

$$\int_{x2M}^{2M} [\alpha + (1 + \beta - \alpha)(\pi + r) - 1] dF(\bar{r}) \geq \int_{x2M}^{2M} f(1 + \beta - \alpha)(\pi + r) dF(\bar{r}).$$

Solving for $x$, we can rewrite the condition as $x \geq \dfrac{1 - \alpha - \pi(1 - f)(1 + \beta - \alpha)}{M(1 - f)(1 + \beta - \alpha)} - 1.$

The fraction $x$ is between 0 and 1. Therefore, imposing this condition, in order to convince depositors that the remaining banks have no incentives to engage in fraud, the coalition must liquidate a fraction $x$ of the member banks, such that $x \geq x^*(\alpha, \pi) \equiv \max\{0, \min\{\dfrac{1 - \alpha - \pi(1 - f)(1 + \beta - \alpha)}{M(1 - f)(1 + \beta - \alpha)} - 1\}\}.$

At date 0, each bank must decide whether to join the coalition, and the coalition must determine the optimal reserve level $\alpha$. For comparison purposes later, the optimal reserve for the coalition is the solution to the following:

$$\text{Max}_\alpha \int_{\pi_L}^{\pi^r} [\alpha + (1 + \beta - \alpha)xQ + (1 + \beta - \alpha)(1 - x)(\pi + (1 + x)M) - 1]\, dF(\tilde{\pi}) +$$

$$\int_{\pi^r}^{\pi^H} [\alpha + (1 + \beta - \alpha)(\pi + M) - 1]\, dF(\tilde{\pi})$$

$$\text{s.t.} \quad \pi^r = \frac{1 - \alpha}{(1 - f)(1 + \beta - \alpha)}$$

$$x = \max\left\{0, \min\left\{1, \frac{1 - \alpha - \pi(1 - f)(1 + \beta - \alpha)}{M(1 - f)(1 + \beta - \alpha)} - 1\right\}\right\}.$$

$$\alpha \in [0, \bar{\alpha}].$$

The coalition system is an intermediate case between the unit bank system and the big bank system. The similarity between the coalition system and the independent unit bank system is that we may observe bank failures (that is, liquidations) when the economy is in a bad state. The similarity between the coalition system and the big bank system is that the coalition can monitor and insure member banks when the economy is in a bad state, while the big bank "monitors" itself by closing branches. The unique feature associated with the coalition is that when a panic occurs, it suspends convertibility and issues certificates. This feature is important because it is a commitment made to depositors that the nonliquidated member banks will not engage in fraud, and it provides incentives for member banks to monitor and insure each other.

### 3.4. Summary

With respect to efficiency, Gorton and Huang show that the big bank system is more efficient than the coalition system, which is more efficient than the independent unit banking system. Realistically, no economy is likely to exactly correspond to the big bank system, though some countries, such as Canada and Germany, may come close. Almost all economies may be expected to have some form of coalition, with the degree of formality being related to the incidence of panics.

A key remaining issue concerns why private coalitions were replaced by the government in the form of deposit insurance and government banks acting as lender of last resort. Gorton and Huang do not explain why government central banks replaced private bank coalitions. In fact, in their model, there is no obvious rationale for the government to step in and provide the lender-of-last-resort function, unless the government has much more power than private agents, more resources than private agents, or there are costs to panics that have not been considered. They consider each of these possibilities in turn and conclude the first two possibilities are unrealistic.

If the government can simply intervene at date 1 and prevent fraud, then the government can improve welfare compared to any of the private arrangements. But this does not seem realistic. Nor is it realistic to assume the government can make transfers at date 2, contingent upon the banks' idiosyncratic shock realizations. Governments are likely to be less informed than the banks themselves.

## 4. GOVERNMENT CENTRAL BANKS VS. PRIVATE BANK COALITIONS

An important role of banks is to provide a transactions medium. This role was not considered in the analysis above. In this section, we extend the model to introduce a transactions role for bank liabilities. This is a natural extension, as bank liabilities do in fact function as a medium of exchange. We then analyze what happens to the transaction capabilities of bank money when there is a banking panic. We show that the transactions system based on bank money is disrupted in a costly way when there is a panic. Moreover, the problem appears to be similar to that discussed by contemporary observers of panics. In particular, during panics the problem is the sudden disappearance of bank liabilities as an acceptable form of exchange—there is a "currency famine."

The incentive-compatible functioning of the coalition requires the existence of panics. But the bank coalition does not take the disruption of the transactions medium into account; it does not internalize this cost. Consequently, we examine a role for government intervention in banking, specifically, to replace the private bank coalitions. We consider two possible government policies. First, the government can set a level of required reserves that takes the costs of panics into account. Panics will still happen, but they will be less frequent than under the private system. With panics still occurring, the coalition will still function. A better system might be to eliminate panics all together. Thus, the second policy is one of deposit insurance. Under this system, panics are eliminated, but the government must replace banks in monitoring. It may be reasonable to assume the government is not as effective as private banks in monitoring; therefore, if the government monitors, there is a cost that may offset the benefits of eliminating panics. We will analyze the welfare implications of these various policies.

### 4.1. Bank Liabilities as a Medium of Exchange

We now introduce a transactions role for bank liabilities, extending the above model as follows. First, we introduce a new set of agents, sellers of goods. Sellers are located at different locations, indexed by $s \in [0, S]$, where $s$ is the distance from the consumers/depositors. Each seller can produce a consumption good at a constant cost of one unit. There are many sellers at each location, so the market for consumption goods at different locations is competitive and the price of a consumption good is always one. We assume the markets for consumption goods close shortly after date 1, and it takes time for consumers to find the consumption goods they prefer. Consumers cannot carry their date-0 endowments to the distant locations because their endowments are perishable. Neither can they trade the withdrawals from banks (at date 1 or date 2) for their preferred consumption goods because if they wait until date 1, there will be no time to locate the sellers before the markets are closed. Therefore, the only way to buy the consumption goods at a distant location is to travel to the place at date 0 and pay for the goods with bank deposits. When a seller sells a good to a depositor/consumer, the seller receives a claim on a distant bank. Clearing bank liabilities is assumed to be costless, so long as sellers accept them.

To capture the idea of a division of labor and a preference over goods of different types, we assume the consumers/depositors prefer products purchased further away from their hometown. So $s$ also represents depositors' taste. We modify the depositors' utility function to include $s$:

$$u(c_1, c_2) = \begin{cases} s + (c_0 + c_1 + c_2) \text{ if} & c_0 + c_1 + c_2 \geq 1 \\ -\infty & \text{if} & c_0 + c_1 + c_2 < 1 \end{cases}$$

Because trade can occur only with bank deposits, we have $s = 0$ if $c_0 > 0$ or if $c_2 > 0$ (that is $s > 0$ only if $c_1 > 0$).

Consumers/depositors have a subsistence level of one unit, but now they prefer larger $s$. If $s = 0$, then the consumer/depositor is simply consuming one unit of the consumption good purchased at the home location, and the utility function is the same as before. According to the utility function, consumers have a taste for goods purchased some distance from home, so they must travel to make purchases. Similar ideas are modeled in Lucas (1980), Wallace (1988), and Gorton (1996). Note that $s$ is not proportional to the quantity of consumption. In addition, we assume there is a round-trip traveling/search cost, $C(s) = \kappa s^2$, which is nonpecuniary. This cost is associated with shopping for the consumption good.

Implicitly, the notion of traveling to shop introduces three new ideas, though they remain in the background. First, we implicitly introduce heterogeneous goods because goods are now indexed by their distance from the consumer/depositor's home location. Linking the type of good to the distance of the search implicitly suggests that searching for goods that the consumer really likes is costly. This is captured by the costs specified above. Second, goods can only be purchased with bank liabilities. We assume consumers cannot carry their own endowments to the distant location and trade with sellers because their endowments are perishable.

So barter is ruled out, which seems realistic. Third, by assuming that markets close shortly after date 1, we assume depositors must find sellers before economic uncertainties are resolved, introducing the possibility that markets might be disrupted. At the time a consumer meets a seller, the information about the macroeconomy arrives. The information affects the seller's decision about whether to accept bank deposits. Imagine the consumer is at the distant location, and there is a state of the macroeconomy in which a panic is needed to prevent bankers from engaging in moral hazard. In that case, the consumer's bank claim (note or deposit) will not be accepted by sellers. Sellers sell to consumers from different places, and they cannot go to different places to run on different banks at the same time. If sellers cannot accept bank claims and run on banks, then depositors themselves have to go back to run on banks. Once they travel back and obtain loan certificates, depositors will not have a second chance to buy their preferred goods at distant locations because they have no time to find a seller before the markets close. Therefore, while a panic is desired to prevent the moral hazard problem, it disrupts the markets for consumption goods at the same time.

Because the model is one of a representative agent, when there is a panic, the consumers/depositors return to their banks and demand that their claims be redeemed for one unit of endowment. There is no issue of the consumers/depositors arriving at different times and having their claims honored sequentially. In fact, this would not matter in any case, because all of their claims can be honored by assumption. Thus, the cause of panics in Diamond and Dybvig (1983), the sequential service constraint, is not an issue here. In the model here, depositors' withdrawals are not motivated by beliefs about (sunspots that are believed to be related to) the actions of other depositors. Rather, they are only motivated by the desire to prevent the moral hazard problem, that is, to monitor bankers. The assumed structure of preferences motivates depositors to avoid the moral hazard problem.

The sequence of events can be recapitulated as follows:

1.  At date 0, consumers/depositors consume their one unit of endowment or save it by depositing it in the bank. They are promised one unit from banks at either date 1 or date 2, at the consumer/depositor's discretion. They decide to search/travel to buy consumption goods (the cost is sunk) at a distant location.

2.  At date 1, while depositors are at the distant location, the macroeconomic state is revealed.

3.  If there is no need for a panic, consumers/depositors pay for their purchases with a bank liability drawn on their home location bank, which is then costlessly cleared. If a panic is needed, then (in equilibrium) depositors have to go back to their home location to liquidate their bank, receiving loan certificates and consuming home location products.

Before we solve the banks' profit-maximization program under different types of banking systems, we first solve for the consumers/depositors' optimal choice of $s$, the distance to travel at date 1, given that the promised payment from the banks is equal to one, and also taking the probability of panic, $\eta$, as given. The probability of panic is determined in equilibrium and will vary depending on the type of banking system we are in, as analyzed below. At date 1, consumers/depositors have one unit on deposit at the bank, which can be spent on consumption goods. They choose $s$ to solve the following optimization problem, recognizing the travel cost is given by $C(s) = \kappa s^2$:

$$\text{Max}_s \ (1 - \eta)(1 + s - \kappa s^2) + \eta(1 - \kappa s^2).$$

The solution is given by:

**LEMMA 1:** *Given a probability of panic, $\eta$, the optimal distance $s^*$ to travel equals* $\dfrac{1 - \eta}{2\kappa}$, *and depositors' utility $U(s^*)$ is equal to* $1 + \dfrac{(1 - \eta)^2}{4\kappa}$.

**PROOF:** It is trivial to show that the objective function is strictly concave in $s$. The first-order condition is $(1 - \eta) - 2\kappa s = 0$; therefore, the optimal $s^*$ is equal to $\dfrac{1 - \eta}{2\kappa}$.

Substituting in $s^*$ to get the maximum value of the objective function, $1 + \dfrac{(1 - \eta)^2}{4\kappa}$. //

For future reference, we note that:

**LEMMA 2:** *The optimal distance to travel and depositors' utility is decreasing in the probability of panic, $\eta$.*

The specification of preferences over distant goods and the cost of traveling to these locations has introduced a cost of a bank panic. Our interpretation is that the payments system is disrupted, causing a decline in utility. This is because when there is a banking panic, distant markets are effectively closed. The private coalition of banks will not consider this additional cost because they have to pay depositors one unit in any case. There is no way for the banks to extract the depositors' additional utility benefit from traveling to the distant locations to shop.

The cost of panics generates a possible reason for the government to intervene in the banking system, possibly eliminate panics, and improve social welfare. There are two distinct costs that arise. First, the possibility of panic introduces the chance there will be no trade at the distant location. Because sellers cannot travel to run on banks, they will not accept bank liabilities in exchange for goods if the macroeconomic state is in a panic. No trade lowers utility. This effect is independent of the cost of traveling/searching, $C(s)$. Second, because of this cost, consumers/

depositors, recognizing there is a chance of no trade occurring, reduce travelling/searching intensity $s$ ex ante (lemma 2).

We now proceed by analyzing the social welfare associated with different regulatory systems. Social welfare is defined as the sum of banks' payoffs and depositors' utility. As mentioned above, we analyze three banking systems. First, we recapitulate the private bank coalition system, analyzed by Gorton and Huang. Next, we consider a system in which the government enforces reserve requirements that reduce the likelihood of panic at date 1. Finally, we analyze a system of government deposit insurance combined with the government monitoring banks at date 1. We seek to learn how the government can improve social welfare.

### 4.2. The Private Bank Coalition

If there is no government intervention, bankers do not internalize the cost of market failure caused by panics. The optimization problem for the bank coalition is given in Gorton and Huang (2001). To be clear, the optimization problem is restated here. When $\pi$ is less than $\pi^r$, panic occurs and the coalition is forced to liquidate a fraction $x$ of its member banks.

$$\text{Max}_\alpha \int_{\pi_L}^{\pi^r} [\alpha + (1 + \beta - \alpha)xQ + (1 + \beta - \alpha)(1 - x)[\pi + (1 + x)M] - 1]\, dF(\tilde{\pi}) +$$

$$\int_{\pi^r}^{\pi^H} [\alpha + (1 + \beta - \alpha)(\pi + M) - 1]\, dF(\tilde{\pi})$$

$$\text{s.t.} \quad \pi^r = \frac{1 - \alpha}{(1 - f)(1 + \beta - \alpha)}$$

$$x = \max\left\{0, \min\left\{1, \frac{1 - \alpha - \pi(1 - f)(1 + \beta - \alpha)}{M(1 - f)(1 + \beta - \alpha)} - 1\right\}\right\}.$$

$$\alpha \in [0, \bar{\alpha}].$$

Gorton and Huang solve the bank coalition problem to determine the optimal level of reserves. That solution does not change here. We use $\alpha^C$ to denote the optimal reserve level. The following proposition gives the social welfare under the private bank coalition system.

**PROPOSITION 1:** *Let $\alpha^C$ denote the optimal reserve level for the private bank coalition system. Panic occurs with probability*

$$\eta^C = A(\pi^r - \pi_L) = A\left(\frac{1 - \alpha^C}{(1 - f)(1 + \beta - \alpha^C)} - \pi_L\right).$$

*Social welfare is equal to*

$$\int_{\pi_L}^{\pi^r} [\alpha^C + (1+\beta-\alpha^C)x^C Q + (1+\beta-\alpha^C)(1-x^C)(\pi+(1+x^C)M] \, dF(\tilde{\pi}) +$$

$$\int_{\pi_r}^{\pi^H} [\alpha^C + (1+\beta-\alpha^C)(\pi+M)-1] \, dF(\tilde{\pi}) + 1 + \frac{(1-\eta^C)^2}{4\kappa}$$

*where*

$$\pi^r = \frac{(1-\alpha^C)}{(1-f)(1+\beta-\alpha^C)},$$

$$x^C = \max\{0, \min\{1, \frac{1-\alpha^C-\pi(1-f)(1+\beta-\alpha^C)}{M(1-f)(1+\beta-\alpha)}-1\}\}.$$

**PROOF:** If $\alpha^C$ is the optimal reserve level, the panic occurs when the macroeconomic state $\pi$ is less than the critical value

$$\pi^r = \frac{1-\alpha^C}{(1-f)(1+\beta-\alpha^C)}.$$

The probability that panic occurs is

$$\eta^C = A(\pi^r - \pi_L) = A\left(\frac{1-\alpha^C}{(1-f)(1+\beta-\alpha^C)} - \pi_L\right).$$

Therefore, depositors' utility is equal to $1 + \dfrac{(1-\eta^C)^2}{4\kappa}$, and social welfare is just the sum of the banks' surplus and the depositors' utility. //

Because the individual banks and their coalition cannot extract the additional utility that depositors get from consuming goods produced at distant locations, the cost of panic is not internalized. The proposition simply calculates the implied probability of panic for that solution so that social welfare can be calculated. We will use this as a benchmark for comparing the government solutions.

### 4.3. A Government-Required Reserve Level

Because the private bank association system fails to internalize the cost of market failure—that is, the failure of the transactions media—the government can internalize the cost by imposing a minimum reserve level for banks at date 0. By imposing such a required reserve level, the government forces banks to hold more reserves, thereby lowering the probability of panic. This results in a decrease in the bankers' payoff and an increase in the depositors' utility. The government chooses the reserve level, $\alpha$, to solve the following problem:

$$\text{Max}_\alpha \int_{\pi_L}^{\pi^r} [\alpha + (1 + \beta - \alpha)xQ + (1 + \beta - \alpha)(1 - x)(\pi + (1 + x)M) - 1] \, dF(\tilde{\pi}) +$$

$$\int_{\pi^r}^{\pi^H} [\alpha + (1 + \beta - \alpha)(\pi + M) - 1] \, dF(\tilde{\pi}) + 1 + \frac{(1 - \eta)^2}{4\kappa}$$

$$\text{s.t.} \quad \pi^r = \frac{1 - \alpha}{(1 - f)(1 + \beta - \alpha)}$$

$$x = \max \{0, \min\{1, \frac{1 - \alpha - \pi (1 - f)(1 + \beta - \alpha)}{M(1 - f)(1 + \beta - \alpha)} - 1\}\}.$$

$$\eta = A(\pi^r - \pi_L) = A \frac{1 - \alpha}{(1 - f)(1 + \beta - \alpha)} - \pi_L .$$

$$\alpha \in [0, \bar{\alpha}].$$

The solution is given by proposition 2.

**PROPOSITION 2:** *The government's objective function has a unique maximum in the interval $[0, \bar{\alpha}]$. Moreover, if $\kappa$ is big enough, the government's objective function is strictly concave in $\alpha$ and there exists a unique solution, $\alpha \in [0, \bar{\alpha}]$, that solves the government's optimization problem.*
**PROOF:** See appendix.

Because the government takes consumers/depositors' welfare into account, unlike the private profit-maximization problem of the banks, it is not surprising that we get the following result.

**PROPOSITION 3:** *Government intervention with the required reserve level dominates the private coalition system by imposing a higher reserve level.*
**PROOF:** See appendix.

By imposing a required reserve level, the government decreases the probability that panic occurs, but it cannot eliminate panics. Panics are still needed for bankers to monitor and to coinsure each other when the economy is in low states, though the set of low states over which there can be a panic is reduced.

Perhaps it would be better to eliminate panics altogether. If panics are eliminated, then some agent must still monitor the banks. Because the role of panics is to cause banks to monitor each other, the elimination of panics must, at the same time, involve a scheme for bank monitoring. Suppose the government took over the task of monitoring the banks. If the government can monitor the banks, it can prevent bankers from engaging in fraud, and there is no need for depositors to run on banks. In other words, the government can make the depositors' deposits safe by monitoring the banks. This is equivalent to the government providing deposit insurance. We proceed to analyze social welfare under such a deposit insurance system.

### 4.4. Deposit Insurance

Suppose the government ensures that deposits will always be worth one unit. To make this claim credible, the government must monitor banks. Reasonably, the government may have a disadvantage in collecting information about the banks' idiosyncratic shocks, $r$. To reflect this disadvantage, we assume there is a cost ($C$) for the government to learn the banks' idiosyncratic shocks and to implement transfers between banks. Let us suppose that each bank holds a reserve level $\alpha$ and that the macroeconomic state is low, so that the government needs to monitor the banks. Then the government works as the banker of a big bank. It closes a fraction $x$ of the banks and taxes some of the $(1 - x)$ nonliquidated banks while subsidizing the other nonliquidated banks. In doing so, the government must meet its budget constraint:

$$\alpha + (1 + \beta - \alpha)\, xQ + (1 + \beta - \alpha)(1 - x)[\pi + (1 + x)\, M] \geq 1 + f(1 + \beta - \alpha)$$

$$(1 - x)[\pi + (1 + x)\, M] + C.$$

The left side consists of three parts: reserve $\alpha$, liquidation proceeds $(1 + \beta - \alpha)xQ$, and the cash flow from nonliquidated banks $(1 + \beta - \alpha)(1 - x)[\pi + (1 + x)\, M]$. The right side also consists of three parts: the one unit promised payment to depositors, a payoff to the nonliquidated banks $f(1 + \beta - \alpha)(1 - x)[\pi + (1 + x)\, M]$, and the government's monitoring cost, $C$. We make the following assumption on information-collection cost ($C$) to ensure there is a unique $x \in [0, 1]$ that will solve the above equation when some banks have incentives to engage in fraud.

**ASSUMPTION 5.** $(1 - f)(1 + \beta)M < C < (1 + \beta)Q - 1.$

At date 1, the government chooses $x$, the fraction of banks to liquidate, to solve the following problem:

$$\text{Max}_x\ \alpha + (1 + \beta - \alpha)\, xQ + (1 + \beta - \alpha)\, (1 - x)[\pi + (1 + x)\, M] - C$$

$$\text{s.t. } \alpha + (1 + \beta - \alpha)\, xQ + (1 + \beta - \alpha)(1 - x)[\pi + (1 + x)\, M] \geq 1 + f(1 + \beta - \alpha)$$

$$(1 - x)[\pi + (1 + x)\, M] + C$$

$$x \in [0, 1].$$

The solution is given by:

**LEMMA 3:** *There is a unique $x \in [0,1]$ that solves the above problem. The unique solution is*

$$x = \frac{Q - (1 - f)\pi - \sqrt{(Q - (1 - f)\pi)^2 - \dfrac{4M(1 - f)(1 + C - \alpha)}{1 + \beta - \alpha} + 4M(1 - f)^2 (\pi + M)}}{2M(1 - f)}$$

*Moreover, x is increasing in C.*

**PROOF:** See appendix.

The government's problem at date 0 can now be written as

$$\text{Max}_\alpha \int_{\pi_L}^{\pi^r} [\alpha + (1 + \beta - \alpha)xQ + (1 + \beta - \alpha)(1 - x)(\pi + (1 + x)M) - 1] \, dF(\tilde{\pi}) +$$

$$\int_{\pi^r}^{\pi^H} [\alpha + (1 + \beta - \alpha)(\pi + M) - 1] \, dF(\tilde{\pi}) + 1 + \frac{1}{4\kappa}$$

$$\text{s.t.} \quad \pi^r = \frac{1 - \alpha}{(1 - f)(1 + \beta - \alpha)}$$

$$x = \frac{Q - (1 - f)\pi - \sqrt{(Q - (1 - f)\pi)^2 - \dfrac{4M(1 - f)(1 + C - \alpha)}{1 + \beta - \alpha} + 4M(1 - f)^2 (\pi + M)}}{2M(1 - f)}$$

$$\alpha \in [0, \bar{\alpha}].$$

Solving the government's problem gives the following proposition:

**PROPOSITION 4:** *The government's objective function has a unique maximum in the interval $[0, \bar{\alpha}]$. Moreover, if C is small enough, the government's objective function is strictly concave in $\alpha$ and there exists a unique solution, $\alpha \in [0, \bar{\alpha}]$, that solves the government's optimization problem.*

**PROOF:** See appendix.

The central bank deposit insurance works as follows: At date 1, the state of the macroeconomy is realized, and the central bank calculates whether there are any banks with an incentive to engage in fraud. If the state of the macroeconomy is low and some banks have incentives to engage in moral hazard, then the central bank monitoring and insurance system is triggered. The central bank first monitors every individual bank to learn the realization of idiosyncratic shocks. Then it closes some of the banks (banks with idiosyncratic shocks in the interval $[0, xM]$) and taxes and subsidizes the remaining banks. Banks with

$$r < \frac{1-\alpha}{(1-f)(1+\beta-\alpha)} - \pi$$

are subsidized, and banks with

$$r < \frac{1-\alpha}{(1-f)(1+\beta-\alpha)} - \pi$$

are taxed. The final payoff to liquidated banks is zero, and to nonliquidated banks with idiosyncratic shock, $r$ is equal to $f(1 + \beta - \alpha)(\pi + r)$. The information-collection cost $C$ is paid from the liquidation proceeds and taxes.

Finally, we need to find out whether the government should provide deposit insurance to get rid of panics. This can be done by comparing the social welfare under the required reserve system with the social welfare under the deposit insurance system.

**PROPOSITION 5:** *The smaller the information collection cost $C$ and the traveling cost $\kappa$ are, the more likely that government deposit insurance is preferred.*

**PROOF:** See appendix.

### 5. CONCLUSION

Banking panics are not an inherent feature of banks. Rather, panics occur in certain kinds of banking systems. Banking panics can cause incentive-compatible private bank coalitions to arise to issue private coalition money, a sort of deposit insurance and lender of last resort. These points are made by Gorton and Huang (2001). We extend their model to show how government intervention in the banking system may be justified when the industrial organization of the banking system is such that there are many small, independent unit banks. Bank liabilities, banknotes, and bank deposits function as a transaction medium. But when there is a panic, this transactions system is disrupted, causing a loss of welfare. Banks do not take this cost into account when they organize their coalition. The government can, however, take this cost into account. If the government can monitor banks at a sufficiently low cost, then a system of deposit insurance can improve welfare. This is the origin of the lender-of-last-resort role of the government.

## APPENDIX

**PROOF OF PROPOSITION 2:** The central bank's optimization problem is

$$\text{Max}_\alpha \quad \int_{\pi_L}^{\pi^r} [\alpha + (1 + \beta - \alpha)xQ + (1 + \beta - \alpha)(1 - x)(\pi + (1 + x)M) - 1] \, dF(\tilde{\pi}) +$$

$$\int_{\pi^r}^{\pi^H} [\alpha + (1 + \beta - \alpha)(\pi + M) - 1] \, dF(\tilde{\pi}) + 1 + \frac{(1 + \eta)^2}{4\kappa}$$

$$\text{s.t.} \quad \pi^r = \frac{1 - \alpha}{(1 - f)(1 + \beta - \alpha)}$$

$$x = \max\left\{0, \min\left\{1, \frac{1 - \alpha - \pi(1 - f)(1 + \beta - \alpha)}{M(1 - f)(1 + \beta - \alpha)} - 1\right\}\right\}.$$

$$\eta = A(\pi^r - \pi_L) = A\left(\frac{1 - \alpha}{(1 - f(1 + \beta - \alpha)} - \pi_L\right).$$

$$\alpha \in [0, \bar{\alpha}].$$

Rewrite the objective function as $G(\alpha) + H(\alpha)$, where

$$G(\alpha) = \int_{\pi_L}^{\pi^r} [\alpha + (1 + \beta - \alpha)xQ + (1 - x)(\pi + (1 + x)M) - 1] \, dF(\tilde{\pi}) +$$

$$\int_{\pi^r}^{\pi^H} [\alpha + (1 + \beta - \alpha)(\pi + M) - 1] \, dF(\tilde{\pi})$$

and $H(\alpha) = 1 + \dfrac{(1 - \eta)^2}{4\kappa} = 1 + \dfrac{[1 - A(\pi^r - \pi_L)]^2}{4\kappa}.$

From the proof of the private coalition's problem (see Gorton and Huang 2001), we know that $G(\alpha)$ is a concave function in $\alpha$. We now show $H(\alpha)$ is convex in $\alpha$.

Because

$$\frac{d\pi^r}{d\alpha} = \frac{-\beta}{(1-f)(1+\beta-\alpha)^2} < 0, \quad \frac{d^2\pi^r}{d\alpha^2} = \frac{-2\beta}{(1-f)(1+\beta-\alpha)^3} < 0,$$

we have

$$H'(\alpha) = -\frac{1}{2\kappa} A[1 - A(\pi^r - \pi_L)] \frac{d\pi^r}{d\alpha} > 0$$

$$H''(\alpha) = \frac{1}{2\kappa} A^2 \left(\frac{d\pi^r}{d\alpha}\right)^2 - \frac{1}{2\kappa} A [1 - A(\pi^r - \pi_L)] \frac{d^2\pi^r}{d\alpha^2} > 0.$$

Therefore, the objective function $G(\alpha) + H(a)$ is not necessarily concave. However, because $G(\alpha) + H(\alpha)$ is continuous in $[0, \bar{\alpha}]$, and it has a finite value when $\alpha = 0$ and $\alpha = \bar{\alpha}$, there is a finite maximum in the interval $[0, \bar{\alpha}]$. $G''(\alpha) + H''(\alpha) < 0$ when $\alpha$ is sufficiently large enough. Therefore there can be a unique interior optimal reserve level, $\alpha \in [0, \bar{\alpha}]$, that solves the coalition's optimization problem. //

**PROOF OF PROPOSITION 3:** The optimal reserve level for the private coalition $\alpha^C$ is feasible for the central bank. When $\alpha < \alpha^C$, we have $G(\alpha) < G(\alpha^C)$ because $G(\alpha)$ reaches its maximum at $\alpha^C$, and we also have $H(\alpha) < H(\alpha^C)$ because $H(\alpha)$ is increasing in $\alpha$. Therefore, the optimal reserve level under central bank intervention is always higher than the one under the private coalition and the central bank intervention with the required reserve level dominates the private coalition. //

**PROOF OF LEMMA 3:** Let $F(x) = \alpha + (1 + \beta - \alpha) xQ + (1 + \beta - \alpha)(1 - f)(1 - x)$ $[\pi + (1 + x) M] - 1 - C$.

$F(x)$ is a continuous quadratic function of $x$. By assumption 5 we have $F(0) < 0$ and $F(1) > 0$. Therefore, solutions exist in the interval $[0, 1]$ for the equation $F(x) = 0$. The solution is the smaller root of the quadratic equation:

$$x = \frac{Q - (1-f)\pi - \sqrt{(Q - (1-f)\pi)^2 - \dfrac{4M(1-f)(1+C-\alpha)}{1+\beta-\alpha} + 4M(1-f)^2(\pi+M)}}{2M(1-f)}$$

Because $\dfrac{4M(1-f)(1+C-\alpha)}{1+\beta-\alpha}$ is increasing in $C$, $x$ is increasing in $C$. //

**PROOF OF PROPOSITION 4:** The central bank's problem at date 0 is

$$\text{Max}_\alpha \int_{\pi_L}^{\pi^r} [\alpha + (1 + \beta - \alpha)xQ + (1 + \beta - \alpha)(1 - x)(\pi + (1 + x)M) - 1 - C] \, dF(\tilde{\pi}) +$$

$$\int_{\pi^r}^{\pi^H} [\alpha + (1 + \beta - \alpha)(\pi + M) - 1] \, dF(\tilde{\pi}) + 1 + \frac{1}{4\kappa}$$

$$\text{s.t.} \quad \pi^r = \frac{1 - \alpha}{(1 - f)(1 + \beta - \alpha)}$$

$$x = \frac{Q - (1 - f)\pi - \sqrt{(Q - (1 - f)\pi)^2 - \dfrac{4M(1 - f)(1 + C - \alpha)}{1 + \beta - \alpha} + 4M(1 - f)^2 (\pi + M)}}{2M(1 - f)}$$

$$\alpha \in [0, \alpha].$$

Rewrite the objective function as

$$V(\alpha) - CA(\pi^r - \pi_L) + 1 + \frac{1}{4\kappa}, \text{ where}$$

$$V(\alpha) \equiv \int_{\pi_L}^{\pi^r} [\alpha + (1 + \beta - \alpha)xQ + (1 + \beta - \alpha)(1 - x)(\pi + (1 + x)M) - 1] \, dF(\tilde{\pi}) +$$

$$\int_{\pi^r}^{\pi^H} [\alpha + (1 + \beta - \alpha)(\pi + M) - 1] \, dF(\tilde{\pi})$$

$$= \alpha + (1 + \beta - \alpha)\left(\frac{\pi_L + \pi_{II}}{2} + M\right) - \int_{\pi_L}^{\pi^r} (1 + \beta - \alpha)x(\pi + xM - Q) \, dF(\pi) - 1.$$

Also rewrite

$$x(\alpha) = C_0 - (C_1 + \frac{C_2}{1 + \beta - \alpha})^{\frac{1}{2}} \text{ , where}$$

$$C_0 = \frac{Q - (1 - f)\pi}{2M - (1 - f)} \text{ ,}$$

$$C_1 = \frac{(Q - (1 - f)\pi)^2 - 4M(1 - f) + 4M(1 - f)^2(\pi + M)}{4M^2 - (1 - f)^2} \text{ ,}$$

$$C_2 = \frac{4M(1 - f)(\beta - C)}{4M^2(1 - f)^2} = \frac{\beta - C}{4M(1 - f)} \text{ .}$$

We have

$$\frac{\partial x}{\partial \alpha} = -\frac{C_2}{2} (C_1 + \frac{C_2}{1 + \beta - \alpha})^{-\frac{1}{2}} (1 + \beta - \alpha)^{-2}$$

and

$$\frac{\partial^2 x}{\partial \alpha^2} = -\frac{C_2^2}{4} (C_1 + \frac{C_2}{1 + \beta - \alpha})^{-\frac{3}{2}} (1 + \beta - \alpha)^{-4} - C_2(C_1 + \frac{C_2}{1 + \beta - \alpha})^{-\frac{1}{2}} (1 + \beta - \alpha)^{-3}$$

$$= \frac{C_2^2}{4} (C_1 + \frac{C_2}{1 + \beta - \alpha})^{-\frac{3}{2}} (1 + \beta - \alpha)^{-4} + 2(1 + \beta - \alpha)^{-1} \frac{\partial x}{\partial \alpha} \text{ .}$$

$$\frac{dV(\alpha)}{d\alpha} = 1 - \frac{\pi_L + \pi_H}{2} + M +$$

$$\int_{\pi_L}^{\pi^r} [\alpha + (1 + \beta - \alpha)xQ + (1 + \beta - \alpha)(1 - x)(\pi + (1 + x)M) - 1] \, dF(\tilde{\pi}) +$$

$$\frac{A\beta}{(1 - f)(1 + \beta - \alpha)} x(\pi^r + xM - Q)$$

$$\frac{d^2V(\alpha)}{d\alpha^2} = \int_{\pi_L}^{\pi^r} (2\frac{\partial x}{\partial \alpha} - (1 + \beta - \alpha)\frac{\partial^2 x}{\partial \alpha^2}) \, (\pi + 2xM - Q) \, dF(\tilde{\pi}) -$$

$$\int_{\pi_L}^{\pi^r} 2M \, (1 + \beta - \alpha)(\frac{\partial x}{\partial \alpha})^2 \, dF \, (\tilde{\pi}) + \frac{2A\beta}{(1 - f)(1 + \beta - \alpha)} \, (\pi^r + 2xM - Q) \frac{\partial x}{\partial \alpha}$$

Because

$$\frac{\partial x}{\partial \alpha} < 0, \quad 2\frac{\partial x}{\partial \alpha} - (1 + \beta - \alpha) \frac{\partial^2 x}{\partial \alpha^2} < 0, \text{ and } \pi + 2Mx - Q > 0,$$

we have

$$\frac{d^2 V(\alpha)}{d\alpha^2} < 0.$$

Therefore, $V(\alpha)$ is a strictly concave function of $\alpha$.

On the other hand, $-CA(\pi^r - \pi_L)$ is convex in $\alpha$ because $\pi^r$ is concave in $\alpha$. Therefore, the objective function is concave in $\alpha$ if and only if $C$ is small enough. Because the objective function is continuous and bounded for $\alpha \in [0, \bar{\alpha}]$, there always exists a unique solution. //

**PROOF OF PROPOSITION 5:** Social welfare under the deposit insurance system is decreasing in the information cost, $C$. Social welfare under the required reserve system is independent of the information cost $C$. Therefore, the smaller $C$ is, the more likely it is that deposit insurance dominates required reserve. On the other hand, if we fix $C$ and let the traveling cost, $\kappa$, change—because then the optimal reserve level in the deposit insurance system does not depend on $\kappa$—the difference in optimal social welfare under the two systems is decreasing in $\kappa$. The smaller $\kappa$ is, the more likely that deposit insurance dominates required reserve. //

### ACKNOWLEDGMENTS

The authors thank Eslyn Jean-Baptiste, Michael Bordo, John Boyd, Ed Green, and participants at the Federal Reserve Bank of Cleveland's Conference on the Origins of Central Banking for their comments and suggestions.

REFERENCES

Andrew, A. Piatt. 1907. The Influence of Crops upon Business in America. *Quarterly Journal of Economics* 20: 323–53.

———. 1908a. Hoarding in the Panic of 1907. *Quarterly Journal of Economics* February: 290–99.

———. 1908b. Substitutes for Cash in the Panic of 1907. *Quarterly Journal of Economics* August: 487–520.

Beck, Thorsten. n.d. Deposit Insurance as a Private Club: Is Germany a Model? World Bank, mimeo.

Bordo, Michael. 1985. The Impact and International Transmission of Financial Crises: Some Historical Evidence, 1870–1933. *Revista di Storia Economica* 2: 41–78.

———. 1986. Financial Crises, Banking Crises, Stock Market Crashes and the Money Supply: Some International Evidence, 1870–1933. In *Financial Crises and the World Banking System*, edited by Forrest Capie and Geoffrey Wood, 190–248. London: Macmillan.

Bordo, Michael, and Angela Redish. 1987. Why Did the Bank of Canada Emerge in 1935? *Journal of Economic History* 47: 405–17.

Bordo, Michael, Hugh Rockoff, and Angela Redish. 1994. The U.S. Banking System from a Northern Exposure: Stability versus Efficiency. *Journal of Economic History* 54: 325–41.

Bordo, Michael, Hugh Rockoff, and Angela Redish. 1995. A Comparison of the Stability and Efficiency of the Canadian and American Banking Systems, 1870–1925. National Bureau of Economic Research, Historical Working Paper no. 67.

Breckenridge, Roeliff Morton. 1910. *The History of Banking in Canada*. Washington, D.C.: Government Printing Office.

Bremer, C.D. 1935. *American Bank Failures*. New York: Columbia University Press.

Calomiris, Charles. 1989. Deposit Insurance: Lessons from the Record. *Federal Reserve Bank of Chicago Economic Perspectives* May/June: 10–30.

———. 1990. Is Deposit Insurance Necessary? A Historical Perspective. *Journal of Economic History* 50: 283–95.

———. 1993. Regulation, Industrial Structure, and Instability in U.S. Banking: An Historical Perspective. In *Structural Change in Banking*, edited by Michael Klausner and Lawrence White, 19–116. Homewood, Ill.: Business One Irwin.

Calomiris, Charles, and Gary Gorton. 1991. The Origins of Banking Panics: Models, Facts, and Bank Regulation. In *Financial Markets and Financial Crises,* edited by Glenn Hubbard, 109–73. Chicago: University of Chicago Press.

Calomiris, Charles, and Charles Kahn. 1996. The Efficiency of Self-Regulated Payments Systems: Learning from the Suffolk System. *Journal of Money, Credit, and Banking* 28: 766–97.

Calomiris, Charles, and Larry Schweikart. 1991. The Panic of 1857: Origins, Transmission, and Containment. *Journal of Economic History* 51: 807–34.

Cannon, James G. 1910. *Clearing Houses.* U.S. National Monetary Commission, 61st Cong., 2d sess., doc. 491. Washington, D.C.: Government Printing Office.

Capie, Forrest. 1997. The Evolution of Central Banking. In *Reforming the Financial System: Some Lessons From History.* Cambridge: Cambridge University Press.

Chapman, John M., and Ray B. Westerfield. 1942. *Branch Banking: Its Historical and Theoretical Position in America and Abroad.* New York: Harper and Brothers.

Curtis, C.A. 1931. Banking Statistics in Canada. In *Statistical Contributions to Canadian Economic History*, vol. 1. Toronto: Macmillan.

Demirgüç-Kunt, Asli, and Tolga Sobaci. 2000. Deposit Insurance around the World: A Data Base. World Bank, mimeo.

Donaldson, R. Glen. 1993. Financing Banking Crises: Lessons form the Panic of 1907. *Journal of Monetary Economics* 31: 69–95.

Diamond, Douglas, and Philip Dybvig. 1983. Bank Runs, Deposit Insurance, and Liquidity. *Journal of Political Economy* 91: 401–19.

Garcia, Gilian. 1999. Deposit Insurance: A Survey of Best Practices. International Monetary Fund, Working Paper no. 99/54.

Goodhart, Charles. 1985. *The Evolution of Central Banks: A Natural Development?* London: London School of Economics.

Gorton, Gary. 1984. Private Clearinghouses and the Origins of Central Banking. *Federal Reserve Bank of Philadelphia Business Review* January/February: 3–12.

———. 1985. Clearinghouses and the Origins of Central Banking in the U.S. *Journal of Economic History* 45: 277–83.

———. 1996. Reputation Formation in Early Bank Note Markets. *Journal of Political Economy* 104: 346–97.

Gorton, Gary, and Lixin Huang. 2001. Banking Panics and the Endogeneity of Central Banking. Wharton School of the University of Pennnsylvania, Working Paper.

Gorton, Gary, and Donald Mullineaux. 1987. The Joint Production of Confidence: Endogenous Regulation and the 19th Century Commercial Bank Clearinghouse. *Journal of Money, Credit, and Banking* 19: 457–68.

Gorton, Gary, and George Pennacchi. 1990. Financial Intermediaries and Liquidity Creation. *Journal of Finance* 45: 49–72.

Gorton, Gary, and Andrew Winton. Forthcoming. Financial Intermediation. In *Handbook of the Economics of Finance*, edited by George Constantinides, Milton Harris, and René Stulz.

Grossman, Richard. 1994. The Shoe that Didn't Drop: Explaining Banking Stability during the Great Depression. *Journal of Economic History* 54: 654–82.

Haubrich, Joseph. 1990. Nonmonetary Effects of Financial Crises: Lessons from the Great Depression in Canada. *Journal of Monetary Economics* 25: 223–52.

Jayanti, S.V., Ann Marie Whyte, and A. Quang Do. 1993. Bank Failures and Contagion Effects: Evidence from Britain, Canada and Germany. Cleveland State University, unpublished manuscript.

Kemmerer, E.M. 1910. *Seasonal Variations in the Relative Demand for Money and Capital in the United States*. U.S. National Monetary Commission, 61st Cong., 2d sess., doc. 588. Washington, D.C.: Government Printing Office.

Livingston, James. 1986. *Origins of the Federal Reserve System: Money, Class, and Corporate Capitalism, 1890–1913*. Ithaca, N.Y.: Cornell University Pres.

Lovell, Michael. 1957. The Role of the Bank of England as Lender of Last Resort in the Crises of the Eighteenth Century. *Explorations in Entrepreneurial History* 10: 8–21.

Lucas, Robert E. 1980. Equilibrium in a Pure Currency Economy. In *Models of Monetary Economics*, edited by John H. Kareken and Neil Wallace. Minneapolis, Mn.: Federal Reserve Bank of Minneapolis.

McGrane, Reginald. 1924. *The Panic of 1837: Some Financial Problems of the Jacksonian Era.* Chicago: University of Chicago Press.

Miron, Jeffrey. 1986. Financial Panics, the Seasonality of the Nominal Interest Rate and the Founding of the Fed. *American Economic Review* 76: 125–40.

Moen, Jon, and Ellis Tallman. 1992. The Bank Panic of 1907: The Role of Trust Companies. *Journal of Economic History* 52: 611–30.

———, and ———. 2000. Clearinghouse Membership and Deposit Contraction during the Panic of 1907. *Journal of Economic History* 60: 145–63.

Mullineaux, Donald. 1987. Competitive Monies and the Suffolk Bank System: A Contractual Perspective. *Southern Economic Journal* 53: 884–98.

Noyes, Alexander D. 1909. A Year After the Panic of 1907. *Quarterly Journal of Economics* 23: 185–212.

Office of the Comptroller of the Currency. 1920. *Annual Report*. Washington, D.C.: Government Printing Office.

Rolnick, Arthur, Bruce Smith, and Warren Weber. 1998a. Lessons from a Laissez-Faire Payments System: The Suffolk Banking System (1825–58). *Federal Reserve Bank of St. Louis Review* 80: 105–16.

———, ———, and ———. 1998b. The Suffolk Bank and the Panic of 1837: How a Private Bank Acted as a Lender-of-Last-Resort. Federal Reserve Bank of Minneapolis, Working Paper no. 592.

Smith, V. 1936. *The Rationale for Central Banking*. London: Whitefriars Press.

Sprague, O.M.W. 1910. *History of Crises under the National Banking System*. Washington, D.C.: Government Printing Office.

Timberlake, Richard. 1984. The Central Banking Role of Clearinghouse Associations. *Journal of Money, Credit, and Banking* 16: 1–15.

———. 1987. *The Origins of Central Banking in the United States.* Cambridge, Mass.: Harvard University Press.

Vreeland, Edward, John Weeks, and Robert Bonynge. 1910. *Interviews on the Banking and Currency Systems of Canada.* National Monetary Commission, 61st Cong., 2d sess., doc. 584. Washington, D.C.: Government Printing Office.

Wallace, Neil. 1988. Another Attempt to Explain an Illiquid Banking System: The Diamond and Dybvig Model With Sequential Service Taken Seriously. *Federal Reserve Bank of Minneapolis Quarterly Review*: 3–15.

Watts, George. 1972. The Origins and Background of Central Banking in Canada. *Bank of Canada Review* May:.

West, Robert Craig. 1974. Banking Reform and the Federal Reserve, 1863–1923. Ithaca, N.Y.: Cornell University Press.

White, Eugene N. 1983. *The Regulation and Reform of the American Banking System, 1900–1929.* Princeton, N.J.: Princeton University Press.

———. 1984. A Reinterpretation of the Banking Crisis of 1930. *Journal of Economic History* 44: 119–38.

Whitney, D. R. 1878. *The Suffolk Bank.* Cambridge, Mass.: Riverside Press.

Wicker, Elmus. 1980. A Reconsideration of the Causes of the Banking Panic of 1930. *Journal of Economic History* 40: 571–83.

———. 1996. *The Banking Panics of the Great Depression.* Cambridge: Cambridge University Press.

———. 2000. *Banking Panics of the Gilded Age.* Cambridge: Cambridge University Press.

Williamson, Stephen. 1989. Bank Failures, Financial Restrictions, and Aggregate Fluctuations: Canada and the United States, 1870–1913. *Federal Reserve Bank of Minneapolis Quarterly Review* Summer: 20–40.

# Commentary

*John H. Boyd*

This study is an interesting blend of banking history and theoretical analysis. It represents a continuation of a long series of papers by Gorton and coauthors (cited in the paper) on the endogenous formation of bank clearinghouses and how they can perform many of the functions of a central bank.

The *historical analysis* is largely based on a comparison of the Canadian and U.S. experience. In the United States, the central bank's function as lender of last resort (liquidity provider) grew out of and imitated private bank clearinghouses. These private clearinghouses entered into coalitions to provide liquidity in anticipation of and during bank panics. They cross-guaranteed, issued private money, and monitored the risk exposure of their members. As discussed in the study, these private arrangements successfully thwarted some—but not all—U.S. bank panics. However, the likelihood of panics, and thus the role of clearinghouses, depends on the industrial organization of banking. In this respect, Canada was and is quite different from the United States. If banks are small and poorly diversified (as they were, historically, in the United States), then panics and failures are more likely, ceteris paribus, than if banks are large and well diversified (as they were and are in Canada). In sum, private bank clearinghouses were not much needed in Canada, but badly needed in the United States.

The theoretical analysis shows that private market arrangements in both countries were efficient, given their respective industrial organizations. When banks are small, as in the United States, clearinghouse coalitions are a welfare-enhancing arrangement: Indeed, it is shown that government intervention cannot improve things. When banks are large and well diversified, as in Canada, private clearinghouses are unnecessary, and, again, government intervention is unnecessary.[1]

These policy conclusions regarding the irrelevance of government depend on the assumptions that (1) there are no externalities unaccounted for by private banking coalitions; and (2) the government does not have access to some technology that is unavailable to private agents. In the last section of the paper, the assumption of "no externalities" is dropped. It is shown that a government-provided system of deposit insurance can (but need not) improve welfare if banking panics result in problems in executing transactions (as was often the case in practice). Whether a deposit insurance system is desirable depends on the government's ability to monitor banks relative to private agents' ability to do so.

---

[1] Several different models are presented. As discussed shortly, the sufficiency of private arrangements may depend on which model is assumed.

Overall, this study is interesting and well executed, and I don't have a lot to say in the form of criticism. However, there are three issues that bothered me somewhat. The first pertains to the "stylized facts" about banking industrial organization and the risk of banks. It is assumed that a highly concentrated system of large banks is better diversified, and thus less risky, than an unconcentrated system of many small banks. Neither assumption is necessarily correct. While large banks generally can diversify more effectively than small banks, that does not mean they necessarily will. Even if large banks are better diversified, they may choose to operate with lower capital ratios, thus offsetting the risk-reducing effects of diversification. There is a large empirical literature on this topic, but it is beyond the scope of this comment to review that literature (see Boyd and Graham 1991; Boyd and Runkle 1993; De Nicolo 2000). I believe a careful reading of the literature reveals that some of the maintained (and important) assumptions of this study are questionable at best. Even the assertion that Canadian banks have been safer than U.S. banks is suspect if one properly accounts for large Canadian banks that did not "fail" (technically), but received massive infusions of government capital.[2]

My second concern pertains to the operations of bank clearinghouses and other endogenous self-regulation mechanisms seen in financial markets. These exist not only in banking, but also in securities, commodities, and options exchanges. While such arrangements may be effective at monitoring and limiting individual and collective risk, they present other policy issues that are ignored and unmodeled in the present study. Specifically, when a large number of firms in an industry coalesces to delimit one another's risk taking, an obvious way to achieve that goal is to assure that all members are as profitable as possible. The commonality of banks' interests, their sharing of private information, their setting of interbank fees, etc., all point to the potential for price fixing and other sorts of cartel-like behavior. This potential problem surely deserves attention in a study that might have policy implications.

My third concern is that, in some ways, the final section of the study reads like a critique of the preceding sections. The last section documents the fact that banking panics have often resulted in negative externalities by raising the cost of executing transactions. Then, this section carefully models an entirely new environment in which bank-issued claims are used for executing transactions. But if that is true—as it obviously is—then what was the point of the preceding analysis? In fairness, the first sections primarily review a different study by the same two authors. But, as it is presented, the paper seems to present two different and essentially competing models. Incidentally, in my view, the last model is the clear winner.

---

[2] Canada experienced a nonsystemic banking crisis during 1983–85. Several of its large banks were reorganized by the regulators and received capital infusions (Caprio and Klingebiel 1997.)

REFERENCES

Boyd, John H., and Stanley Graham. 1991. Investigating the Banking Consolidation Trend. *Federal Reserve Bank of Minneapolis Quarterly Review* Spring: 3–15.

Boyd, John H., and David Runkle. 1993. Size and Performance in Banking Firms: Testing the Predictions of Theory. *Journal of Monetary Economics* 31: 47–68.

Caprio, Gerard Jr., and Daniela Klingebiel. 1997. Bank Insolvency: Bad Luck, Bad Policy, or Bad Banking? In *Annual World Bank Conference on Development Economics*, edited by Michael Bruno and Boris Pleskovic. Washington, D.C.: World Bank.

De Nicolo, Gianni. 2000. Size, Charter Value and Risk in Banking: An International Perspective. Board of Governors of the Federal Reserve System, International Finance Discussion Paper no. 689, December.

# Commentary

*Edward J. Green*

Gorton and Huang study three possible industry structures for banking, which they model as a business of taking demand deposits to fund risky projects. The structures are:

- An *atomistic industry* of small, wholly independent banks
- A large number of banks that combine in a *voluntary coalition*—such as a central bank may implement—that can coordinate the banks in actions to which they unanimously agree
- A *monopoly bank* (or perhaps more generally, a tightly coordinated oligopoly) or a powerful industry coalition that can exercise coercive powers over its member banks.

Gorton and Huang give a summary description of a model, according to which the voluntary coalition provides more insulation against bank failures during banking panics than is provided by an atomistic industry; a monopoly bank or coercive coalition provides still greater insulation. The authors suggest that roughly a century ago, the U.S. banking industry approximated the voluntary coalition structure, while the Canadian industry approximated the monopoly bank structure. They note that Canada was less troubled by banking panics than the United States, and they view this cross-country comparison as corroborating their model.

Let me make two remarks about Gorton and Huang's theoretical model before turning to questions about its application. First, Gorton and Huang emphasize the importance of the structure of the asset side of banks' balance sheets as a factor that can predispose a banking industry to panics or crises. In this respect, their model differs from models like that of Diamond and Dybvig (1983), which emphasizes the liability side of the banks' balance sheets and abstracts from the riskiness of the bank's assets. I agree with Gorton and Huang's judgment that asset-quality considerations must have been a part of what drove nineteenth-century banking crises. Sprague (1910) has documented supporting evidence that, at the outset of intervention by a clearinghouse, the clearinghouse would audit its members' assets. If the value of assets were not in question, then such auditing would have been an unnecessary cost that could not have contributed to the restoration of confidence in the banks. Gorton and Huang's model also reflects Sprague's judgment that the major welfare cost of U.S. banking crises was the disruption of intercity trade while financial intermediation through banks was unavailable.

Three assumptions seem to be driving the theoretical result:

1. The atomistic industry has multiple Nash equilibria.
2. One of these equilibria is more robust to "bank failures" than another, and the more robust equilibrium yields higher welfare.
3. Neither of the noncooperative equilibria is as robust to panics as an enforced cooperative solution would be. Thus, voluntary coordination on the preferred Nash equilibrium is superior to selecting one of the equilibria at random. Enforced cooperation—which is achieved by merger to monopoly in the banking industry—is superior to voluntary coordination in point of avoiding failures.

These general considerations of multiplicity and inefficiency of noncooperative equilibria, rather than specific considerations about the relative importance of the asset or liability sides of the banking system's portfolio, are the essential assumptions from which Gorton and Huang's ranking of banking regimes is derived.

In the following three paragraphs, I offer some comments on the three assumptions I have just stated.

While it is interesting to study the implications of the multiple-equilibria assumption, that assumption is plausible but not certain. The theoretical models in which banking has multiple Nash equilibria, including Gorton and Huang's model, assume that banks' liabilities are demand deposits, which require the bank to pay on demand an amount that is not state contingent. Demand deposits and other short-term deposits do make up a large part of banks' liabilities, and the amounts payable on demand are ostensibly not state contingent. However, Green and Oh (1991) and Bolton and Rosenthal (2001) emphasize that demand-deposit contracts are written in the context of a legal and regulatory regime that makes them state contingent in practice, particularly during business cycle downturns. Green and Lin (1999) show—in a straightforward reformulation of the Diamond–Dybvig model, where the form of the deposit contract is determined by optimization—that there is a unique equilibrium and the banking institution implements an efficient allocation. Peck and Shell (2001) show that different assumptions about depositors' preferences and information restore the Diamond–Dybvig multiplicity and Pareto ranking of equilibrium in an optimal-contract model. In short, Gorton and Huang's assumption about the multiplicity of equilibria conforms to some models but conflicts with another; these models with opposite implications are sufficiently similar that casual citation of historical evidence cannot discriminate between them. Further research, of a more statistically disciplined sort than the historical research that is typically cited to motivate theoretical models of banking, must be conducted before the multiple-equilibria assumption can be considered a proven fact.

Gorton and Huang note Sprague's conclusion that a major cost of crises under the national banking system was the disruption of intercity trade. They seem to assume—given that such a welfare cost exists—that a regime with fewer crises will achieve higher welfare. Regardless of whether that conclusion is true, though, it cannot be inferred soundly from Sprague's observation alone. For example, a banking regime that suffers brief crises every few years may provide better conditions for faster economic growth than a regime that avoids banking crises. Indeed, the end of the nineteenth century was a period of both exceptionally frequent banking crises and exceptionally fast economic growth. This is not to say that the national banking system was necessarily more favorable to economic growth than it was to other banking regimes; rather, a general point about welfare comparisons among economic regimes ought to be made. Namely, the overall effect of each regime must be understood (on the basis of theoretical understanding, historical evidence, and perhaps other sorts of study such as calibration and experiment), and then the regimes with the best overall performance should be considered superior. Without embedding Gorton and Huang's model (or some other static model of banking) in a growth model, for instance, one cannot draw strong conclusions about the welfare properties of various historical banking regimes.

Gorton and Huang model a monopoly bank as being more resistant to failure than an atomistic banking system because of its ability to diversify and to act in ways that would require coercive coordination of the firms in an atomistic banking industry. There is an alternative reason why a monopoly bank might be relatively resistant to failure—namely, that it receives a stream of monopoly rents that can be capitalized in the financial markets, if necessary, to cover the loss of value of its assets. If this explanation is significant (even though Gorton and Huang's explanation may also be a part of the story), then a welfare comparison between an atomistic banking market and a monopoly bank should be based on comparing the welfare loss from monopoly to the expected welfare loss that would accrue from bank failure. Gorton and Huang's model seems to abstract from the welfare loss due to monopoly in banking, so it does not make such a comparison. Banking policy that tolerates or encourages monopoly might be advisable on economic grounds if demand for banking services were inelastic and the welfare loss from monopoly were small; otherwise, a competitive bank market (either without regulation or with deposit insurance and regulation) might be preferable, even though such a market structure and policy regime would also have some welfare costs relative to an ideal world.

Gorton and Huang provide a model that formalizes one prevalent view of the comparison between three banking industry structures. Formalization makes a contribution here by providing clarity and precision and by ensuring logical consistency. The assumptions of the model are plausible, but some equally plausible alternative assumptions may have very different implications for policy and welfare. Theoretical contributions from a more fundamental general-equilibrium and optimal-institution-design perspective than is traditional in the study of banking industry structure, and historical studies that are more explicitly informed by the alternative models and that involve more explicit statistical analysis, would help to attain better understanding of these issues.

REFERENCES

Diamond, Douglas W., and Philip H. Dybvig. 1983. Bank Runs, Deposit Insurance, and Liquidity. *Journal of Political Economy* 91: 401–19.

Bolton, Patrick, and Howard Rosenthal. 2001. Political Intervention in Debt Contracts. Unpublished manuscript. Available at *www.princeton.edu/~rosentha/jpe.pdf* [17 January 2002].

Green, Edward J., and Ping Lin. 1999. Implementing Efficient Allocations in a Model of Financial Intermediation. Unpublished manuscript. Available at *www.library.ln.edu.hk/etext/caws/cpps_0092.pdf* [2 January 2002].

Green, Edward J., and Soonam Oh. 1991. Can a "Credit Crunch" Be Efficient? *Federal Reserve Bank of Minneapolis Quarterly Review* 15: 3–17.

Peck, James, and Karl Shell. 2001. Equilibrium Bank Runs. Unpublished manuscript. Available at *www.arts.cornell.edu/econ/cae/bankrun1.pdf* [2 January 2002].

Sprague, O.M.W. 1910. *History of Crises under the National Banking System.* Washington, D.C.: U.S. Government Printing Office.

# 6

# Establishing a Monetary Union in the United States

*Arthur J. Rolnick, Bruce D. Smith, and Warren E. Weber*

## 1. INTRODUCTION

Before 1789, the individual colonies that would ultimately make up the United States were free to issue their own currencies, and all of them did.[1] The U.S. Constitution, adopted in 1789, took this power away from the individual states. Thus, it might appear that the Constitution left the federal government, which minted gold and silver coins, as the sole creator of currency in the new country.

However, this did not turn out to be the case. Although the Constitution took away the power of states to issue money, it left them with the power to charter and regulate note-issuing banks. All of the states ultimately utilized this power, and some went as far as wholly or partially owning banks. In addition, the federal government chartered the (First) Bank of the United States from 1791 to 1811 and the (Second) Bank of the United States from 1816 to 1836. Virtually all of these banks issued notes, and these notes circulated as currency. Thus, by the early 1800s, there were far more entities issuing currency in the United States than there had ever been before 1789. The regulation of these currency issuers varied from place to place and from time to time.

We have argued elsewhere (Rolnick, Smith, and Weber 1994) that the intention of the framers of the Constitution was to make the United States a monetary union or a uniform currency area. If this is correct, then their goal was not achieved before the passage of the National Banking Act in 1863. Before this act, most banknotes circulated against each other and against specie at discounts or premiums that varied across time and space. The United States did not have a uniform currency.

Why did the initial attempt to provide the United States with a uniform currency fail? Our answer is that the regulation of banknote issues was flawed. In our view, and under conditions we describe, a necessary and sufficient condition for the achievement of a uniform currency with private currency issuers is that *holders* of currency can costlessly redeem private notes for outside money at par on demand. When a currency can be costlessly redeemed for outside money at par on demand, it becomes a perfect substitute for outside money and will, therefore, trade at a fixed exchange rate with that currency. When all private currencies satisfy this condition,

---

[1] See Rolnick, Smith, and Weber (1994) for a summary of the monetary arrangements prevailing among the states/colonies before 1789.

they will all trade at a fixed rate with outside money and, as a result, at par with each other.

At no time in the antebellum United States did bank regulation provide adequately for par redemption on demand that was costless to the holders of banknotes. Par redemption was not guaranteed. Banks could go out of business without sufficient assets to pay off note liabilities. Further, general suspensions of specie payments were, at various times, sanctioned by state governments. And even during periods in which banks generally were redeeming notes in specie, note holders had to bear costs in terms of time and effort in order to redeem their notes. As a result, banknotes circulated at something other than their face value.

The rest of this paper illustrates how important costless redemption of currencies at par on demand is for a uniform currency with private issuers to exist. Although such a situation never existed in the United States before the passage of the National Banking Act of 1863, we show that the size and regional variability of banknote discounts were smaller, the closer this criterion was to being met. We also examine how other problems in achieving a common currency—such as incentives to overissue notes—were affected by how close banknote redemption was to being costless.

Specifically, we examine two mechanisms used during the antebellum period that affected the redemption costs borne by the holders of banknotes. One is the Suffolk Banking System. This system for net clearing of banknotes existed in New England from the mid-1820s to the 1850s. It eliminated much of the cost to banks of redeeming the notes of other banks. If our view is correct, the notes of the banks participating in the Suffolk Banking System should have behaved more like a common currency than did banknotes in other parts of the country at the same time. We show this was the case. Thus, although achieving a uniform currency was not a goal of the Suffolk Banking System, it had the effect of providing a uniform currency in New England. We also argue that the design of the Suffolk Banking System included mechanisms that were sufficient to remove banks' incentives to overissue notes.

The other mechanism is the strategy for dealing with the notes of state banks used by the Second Bank of the United States from 1823 to 1836. This strategy was to immediately present to the issuing bank, for redemption in specie, all state banknotes it received. Although the stated objective of this policy was to achieve a uniform currency, we argue it did not provide much cost reduction for the holders of banknotes and, therefore, did not establish a uniform currency. We also have some reasons to doubt that this mechanism was adequate to control the potential for the overissue of notes.[2]

---

[2]  See, for instance, the discussion in Smith (1936, 85–88).

All of our discussion takes for granted that the achievement of a uniform currency was an objective—at least of the federal government—throughout U.S. history. We do not consider whether the achievement of a uniform currency *should* have been such an objective. Theoretical treatments do not necessarily suggest that the existence of discounts or premiums—even fluctuating discounts or premiums—on notes with the same face value are undesirable from a welfare perspective (Smith and Weber 1999; Wallace 2002). And whether the antebellum United States constituted an optimal currency area is an open question (Rockoff 2000; Bencivenga, Huybens, and Smith 2001).

The paper proceeds as follows: In section 2, we discuss in more detail our hypothesis that costless par redemption is required to achieve a uniform currency. In section 3, we discuss the Suffolk Banking System. The Second Bank of the United States is discussed in section 4. Interestingly, the experience of the Second Bank itself illustrates how a failure of the par-redemption requirement for note issuers provides incentives for note overissue. These incentives are discussed in section 5. The final section concludes.

## 2. ACHIEVING A UNIFORM CURRENCY WITH PRIVATE ISSUERS

In this section, we consider an economy in which notes issued by private agents coexist with a stock of outside money. We state three conditions that we think were satisfied in early U.S. monetary history. We then argue that, under these conditions, a necessary and sufficient condition for uniformity of currency is that private notes be redeemable in outside money at par on demand, and that this redemption be costless to the holders of the notes. Throughout, what we mean by *uniform currency* is that currencies of different issuers bearing the same denomination trade at par with each other and with whatever outside money is in circulation.

### 2.1. Three Conditions for Monetary Exchange with Private Note Issuers

We begin by considering an economy in which monetary exchange is accomplished using a combination of outside money and a stock of privately issued banknotes. Three conditions were certainly satisfied in early U.S. monetary history and, we think, are likely to be satisfied in any economy with a similar set of monetary arrangements.

The first condition is that private currencies in such a system are representative monies. That is, they are redeemable in some form of outside money with positive probability. Although par redemption with certainty was far from the norm in the early United States, most banknotes could be redeemed for some positive amount of specie most of the time.

The second condition is that redemption inevitably involves some expenditure of time or resources on the part of the holder of the note, the issuer of the note, or both. Note holders might have to ship notes and specie as a part of the redemption process, and banks might have to install vaults to hold specie reserves and employ tellers to facilitate note redemption.

The third condition is that monetary arrangements require the use of both specie and banknotes. On certain occasions, some agents must convert specie into banknotes and, conversely, banknotes into specie. It is, of course, plausible that banknotes could be used to supplement the use of specie: Specie is relatively scarce and costly to use in transactions, and the use of commodity monies involves a well-understood opportunity cost. At the same time, other transactions—particularly payments for imports or payments of certain kinds of taxes—might well require specie. At various times, banks could face the need to redeem any notes they receive that were issued by other banks in order to augment their specie reserves. In summary, some agents are confronted with the necessity of regularly converting banknotes into specie and specie into banknotes. We now consider what is required for all currencies issued by different entities to circulate at par.

### 2.2. Necessary and Sufficient Conditions for Uniformity of the Currency

Under the conditions just stated, our assertion in this paper is that a necessary and sufficient condition for a uniform currency with private issuers is that note issuers redeem their notes at par on demand, with no cost to the holders of their notes. In other words, a uniform currency will be observed if and only if the holders of that currency can instantaneously get the par value of the currency without expending any resources. In particular, private currencies must be redeemable on demand with certainty, and holders of currency must experience no (or minimal) time delay in exchanging the private currency for the outside money at par. Stated slightly differently, our claim is that a uniform currency with private issuers will exist if and only if redemption is certain and redemption costs are borne entirely by note issuers (as was the case under the national banking system) or by some other entity, such as the government.[3]

When the redemption costs are borne by the agents holding a currency and when agents have a positive probability of having to make redemptions, then a currency will circulate at a discount against specie. Discounts on banknotes, which reflect the expected redemption costs for note holders, are required for banknotes and specie to have the same expected rates of return. Further, if redemption costs or probabilities vary by the location of the issuer, discounts at a given location can be different for different currencies.

---

[3] Bullard and Smith (2001) provide a theoretical model in which this claim can be established. Their economy satisfies our three conditions and allows for costly redemption of notes.

The rates of exchange between banknotes of various issuers and between banknotes and specie can fluctuate for reasons unrelated to fundamentals, as long as these rates of exchange do not imply an arbitrage opportunity associated with purchasing and redeeming notes. This is essentially the gold points argument for why exchange rates between sovereign currencies can fluctuate under a commodity standard. Because such discounts or premiums can occur for reasons that are unrelated to fundamentals but that can affect allocations and use resources,[4] they are inimical to a uniform currency system.

### 2.3. What Limits Private Note Issue?

When redemption at par is not required of the issuers of banknotes, then the uniformity of the currency may be threatened in another way. Suppose the currencies of various private issuers (for example, banks, states, or countries) are treated as a uniform currency in the absence of a redemption requirement. Because the various currencies trade at par with each other, money holders will treat the various currencies as perfect substitutes. In this situation, any issuer of currency can collect seigniorage from the holders not only of its own liabilities, but of other liabilities as well.[5]

Further, the entity whose note circulation grows most rapidly will, asymptotically, collect the bulk of the seigniorage generated within the monetary union. This fact gives each issuer of a uniform currency a strong incentive to capture seigniorage by printing its notes at a rapid rate. We call this the seigniorage incentive problem. Moreover, failure to control this problem threatens the viability of a monetary union because the resulting high rates of inflation can dilute or overturn the benefits of monetary unification. Additionally, when seigniorage incentive problems arise, currency issuers have incentives to take strategic actions to strengthen the demand for their own liabilities.[6] Such actions are detrimental to the existence of a common currency area because they undermine its intention, which is to make all currencies perfectly substitutable.

Requiring redemption at par on demand offers a solution to the seigniorage incentive problem. When note issuers must redeem their liabilities on demand, they have no control over the quantity of their liabilities outstanding. While they can still raise seigniorage, they can take no strategic actions to enhance their seigniorage income. As a result, the seigniorage incentive problem disappears. However, if some currency issuers are not required to redeem on demand, perhaps because they operate under different regulations, then the seigniorage incentive problem remains.

---

[4]   See Manuelli and Peck (1990) and King, Wallace, and Weber (1992).
[5]   See Kareken and Wallace (1981) and Cooper and Kempf (2000) for a discussion of this point when different countries issue a nonredeemable currency.
[6]   A modern example of attempts to avoid immediate and costless liability redemption arises when agents try to arrange payments to earn float. This is a small instance of how strategic actions can be undertaken that allow issuers of liabilities to increase their earnings at the expense of other agents.

### 2.4. Why Wasn't Note Redemption Costless?

Costless redemption at par on demand was far from the norm in early U.S. bank regulation. The enforcement of the regulations against nonredemption and the penalties imposed for nonredemption varied from state to state and from time to time. For example, many states did not require banks to redeem notes promptly, or they imposed only nominal penalties for failure to redeem notes on demand. According to Dewey (1910, 73), "In the earliest charters there was no express provision made for the redemption of notes, nor was there any penalty for nonredemption."[7] And even when state laws or charters expressly required that banknotes be convertible into specie on demand, many states imposed no penalties for nonredemption. Relying once again on Dewey (1910, 76): "With few exceptions previous to 1830 there were no penalties in southern charters for not redeeming notes. Banks were under no legal obligation to pay demands *except by suit* [our emphasis], and note holders were in the same position as other creditors."

Given the importance of note redemption, why did the states not insist on and enforce the prompt and certain redemption of banknotes on demand? While this question undoubtedly has many answers, an important consideration was certainly revenue. The Constitution not only took away the states' ability to print money, it also eliminated several traditional sources of revenue (derived, for example, through the taxation of interstate commerce). Thus, we expect the states would have attempted to raise revenue from their power to create note-issuing banks. Indeed, this source of revenue was rapidly exploited. In several instances, states took an ownership position in the banks they chartered; in other instances, taxation of bank profits was a major source of state revenue. According to Sylla, Legler, and Wallis (1987), from 1796 to 1800, Pennsylvania collected 43 percent of its total revenue from its banks. Furthermore, in a study of 15 states, the same authors report that from 1821 to 1825 (the first years for which data are available for all states), seven states collected more than 20 percent of their total revenue from their banking systems. From 1831 to 1835, 10 states collected more than 20 percent and six states collected more than one-third of their revenue from their banking systems.

Thus, states could and did perceive strong incentives to allow banks to earn profits. If this revenue could be enhanced by taking a casual attitude toward note redemption—an attitude certainly taken by many states—the state would profit as a result. Additionally, if states took a more casual attitude toward note redemption in cyclical downturns than at other times—as they certainly did in practice—this would permit them to allow an expansion of the money stock, at least relative to

---

[7]  See also Huntington (1915, 33).

what would have occurred with note redemption in place. Thus, a desire to run countercyclical monetary policies would give states incentives to take a relaxed attitude toward note redemption, at least at certain times.

Having said this, we think it is important to observe that great importance was attached to the achievement of a uniform currency throughout the early history of the United States. Thus, to the extent that uniformity of currency has value, the states in the early United States confronted a trade-off. They could raise revenue by taking a casual attitude toward the redemption of banknotes, but this damaged the uniformity of the currency. Thus, not surprisingly, not all states adopted an equally lax attitude toward note redemption. Moreover, our impression is that the federal government attached much greater importance to uniformity of the currency than did most of the states.[8] In particular, the federal government was concerned about problems that might arise from collecting tax payments made in state banknotes that might go at a discount. Thus, attitudes toward note redemption might differ greatly at different levels of government. However, for whatever reason, the enforcement of par redemption on demand—if not necessarily par redemption that was costless to the holder of the note—became more common as time passed throughout most of the United States.

### 3. THE SUFFOLK BANKING SYSTEM[9]

We now turn to an examination of the Suffolk Banking System to show how it effectively reduced the redemption costs borne by the holders of banknotes to zero. Under our hypothesis, such a redemption mechanism should have caused the notes of banks participating in this system to behave like a uniform currency. We show this was the case, and by the mid-1830s, a uniform currency area existed in New England.[10]

### 3.1. Its Beginnings

On February 10, 1818, the Suffolk Bank became the seventh bank to be chartered in Boston. Within a year, it entered the note-brokering business—the buying and selling of country (non-Boston) banknotes, also known as *foreign money*. While the Suffolk Bank's note-brokering business was never profitable, it provided the testing ground for the development of a profitable, regionwide note-clearing system.

---

8   For instance, the creation of the federally chartered Second Bank of the United States was motivated largely by the federal government's desire to achieve a uniform currency.
9   See Rolnick, Smith, and Weber (1998) for a more detailed discussion of the operation of the Suffolk Banking System and some issues related to its organization.
10  The Suffolk System probably also reduced the general costs of note redemption, but this point is not essential to our argument.

By 1824, the Suffolk Bank had given up the note-brokering business and devised a new strategy for dealing with foreign money. The Suffolk Bank formed a coalition with the six other Boston banks. Members of the coalition pooled their resources at the Suffolk Bank in order to purchase and export country banknotes for redemption, with the hope of ultimately eliminating these notes from circulation in the city of Boston. To that end, the Suffolk Bank would actively purchase, at the market discount, large quantities of foreign notes and send them back to the issuing country banks for redemption. These activities were nothing more than an attempt to increase the share of the Boston banks' notes in the total note circulation in Boston. However, the new note-purchasing strategy was unsuccessful in achieving this objective and was ultimately abandoned.

### 3.2. How the Suffolk System Operated

In May of 1825, the coalition of Boston banks suggested that the Suffolk Bank begin a new note-clearing business. The Suffolk Bank would allow banks to deposit their foreign money, and it would accept, at par, the notes of all country banks that chose to participate in this new arrangement. By 1826, the Boston banks had withdrawn from the original note-brokering coalition and become members of the new *Suffolk Banking System* (Suffolk Bank 1826; Mullineaux 1987, 890).

For a New England bank to be a member of the Suffolk Banking System, it had to maintain a permanent, non-interest-bearing deposit with the Suffolk Bank: For each $100,000 of capital, the country bank had to hold $2,000 on deposit. A country bank also had to maintain an additional non-interest-bearing deposit that was, on average, sufficient to redeem its notes received by the Suffolk Banking System. Boston banks had to maintain only a permanent, non-interest-bearing deposit. This deposit was initially set at $30,000, but was gradually reduced to $5,000. The original deposit with the Suffolk Bank had to be in specie.

It should be noted that the Suffolk Bank did not require a country bank to be a member as a condition of receiving that bank's notes at par. The country bank was only required to have its notes redeemable at par at a Boston bank (Dewey 1910, 87).

This new arrangement produced an important innovation: Banknotes were cleared, at par, by netting the accounts of member banks (Redlich 1947, 74). Before this time, no net-clearing system for banknotes had been established in the United States. The netting of banknotes worked as follows: Each day, the notes deposited by participating banks at the Suffolk Bank were sorted. If a bank deposited more notes of other banks than the amount of its notes presented by other banks, then the bank received a credit to its account with the Suffolk Bank for the difference. In the opposite situation, the bank's account with Suffolk was debited for the difference. In computing these differences, the notes of all banks that were members of the

Suffolk Banking System were valued identically at par. The actual debiting and crediting of accounts occurred on the day after the notes were sorted. Once the posting to accounts was accomplished, the notes were returned to the issuing banks.

Notes of banks outside New England and notes of the few New England banks that did not participate in the Suffolk System were also accepted by the Suffolk Bank.[11] However, they were not accepted at par and were returned to the issuing bank for redemption as quickly as possible.

In its early stages, the note-clearing operations of the Suffolk System were relatively small. In the summer of 1824, the Suffolk Bank received about $300,000 a month in country banknotes. This amount grew to $2 million a month by the end of 1825, and to well over $6 million a month by 1837 (Trivoli 1979, 15, 21). To put these numbers in perspective, monthly clearing in 1825 amounted to approximately one-half of the stock of notes in circulation in Massachusetts; by 1837, monthly clearing was close to the entire stock. And by 1837, virtually all the banks in New England were members of the Suffolk Banking System.

### 3.3. Evidence on Currency Uniformity

The existence of the Suffolk Banking System reduced the cost of redemption to the holders of country banknotes. Now a New England bank did not have to take notes of other banks that it received in the normal course of business back to the issuing bank and then bear the cost of shipping the specie received back home. Instead, the Suffolk System gave banks the option of depositing these notes at par in the Suffolk Bank (or another Boston bank). Banks could then forgo the shipping of specie because the deposit could be used to redeem their notes. Thus, the cost of note redemption for a note-holding bank was reduced essentially to zero. Under our hypothesis, the prediction is that the notes of New England banks that were members of the Suffolk System would go at par against each other.

Three pieces of evidence support the prediction of par circulation. The first is contemporary accounts, as in this passage from Dewey (1910, 91–92):

> It [the Suffolk Banking System] was also an advantage to a merchant in the interior who wished to purchase merchandise in Boston, for he could carry with him country bank bills without resorting to specie or the purchase of a draft on Boston, for he knew that his bank bills were at par there *(Merchants' Magazine,* 1851, 24:79).

The second is the report of exchange rates for notes circulating in Hartford, Connecticut, on May 16, 1838 (House Doc. 457). The notes of all New England banks that were members of the Suffolk Banking System exchanged at par. By

---

1 After 1837, the New England banks outside Rhode Island that did not participate in the Suffolk System were almost exclusively located in remote parts of Maine that had their major trading links with Canada rather than with Boston.

contrast, the notes of banks that were *not* members of Suffolk (at that time, these were almost all of the Rhode Island banks, 13 Maine banks, and roughly 17 other New England banks) circulated at a discount, with discounts ranging from 1 percent to 55 percent.

The third is the discounts on banknotes reported in the *Van Court's Counterfeit Detector, and Bank Note List*. This monthly publication contained the discounts on the notes of banks from all states in the country in terms of notes of Philadelphia banks. Data are available for February 1839 through December 1858, a period of 239 months.[12] In all but 16 months, the modal discounts on the notes of New England banks, with the exception of Rhode Island, were identical.[13] Because the notes were treated as having the same value in terms of Philadelphia notes, we infer they were going at par against each other in New England.[14] No other region of the country had such uniformity of modal discounts over this period. In fact, in states such as New York, New Jersey, and Pennsylvania, discounts varied by the part of the state in which banks were located.[15]

According to our arguments, it is also important that the Suffolk System evolved mechanisms for controlling the seigniorage-incentive problem. This was done in two ways. First, the Suffolk System required member banks to redeem notes at par on demand. Second, Suffolk System members were required to maintain a non-interest-bearing deposit with the Suffolk Bank (or another Boston bank) that was adequate, on average, to redeem their notes received by the Suffolk Bank. If, at the margin, an additional dollar of note issue led to an additional dollar of note redemption, then every additional dollar of notes issued required that an additional dollar be held in a non-interest-bearing Suffolk Bank account. In this case, at the margin, the issue of additional notes did not generate additional seigniorage for the issuing bank. Smith and Weber (1999) argue this was important in ensuring that the notes of Suffolk System members would circulate at par.

---

[12] These discounts were originally collected in electronic form by Gary Gorton. They have been corrected and amended by Warren Weber and are available at *http://minneapolisfed.org/research/economists/ wewproj.html*.

[13] The exceptions were October and November 1839, January through May 1851, May through November 1854, and March and April 1855.

[14] There is some evidence that the currency in New England was not completely uniform, however. *Clapp, Fuller & Browne's Bank Note Reporter, and Counterfeit Detector* for July 1858 reports discounts on New England country banknotes of 1/10 percent, whereas the notes of Boston banks were trading at par. Despite this observation, we think the conclusion of par circulation is generally correct for this period.

[15] While the design of the Suffolk Banking System was not duplicated elsewhere in the United States, mechanisms were developed in other regions for reducing the cost of note redemption. In New York, country banks were required to have redemption agents in New York City or Albany (Redlich 1947). Fenstermaker (1965, 84) suggests that similar mechanisms evolved in parts of Virginia. Weber (2001) also presents evidence that many country banks had arrangements with banks in financial centers to have their notes redeemed at par in those centers, again reducing the redemption costs to note holders.

## 4. THE SECOND BANK OF THE UNITED STATES

We now examine the Second Bank of the United States. One objective of this institution was to provide the country with a uniform currency. We discuss the mechanism that the Second Bank used to attempt to achieve this objective and argue that it did not produce much, if any, reduction in the cost of redemption to note holders. We then present evidence that a uniform currency was not achieved by the actions of the Second Bank.

### 4.1. Banknote Discounts before the Second Bank

The Bank of North America in Philadelphia was the first bank chartered by a state after the United States achieved independence from England. It was chartered in 1782. Shortly thereafter, other states also chartered banks, and by the early 1800s banks existed in all of the states. Virtually every one of these banks issued banknotes that were, at least nominally, convertible into specie on demand. Although we do not have explicit data, we believe banknotes circulated outside the local area at discounts and premiums against the notes of local banks and circulated at a discount against specie everywhere.

This situation with regard to the convertibility of banknotes lasted until the latter part of April 1814, when banks in New Orleans suspended payments. Banks in Philadelphia followed on August 30, 1814, and banks in the middle Atlantic and southern states followed shortly thereafter. By the beginning of 1815, the suspension of convertibility was general throughout the United States, with the exception of New England. (Because the charter of the First Bank of the United States had lapsed in 1811, there were no federally chartered banks at this time.) Substantial discounts on the notes of state banks relative to specie became commonplace, with these discounts varying significantly across the notes of different banks.

Some evidence on this is presented in figure 1, where we plot the discounts on notes of banks in various states in terms of notes of Philadelphia banks. The figure clearly shows the United States did not have a uniform currency in any meaningful sense. From 1815 through 1817, the notes of Baltimore banks were at a 2 percent to 6 percent discount. During 1816 and 1817, discounts on the notes of North Carolina and District of Columbia banks were between 2 percent and 8 percent. There is also evidence that the notes of banks in Ohio were running at a 6 percent to 8 percent discount during this period.

The figure also shows that the notes of Boston banks were at a substantial premium, sometimes as high as 17 percent, against Philadelphia banknotes in Philadelphia during this time. The reason is that Boston banks had not suspended specie payments, whereas Philadelphia banks had. The premiums on Boston banknotes were roughly the same as the premium on specie in Philadelphia, as would be expected.

**Figure 1:  Discounts on Banknotes in Philadelphia, 1815–18**

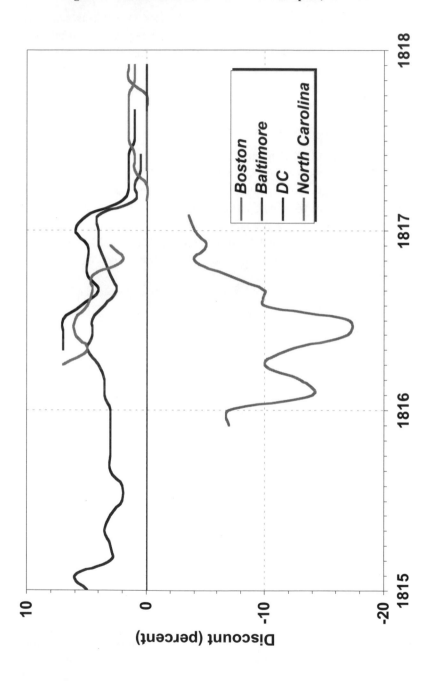

In 1816, the federal government chartered the Second Bank of the United States, largely in the hope that such a bank would promote the resumption of specie convertibility by the state banks. This bank had capital of $35 million, more than 10 times larger than any other bank in existence at the time. Of this $35 million, the federal government subscribed $7 million; individuals purchased the rest. The Second Bank had its headquarters in Philadelphia. Initially, it had 19 branches; ultimately, it had 27 branches and two agencies, which were located in all parts of the country.

Although the Second Bank was unable to require state banks to resume specie payments, it eventually offered enough financial incentives so that by February 20, 1817, state banks had voluntarily resumed specie convertibility (Catterall 1902, 24–25). The effect is shown dramatically in figure 1. After February 1817, the discounts on Baltimore, District of Columbia, and North Carolina banknotes fell to $1\frac{1}{2}$ percent or less. The premium on Boston notes also decreased. Thus, the resumption of convertibility moved the country much closer to a uniform currency.

The resumption of convertibility did not last long, however. In 1819, a suspension of convertibility of state banknotes became general in the United States (outside New England) as the country experienced its first bank panic.

From 1819 through much of 1821, the state banks (except those in New England) were not even nominally redeeming their notes for specie. As a result, discounts increased on the notes of most state banks in Philadelphia (see figures 2–5). These discounts also varied widely by location. Notes of Maryland banks outside Baltimore went at discounts that were 1 percent to 3 percent higher than banks in that city. The notes of North Carolina banks went at discounts as high as 16 percent, whereas discounts on the notes of South Carolina banks never exceeded 8 percent, and discounts on the notes of Virginia banks never exceeded 5 percent. Further, the discount on the notes of a particular state's banks could vary widely over time (witness the three southern states in figures 3 and 4). Thus, this period illustrates how the total relaxation of the enforcement of par redemption led to currencies being much less uniform.

In view of the removal of any checks associated with the necessity of redeeming notes, it is not surprising that the issues of some state banks expanded dramatically. Indeed, the desire of several states for seigniorage manifested itself in the establishment of wholly state-owned, non-specie-paying, note-issuing banks in Alabama, Kentucky, Illinois, Missouri, and Tennessee. In addition, some states, such as Michigan, issued scrip. In several of these states, laws were passed to force people to hold state banknotes—and to take them at rates in excess of their market value. This is a manifestation of a seigniorage incentive problem: States were taking strategic actions to enhance their own seigniorage income.

**Figure 2:  Discounts on Maryland Banknotes in Philadelphia, 1815–30**

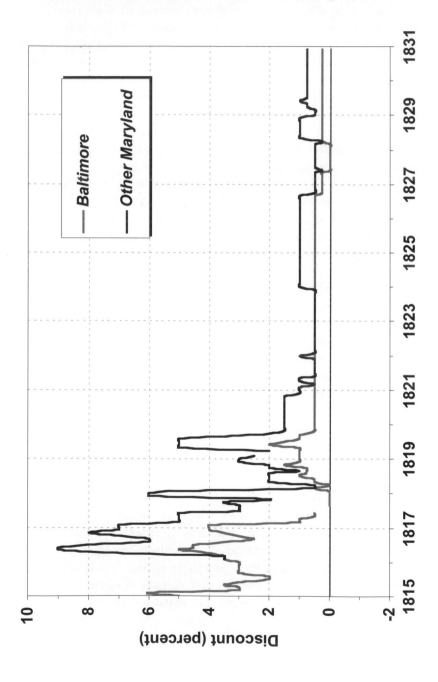

Figure 3: Discounts on Carolina Banknotes in Philadelphia, 1817–30

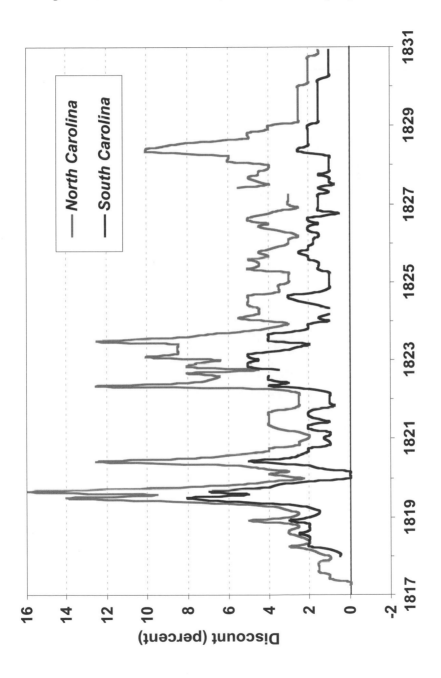

**Figure 4: Discounts on Virginia Banknotes in Philadelphia, 1819–30**

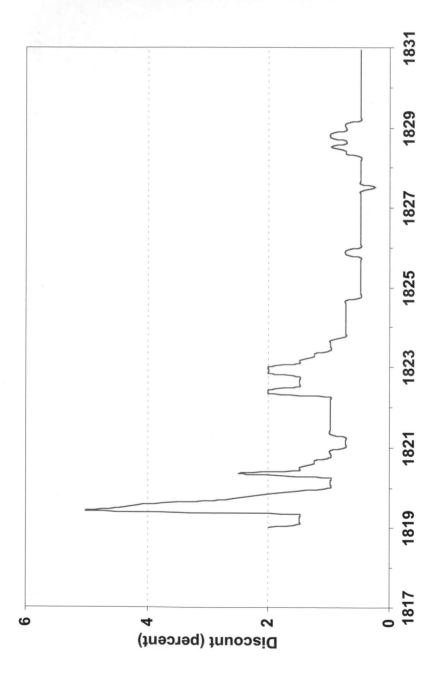

**Figure 5:  Discounts on Kentucky Banknotes in Philadelphia, 1816–30**

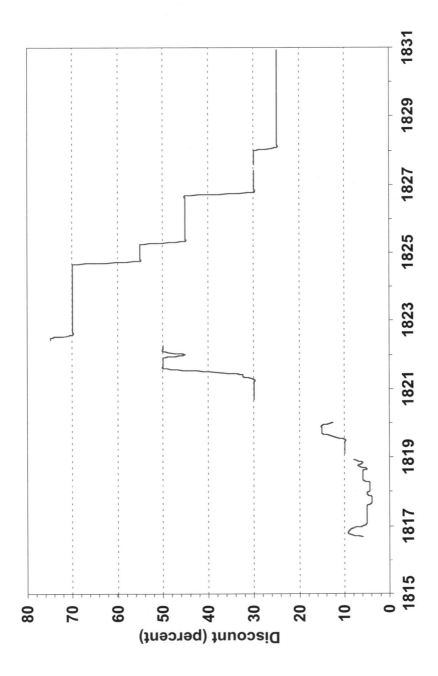

The most dramatic example of this occurred in Kentucky. Before 1819, Kentucky had relatively lax bank regulation. In 1817–18, state banks were authorized to redeem their notes with Bank of Kentucky notes rather than specie, and for the Bank of Kentucky and its 13 branches, none was required to take the notes of another (Duke 1895, 16–17).[16] In November 1820, the state chartered the wholly state-owned Bank of the Commonwealth of Kentucky, which did not redeem its notes in specie. Moreover, the notes of this bank were given several advantages in transactions. For example, the state had passed a law imposing a mandatory stay of one year if creditors accepted Bank of Kentucky notes at par, and a two-year stay otherwise. When the Bank of the Commonwealth was created, creditors accepting its notes at par faced only a three-month stay (Rothbard 1962, 53). The notes of this bank soon were depreciated 50 percent relative to specie (and even more in Philadelphia), and this situation persisted for some time.

In Illinois, another wholly state-owned bank was created and was authorized to issue $300,000. "The bank notes were backed by a stay law, delaying all executions for three years unless the creditor agreed to receive the state bank notes. Thus, the state did its best to place the notes on as close to a legal tender basis as constitutionally seemed possible" (Rothbard 1962, 83). The bank's notes depreciated rapidly, and Rothbard reports they ceased to circulate by the end of 1823.

In Alabama, "the legislature refused to abide by the existing law which forbade accepting notes of non-specie paying banks in taxes. . . . The Alabama legislature went further and issued Treasury notes payable in the depreciating currency of the Huntsville Bank. Under the government umbrella, the Huntsville Bank issued large quantities of notes, which sank to a 25–50 percent discount" (Rothbard 1962, 58). In 1823, Alabama chartered a state-owned, note-issuing bank as well.

In Tennessee, a state-owned bank was created in 1819, and a stay law was passed providing that "when a *bank* was the creditor and refused to accept at par . . . either its own notes or the notes of the two leading banks in Tennessee, the execution would be stayed for two years" (Rothbard 1962, 48). In Missouri, the state established a loan office and a "supplementary stay law, which gave the creditor the choice of accepting two-thirds of the appraised value of the property *in loan-office certificates* at par or suffer a two-and-one-half-year stay" (Rothbard 1962, 45).

In short, an absence of note redemption led to widely varying discounts and premiums on notes and to a serious seigniorage incentive problem. Moreover, the situation of several states issuing their own notes (here, indirectly through state-owned banks) and using legislative interference with contracts to enforce their circulation and enhance their value replicated, in certain respects, the experience of the United

---

[16] In 1820, the charters of several state banks were revoked because they did not redeem their notes even in this form.

States under the Articles of Confederation. It was this exact set of circumstances that had resulted in the constitutional prohibition of currency issues by the states in the first place.

## 4.2. Biddle's Banknote Redemption Policy

In January 1823, Nicholas Biddle succeeded Langdon Cheves as president of the Second Bank. By this time, the banks of many, but by no means all, of the states had resumed the redemption of their notes in specie.[17] Even so, substantial discounts remained on the notes of banks of many states (see figures 2–5) because, as we have argued, requiring note holders to bear the costs of redemption allows discounts to be observed.

Biddle sought to reduce discounts on the notes of state banks in order to achieve the desired objective of having a uniform currency. To attempt to accomplish this, he changed the policy of his predecessor with regard to the notes of state banks. During Cheves' presidency, the Second Bank paid out state banknotes whenever possible in its own lending operations and to its own depositors. Biddle reversed this policy; the bank paid out its own notes whenever possible. Indeed, even deposits made in state banknotes were repaid using Second Bank notes.[18] The state banknotes that the Second Bank received in the normal course of business were presented to their issuers for redemption as soon as possible.

It seems plausible that Biddle's policy was a method for reducing the effective costs of note redemption perceived by most holders of state banknotes. Instead of having to return a state banknote to the issuing bank, a holder could deposit it with a Second Bank branch and obtain a Second Bank note that was more widely and easily redeemable at par.[19] However, a critical question is whether the Second Bank was accepting state banknotes at par or at a discount. In other words, was the Second Bank acting like the Suffolk Bank, or was it acting like a note broker? If the former, then under our hypothesis, its policy should have provided the country with a uniform currency. If the latter, state banknotes would have gone at discounts.

We have no direct evidence on how the Second Bank behaved with regard to the state banknotes presented to it. We know the Second Bank was required to accept the notes of specie-paying banks at par from the federal government and for purchases of federal lands. However, we doubt that most branches did this for state banknotes presented for deposit or loan repayment. That is, we think the Second Bank acted like a note broker rather than like the Suffolk Bank.

---

[17] South Carolina banks did not resume specie convertibility until 1823. In several western states, resumption also failed to occur until well after 1821.

[18] According to Catterall (1902, 437–38), "It was customary to receive from individuals the notes of state banks on deposit and pay the deposit in branch notes."

[19] For example, after 1824, these notes were taken at par in Philadelphia.

We have two reasons for thinking this way: One is that it is well known that many branches of the Second Bank did not even accept the notes of other Second Bank branches at par (see below). From August 28, 1818, until July 1824, each branch was forbidden to redeem any notes but its own.[20] Notes of Second Bank branches were quoted at a discount of 1 percent in Philadelphia between August 1818 and March 1819. The notes of most branches went at discounts of $\frac{1}{2}$ percent from then until July 1824. Notes of some other branches carried even larger discounts in Philadelphia. Notes of the Portsmouth, New Hampshire, branch, for example, were discounted 4 percent in September and October 1820 and 2 percent from September 1820 through 1821; the notes of the Middletown, Connecticut, branch were discounted 4 percent in September 1820.[21]

After July 1824, if branches were accepting the notes of other branches at par, then all branch notes should have gone at par in all cities where there was a branch. The evidence from banknote reporters on whether this was the case is mixed. *Day's New-York Bank Note List, Counterfeit Detector and Price Current* for July 4, 1828, and for June 15, 1830, lists the notes of the "Bank of the United States and all its branches" at par to a $\frac{1}{4}$ percent discount. *Sylvester's Reporter, Counterfeit Detector, New-York Price Current, & General Advertiser* for October 3, 1832, has the notes of the Second Bank in Philadelphia and all branches listed at a $\frac{1}{4}$ percent discount. *Day's* for December 2, 1834, has all of the notes of the Second Bank and its branches going at par. Given this evidence about how the Second Bank treated the notes of its own branches, it seems unlikely that it was indiscriminately taking state banknotes at par.[22]

The other reason we think the Second Bank acted more like a note broker than like the Suffolk Bank is this: Suppose the Second Bank took state banknotes at par and then presented them for redemption. Then it, rather than the issuing bank, would have borne the major portion of the cost of redeeming state banknotes. Given that the Second Bank was in business to maximize the profits of its shareholders—not the profits of the owners of state banks—it seems unlikely it would have enacted such a policy.

---

[20] Except in payments of debts owed to the federal government.

[21] According to Catterall (1902, 416), "Why the paper of these branches should have suffered greater depreciation than that of the others it is not possible to say."

[22] In addition, according to Catterall (1902, 417), "It is certain that some [Second Bank] branches sometimes refused to receive the notes of other branches even at a discount."

### 4.3. Evidence on Currency Uniformity

Given that the Second Bank acted like a note broker, under our hypothesis Biddle's policy should not have reduced the discounts on state banknotes below what they were when this policy was not in effect. At first glance, the evidence appears to contradict this view. The discounts plotted in figures 2–5 show a general tendency to be lower after 1823 than in the period before 1823. However, a closer examination of the evidence indicates that the reduction in discounts was (almost) entirely due to the fact that banks in the states shown in these figures had resumed specie payments. Biddle's policy of acting like a nationwide note broker had no effect, as our hypothesis would suggest.

Specifically, a closer inspection of the evidence indicates that in many cases, the level of discounts after 1823 was not below the discount levels of 1817–18, when banks were also paying specie for their banknotes. For example, during 1817 and 1818, South Carolina banknotes were at about a 2 percent to 4 percent discount (see figure 3). After 1824, they were at discounts in about the same range. North Carolina notes were also at about a 2 percent to 4 percent discount in 1817 and 1818; after 1824, these discounts were more in the 3 percent to 5 percent range. Discounts on the notes of Baltimore banks were also higher after 1823 than they were during the 1817–18 period (see figure 2).

Further, although the discounts on the notes of Maryland banks outside Baltimore were lower after 1823 than during the 1817–18 period (again, see figure 2), the timing of the reduction is off. The decline occurred in 1821, two years before Biddle's policy was put into place.

That leaves the evidence from Virginia (figure 4) and Kentucky (figure 5) as possibly refuting our hypothesis. Virginia is problematic because we have no discounts from 1817 and 1818 to use for comparison, and it can be argued that the reduction in the discounts on Kentucky banknotes was more the result of changes in Kentucky banking than Biddle's policy.

Other evidence against the view that Biddle's policy effected a more uniform currency is found in the discounts on banknotes during the 1840s and 1850s, after the Second Bank had lost its charter and ceased to exist. The mean monthly discounts on banknotes in Philadelphia for Baltimore and four states for the period 1823–58 are presented in table 1. The evidence shows that, with the exception of Virginia, discounts on banknotes were lower in the 1840s and 1850s than they were from 1823 to 1832, when Biddle's policy was in effect. Of course, this observation could be explained by improvements in transportation and communication that reduced the costs of note redemption. However, it is also consistent with our view that the reduction in discounts after Biddle's policy went into effect was due to the fact that most banks resumed specie payments at or before that time.

**Table 1: Discounts on State Banknotes**

|  | **Baltimore** | **MD** | **VA** | **NC** | **SC** |
|---|---|---|---|---|---|
| Second Bank (1823–35) | .33 | .75 | .66 | 3.4 | 1.8 |
| Post–Second Bank (1843–58) | .28 | .66 | 1.1 | 1.7 | 1.2 |

The question arises: Why, given that one of its objectives was to provide a uniform currency, did the Second Bank not set up a system of redemption accounts for state banks, along the lines of that established by the Suffolk Bank? One answer is that it would not have been technically feasible, given the large number of banks and the widespread counterfeiting of banknotes during this period. However, we think another answer is that Biddle wanted the Second Bank to be a creditor to other banks, rather than a debtor. A Suffolk-type system requires the bank running it to be a debtor to other banks. Finally, we think the lack of fully centralized control over the Second Bank branches should not be discounted. We expand on this lack of control in the next section.

## 5. A SEIGNIORAGE INCENTIVE PROBLEM WITHIN THE SECOND BANK

We have already seen the seigniorage incentive problem—the problem of over-issuing notes and taking strategic actions to enhance their circulation—manifest itself during a period of general suspension of note convertibility. However, this problem can be even more extreme in a context where many entities are issuing notes that are fully intended to be perfect substitutes. Indeed, the seigniorage incentive problem arose in a particularly significant way in the early history of the Second Bank, and addressing it became a central issue within the bank itself. We now examine this problem and look at the two solutions that were implemented to control it.

The Second Bank was created with 19 branches. Each branch issued notes of the Second Bank, so that the bank itself was an example of a multiple-issuer system, with all issuers printing the same currency. Until August 1818, all notes—issued by any branch—were nominally redeemable at par at any other branch of the bank. However, patterns of funds flows imply that notes issued by southern and western branches were primarily redeemed in the North and East. Thus, without an adequate scheme for controlling note issue by an individual branch, the Second Bank should have been subject to an *internal* seigniorage incentive problem in the sense that one branch bank was able to extract revenue from other branches through note issue.[23] In fact, this problem proved to be severe.

---

[23] Or, more specifically, the directors of some branches were able to extract resources from the directors of other branches.

Why did the Second Bank have branches? The primary reason is that as a fiscal agent for the federal government, the bank needed to be able to collect and disburse funds in disparate regions and to be able to engage in interregional funds transfers. The existence of a branch system also facilitated the bank as a mechanism for creating a uniform currency. The existence of branches enabled the Second Bank to collect the notes of a wide variety of state banks and present them for redemption in a timely manner at a lower cost than without branches.

In its early incarnation, there was relatively little control over the individual branches. The first president of the bank, William Jones, was opposed to assigning a specific amount of capital to each (or any) branch (Catterall 1902, 380). Nor were there any mechanisms put in place for settling accounts between different branches of the Second Bank (Catterall 1902, 30). In addition, branch practices might not be known by the president. For example, in 1817, the Lexington branch of the bank sold its own notes at a premium of $1\frac{1}{2}$ percent and paid out the notes of local banks in its other transactions. Schur (1960, 123) suggests this practice was unknown to Jones until October of that year. This state of affairs led the bank's second president, Langdon Cheves, to write, "I am perfectly satisfied that with the present organization of the Bank it can never be managed well. We have too many branches, and the directors are frequently governed by individual and local interests." (Catterall 1902, 381, fn. 4). Moreover, while both Cheves and Biddle regarded the lending operations of western branches as unprofitable, under Jones, several branches explicitly ignored directions from Philadelphia to curtail their lending (Catterall 1902, 52–54). This is perhaps not surprising in view of the fact that branch directors were often significant borrowers (Catterall 1902, 101).

In a system of this type, the branch(es) with the fastest growing note issues could collect resources from the rest of the banks. Those branches were primarily located in the South and West, as well as in Baltimore, where the branch directors were engaged in active fraud. In June 1818, the Cincinnati branch made over $1,800,000 in loans, while the branch at Lexington loaned $1,619,000 (Catterall 1902, 34).[24] The result was that "the entire capital of the institution was rapidly being shifted to the South and West. Out of the total capital stock of $35,000,000, the office at Baltimore held $5,646,000 in May 1819; Richmond, $1,760,000; Savannah, $1,420,000, and Charleston, $1,935,000. . . . Lexington had $1,502,000, Louisville, $1,129,000, and Cincinnati $2,400,000, while New York had a capital of $245,000, and Boston had none whatever" (Catterall 1902, 55–56).

---

[24] According to Catterall, these loan volumes approximated those made by the much larger branches in Boston and New York.

In response to this state of affairs, Jones ordered discounts to be reduced by $5 million throughout the Second Bank. This was actually accomplished, but in a way that illustrates the lack of centralized control over the western branches. Those "offices, instead of diminishing, increased their loans to the extent of $500,000" (Catterall 1902, 54). As a result, Philadelphia, New York, and Boston were forced to curtail loan activity; New York and Boston had not been assigned any loan reductions.

In principle, there should have been a mechanism in place to check the activities of the offending branches; their notes could have been presented for redemption (at the branch of issue) by other branches of the bank (or by individuals). In practice, however, "the southern and western branches could not and did not furnish means for their redemption" (Catterall 1902, 412). To the extent these notes were redeemed anywhere, they were redeemed in the Northeast.

The consequence of this lack of uniform regulation over the branches was that the southern and western branches faced no effective check on their ability to raise seigniorage. As they collected seigniorage from the rest of the Second Bank, they could use the resources acquired either for the benefit of the individual branch directors, as in Baltimore,[25] or for the benefit of their own regional economy, at the expense of other regions.

Without any other means of controlling the seigniorage incentive problem, Jones acted to make the notes issued by the various branches imperfect substitutes: On August 28, 1818, each branch was forbidden to redeem any notes but its own.[26] We have already seen what this implied about discounts on the notes of various branches. As a result, from August 1818 on, the Second Bank did not even issue an internally uniform currency. "Once more there was no common medium of exchange, and thus the first attempt to give the country a better currency through the agency of the Bank of the United States ended in failure" (Catterall 1902, 405). The seigniorage incentive problem had prevented even the Second Bank itself from acting as a true monetary union.

In 1819, Cheves replaced Jones as the president of the bank and, in that year, began to implement a new set of policies designed to control the seigniorage incentive problem within the Second Bank. However, this was done by nearly eliminating the note issues of the southern and western branches altogether. Indeed, while the bank resumed the redemption of its small-denomination ($5) notes at branches other than the branch of issue,[27] and while Cheves took actions to restore central control of the bank's branches—eliminating one branch (Cincinnati) and preventing western branches from issuing any notes at all—"by January 1823, the

---

[25] See the discussion in Catterall (1902, 42–48).
[26] Except in payment of debts owed to the federal government.
[27] Notes in this denomination constituted about one-sixth of the bank's outstanding note issue.

active western offices issued only $45,820, and in December of the same year only $16,785—insignificant sums which hardly permit one to speak of western issues" (Catterall 1902, 411). This certainly was another means of controlling the seigniorage incentive problem that existed within the bank, but it had the consequence that large parts of the country were left with only the notes of state banks as currency. Outside New England, state banks were not redeeming their notes at this time, often their notes were heavily discounted, and a seigniorage incentive problem of a different sort was disrupting the monetary system. Again, the United States did not have a uniform currency.

When Nicholas Biddle became president of the Second Bank, he was determined to expand the note issues of the southern and western branches. This policy stood in marked contrast to that of Cheves. Biddle's solution to the seigniorage incentive problem within the bank was similar in spirit to the mechanism of having notes be redeemable in specie on demand. The branches were to be allowed to issue notes, but they were to give up a large amount of discretion regarding the volume of their own notes outstanding. The specific mechanism employed was that the branches were allowed to use their own notes to purchase "inland bills of exchange." According to Catterall (1902, 406), "By the buying of bills when notes were issued, a fund was provided out of which the notes were paid when they were presented at the Atlantic offices. In this way the danger of having the bank's capital shifted to the West and South was avoided." In particular, the branches were permitted to issue notes, but only in a way that created a fund allowing for their redemption.[28] By maintaining this redemption, the Second Bank branches lost the power to take strategic actions to enhance their own seigniorage income. Biddle also took several actions to increase the degree of centralized control over the operations of the individual branches (Catterall 1902, 102–4).

Evidently, these policies still allowed the southern and western branches to substantially expand their note issues without threatening the rest of the bank. In December 1823, notes of branches in southern, southwestern, and western states were approximately $3.44 million (70 percent) of the total note issue of approximately $4.93 million. By September 1830, the notes of these branches had increased to $11.50 million and made up 75 percent of the total note issues of approximately $15.3 million. Clearly, while note issues by the bank expanded dramatically in all regions, issues by branches in the South and West represented a larger proportion of the expansion (Catterall 1902, 408).

---

[28] The bills of exchange purchased by the branches "were to be drawn on New Orleans or the Atlantic cities . . . so that they might come to maturity and be paid at these places simultaneously with the notes" (Catterall 1902, 115). Thus, redemption was not only possible, but fairly automatic, "provided the bills of exchange were promptly paid" (Catterall 1902, 115).

Obviously, the corporate governance of the Second Bank was severely flawed. Its internal organization allowed various branches to issue claims which were, in many instances, paid off by other branches of the bank. Not surprisingly, this permitted such claims to be overissued. Nonetheless, the main point remains: When notes were not redeemed by certain issuing branches, they were issued in relatively large quantities. The insistence on note redemption by issuing branches—as under Biddle's policy regarding the use of inland bills of exchange—did quite a bit to control the Second Bank's internal seigniorage incentive problem.

## 6. CONCLUSIONS

A comparison of the operation of the Suffolk Banking System with the activities of the Second Bank of the United States suggests several conclusions. First, the attainment of a genuine monetary union with multiple issuers of currency can be guaranteed only if notes are costlessly redeemable at par on demand. In the Suffolk System, the costs of note redemption were effectively transferred to the issuers of notes, which paid the costs of operation of the Suffolk System. Under the Second Bank, the costs of note redemption were never fully transferred away from note holders on a national basis. The Suffolk Banking System came much closer to providing a uniform currency than did the system used by the Second Bank.

Second, the attainment of a successful monetary union with multiple currency issuers requires that these issuers not perceive incentives to overissue notes or to take strategic actions to expand their note circulation. Appropriate incentives in this regard were not present in the early history of the Second Bank. They were provided under Cheves' presidency only by virtually eliminating the note issues of southern and western branches—hardly a state of affairs conducive to the existence of a uniform currency. In contrast, the Suffolk System provided at least two separate mechanisms—par redemption of notes on demand and the holding of non-interest-bearing centralized clearing balances—as a means of checking seigniorage incentive problems. The means devised by the Suffolk System for addressing the seigniorage incentive problem appear to have been highly successful.

With the lapse of its federal charter in 1836, the Second Bank ceased to operate on anything other than a local basis.[29] The Suffolk System continued in operation until 1858. The uniformity of the currency in New England was preserved until that date. The rest of the United States never achieved a uniform currency until the passage of the National Banking Act in 1863. That act forced note issuers to bear redemption costs, as under the Suffolk System, and it solved the seigniorage incentive problem by making notes redeemable at par on demand.

---

[29] The Second Bank operated under a state of Pennsylvania charter until 1841. See Holdsworth (1928).

We believe these lessons from U.S. monetary history have broad current applicability in areas that are now in the process of establishing monetary unions. Part of the problem in attaining a uniform currency in the United States before the Civil War was the lack of uniform bank regulation. As we have noted, individual states regulated the activities of banks, and these regulations were far from uniform in terms of requiring par redemption of notes on demand. Even within the Second Bank, branches did not operate in a uniform way or under uniform regulation.

In the current constitution of the European Monetary Union, for instance, bank regulation is left to the individual member nations. This allows for the possibility that national governments will manipulate regulations in a way that allows seigniorage incentive problems to arise. Alternatively, as more entities—nonbanks as well as banks—issue currency-like liabilities (possibly in the form of e-cash) in the United States under the aegis of different regulatory institutions, the same possibility arises. In our view, this suggests the importance of the lessons learned in the early United States with respect to the formation of a monetary union.

Of course, there have been a number of attempts in other places at other times to establish a monetary union.[30] It would be interesting to do a systematic study of the extent to which costless convertibility of currencies was maintained in such attempts, and of the extent to which this costless convertibility was correlated with the success of the monetary union.

## ACKNOWLEDGMENTS

The authors thank Michael Bordo, Bruce Champ, Geoffrey Miller, and Neil Wallace for their very helpful comments on an earlier version of this paper. The views expressed herein are those of the authors and not necessarily those of the Federal Reserve Bank of Minneapolis or the Federal Reserve System.

---

[30] See Bordo and Jonung (2000) for a number of descriptions.

## References

Bencivenga, Valerie R., Elisabeth Huybens, and Bruce D. Smith. 2001. Dollarization and the Integration of International Capital Markets: A Contribution to the Theory of Optimal Currency Areas. *Journal of Money, Credit, and Banking* 33: 548–89.

Bordo, Michael D., and Lars Jonung. 2000. *Lessons for EMU From the History of Monetary Unions*. London: Institute of Economic Affairs.

Bullard, James B., and Bruce D. Smith. 2001. Intermediaries and Payments Instruments. Federal Reserve Bank of St. Louis, unpublished manuscript.

Catterall, Ralph C.H. 1902. *The Second Bank of the United States*. Chicago: University of Chicago Press.

Cooper, Russell, and Hubert Kempf. 2000. Establishing a Monetary Union. Boston University, unpublished manuscript.

Dewey, Davis R. 1910. *State Banking Before the Civil War*. Washington, D.C.: Government Printing Office.

Duke, Basil W. 1895. *History of the Bank of Kentucky*. Louisville, Ky.: John P. Morton and Co.

Fenstermaker, Joseph Van. 1965. *The Development of American Commercial Banking, 1782–1837*. Kent, Oh.: Kent State University.

Holdsworth, John Thom. 1928. *Financing an Empire: History of Banking in Pennsylvania*. Chicago: S.J. Clarke.

Huntington, C.C. 1915. A History of Banking and Currency in Ohio before the Civil War. *Ohio Archaeological and Historical Quarterly* 24: 235–539.

Kareken, John, and Neil Wallace. 1981. On the Indeterminacy of Equilibrium Exchange Rates. *Quarterly Journal of Economics* 96: 207–22.

King, Robert G., Neil Wallace, and Warren E. Weber. 1992. Nonfundamental Uncertainty and Exchange Rates. *Journal of International Economics* 32: 83–108.

Manuelli, Rodolfo E., and James Peck. 1990. Exchange Rate Volatility in an Equilibrium Asset Pricing Model. *International Economic Review* 31: 559–74.

Mullineaux, Donald J. 1987. Competitive Monies and the Suffolk Bank System: A Contractual Perspective. *Southern Economic Journal* 53: 884–98.

Redlich, Fritz. 1947. *The Molding of American Banking: Men and Ideas*. New York: Hafner.

Rockoff, Hugh. 2000. How Long Did It Take the United States to Become an Optimal Currency Area? Rutgers University, unpublished manuscript.

Rolnick, Arthur J., Bruce D. Smith, and Warren E. Weber. 1994. In Order to Form a More Perfect Monetary Union. *Federal Reserve Bank of Minneapolis Quarterly Review* 17: 2–13.

———, ———, and ———. 1998. Lessons from a Laissez-faire Payments System: The Suffolk Banking System (1825–58). *Federal Reserve Bank of St. Louis Review* 80: 105–16.

Rothbard, Murray N. 1962. *The Panic of 1819: Reactions and Policies.* New York: Columbia University Press.

Schur, Leon M. 1960. The Second Bank of the United States and the Inflation after the War of 1812. *Journal of Political Economy* 68: 118–34.

Smith, Bruce D., and Warren E. Weber. 1999. Private Money Creation and the Suffolk Banking System. *Journal of Money, Credit, and Banking* 31: 624–59.

Smith, Vera C. [1936] 1990. *The Rationale of Central Banking and the Free Banking Alternative.* Reprint, Indianapolis: Liberty Press.

Suffolk Bank. 1826. Directors' records. Baker Library, Harvard Business School, Cambridge, Mass.

Sylla, Richard, John B. Legler, and John J. Wallis. 1987. Banks and State Public Finance in the New Republic: The United States, 1790–1860. *Journal of Economic History* 47: 391–403.

Trivoli, George. 1979. *The Suffolk Bank: A Study of a Free-Enterprise Clearing System.* London: Adam Smith Institute.

Wallace, Neil. 2002. Commentary. In *Evolution and Procedures in Central Banking,* edited by David E. Altig and Bruce D. Smith. New York: Cambridge University Press.

Weber, Warren E. 2001. Interbank Payments Relationships in the Antebellum United States. Federal Reserve Bank of Minneapolis, unpublished manuscript.

# Commentary

*Neil Wallace*

## 1. INTRODUCTION

Rolnick, Smith, and Weber describe features of the monetary system in the United States prior to the Civil War and, hence, prior to the establishment of the national banking system in 1863. They focus on the systems in place for the issue of bank notes. Some banks were state-chartered banks, and some, the First and Second Banks of the United States, were federally chartered. The authors devote most of their paper to contrasting the operations of the Suffolk Banking System in New England with those of the Second Bank. They take as given that the goal was a nationwide system in which bank notes were uniform in two senses: Notes issued by different banks were perfect substitutes, and such notes were valued at par, meaning that notes did not trade at a discount or at a premium relative to their stated denomination in units of account. In their view, Suffolk approximated such uniformity in New England, but the activities of the Second Bank did not do so for the country as a whole.

I will set out a model that can be used to consider whether and in what sense such uniformity is good. There are at least two reasons for doing so. First, uniformity in the above sense is not an ultimate goal. Therefore, we are left with two options: We can rely on data and natural experiments to judge whether uniformity is good in terms of ultimate goals such as consumption, or we can use a model within which the uniformity experiments can be performed. The modeling alternative is easier and cheaper.

Second, Rolnick, Smith, and Weber make repeated use of arbitrage arguments, which may or may not be consistent with the frictions that give bank notes a significant role. In addition, they label bank notes "currency." If they were, instead, labeled "payable-to-the-bearer securities," we might be more reluctant to accept the conclusion that they should trade at par. In this regard, although it is hardly mentioned in this paper, bank notes tended to be issued in large denominations. The number five seems to have had a magical status, perhaps because Adam Smith said that bank notes issued by private banks in England and Scotland should have a £5 minimum denomination. In any case, $5 was often used as a minimum denomination in the United States. Historians among us can better interpret the magnitude of the $5 note in the first half of the nineteenth century; I suspect that, relative to per capita income, $5 was substantially larger than the largest unit of U.S. currency circulating today.

I will show how to pose the following questions within a model of private money that Ricardo Cavalcanti and I formulated and studied (see Cavalcanti and Wallace 1999a,b). Is it good if banks redeem each other's notes, as was done, in effect, within New England under the Suffolk Banking System? Is it good if bank notes circulate at par, rather than at a discount or a premium? Are the answers to these questions likely to change if we complicate the model by making it a model of regions?

## 2. THE CAVALCANTI–WALLACE MODEL

The background environment is borrowed from Shi (1995) and Trejos and Wright (1995). Time is discrete and the horizon is infinite. There are $S > 2$ perishable goods at each date and a $[0, 1]$ continuum of each of $S$ types of people. A type $s$ person consumes only good $s$ and is able to produce only good $s + 1$ (modulo $S$). Each person maximizes expected discounted utility with a discount parameter $\beta \in (0, 1)$. The period utility function is $u(x) - y$, where $x$ is the consumption of the relevant good, and $y$ is the production of the relevant good. The function $u$ is strictly concave and increasing, and it satisfies $u(0) = 0$, $u'(0) = \infty$, and $u'(\infty) = 0$. At each date, each person meets one other person at random.

Cavalcanti and Wallace split the $[0, 1]$ continuum of each type into two intervals: The interval $[0, B]$ consists of those whose previous actions are perfectly monitored and, therefore, are common knowledge. They are called *bankers*. The rest, the interval $[B, 1]$, are not monitored at all, so their previous actions are private. They are called *nonbankers*. The parameter $B$ can be interpreted as the society's monitoring capacity. A person's specialization type and banker/nonbanker status are common knowledge, and people cannot commit to future actions.

Each banker has a printing press that turns out uniform, indivisible, and perfectly durable objects that we call notes. The notes of any banker can be distinguished from those of any other banker. These notes are the only durable assets. Finally, each person can carry at most one note from one date to the next.

Although I will continue to use the labels *bankers* and *nonbankers*, a more straightforward interpretation of this model is that it is a model of payable-to-the-bearer trade credit instruments. When a nonbanker produces for a banker and receives a note, the nonbanker is like a worker or a supplier of goods to a firm that is paid in the form of a trade credit instrument. Thus, the questions about uniformity that I will address can be regarded as ones about trade credit instruments. Should these circulate at par, and should the trade credit of one issuer be redeemed by others?

### 3. SYMMETRIC, STATIONARY, PURE
### STRATEGY, IMPLEMENTABLE ALLOCATIONS

Here, I limit consideration to a very small class of allocations, even smaller than was studied originally. I assume that all trades, except those between two bankers, involve a transfer of one bank note, without regard to which bank issued it. Bankers give gifts to each other and never trade notes among themselves. There are, then, four potentially distinct output levels. Let $y_{ij}$ denote output where $i \in [b,n]$ is the identity ($b$ for banker, $n$ for nonbanker) of the producer and $j \in [b, n]$ is the identity of the consumer.[1] Because each output level (except $y_{bb}$) is exchanged for one bank note, $y_{nb}$ is the issue value (in goods) of a note, $y_{bn}$ is the redemption value, and $y_{nn}$ is the circulation value. In this context, issue, circulation, and redemption at par mean only that all three are equal. Circulation at a discount (relative to redemption), which Rolnick, Smith, and Weber report was sometimes the case, is $y_{nn} < y_{bn}$. Issue at a discount, which may well have occurred, means $y_{nb} < y_{bn}$ or $y_{nb} < y_{nn}$. A low redemption value could be interpreted as $y_{bn} < y_{nn}$ or $y_{bn} < y_{nb}$.

To consider the question of whether it is good for banks to redeem each other's notes, I proceed as follows: I subdivide each $[0, B]$ interval of bankers into $K$ equal subintervals and assume each bank redeems only the notes issued by banks in its subinterval. If banks only redeem notes from banks in their subinterval, then a particular nonbanker consumer with a note who meets a banker producer will trade the note for $y_{bn}$ with probability $\frac{1}{K}$ and will not trade with probability $1 - \frac{1}{K}$. (Given the random meetings, this scheme is consistent with the symmetrical treatment of all notes.) The extent to which banks redeem each other's notes is modeled by varying $K$.

Of course, $K$ has an effect on the steady-state stock of notes, unless I make some other adjustment. If banks always issue notes in meetings with potential nonbank producers but only redeem notes with probability $\frac{1}{K}$, then the steady-state fraction of nonbankers with notes is $\frac{K}{K+1}$. This effect of $K$ on the stock of notes is an unpleasant consequence of the bound on individual holdings. To avoid it, I make note issue probabilistic and assume that $\frac{1}{K}$ is also the probability that a banker issues a note in a meeting with a potential nonbanker producer. This assumption makes the steady-state stock of notes in the hands of nonbankers independent of $K$: In particular, half of nonbankers have a note.

In this simple version, an allocation consists of the four output levels and $K$. To describe those that are implementable, it is convenient to first set out expected discounted utilities as functions of the allocation, under the assumption that

---

[1]  An even simpler version would assume that bankers do not meet each other. In the original formulation, we also considered outright gifts from bankers to nonbankers.

everyone trades according to the allocation. For such allocations, a banker has no state. Thus, I let $v_b$ denote the expected utility of a banker, $v_0$ that of a nonbanker without a note, and $v_1$ that of a nonbanker with a note—all at the start of a date prior to meetings. These values satisfy

(1) $\quad v_b = \beta v_b + \dfrac{B}{S} [u(y_{bb}) - y_{bb}] + \dfrac{(1-B)}{2SK} [u(y_{nb}) - y_{bn}]$

(2) $\quad v_0 = \beta v_0 + \dfrac{B}{SK} (-y_{nb} + \beta \Delta) + \dfrac{(1-B)}{2S} (-y_{nn} + \beta \Delta)$

(3) $\quad v_1 = \beta v_1 + \dfrac{B}{SK} [u(y_{bn}) - \beta \Delta] + \dfrac{(1-B)}{2S} [u(y_{nn}) - \beta \Delta]$,

where $\Delta \equiv v_1 - v_0$.[2] I call an allocation "implementable" if individuals who take next-period values as given do not want to individually defect to autarky in the meeting. The information assumptions preclude the punishment of individual nonbankers. By assumption, I rule out positive-measure punishment responses to individual defections. That, in turn, implies that nonbankers can choose autarky in a meeting with impunity. Hence, they participate if and only if they receive non-negative gains from trade. I also assume that a banker who defects to autarky in a meeting can do so, but he faces permanent autarky (a zero payoff) as a consequence. It follows that bankers are tempted to defect only when they are asked to produce. These assumptions give rise to the following constraints:

(4) $\quad \max \{y_{bb}, y_{bn}\} \le \beta v_b$

and

(5) $\quad \max \{y_{nn}, y_{nb}\} \le \beta \Delta \le \min \{u(y_{bn}), u(y_{nn})\}$.

The first restricts banker production, while the second assures non-negative gains from trade for nonbankers in all meetings.

One welfare criterion is representative-agent welfare, given by

$$w \equiv B v_b + \frac{(1-B)}{2} (v_0 + v_1).$$

Alternatively, I could distinguish between bankers and nonbankers and consider Pareto efficient allocations, or I could go even further and distinguish nonbankers by money holdings. I will use the representative-agent criterion because it is most likely to yield strong results. It follows from equations (1)–(3) that

(6) $\quad w = \dfrac{B^2}{S(1-\beta)} z(y_{bb}) + \dfrac{(1-B)B}{2KS(1-\beta)} [z(y_{nb}) + z(y_{bn})] + \dfrac{(1-B)^2}{4S(1-\beta)} z(y_{nn})$,

where $z(y) \equiv u(y) - y$.

---

[2] Given the four outputs and $K$, $v$ is uniquely determined.

Thus, the welfare problem is to maximize $w$ by choice of the four output levels and $K \geq 1$, subject to equations (4) and (5). Let $y^*$ denote the output that maximizes $z$. Obviously, according to equation (6), the unconstrained optimum of $w$ is $y_{ij} \equiv y^*$ and $K = 1$.

## 4. SHOULD BANKS REDEEM EACH OTHER'S NOTES?

That is, should $K$ be unity? If the unconstrained optimum is implementable—that is, satisfies (4) and (5)—then the answer is yes. If not, then the answer is not so obvious. If $u(y_{nb}) - y_{bn} \geq 0$, then $v_b$ is decreasing in $K$, and the first constraint would be made more slack by decreasing $K$ while holding outputs fixed. The inequality $u(y_{nb}) - y_{bn} \geq 0$ would be necessary for $v_b \geq 0$ if bankers did not meet each other. Alternatively, it could be interpreted as a condition for voluntary participation in the note issue and redemption scheme. It follows from equations (2) and (3) that $\delta$ is decreasing in $K$. That tells us the producer constraints in (5) are made more slack as $K$ is reduced for given outputs. It follows that if optimum outputs for a given arbitrary $K$ imply slack consumer constraints in (5) and $u(y_{nb}) - y_{bn} \geq 0$, then reducing $K$ improves welfare. There is some hope for establishing the slack consumer-constraint condition.

If an allocation with $y_{ij} \equiv y^*$ and an arbitrary $K$ is not implementable, then it violates one of the producer constraints, either the one for bankers or the one for nonbankers. More generally, if all outputs are identical at some amount, then nonbankers alternate between consuming and producing that amount. Satisfaction of the nonbanker producer constraint requires the utility of consuming that amount to be sufficiently greater than the disutility of producing it, because there is random delay and discounting. It follows that satisfaction of the producer constraint at such an amount implies the consumer constraint is slack. Therefore, it may be possible to arrive at a general affirmative answer to whether the optimum has banks redeeming each other's notes.

## 5. SHOULD ISSUE, CIRCULATION, AND REDEMPTION VALUES BE IDENTICAL?

Again, if the unconstrained optimum is implementable, then the answer is yes. But what if some constraints are binding? If the unconstrained optimum is not implementable, then some producer constraint is violated. For many parameters, the binding constraint will be a nonbanker producer constraint. (A sufficiently small magnitude for $\frac{\beta}{S}$ implies binding producer constraints.) If so, that constraint would be made more slack—and, hence, welfare improved—if interest could be paid on notes. This model allows for a probabilistic version of interest on notes. It is achieved by having the issue value and/or the circulation value be less than the redemption value. Although I have not produced a complete argument, I am confident that such outcomes are optimal for a substantial region of the parameter space.

## 6. PUTTING REGIONS INTO THE MODEL

The existence of different geographic regions plays an important role in the descriptions given by Rolnick, Smith, and Weber. Therefore, I will briefly indicate how to convert the above model into a model of regions. For outside money, this has already been done, and the same device can be used here. Matsuyama, Kiyotaki, and Matsui (1993) consider two regions: People who live in one region meet others more frequently than they meet people from the other region. This device, which I find to be an attractive way to think of regions for studying currency substitution and related matters, could be embedded in the above model.

In particular, a symmetrical two-region version would have two identical regions with people in each region meeting each other with probability $\theta$ and meeting people in the other region with probability $1 - \theta$. Although optimum problems are not explicitly considered in Matsuyama, Kiyotaki, and Matsui (1993) (and in the related work of Trejos and Wright [1996] and Zhou [1997]), and although they study outside money, their results strongly suggest that if $\theta$ is near enough to unity, there are feasible outcomes in which there is no trade across regions, in which people hold only the notes of the banks in their region, and in which banks in one region only redeem notes issued by banks in the region. However, such outcomes, which have different regions using different monies and not trading with each other, are almost certainly worse in terms of welfare than one in which there is a uniform currency across regions. One aspect of the uniformity would be banks redeeming the notes of all other banks. Hence, adding regions would not seem to weaken the surmise that good systems have banks redeeming each other's notes. And adding regions would not seem to have any special consequences for whether issue, circulation, and redemption values should or should not be identical.

## 7. CONCLUSION

In his review of Friedman and Schwartz (1963), Tobin (1965) criticizes the authors for not setting out an explicit theoretical framework. Is there a widely accepted framework that can be used to deal with the variety of monetary experiences that Friedman and Schwartz describe or that Rolnick, Smith, and Weber describe? I do not think so. That leaves Friedman and Schwartz and Rolnick, Smith, and Weber appealing to bits and pieces of theory—some price theory including arbitrage arguments, augmented by assumed demands for assets labeled money. The problem with such theorizing is that the bits and pieces are not likely to fit together.

They are unlikely to be consistent with a single coherent underlying model. The model I have set out above includes some extreme and unpalatable assumptions. But because those assumptions form a coherent model, the model can be discussed, amended, and generalized. Even as it stands, I find it helpful for thinking about some of the issues that Rolnick, Smith, and Weber discuss.

## ACKNOWLEDGMENTS

The author thanks the Pennsylvania State University. He is indebted to Ricardo Cavalcanti for helpful comments on a preliminary draft.

## REFERENCES

Cavalcanti, Ricardo, and Neil Wallace. 1999a. A Model of Private Bank Note Issue. *Review of Economic Dynamics* 2: 104–36.

———, and ———. 1999b. Inside and Outside Money as Alternative Media of Exchange. *Journal of Money, Credit, and Banking* 31: 443–57.

Friedman, Milton, and Anna J. Schwartz. 1963. *A Monetary History of the United States*. Princeton, N.J.: Princeton University Press.

Matsuyama, Kiminori, Nobuhiro Kiyotaki, and Akihiko Matsui. 1993. Toward a Theory of International Currency. *Review of Economic Studies* 60: 283–307.

Shi, Shonyong. 1995. Money and Prices: Akihiko Model of Search and Bargaining. *Journal of Economic Theory* 67: 467–98.

Tobin, James. 1965. The Monetary Interpretation of History. *American Economic Review* 55: 464–85.

Trejos, Alberto, and Randall Wright. 1995. Search, Bargaining, Money, and Prices. *Journal of Political Economy* 103: 118–41.

———, and ———. 1996. Search-Theoretic Models of International Currency. *Federal Reserve Bank of St. Louis Review* May: 117–32.

Zhou, R. 1997. Currency Exchange in a Random Search Model. *Review of Economic Studies* 64: 289–310.

# Commentary

*Bruce Champ*

### 1. INTRODUCTION

Rolnick, Smith, and Weber provide a fascinating description of attempts to provide a uniform currency during the early period of the United States. They also present an interesting summary of the problems that can exist when a uniform currency is lacking.

### 1. THE ELUSIVE GOAL: ESTABLISHMENT OF A UNIFORM CURRENCY

Why was so much importance placed on the establishment of a uniform currency in the early period of the United States? This emphasis appears to be motivated by the country's experience during its formative years.

Irredeemable bills of credit issued by the colonies and by the states fluctuated in value against specie and against each other. This exchange rate variability created high transaction costs and was viewed as disruptive to trade between the colonies and, later, between the states.

Furthermore, a significant seigniorage incentive problem existed whereby colonial and state governments attempted to extract seigniorage revenue from their neighbors (for instance, Rhode Island during the colonial period and several states during the period of Confederation), a fact that is well documented by Rolnick, Smith, and Weber (1993). As an example, by 1744, 43 percent of New England's money was issued by Rhode Island.

Even after the constitutional prohibition on the issuance of bills of credit by the states, problems persisted. Exchange rate variability continued with the issuance of state banknotes. This was evidenced by widely varying discounts on state banknotes across regions of the country.

The problems associated with a currency lacking in uniformity were well recognized by contemporaries. For example, the importance of establishing a uniform currency was a common theme during the discussion of the chartering of the Second Bank of the United States.

> It is, however, essential to every modification of the finances that the benefits of an uniform national currency should be restored to the community (Madison 1815).

> In referring to the causes which had the most decided influence in calling the United States Bank into existence, the inconveniences resulting to the community from the inequality in the rate of exchange between the different sections of the Union stand eminently prominent. (Crawford 1817, 540)

This second quotation clearly makes reference to the problems that the lack of a uniform currency created with respect to interregional trade.

## 2. PROVISION OF A UNIFORM CURRENCY

According to Rolnick, Smith, and Weber, the achievement of a uniform currency requires two features:

- At par redemption on demand (with certainty) in the form of outside money.
- The note holder should not bear the cost of redemption.

Prior to the national banking system, these conditions typically were not met.

Although penalties existed for an institution's failure to redeem notes—ranging from interest payments to closure of the bank—enforcement of these provisions by most states was lax, at best. States benefited in terms of revenue by not enforcing redemption. As the authors point out, the Constitution took away many means for states to collect revenue. It was a natural response for states to find alternative revenue sources.

In addition, before the national banking system, note redemption costs were almost always borne by the holder. A note holder was required to redeem the note at the bank of issue, a costly action for the bearer. Alternatively, the bearer bore the cost in terms of a discount on the note in trade.

The National Banking Act (1863) provided a uniform currency. Under this act, banks were required to redeem their own notes at par in lawful money and to accept the notes of other banks at par, and the costs of note redemption were borne by the issuing bank, not by the bearer. However, even during the national banking system, at par circulation of all forms of money was not achieved until the resumption of specie payment in 1879.

## 3. DISCOUNTS ON NOTES

During the early 1800s, state banknotes displayed significant variations in discounts across banks and over time. These discounts reflected all of the expected costs of redemption. Three factors affected the discounts:

- The probability of a note holder demanding redemption. These probabilities definitely were positive during this period since certain transactions required specie (international transactions and payment of some forms of taxes).
- The cost to a note holder of redeeming notes.
- Note default risk. This refers to the ability of the note issuer to keep the promise to redeem. States often sanctioned suspensions of specie payment. Furthermore, without perfect insurance of notes, doubts about the solvency of a bank could lead to discounts. Here, credibility is also important. If note holders questioned the ability of the issuer to redeem in full, discounts could arise. During the state banking period, notes generally were paid back in the case of failure at par or at a small discount. However, notable exceptions to this rule certainly existed (see Rolnick and Weber 1982, 1983).

Fluctuations in these factors led to variations in discounts. Variations in discounts could arise even without these factors varying just so long as rates of exchange did not get too far out of line so that arbitrage possibilities existed.

## 4. SEIGNIORAGE INCENTIVE PROBLEM

In addition to discounts on notes, another problem that arises with the private issuance of banknotes is the seigniorage incentive problem. With notes trading at fixed rates of exchange, notes become perfect substitutes and have the same rate of return. This gives rise to a seigniorage incentive problem when currencies are not redeemable. The issuer with the highest rate of money creation can extract seigniorage revenue from the holders of all currency.

As Rolnick, Smith, and Weber point out, the seigniorage incentive problem was present among state banks during the early 1800s and between the branches of the Second Bank of the United States. Debatably, this may have been one of Hamilton's worries when, in his proposal for the establishment of the First Bank of the United States, he argued against establishing branches:

> The argument against it is, that each branch must be under a distinct, though subordinate direction, to which a considerable latitude of discretion must of necessity be entrusted. And as the property of the whole institution would be liable for the engagements of each part, that and its credit would be at stake, upon the prudence of the directors of every part. The mismanagement of either branch might hazard serious disorder in the whole. (Quoted in Wettereau 1942, 70)

The inflation that arises from the seigniorage incentive problem obviates the advantages of a uniform currency. To minimize this problem, issuers may attempt to differentiate their currencies to make them imperfect substitutes. For example, the colony of Connecticut prohibited the circulation of Rhode Island notes in 1752. However, such attempts to differentiate currencies also undermine the advantages of a uniform currency.

Redemption of notes at par alleviates the seigniorage incentive problem. Banks have the incentive to redeem notes of their overissuing counterparts. An overissuing bank will find its notes promptly redeemed for specie, forcing a contraction of its issue.

## 5. ATTEMPTS TO PROVIDE A UNIFORM CURRENCY

### 5.1. Suffolk System (1825–58)

The Suffolk System was the first system of net clearing of regional banknotes in the United States. The banknotes of participating banks were cleared at par by netting the accounts of the participating banks. Notes of nonparticipating banks were promptly redeemed by the Suffolk System. Due to net clearing, the system lowered the cost of redeeming banknotes by minimizing the shipment of specie. For participating banks, the cost of redeeming notes essentially was driven to zero.

The evidence supports the success of the Suffolk System in that the notes of participating banks traded at par. Hence, it did achieve the goal of uniform currency, but only in the New England region where it operated.

### 5.2. Second Bank of the United States (1816–36)

When the Second Bank of the United States was formed in 1816, the nation was far from a situation of currency uniformity. In the midst of the War of 1812, state banks around the country—with the exception of New England banks—began suspending specie payment in April 1814. This forced the "government to receive its revenues in state-bank paper and treasury notes of all degrees of depreciation" (Catterall 1902, 4) and greatly impeded the financing of the war effort.

Originally opposed to the formation of the First Bank of the United States, President Madison rejected a bill proposing the chartering of a second national bank. However, his Secretary of the Treasury, Alexander Dallas, claimed the only way to restore specie payment and to create a uniform currency was to establish a national bank. In his 1815 annual report, Dallas stated,

> It is a fact, however, incontestably proved, that those institutions [state banks] cannot, at this time, be successfully employed to provide a uniform national currency.... A national bank will, therefore, possess the

means and the opportunity of supplying a circulating medium of equal
use and value in every State, and in every district of every State.

Madison ultimately concurred in his State of the Nation address in 1815. The
bill establishing the Second Bank of the United States (SBUS) passed Congress in
April 1816 and was signed into law by Madison.

In a series of proposals to state banks, Dallas and his successor, William
Crawford, began the difficult process of providing for the restoration of specie payments. An agreement between the SBUS and the state banks was finally achieved
on February 1, 1817, with specie payments to resume February 20, 1817. However,
this goal was not completely achieved. The panic of 1819 brought renewed suspension of convertibility of state banknotes. State banks often refused to pay out
specie when the SBUS presented its notes for redemption. In fact, the U.S.
Treasury frequently urged leniency on the part of the SBUS regarding the redemption of state banknotes. Catterall (1902, 37) provides evidence that discounts on
state banknotes remained high in certain regions. Secretary of the Treasury
Crawford admitted that "the convertibility of banknotes into specie has been rather
nominal than real in the largest portion of the Union" (Catterall 1902, 38).

The SBUS itself only maintained redeemability of its own notes at each of its
branches during 1817–18. This practice was stopped on August 28, 1818, and the
notes of the separate branches were quoted at discounts of up to 4 percent (Catterall
1902, 416). As Catterall states, "There were now nineteen distinct currencies of the
Bank of the United States, and to a considerable extent the country lost one of the
principal benefits sought in the establishment of the bank" (415). The Bank's action
prompted a congressional investigation. Secretary of the Treasury Crawford also
came down hard on the SBUS for this action, threatening its extinction. In 1819,
"the bank restored the quality of universal redeemability in respect to its five-
dollar notes" (Catterall 1902, 415), but notes of larger denominations were not
universally accepted at par. In fact, at times the branches of the SBUS refused to
accept the notes of the other branches at all.

Nicholas Biddle assumed the presidency of the SBUS in 1823. Biddle took
seriously the Bank's role in providing a uniform currency. He believed the only
way to accomplish this was to become a net creditor to the state banks and to
promptly redeem state banknotes in specie. This action would lower state bank
reserves, curtail lending by state banks, and provide restraint against overissue. In
the process, the SBUS notes would displace those of the state banks, an action that
would lead to a more uniform currency. According to Catterall, Biddle achieved
some degree of success toward this goal: "The state banks were compelled to
redeem their notes frequently, and the currency showed a progressive improvement" (99). Catterall goes on to claim that the SBUS "put an end to most of the
depreciated state-bank currencies" (113).

Biddle himself claimed success at establishing a uniform currency, stating that

> The experiment was interesting and hazardous. It was to try how far
> the institution could succeed ... in diffusing over so wide a surface of
> country a currency of large amount and of uniform value at all places
> and under all circumstances. [The bank has fulfilled] all the purposes
> for which it was created. At present these exchanges are generally
> either at par, or at the utmost one-half of one percent.
> (*Niles Register*, quoted in Catterall 1902, 132–33)

A report by the House Ways and Means Committee concurred, claiming that
the Bank "actually furnished a circulating medium more uniform than specie"
because it lowered the rates of exchange across the regions of the country by
saving the costs of shipping specie (Report of April 13, 1830, H.R. 358, 21st
Cong., 1st sess., p. 14). President Jackson, however, disagreed: In his State of the
Nation address of 1829, which prompted the House study, he said, "it must
be admitted by all that [the Bank] has failed in the great end of establishing a
uniform and sound currency."

In principle, it seemed as if the SBUS was in a position to make significant
advances toward the provision of a uniform currency, and many contemporaries
believed it had succeeded at doing so. However, Rolnick, Smith, and Weber find
that the SBUS did not significantly reduce the costs of redemption for holders of
state banknotes. Therefore, they conclude that the SBUS failed in its attempt to provide a uniform currency. This author must concur, with some reservation. Although
the SBUS went part of the way toward establishing a uniform currency by lowering interregional rates of exchange, its impact on the degree of discounts among
state banknotes does not appear dramatic when confronted with the data. The
resumption of specie payments by the state banks appears to have been the driving
force behind the reduction in state banknote discounts. The policies of the SBUS
seem to have played a minimal role in the reduction of discounts. Nonetheless, one
must not diminish the role played by the SBUS in the restoration of specie payment
by state banks. On numerous occasions, it attempted to force state banks to redeem
their notes in specie. Catterall (1902, 440–44) details the efforts of the SBUS in
forcing the convertibility of state banknotes.

## 6. AT PAR REDEMPTION

Rolnick, Smith, and Weber claim that at par redemption is a necessary factor for the establishment of a uniform currency. However, in reading their paper, one might wonder, what is special about par? In other words, which is most important: at par redemption, or fixed exchange rates between the existing currencies?

Suppose we look at the plots of discounts for various banknotes and observe, contrary to reality, that these discounts were constant over time. Would we call that a uniform currency system? Such an argument seems plausible. Such a system would merely be one with many denominations of the same currency. In fact, at times the discounts do remain fairly constant. It seems that eliminating exchange rate risk is the most important factor. This issue is important because Rolnick, Smith, and Weber often associate the mere presence of discounts with the lack of a uniform currency. I would focus more on the fluctuations in discounts.

In fact, at par redemption may not be the most efficient outcome, given that the costs of shipping specie varied across banks. Catterall (1902) and others[1] imply that discounts on notes issued by the SBUS were to be expected for this reason.

So why do Rolnick, Smith, and Weber emphasize the notion of at par redemption? On closer examination, it is probably reasonable for a number of reasons. Certainly, contemporary references to a "uniform currency" were trading at par with respect to all currencies.

Furthermore, at par redemption is desirable from the viewpoint of convenience. There is a tremendous informational advantage to having at par redemption. Without it, one needs to have information on the wide number of different discounts at which notes trade. Such information would come at a cost. With at par redemption, however, this information is unnecessary.

In addition, how do you make change? Coin and currencies possessed indivisibilities. Exchanging one note that has a premium of, say, 1.395 relative to another may be impossible due to these indivisibilities.

## 7. AREAS FOR FURTHER RESEARCH

This paper provides an interesting description of early attempts to provide a uniform currency in the United States. It does leave open a number of questions that merit further research.

### 7.1. Can Private Markets Provide a Uniform Currency?

One question that naturally arises is, can competitive private markets alone provide a uniform currency? At first glance, looking at the Suffolk System, one

---

1 See, for example, the Report of the the House Ways and Means Committee on the Bank of the United States (Report of April 13, 1830, H.R. 358, 21st Cong., 1st session, pp. 13–14).

may be tempted to say yes. Certainly, it does not appear that state governments in the region purposely created laws with the intent of providing a uniform currency. State banks themselves took the initiative to provide at par clearing of notes. However, it does appear that Suffolk had some government protection of its note-clearing monopoly and tax incentives were given to participants (Vermont, for example).

Certainly, there is no direct evidence that a Suffolk-like system was repeated elsewhere in the United States, although a similar system existed in Mexico with the Banco Central System. According to Patrice Robitaille (1997, 1), "Banco Central redeemed member bank notes for specie (gold or silver coin) at par and acted as their agent in the clearing of other payments. Because of Banco Central's role in the arrangement, I call it the Banco Central System (BCS). The BCS lasted until 1913, two years after the revolution began."

But why wasn't the Suffolk System duplicated elsewhere in the United States? It appeared to have several advantages:

- The Suffolk System was profitable for the organizing bank (Rolnick, Smith, and Weber 1998).
- Such a system generated significant efficiencies in the redemption process through net clearing.
- The net-clearing aspect of the system saved costs by not requiring the shipment of specie.
- The Suffolk System provided a more efficient monitoring of note default risk. Rather than all note holders bearing the costs of monitoring note default risk, the Suffolk bank became the sole monitor of risk. This undoubtedly saved resources.
- A successful Suffolk-like system made the notes of participating banks more attractive. This allowed them a greater range of circulation and a longer period of circulation before redemption.

One must wonder whether government restrictions prevented the establishment of Suffolk-like systems elsewhere.

Were there less formal note-clearing arrangements present in other areas of the country? Looking at the data, one cannot overlook the possibility. Notes within states often traded at the same discount. This suggests that within these states, notes were trading at par relative to one another. Table 1 presents data on time periods within certain states that all state banknotes traded at the same discount.[2] The data presented in this table are fairly conservative. I'm looking only at situations in which all banks in a state had the same discount. There are additional examples where most banknotes within a state had the same discount.

2  The data are originally from *Van Court's Counterfeit Detector and Bank Note List*. Gary Gorton collected the data in electronic form. Amendments to the data, assembled by Warren Weber, are available at www.minneapolisfed.org/research/economists/wewproj.html.

**Table 1: States With Common Discounts on State Banknotes**

| State | Period |
|---|---|
| Delaware | February 1839–October 1852, September 1854–December 1858 |
| Louisiana | June 1849–December 1858 |
| Nebraska | January 1848–December 1858 |
| North Carolina | February 1839–August 1853 |

There is some evidence that casual attempts were made to improve the clearing of banknotes. Fenstermaker (1965, 80) notes correspondent relations between New England banks and New York banks, stating "Some New England banks also kept balances in correspondent banks at Troy, Albany, and New York City to maintain their banknote quality." He also states, "In 1823, the Virginia banks established a system of interbank deposits which kept their notes near par at major commercial centers" (84). Weber (2001) finds correspondent relations among Pennsylvania banks in which country banknotes were accepted at par by correspondent banks in the large cities.

However, more investigation is needed as to the extent to which notes were accepted at par under these varied correspondent arrangements. The evidence on discounts seems to imply these schemes were not successful in general. However, more research is needed into the effect that correspondent relationships had on the provision of at par redemption of notes.

### 7.2 The Importance of Denomination Restrictions in Privately Issued Currencies

To promote redemption, Smith ([1776] 1994) advocated minimum denomination restrictions on privately issued currencies. Note holders would have a greater incentive to monitor the redemption of large-denomination notes. This view permeates many of the banking laws of the United States and other countries in which minimum denomination restrictions were common features of banking laws.

However, to what extent was this advice followed during the period under study? Catterall notes the existence of "an immense circulation of notes of less value than $5—calculated, indeed, at almost one-fourth of the amount of currency issued by the state banks" (1902, 446). In fact, note issues as small as $6^{1}\!/_{2}$ cents were observed in the two Carolinas. Even after resumption, we observe continued relatively high discounts in North Carolina. One must question whether the presence of small-denomination notes inhibited redemption and led to overissue.

### 7.3 The Importance of Branch Banking Laws

The degree of branching varied significantly across states, with branch banking systems more prevalent in the South and West. One might expect a high degree of branching to be more supportive of a uniform currency within that state. However, it needs to be investigated as to the degree that branch banks accepted the notes of other branches at par and, hence, altered the cost to note holders of redeeming notes. Certainly, most of the time, even the branches of the SBUS did not accept the notes of other branches at par.

## 8. CONCLUSION

This paper presents an interesting perspective on the attempts by the Suffolk System and the Second Bank of the United States to provide a uniform currency. Both of these attempts did not achieve this goal with complete success. The Suffolk System only provided a uniform currency among the regional banks that participated in the system. The Second Bank of the United States, although in a better position to provide a uniform currency due to its national reach, failed to achieve a truly uniform currency. Discounts on state banknotes did not diminish significantly during its existence and actually appeared to be smaller in many cases after the SBUS lost it charter.

This paper suggests numerous possibilities for future research. Evidence exists that correspondent relationships existed which might have promoted greater uniformity in the currency issued by state banks. Issues regarding the effects of branch banking laws and denominational restrictions on banknote issue also deserve further attention.

## References

Catterall, Ralph C.H. 1902. *The Second Bank of the United States*. Chicago: University of Chicago Press.

Crawford, William. 1817. Letter to William Jones, July 3. *American State Papers: Finance*. Vol. IV.

Dallas, Alexander. 1815. *Annual Report on a National Bank*. December 6.

Fenstermaker, Joseph Van. 1965. *The Development of American Commercial Banking: 1782–1837*. Kent, Oh.: Kent State University.

Kaplan, Edward S. 1999. *The Bank of the United States and the American Economy*. Westport, Conn.: Greenwood Press.

Madison, James. 1815. Seventh Annual Message to Congress. December 5.

Robitaille, Patrice. 1997. Private Payments Systems in Historical Perspective: The Banco Central System of Mexico. Board of Governors of the Federal Reserve System, *International Finance Discussion Papers,* no. 1997-599.

Rolnick, Arthur J., and Warren E. Weber. 1982. Free Banking, Wildcat Banking, and Shinplasters. *Federal Reserve Bank of Minneapolis Quarterly Review* 6: 10–19.

Rolnick, Arthur J., and Warren E. Weber. 1983. New Evidence on the Free Banking Era. *American Economic Review* 73: 1080–91.

1993. In Order to Form a More Perfect Monetary Union. *Federal Reserve Bank of Minneapolis Quarterly Review* 17: 2–13.

Rolnick, Arthur J., Bruce D. Smith, and Warren E. Weber. 1998. Lessons from a Laissez-faire Payments System: The Suffolk Banking System (1825–58). *Federal Reserve Bank of St. Louis Review* 80: 105–16. [1776] 1994.

Smith, Adam. [1776] 1994. *An Inquiry into the Nature and Causes of the Wealth of Nations*. New York: Modern Library.

Schur, Leon M. 1960. The Second Bank of the United States and the Inflation after the War of 1812. *Journal of Political Economy* 68: 118–34.

Weber, Warren E. 2001. Interbank Payments Relationships in the Antebellum United States. Federal Reserve Bank of Minneapolis, unpublished manuscript.

Wettereau, James O. 1942. The Branches of the First Bank of the United States. *Journal of Economic History* 2: 66–100.

# Currency Competition in the Digital Age

*Randall S. Kroszner*

## 1. INTRODUCTION

A striking macroeconomic fact is the dramatic recent decline in worldwide inflation. What accounts for this newfound discipline by central banks around the
globe? I argue that an important but largely overlooked factor is technological
innovation in transactions and payments services. Such innovations have significantly reduced the costs of using alternative means of payment when the local
currency is rapidly depreciating in value. A quarter-century ago, Hayek (1978)
argued that breaking a central bank's monopoly of issue is necessary to protect
against the inflationary excesses to which government central banks have
succumbed throughout history.[1] To achieve this end, Hayek proposed the abolition
of legal tender laws and the elimination of government controls on monetary movements around the globe. I argue that advances in transactions and payments
technology have eroded the local monopoly of issue and have resulted in greater
discipline on central bank behavior. In addition, these advances have enhanced the
feasibility of private-sector provision of monetary services.

I first document the trends in worldwide inflation during the last 40 years.
I then discuss alternative explanations for the recent reduction, including the rise of
central bank independence, the role of fixed exchange rates as discipline devices,
and various political and fiscal factors. I also explain the role of technology in more
detail. This will form the basis of a more speculative discussion of what the evolution of these transactions technologies implies for the feasibility of private
provision of monetary services and the forms that such competition to central bank
issue would likely take.

## 2. THE RISE AND DECLINE OF INFLATION
## AROUND THE WORLD SINCE 1960

Figure 1 presents the median annual rate of inflation for all of the countries in the
International Monetary Fund's *International Financial Statistics* database from
1960 to 1999. The number of countries ranges from a minimum of 68 in 1960 to a

---

[1]  See Klein (1974) and Vaubel (1977) for models of private competitive currency supply.

maximum of 159 in 1996. In all of the figures and tables, inflation is measured by the nation's consumer price index.[2] Figure 2 depicts median inflation rates by region.

Median world inflation began its upward trend during the last years of the Bretton Woods system. In the early 1970s, median world inflation jumped as that system collapsed and the OPEC oil price shock hit. Median world inflation rose again in the early 1980s and then drifted lower until the early 1990s, when median world inflation began to move up. The increase in the 1990s was driven by the entry of the countries of the former Soviet Union into the sample. As figure 2 shows, the countries of Europe and Central Asia experienced bouts of high inflation in the early 1990s.[3]

**Figure 1:  Median and Deciles of Inflation across all Countries (1960–99)**

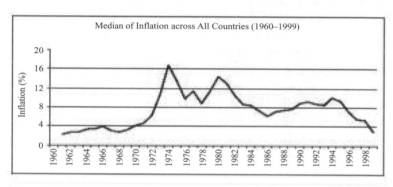

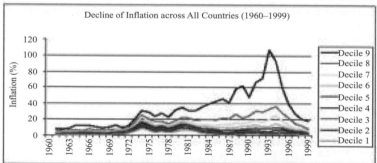

Note:  The number of countries ranges from 68 to 159. Inflation is defined as a change in the consumer price index.
Source: *International Financial Statistics.*

---

[2]  The patterns appear the same when the GDP deflator is used as the measure of inflation.
[3]  A temporary spike also occurred in sub-Saharan Africa at the end of the CFA-Franc era.

**Figure 2: Medians of Inflation Categorized by Region (1960–99)**

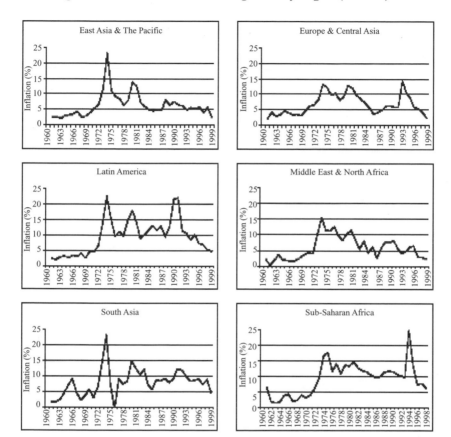

Note: The number of countries ranges from 68 to 159. Inflation is defined as a change in the consumer price index.
Source: *International Financial Statistics.*

What is most striking in the data is the steep, steady decline in worldwide inflation during the last five years to levels not seen since the end of the Bretton Woods era. In 1999, the world median annual inflation rate was 3 percent. This decline occurred despite tumultuous conditions in many parts of the world, from the Asian crisis in 1997, to the Russian crisis in 1998, to the devaluation in Brazil in 1999. In the past, financial and fiscal crises were often associated with episodes of high inflation; clearly, this has not generally been the case recently.

The lower panel of figure 1 shows the distribution of inflation performance across countries. Rather than reporting the median for all countries, this panel breaks down inflation rates by decile. The line for decile 9, for example, represents the inflation rate of the country that experienced the top-decile inflation in each year (that is, 90 percent of countries had lower inflation in that year). By examining the experience of the top-decile country, we can observe how countries with the most extreme inflation performance have evolved over time. In 1999, the top-decile annual inflation rate was 18 percent; the inflation performance of the top decile has not been this low since the end of Bretton Woods.

This recent reduction in inflation stands in sharp contrast to the overall abysmal worldwide inflation experience of the post–Bretton Woods era. Table 1 reports the change in the consumer price index and the extent of the decline in purchasing power of each national currency during 1972–99. Not a single currency maintained even half its purchasing power over the period. As figure 3 shows, more than half the countries experienced a reduction in purchasing power of more than 90 percent (that is, the price level was more than 10 times higher in 1999 than it was at the end of 1972).[4] Next I will consider alternative explanations for why inflation performance has improved so much relative to the period spanning the early 1970s to the early 1990s.

**Figure 3:  Countries Categorized by the Extent of the Decline in
the Purchasing Power of their Currency, 1972–99**

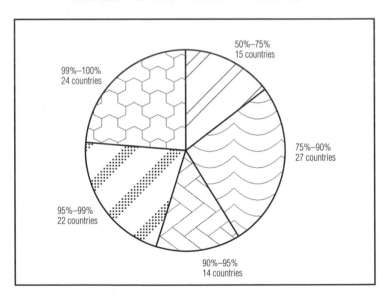

Note:  The total number of countries is 102.
Source:  Table 1.

---

[4]  For more details on currency debasement in the post–World War II era, see Mas (1995).

Table 1: **Inflation and Decline in Purchasing Power of Currency, 1972–99**

| Country | Increase in CPI, 1972–99 | Decline in Purchasing, Power, 1972–99 |
|---|---|---|
| GERMANY | 134% | –57.28% |
| SWITZERLAND | 138% | –58.02% |
| PANAMA | 143% | –58.82% |
| SINGAPORE | 163% | –62.03% |
| NETHERLANDS | 177% | –63.87% |
| JAPAN | 184% | –64.74% |
| AUSTRIA | 186% | –65.08% |
| MALTA | 193% | –65.83% |
| SAUDI ARABIA | 217% | –68.46% |
| LUXEMBOURG | 220% | –68.72% |
| MALAYSIA | 229% | –69.65% |
| KUWAIT | 242% | 70.80% |
| BELGIUM | 245% | –70.99% |
| BAHAMAS, THE | 296% | –74.74% |
| UNITED STATES | 298% | –74.89% |
| NETHERLANDS ANTILLES | 308% | –75.50% |
| CANADA | 324% | –76.41% |
| CYPRUS | 338% | –77.18% |
| INDUSTRIAL COUNTRIES | 340% | –77.28% |
| NIGER | 347% | –77.62% |
| FRANCE | 382% | –79.27% |
| DENMARK | 383% | –79.28% |
| NORWAY | 401% | –80.03% |
| SEYCHELLES | 422% | –80.84% |
| SWEDEN | 448% | –81.74% |
| THAILAND | 466% | –82.35% |
| FINLAND | 467% | –82.37% |
| FIJI | 501% | –83.35% |
| MOROCCO | 510% | –83.61% |
| TOGO | 513% | –83.70% |
| SENEGAL | 521% | –83.90% |
| AUSTRALIA | 523% | –83.94% |
| ST. LUCIA | 526% | –84.04% |
| BARBADOS | 604% | –85.79% |
| DOMINICA | 611% | –85.93% |
| JORDAN | 639% | –86.46% |
| UNITED KINGDOM | 661% | –86.86% |
| IRELAND | 676% | –87.12% |
| PAPUA NEW GUINEA | 684% | –87.24% |
| CAMEROON | 781% | –88.64% |
| NEW ZEALAND | 788% | –88.74% |
| COTE D IVOIRE | 809% | –89.00% |
| INDIA | 927% | –90.26% |
| KOREA | 948% | –90.45% |
| SAMOA | 1024% | –91.10% |
| ITALY | 1061% | –91.39% |
| NEPAL | 1072% | –91.47% |
| SPAIN | 1119% | –91.79% |
| PAKISTAN | 1195% | –92.28% |
| TRINIDAD AND TOBAGO | 1309% | –92.90% |
| MAURITIUS | 1373% | –93.21% |
| SOLOMON ISLANDS | 1476% | –93.65% |

Table 1:  Inflation and Decline in Purchasing Power of Currency, 1972–99

| Country | Increase in CPI, 1972–99 | Decline in Purchasing, Power, 1972–99 |
|---|---|---|
| SRI LANKA | 1485% | −93.69% |
| GAMBIA, THE | 1667% | −94.34% |
| RWANDA | 1684% | −94.40% |
| BURUNDI | 1772% | −94.66% |
| HONDURAS | 1982% | −95.20% |
| SOUTH AFRICA | 2034% | −95.31% |
| PHILIPPINES | 2114% | −95.48% |
| HUNGARY | 2229% | −95.71% |
| ALGERIA | 2309% | −95.85% |
| SWAZILAND | 2331% | −95.89% |
| EGYPT | 2446% | −96.07% |
| GUATEMALA | 2469% | −96.11% |
| HAITI | 2478% | −96.12% |
| SYRIAN ARAB REPUBLIC | 3205% | −96.97% |
| INDONESIA\ | 3209% | −96.98% |
| EL SALVADOR | 3244% | −97.01% |
| KENYA | 3264% | −97.03% |
| PORTUGAL | 3347% | −97.10% |
| MIDDLE EAST | 4272% | −97.71% |
| MADAGASCAR | 4479% | −97.82% |
| GREECE | 4626% | −97.88% |
| DOMINICAN REPUBLIC | 4645% | −97.89% |
| MYANMAR | 6494% | −98.48% |
| PARAGUAY | 6802% | −98.55% |
| ZIMBABWE | 7127% | −98.62% |
| COSTA RICA | 9847% | −98.99% |
| IRAN, I.R. OF | 11922% | −99.17% |
| JAMAICA | 15923% | −99.38% |
| TANZANIA | 25625% | −99.61% |
| COLOMBIA | 26585% | −99.63% |
| NIGERIA | 27132% | −99.63% |
| ICELAND | 34723% | −99.71% |
| VENEZUELA, REP. BOL. | 53588% | −99.81% |
| ECUADOR | 108910% | −99.91% |
| DEVELOPING COUNTRIES | 115537% | −99.91% |
| SURINAME | 144311% | −99.93% |
| MEXICO | 309693% | −99.97% |
| POLAND | 319677% | −99.97% |
| GHANA | 682496% | −99.99% |
| SIERRA LEONE | 821323% | −99.99% |
| SUDAN | 1881780% | −99.99% |
| CHILE | 3010882% | −100.00% |
| ISRAEL | 4120433% | −100.00% |
| TURKEY | 9167376% | −100.00% |
| URUGUAY | 13207282% | −100.00% |
| BOLIVIA | 141514922% | −100.00% |
| PERU | 67235426470% | −100.00% |
| NICARAGUA | 8067632087241% | −100.00% |
| ARGENTINA | 9935301973387% | −100.00% |
| BRAZIL | 273051504844993% | −100.00% |

Note:  Inflation rates are computed as a change in consumer price index over 1972–98 for all countries except for Brazil. The numbers for Brazil are computed from GDP deflator during 1972–98.
Source: *International Financial Statistics.*

## 3. ALTERNATIVE EXPLANATIONS FOR THE RECENT DECLINE IN WORLDWIDE INFLATION

### 3.1. Central Bank Independence

A popular remedy for poor central bank performance is to increase the central bank's independence from the rest of the government (see Alesina and Summers 1993). In principle, such a separation reduces political pressures on the central bank to monetize government debt or to manipulate economic performance for political purposes (for example, prior to an election). Greater independence may also increase the central bank's credibility with the public. Enhanced inflation-fighting credibility then mitigates the "time-consistency" problem that can result in high inflation, even though neither the public nor the central bank prefers such an outcome (see Barro and Gordon 1983).

The consistent, inverse correlation between measures of central bank independence and inflation have led to policy recommendations in favor of greater central bank independence (Alesina and Summers 1993), and these recommendations have led to greater independence in practice during the last decade. The European Union, for example, required independence to be eligible to join the euro, and, as a result, central banks in Europe became more independent of the governments. The Bundesbank, one of the highest ranked in terms of independence, was the model for the European Central Bank, and this structure was consciously chosen to enhance credibility. The World Bank and the International Monetary Fund have also urged emerging and transition economies to adopt independent central banks, and many have done so.

While the recent trend toward greater central bank independence is correlated with improved inflation performance around the world, I believe that central bank independence can provide no more than a partial explanation. First, in order for central bank independence to lead to lower inflation, the independent central banker must have a preference for lower inflation. This proposition may apply to central bankers who have been appointed in OECD countries in recent years, but it cannot be assumed for emerging and transition economies. In Russia, for example, the central bank and its employees enjoyed direct benefits from inflation because it was able to keep some of the profits from high inflation for its management and staff (Shleifer and Treisman 2000). During part of the 1990s, the Russian central bank's independence from political control was an obstacle to inflation control. In other countries, "independent" central bankers may effectively represent particular constituencies that prefer high to low inflation.

Second, the inverse correlation between independence and inflation does not necessarily imply causation. Posen (1995a), for example, argues that the costs of disinflation are no lower and disinflation occurs no faster when central banks have high independence rankings. Posen also finds that governments' seigniorage revenue does not decline with central bank independence. These results suggest that central bank independence may be the result of a coalition of anti-inflation interests or a deeper political consensus against inflation, rather than a separate anti-inflation force (see Posen 1995b).[5]

Third, the concept of central bank independence is fragile and difficult to define. At the Bundesbank, for example, the finance minister was an ex officio member of the committee that set monetary policy (in sharp contrast to the United States), though it was typically ranked among the most independent central banks. A simple vote in the German parliament could have altered the Bundesbank's structure. With the reunification of Germany, it was the German parliament—over the strenuous objection of the Bundesbank—that determined that the conversion of the ostmark into the deutschmark would take place at a one-to-one ratio. Because the market rate of the ostmark was substantially below one-to-one, the government effectively forced the Bundesbank to engage in a large increase in the money supply. Finally, it might be very difficult to create an index of central bank independence that is not affected by the historical inflation performance of the central banks.

### 3.2. Fixed Exchange Rates as a Disciplinary Device

Following World War II, there was a consensus that a fixed exchange rate regime such as Bretton Woods would provide an effective way to discipline the central bank and to check inflation. Bretton Woods broke down in the early 1970s, precisely because central banks (in particular, the Federal Reserve) were pursuing faster money growth than was consistent with Bretton Woods parities. As figure 1 shows, worldwide inflation was increasing during the 1960s but took off sharply after the end of Bretton Woods in 1973. The lesson that some economists and policymakers have drawn from this is that some form of exchange rate peg can provide an effective means of reining in domestic inflation forces.[6]

In certain circumstances, some form of pegging has been effective. The currency boards of Hong Kong and Estonia, for example, have been effective means of reducing inflation. The recent trend toward lower inflation, however, has been accompanied by less reliance on fixed or pegged regimes around the world

---

[5]  Actual experience with high inflation makes voters aware of its costs in a way that no argument from an economist can. The experience can provide information to voters so that citizens (hence, the median voter) put a more negative weight on inflation.

[6]  In recent years, the International Monetary Fund does not seem to be of a single mind on this issue, evidenced by the fact that it encourages maintaining exchange rate pegs in some situations but floating rates in others.

(figure 4). In addition, the end of exchange rate pegs in recent years has generally not led to significantly higher sustained inflation after devaluation.

**Figure 4: Fraction of All Countries Using Fixed Exchange Rate**

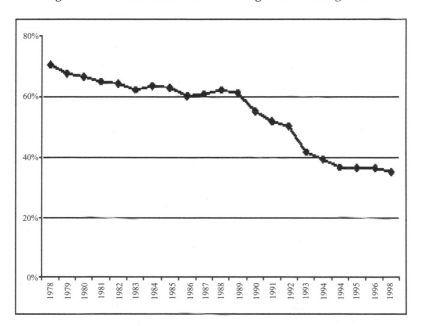

Note: The number of the countries ranges from 136 to 182 countries. The currency is under the fixed exchange rate regime if it is pegged to another single currency or to a composite of currencies.
Source: *International Financial Statistics*.

Consider the case of the Brazilian devaluation in early 1999. Given Brazil's history of hyperinflation and the important role that many believed the peg to the dollar played in bringing inflation down in the mid-1990s (figure 5), there was much concern about high inflation following the devaluation and floating of the currency. As the lower panel of figure 5 shows, however, Brazil's inflation performance was little different after the devaluation than it was in the years following the peg in 1994. There has been no sign of a return to the hyperinflation of the late 1980s and early 1990s.

Russia provides a similar example. After experiencing extremely high inflation in the early 1990s, Russia was able to stabilize the value of the ruble and peg it to the dollar. The peg was seen as an important commitment device, which helped to achieve low inflation through 1996 and 1997 (figure 6). A series of adverse shocks and fiscal problems during 1998 caused a serious deterioration of Russia's economic conditions, setting the stage for a crisis. At the height of the crisis in August 1998, Russia stopped payment on some of its debt and broke the peg,

**Figure 5:  Brazil Monthly Inflation (1980–2000)**

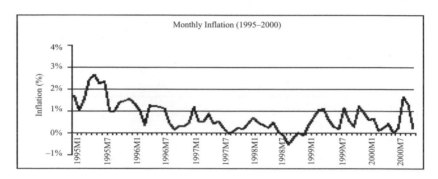

Note:  Monthly inflation is defined as a change of the consumer price index from the previous month.
Source:  *International Financial Statistics.*

**Figure 6:  Russia Monthly Inflation (1992–2000)**

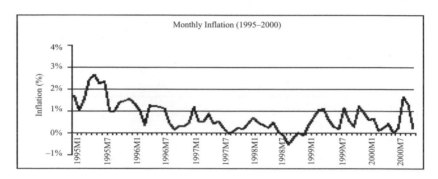

Note:  Monthly inflation is defined as a change of the consumer price index from the previous month.
Source:  *International Financial Statistics.*

causing the ruble to fall nearly 70 percent against the dollar. As figure 6 shows, however, the devaluation led to an initial sharp increase in the price level (as imports became more expensive in local terms), but it did not lead to sustained inflation. Subsequent inflation performance has been similar to that experienced during the low-inflation years of the peg. These examples illustrate that within the last few years, moving from a pegged to a floating exchange rate—even during a financial "crisis"—need not result in poorer inflation performance. Other forces, in addition to the discipline of an exchange rate peg, keep central banks from pursuing high-inflation policies.

### 3.3. Reductions in Transactions Costs and Currency Competition

A generally overlooked explanation for the recent decline in worldwide inflation is the effective erosion of the local central bank monopoly on the provision of monetary services. Advances in electronic payments technologies during the last decade and the widespread availability of alternative instruments for hand-to-hand transactions now permit competition among currencies and means of payment.[7] Dramatic cost reductions and increases in the reliability of information gathering, processing, and dissemination in the financial markets have made it possible to bypass locally issued money for undertaking both small and large transactions. A combination of the emergence of credit card networks and the Internet, lower telecommunication and computing costs, and greater security and reliability of electronic transactions now makes holding assets and transacting in U.S. dollars, for example, possible for a much larger number of individuals and businesses outside the U.S. than was the case a decade ago. While these are not the only forces putting greater discipline on central banks, I believe that increased competition through technological advances plays a significant role, and these forces are likely to grow in importance in the future.[8]

These innovations affect the central bank's ability and incentives to pursue a policy of high inflation. When few low-cost alternatives to central bank money exist for undertaking transactions in an economy, the government can raise more revenue through the inflation tax on real balances (seigniorage) than it can when feasible alternatives exist. Individuals and businesses may tolerate a "tax" on the national currency because of the inconvenience of using means other than the national currency for transactions. They will tolerate this tax to the extent the convenience of using the national currency outweighs the burden of the tax.

---

7 Many alternative currencies circulated in Weimar Germany during the hyperinflation, but they did not exercise an important disciplinary force on the Reichsbank. Thus, the availability of currencies for hand-to-hand transactions does not appear to be sufficient to keep a central bank in check.
8 An unsigned essay on "Governments and Money" in the Federal Reserve Bank of Cleveland's 1995 annual report anticipated some of the themes on currency competition. I thank David Altig for alerting me to this reference.

As technological innovation reduces the cost and inconvenience of using alternatives to the national currency, however, individuals and businesses will switch more of their transactions away from the national currency for each level of the inflation tax. With improved transactions technology and the availability of physical dollars for smaller transactions, for example, demand for the national currency becomes more sensitive to the inflation rate. In this setting, the central bank's attempt to increase its inflation rate will lead to substitution toward more stable currencies.

This argument is analogous to Hayek's vision of competition among privately issued monies—that is, if the available media have similar transactional-convenience properties, competition will lead people to shun the depreciating media and to demand the more stable media (see Hayek 1978, 38–39, quoted below). Hayek assumes that the competing currencies had similar transactional-convenience properties. I argue, however, that technological innovation has changed the relative convenience of using the national currency, so that this type of currency competition is now operating to a greater extent among central bank monies.

The greater elasticity of demand resulting from technological innovation reduces the amount of revenue the government can raise for each unit of inflation. In addition, the larger the pre-existing holdings of foreign currency for a given level of national economic activity (perhaps due to past inflation experiences or concerns about the credibility of the national central bank), the lower the amount of seigniorage revenue that can be earned for each unit of inflation.[9] Thus, inflation becomes a much less efficient means of raising revenue for the national government, and the government has less incentive to tax through inflation. If there is a fixed cost involved in switching (or developing and implementing the technology to facilitate the usage of an alternative money), seigniorage revenues for a unit of inflation would decline rapidly for greater levels of inflation, again undercutting the incentive for high inflation.

Increased monetary competition helps to explain why Brazil and Russia did not experience high inflation after their exchange rate pegs ended in 1998 and 1999. In the mid-1990s, Brazilian banks developed an advanced electronic payments network to permit businesses and individuals with bank accounts to move their funds into dollar-denominated or dollar-indexed funds. This technology did not exist during the late 1980s and early 1990s, when Brazilian inflation was out of control. Similarly, a reliable electronic payments network with international linkages was not available to most individuals and enterprises in the early years of the new Russia, but it had developed by the late 1990s.

---

[9]    See Jeremy Stein's comment following this essay for an illustration of this proposition.

In both countries, the availability of U.S. dollars (and deutschmarks in the former Soviet states) for hand-to-hand transactions increased rapidly during the decade, so that by the late 1990s, low-cost alternatives to using the local currency were readily available. The demand for foreign currency is a legacy of previous bouts of inflation, and it shows that the national currency did not regain its effective monopoly after inflation came down for a few years. The inflation spike in Russia, for example, was short-lived, at least partly because feasible alternative transactions media were at hand. The next section describes the sharp worldwide increase in international holdings of U.S. dollars and deutschmarks during the 1990s.

### 3.4. Rapid Growth of International Currency Holdings of Dollars and Deutschmarks

One aspect of the growing currency competition is that economic actors have access to an alternative money in which to undertake transactions. Recent studies suggest the availability of relatively stable currencies (such as the U.S. dollar and the deutschmark) outside their domestic markets is large and increasing (Doyle 2001). Compared with most other countries, the United States and Germany have very high levels of currency per capita, if the denominator is taken to be the domestic population. Table 2 compares the total amount of currency outstanding and currency per capita for a number of countries. Currency in circulation is roughly $1,750 per capita for the United States and roughly $2,000 per capita for Germany.

These extremely high levels of cash holdings, as well as the obvious availability of U.S. dollars and deutschmarks in other countries, have led economists to try to calculate how much of these currencies are held abroad.[10] Porter and Judson (1996), for example, estimate that 50 percent to 70 percent of the stock of U.S. currency is outside the United States, whereas Feige (1997), using direct data on currency shipments out of the country, estimates 30 percent of U.S. currency is abroad. For Germany, the share of deutschmarks abroad is estimated to be between 40 percent (Seitz 1995) and 70 percent (Doyle 2001).

Given the large currency stocks of the United States and Germany, these estimates imply a significant degree of competition exists within countries between the U.S. dollar and the deutschmark and domestic currencies around the world. To argue that such competition is a factor in the recent decline in inflation rates, however, requires evidence that the competition has been increasing. While most of the estimates just cited are averages for recent time periods, Doyle (2001) examines currency substitution from the 1960s to the 1990s and finds that currency substitution in the form of cash tripled during the 1990s in constant-dollar terms.

---

[10] When U.S. households and businesses are asked about their currency holdings, the numbers they report imply that only 8 percent to 18 percent of this amount is in their hands (see Doyle 2001).

Figure 7 illustrates the sharp increase in dollars estimated to be held outside the United States during the 1990s. The total amount of U.S. and German currency held by foreigners in 1996 was roughly $220 billion in 1990 dollars.[11]

### Table 2: Currency per Capita, 1998

| Country | Current (Billion U.S. Dollar) | Population (Million) | Currency per capita (U.S. Dollar) |
|---|---|---|---|
| Argentina | 13.51 | 36.12 | 374.02 |
| Australia | 13.99 | 18.73 | 746.77 |
| Brazil | 17.53 | 161.79 | 108.33 |
| Canada | 21.12 | 30.25 | 698.03 |
| Chile | 2.06 | 14.82 | 139.19 |
| Czech Republic | 4.26 | 10.29 | 413.92 |
| Denmark | 5.40 | 5.30 | 1,018.95 |
| France | 51.03 | 58.85 | 867.13 |
| Germany | 161.97 | 82.02 | 1,974.80 |
| Hungary | 3.05 | 10.11 | 301.22 |
| Iceland | 0.09 | 0.27 | 337.78 |
| India | 38.24 | 970.93 | 39.39 |
| Ireland | 4.52 | 3.70 | 1,222.00 |
| Italy | 75.54 | 57.59 | 1,311.69 |
| Japan | 469.81 | 126.41 | 3,716.56 |
| Mexico | 11.77 | 95.83 | 122.79 |
| Netherlands | 21.65 | 15.71 | 1,378.32 |
| New Zealand | 0.91 | 3.79 | 239.66 |
| Poland | 8.63 | 38.67 | 223.07 |
| Russia | 9.10 | 146.54 | 62.08 |
| Saudi Arabia | 12.02 | 20.18 | 595.69 |
| Slovenia | 0.58 | 1.98 | 293.43 |
| South Africa | 3.16 | 42.13 | 74.97 |
| Switzerland | 25.74 | 7.11 | 3,620.42 |
| Thailand | 8.67 | 61.20 | 141.75 |
| United Kingdom | 31.61 | 58.85 | 537.07 |
| United States | 473.19 | 270.56 | 1,748.93 |

Note: Currency in U.S. dollar is the currency in national unit converted by the exchange rate of the U.S. dollar against the national currency. All data are end-of-the-year data.
Source: *International Financial Statistics*.

As figure 8 shows, from the 1960s until the early 1970s, the fraction of U.S. dollar and deutschmark currency stocks held by foreigners drifted downward. In the late 1970s and early 1980s, this number moved up sharply as inflation picked up in Latin America. Foreign currency holdings then jumped again in the late 1980s and early 1990s and continued to rise sharply through the 1990s, coinciding with high inflations in Latin America and the former Soviet bloc.[12]

---

[11] Doyle (2001) also calculates the amount of Swiss currency held by foreigners to be roughly $21 billion in 1990 dollars.

[12] Doyle (2001) also has some suggestive information as to who is using this money. He finds evidence of relatively large seasonal components in the demand for foreign holdings. Drug smuggling and other illegal activities, however, are unlikely to have strong seasonal components. If other countries a have a seasonal currency demand that is similar to the U.S. pattern, Doyle's results suggest that households and businesses in foreign countries (rather than illegal operations) are key players in the demand for currency.

**Figure 7: World Dollarization (in 1990 U.S. Dollars)**

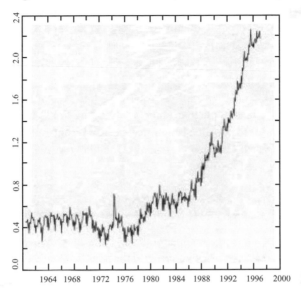

Source: Doyle (2001).

**Figure 8: Foreign Holdings as a Percentage of the Currency Stock for the U.S. and Germany**

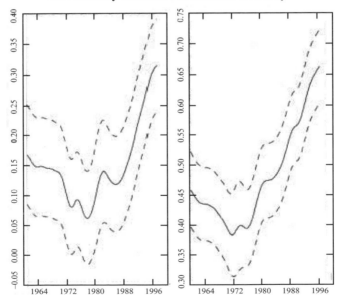

Note: The dashed lines represent 2 standard error bands.
Source: Doyle (2001).

A notable feature of the estimates is that foreign holdings of U.S. dollars and deutchmarks do not appear to have fallen after inflation rates declined. Figure 8 shows only a slight dip in the fraction of foreign holdings during the mid- to late 1980s before climbing sharply through the 1990s, even as domestic inflation rates began to fall. This suggests that domestic currencies, even after domestic inflation comes down, do not regain anything close to their previous market share of domestic transactions. The persistence of the use of the foreign currencies (or "hysteresis") seems to have been particularly important during the last decade, as foreign currency holdings have remained high despite the recent reduction in domestic inflation rates. The national central banks are unlikely to regain their monopoly position in the foreseeable future.

## 4. CHALLENGES TO CENTRAL BANKS FROM THE PRIVATE SECTOR FOLLOWING IMPROVEMENTS IN TRANSACTIONS TECHNOLOGY

This discussion of currency competition has focused primarily on competition among different government fiat monies and the beneficial effect of increased competition on central bank behavior. Next, I would like to speculate on how the same forces of technological innovation in payments and transactions services increase the feasibility of private-sector competition to government fiat money.

### 4.1. Concerns about the Feasibility of Currency Competition and the Role of Transactions Costs

A number of questions have been raised about the feasibility of full-fledged currency competition (see Issing 2000). One concern arises from the currency-substitution literature, which says that multiple competing monies in one economy could produce an explosion of velocity and instability/indeterminacy of money demand (see Girton and Roper 1981; Giovannini and Turtelboom 1994). If my argument is correct—increased competition among fiat monies has led to greater price-level stability—then this concern does not appear to have much empirical relevance. It is unclear why private, parallel fiat monies would pose any more problems for the stability of money demand than parallel government fiat currencies (if private provision of monetary services takes the form of "unbacked" issues—see below for alternatives).

Gresham's law that "bad money will drive out good" is another concern that has been raised about private currency competition. Would market competition in money simply lead to a race to the bottom? Hayek (1978, 38–39) argues that the competitive process would result in a race to the top:

Gresham's law will apply *only* to difference kinds of money between which a fixed rate of exchange is enforced by *law*. If the law makes two kinds of money perfect substitutes for the payment of debts and forces creditors to accept a coin of a smaller content of gold in the place of one with a larger content, debtors will, of course, pay only in the former and find profitable use for the substance of the latter.

With variable exchange rates, however, the inferior quality money would be valued at a lower rate and, particularly if it threatened to fall further in value, people would try to get rid of it as quickly as possible. The selection process would go on towards whatever they regarded as the best sort of money among those issued by the various agencies, and it would rapidly drive out money found to be inconvenient or worthless. [italics in original]

Transactions costs and convenience, which Hayek mentions in his last sentence, are fundamental to how the competition will operate. As Rolnick and Weber (1986) have emphasized, it is rare to have a nonmarket fixed rate of exchange between currencies enforced in practice. "Black" and "gray" markets develop. Historically, both "good" and "bad" monies tend to circulate simultaneously, and it is unusual for one to completely drive out the other. Economic agents would attempt to price the gold or silver content relative to par—for example, a silver dollar would be worth 104.2 cents in gold, and a silver nickel would be worth 5.21 cents in gold. If there is a fixed transactions cost involved in the non-par pricing of the coins (that is, the cost is independent of the denomination), then traders may not be willing to pay the premium on the silver nickel, but they would do so on the silver dollar. If that were the case, the silver dollar would continue to circulate along with the gold coins, but the silver nickel would not. A corrected version of Gresham's law can be based on a fixed transactions cost rather than a fixed rate of exchange: "Bad money drives good money out of circulation only when the costs of using the good money at a premium are significant" (Rolnick and Weber 1986, 198).

Advances in transactions technologies and increases in the liquidity of markets have dramatically reduced the costs of pricing a wide variety of potential payments media. Reductions in the costs of monitoring the value of privately issued instruments and the costs of converting from one instrument to another play an important role in determining the feasibility and form of private-sector competition in money.

### 4.2. Alternative Approaches to Currency Competition and "Free Banking"

Alternative approaches to currency competition fit into three broad categories that correspond to three models of so-called "free banking" (Selgin and White 1994; Hayek 1978; Cowen and Kroszner 1994). The key aspect in each approach is that government involvement in the money and payments system is dramatically reduced or eliminated, and the role of private producers of monetary services is greatly enhanced. At the core of each approach is the ability of private banks, firms, or individuals to issue instruments that will be used as means of payment (media of exchange). Monetary policy, to the extent that such a concept is operative when monetary issues are decentralized, would be largely in the hands of the private sector. I will provide only an extremely compact summary here, with special attention to how technology affects the feasibility of the alternative approaches.[13]

In the first scenario, the economy has a common medium of settlement, that is, all monetary instruments are ultimately redeemable in a single base (or "outside") money at a fixed rate. The base money also serves as the common unit of account in the economy; gold, silver, or other commodities could serve as the base money. Selgin (1988) even proposes freezing the total quantity of government-issued fiat money at a particular point and then using that as the medium of settlement in a free-banking economy. Private firms then issue notes that are redeemable and denominated in the base money. Historical episodes of so-called "free banking," such as the eighteenth and nineteenth centuries in Scotland, generally operated in this manner (Cowen and Kroszner 1989, 1992; White 1984). Periodic clearing of balancing among issuers and the right of redemption were the keys to preventing excess private-note issuance.

A second approach involves private firms issuing competing base monies (this is the scenario that Hayek proposes). Firms effectively issue private fiat monies because their issues are not redeemable. The issuers make commitments either to limit the quantity of issue or to maintain the purchasing power in terms of some index. Hayek appears to have had in mind that there would be a common unit of account. The reputation of the issuers and monitoring of the quantity issued by the market are the key factors in making this competition feasible.[14] Illustrated by the quotation in the previous section, Hayek argued that people would not hold unstable and depreciating monies so that competition would generate monetary stability.

While improvements in monitoring technology and reductions in the transactions costs of using alternative media are important to improving the chances for successful operation of private monetary competition in the first two scenarios, the third relies more heavily on technological advances. This scenario involves a more fundamental change in how the monetary system operates because there is a separation of the medium of exchange from the unit of account. This approach can be characterized as developing from the "legal restrictions theory of money" and the "new monetary economics" and involving "sophisticated barter" (Fama 1980; Hall 1982; Greenfield and Yeager 1983; Wallace 1983; Cowen and Kroszner 1994).

---

[13] For book-length treatments, see White (1984), Selgin (1988), and Cowen and Kroszner (1994). Friedman and Macintosh (forthcoming) analyze how technological innovation undercuts traditional objections to "free banking."

[14] In principle, there should not be greater acceptability problems for alternative monies than for alternative credit cards: For instance, some establishments accept only cash or Visa and Mastercard, but not American Express, Discover, or Diner's Club, or charge a fee to use one or the other.

In such a sophisticated barter system, the media of exchange are explicit and continuously priced. Marketable financial assets serve as media of exchange and offer dividends and interest, as well as capital gains and losses. Electronic information and transfer systems might be used to price these media conveniently and at a low cost. Crediting or debiting of accounts can take place at prevailing "exchange rates" among the various media. Issuers of financial assets have an incentive to increase the liquidity and marketability of their instruments in order to enhance their demand as media of exchange. Individuals and firms can choose to hold whichever assets best satisfy their risk-return preferences, and they do not have to forgo a return on the assets they use as exchange media. The desire to obtain pecuniary returns motivates the displacement of non-return-bearing money as we know it in a deregulated environment. Returns also could be provided through various "discounts" on exchange media, which would provide implicit interest (see Smith and Weber 1999). Physical forms of exchange media could eventually disappear as transactions technology improves.[15]

The distinction between money and other highly liquid assets is increasingly difficult to draw. Financial intermediaries might evolve away from traditional depository institutions toward institutions that more closely resemble mutual funds (Cowen and Kroszner 1990). Other intermediaries would engage in lending that we traditionally associate with banks, much as finance companies do today, and then repackage and securitize their assets and sell them to the market.[16] If the banking intermediaries are effectively mutual funds holding liquid assets, then the problem of a bank "run" is minimized because the value of the deposit shares issued by the institution is continuously priced based on the value of the assets in the portfolio.

The explicit pricing of exchange media could even occur in terms of multiple units of account. To the extent that transactions and information technology allows low-cost pricing—of groceries to bonds—multiple units of account could arise within an economy.[17] Wireless devices can report prices in any unit at a low cost in retail outlets using "digital price tags." "Currency-transparent" browsers can read prices from a seller's Web page in one unit, convert the prices to the units desired by the buyer using a conversion rate from the seller's financial institution, and display them for the buyer in the preferred unit (see Friedman and Macintosh forthcoming). While any discussion of how payments and pricing systems of the

---

[15] If there is a desire for anonymity or distrust of the electronic network, bearer bonds could provide a medium for such exchanges.

[16] This raises the question of whether the liquidity-supply function associated with traditional banking could be supplied through these other intermediaries. See Kashyap, Rajan, and Stein (1999) for a discussion of the role of traditional banks as liquidity providers.

[17] In Chile, for example, an "indexed" unit of account—"UF"—is calculated daily and reported in the newspapers in addition to the peso. Many long-term contracts are denominated in UFs.

future may evolve is speculative, such an inquiry highlights the importance of technology for affecting the costs—and hence the feasibility—of transacting with alternatives to central bank money.

## 5. SUMMARY AND CONCLUSIONS

To explain the recent decline in inflation rates around the globe, I have emphasized the role of increased currency competition. This enhanced competition has been made feasible and effective, I argue, by innovations in payments technology and information processing and dissemination. Greater international competition among monies has put discipline on the behavior of national central banks because attempting to raise revenue through seigniorage is less effective and more costly than it once was. Even countries with notorious recent histories of high inflation, such as Brazil and Russia, have kept inflation in check even after breaking their pegs to the U.S. dollar.

I then considered the implications of payments innovations and increased competition among government fiat monies for future competition from the private sector in the provision of monetary services. Technological advances appear to be making competition from the private sector increasingly feasible. National central banks' local monopolies are being eroded by competition from other central banks and from the private sector.[18] How payments technologies evolve will play a key role in determining the forms of private monetary competition that will develop and the future challenges that central banks will face.

## ACKNOWLEDGMENTS

The author thanks Jeffrey Lacker, Jeremy Stein, David Altig, Brian Doyle, conference participants, and anonymous referees for their comments.

---

[18] I do not consider here the political economy of these changes and the likely response. This is an important topic, but it is beyond the scope of this paper (see Kroszner 2000). One speculation is that the reduction in feasible seigniorage revenue from central bank activities that has already occurred and cannot be legislated back might reduce the ability of central bankers to convince legislators to help them to maintain their monopolies.

## REFERENCES

Alesina, Alberto, and Lawrence Summers. 1993. Central Bank Independence and Macroeconomic Performance: Some Comparative Evidence. *Journal of Money, Credit, and Banking* 25: 151–62.

Barro, Robert J., and David B. Gordon. 1983. Rules, Discretion, and Reputation in a Model of Monetary Policy. *Journal of Monetary Economics* 12: 101–22.

Cowen, Tyler, and Randall Kroszner. 1989. Scottish Banking before 1845: A Model for Laissez-Faire? *Journal of Money, Credit, and Banking* 21: 221–31.

———. 1990. Mutual Fund Banking: A Market Approach. *Cato Journal* 10: 223–37.

———. 1992. Scottish Free Banking. In *The New Palgrave Dictionary of Money and Finance*, edited by John Eatwell, Murray Milgate, and Peter Newman, 398–400. London: Macmillan.

———. 1994. *Explorations in the New Monetary Economics*. Cambridge: Basil Blackwell.

Doyle, Brian. 2001. "Here, Dollars, Dollars..."—Estimating Currency Demand and Worldwide Currency Substitution. Board of Governors of the Federal Reserve System, International Finance Discussion Paper no. 657, February.

Fama, Eugue. 1980. Banking in the Theory of Finance. *Journal of Monetary Economics* 6: 39–57.

Feige, Edgar. 1997. Revised Estimates of the Underground Economy: Implications of U.S. Currency Held Abroad. In *The Underground Economy: Global Evidence of its Size and Impact*, edited by Owen Lippert and Michael Walker. Vancouver: Fraser Institute.

Friedman, David, and Kerry Macintosh. Forthcoming. Technology and the Case for Free Banking. In *The Half-Life of Policy Rationales: How New Technology Affects Old Policy Issues*, edited by Daniel Klein. New York: New York University Press.

Giovannini, Alberto, and Bart Turtelboom. 1994. Currency Substitution. In *The Handbook of International Macroeconomics*, edited by Frederick van der Ploeg. Oxford: Basil Blackwell.

Girton, Lance, and Don Roper. 1981. Theory and Implications of Currency Substitution. *Journal of Money, Credit, and Banking* 13: 12–30.

Greenfield, Robert, and Leland Yeager. 1983. A Laissez-Faire Approach to Monetary Stability. *Journal of Money, Credit, and Banking* 15: 302–15.

Hall, Robert. 1982. Monetary Trends in the United States and the United Kingdom: A Review from the Perspective of New Developments in Monetary Economics. *Journal of Economic Literature* 20: 1552–56.

Hayek, Frederick von. 1978. *Denationalization of Money: An Analysis of the Theory and Practice of Concurrent Currencies*. 2nd ed. London: Institute of Economic Affairs.

Issing, Otmar. 2000. Hayek, Currency Competition, and European Monetary Union. Institute for Economic Affairs, Occasional Paper no. 111.

Kashyap, Anil, Raghuram Rajan, and Jeremy Stein. 1999. Banks as Liquidity Providers: An Explanation for the Co-Existence of Lending and Deposit Taking. National Bureau of Economic Research, Working Paper no. 6962, February.

Klein, Benjamin. 1974. The Competitive Supply of Money. *Journal of Money, Credit, and Banking* 6: 423–53.

Kroszner, Randall. 2000. The Economics and Politics of Financial Modernization. *Federal Reserve Bank of New York Economic Policy Review* 6: 25–37.

Mas, Ignacio. 1995. Things Governments Do to Money: A Recent History of Currency Reform Schemes and Scams. *Kyklos* 48: 483–512.

Porter, Richard, and Ruth Judson. 1996. The Location of U.S. Currency: How Much is Abroad? Board of Governors of the Federal Reserve System, unpublished manuscript, April 15.

Posen, Adam. 1995a. Central Bank Independence and Disinflationary Credibility: A Missing Link? Federal Reserve Bank of New York, Staff Report, May.

———. 1995b. Declarations Are Not Enough: Financial Sector Sources of Central Bank Independence. In *NBER Macroeconomics Annual 1995*, 253–74. Cambridge: MIT Press.

Rolnick, Arthur, and Warren Weber. 1986. Gresham's Law or Gresham's Fallacy? *Journal of Political Economy* 94: 185–99.

Seitz, Franz. 1995. The Circulation of Deutsche Marks Abroad. Deutsche Bundesbank, Discussion Paper no. 1/95, May.

Selgin, George. 1988. *The Theory of Free Banking*. Totowa, N.J.: Rowman and Littlefield.

———, and Lawrence White. 1994. How Would the Invisible Hand Handle Money? *Journal of Economic Literature* 32: 1718–49.

Shleifer, Andrei, and Daniel Treisman. 2000. *Without A Map: Political Tactics and Economic Reform in Russia*. Cambridge: MIT Press.

Smith, Bruce, and Warren Weber. 1999. Private Money Creation and the Suffolk Banking System. *Journal of Money, Credit, and Banking* 31: 624–59.

Vaubel, Roland. 1977. Free Currency Competition. *Weltwirtschaftliches Archiv* 113: 435–59.

Wallace, Neil. 1983. A Legal Restrictions Theory of the Demand for "Money" and the Role of Monetary Policy. *Federal Reserve Bank of Minneapolis Quarterly Review* 7: 1–7.

White, Lawrence. 1984. *Free Banking in Britain: Theory, Experience, and Debate, 1800–1845*. Cambridge: Cambridge University Press.

# Commentary

*Jeremy C. Stein*

This very interesting paper by Randy Kroszner has two parts. The first part sketches a novel theory, namely that competition from foreign currencies (such as the U.S. dollar and the deutschmark) has helped to reduce worldwide inflation in recent years. The second part speculates on the future of financial innovation and the potential for private monies to become an increasingly important substitute for central bank money. In my comments, I will focus on the first part of the paper.

As I understand it, Kroszner's theoretical story goes something like this: Governments like to raise revenue through seigniorage. When private agents have no alternatives to domestic central bank money for their transactional needs, it is easy for the government to engage in seigniorage. In contrast, when agents can switch to dollars, for example, when making transactions, the government cannot raise as much seigniorage revenue for a given amount of inflation. If we further assume that the government trades the benefits of seigniorage against some other (unspecified) costs of inflation in a fixed way, it should inflate less.

An example may help to illustrate the logic behind the theory. In scenario A, imagine that Russian households initially hold 100 rubles as their only form of transaction balance, and the only good in the Russian economy is 100 units of corn. The price of corn is one ruble. Starting from this position, suppose the Russian central bank prints 100 more rubles. The government will extract real seigniorage revenue equal to 50 units of corn and the price level will double, so that each unit of corn now costs two rubles.

Alternatively, consider scenario B: The Russian economy is partially dollarized and households hold 50 rubles and 50 dollars, and there are still 100 units of corn. The initial price of corn is equal to either one ruble or one dollar. Now, suppose the Russian central bank prints another 50 rubles. In this case, the real seigniorage revenue is only 25 units of corn—that is, just half what it was in scenario A. But there is just as much ruble inflation as there was before, because the quantity of rubles has once again doubled—that is, the price of corn goes from one ruble to two rubles.

This example helps to clarify the assumptions that are required for Kroszner's story. On one hand, it seems plausible that if Russian citizens get burned once holding rubles, they will be less inclined to do so in the future, and they may prefer to hold dollars instead. In other words, it is plausible that, following a period of high inflation, the Russian economy could transition from scenario A to scenario B. However, this is not sufficient for the reduced-future-inflation result; the government also must have preferences that trade seigniorage revenues for inflation in a particular way.

Specifically, if the government's objective function puts fixed weights on seigniorage revenues and inflation, Kroszner's result will emerge—there will be less inflation in scenario B because the Russian government gets less real revenue for a given amount of inflation. However, apparently reasonable modifications to the government's objective function can significantly alter the conclusion. First of all, one might wonder why there should be a fixed distaste for inflation that is invariant to the level of ruble balances held by households. Perhaps some of the distortions that accompany inflation (for example, arbitrary transfers of wealth) are less pronounced when private agents hold lower balances of rubles. If so, the government has less reason to worry about inflation in scenario B, and we might get as much or more inflation in this scenario.

As an extreme version of this critique, consider what happens when the government's *only* objective is to generate seigniorage revenue, and it does not attach any direct disutility to inflation. (Perhaps its ability to collect taxes is badly impaired, and so seigniorage is the only way it can continue to fund itself.) In the language of the previous example, suppose the Russian government simply diverts real seigniorage revenue of 50 units of corn to itself. In scenario A, it can do so by doubling the quantity of rubles outstanding, and hence doubling the price level. In scenario B, the quantity of rubles must be infinitely large, thus creating an unbounded level of inflation. The bottom line is that with less domestic currency outstanding, the desire to generate a given target level of real seigniorage revenue leads to more—not less—inflation.

This example is intentionally extreme, but it makes the point that the model's conclusions hinge on a particular form for the government's objectives. It would be nice to have some further theory or some evidence to help us think about whether these sorts of government preferences are reasonable.

Despite this quibble, there is much to like about the theory. Most notably, it makes a number of novel and sharp empirical predictions. To take just one example, it suggests that, in a cross-section of countries, the extent to which a country's economy dollarizes in period $t$ should forecast the degree to which its inflation rate comes down in subsequent periods. Of course, one must take care in implementing any test of this proposition, because there are obvious endogeneity problems—for example, an agent's desire to hold dollars undoubtedly depends partly on his expectations of future inflation. Still, it seems there is plenty of scope for taking the theory seriously from an empirical perspective.

A related observation that may be helpful in this regard is that the theory can also be tested using cross-country or time-series variations in domestic currency balances that are attributable to factors other than dollarization. Conceptually, the effect of dollarization is no different in the example above than it is for any other financial innovation (for example, a money market fund with a debit card) that allows households to get by with lower real balances of domestic currency. Anything that leads to lower domestic currency balances reduces the government's ability to generate seigniorage revenue in exactly the same way.

Finally, let me venture one quick thought on the second part of the paper. Kroszner speculates on the future, and he asks whether one should be concerned that further development of private monies (or other related innovations) might erode the central bank's traditional monopoly over money creation, compromising the effectiveness of monetary policy.

On one hand, it is hard to argue with the premise that financial innovation is likely to reduce households' demand for the central-bank-created monetary base (that is, currency) and to make this demand more elastic. What is less clear is the extent to which this matters at all for monetary policy. Most likely, the answer depends on one's model of how monetary policy affects the economy. Perhaps if one takes the traditional IS/LM view—according to which imperfect household substitutability across central-bank-provided money and other assets is the sole key to the central bank's ability to move interest rates—then financial innovation might arguably have a meaningful impact.

But if one takes a more bankcentric view of the transmission mechanism, the sorts of innovations that Kroszner discusses seem less significant for monetary policy. According to this view, the central bank's monopoly power—hence, its ability to influence interest rates and, ultimately, real activity—stems not from household currency demand, but from commercial banks' demands for reserves. Banks value reserves because by holding reserves, they can issue demand deposits and gain access to federal deposit insurance. This seems to be an easier monopoly for the central bank to defend.

The central bank may not be able to prevent households from economizing on currency, or even from abandoning the use of currency altogether. But as long as it can stipulate that banks wishing to have access to deposit insurance must hold a portion of their reserves in the form of central-bank-provided monetary base (rather than some privately provided substitute), its traditional monopoly position should not be significantly eroded.

# Commentary

*Jeffrey M. Lacker*

This is a provocative and intriguing paper. The author argues that the decline in average inflation rates over the last decade or so might be the result, at least in part, of an inward shift in the demand for locally issued money that is caused by innovations in payments technologies. The idea is that governments now find it more difficult to raise revenue through the inflation tax, and so, to some extent, they've simply given up. My approach to this subject is quite sympathetic to the idea that payments-system developments might have discernable macroeconomic effects; however, Kroszner's conjecture is fairly ambitious, and it would take a significant amount of further research to convince the profession of its validity. Instead, his paper has the more modest goal of simply putting an intriguing hypothesis on the table for consideration. This leaves a discussant free to appraise the prospects for future research.

Kroszner's hypothesis naturally breaks down into two distinct questions. The first is a factual question: Have payments technologies changed in such a way as to reduce the ability or desire of governments to earn seigniorage through the inflation tax? The second is a political economy question: Is this why some countries have selected lower inflation rates? I will discuss these questions before turning to some competing hypotheses that I think should figure in future research.

The essential factual question is whether money demand became significantly more elastic in the 1990s, because the elasticity of money demand determines whether it is difficult to raise total seigniorage revenue by increasing the inflation rate. Larger elasticity of money demand implies a lower seigniorage-maximizing rate of inflation and a greater rate of revenue loss in response to increased inflation.

First, it is important to be clear about exactly what margins of substitution we are talking about. Consider a simple fourfold categorization of payment instruments. Instruments are either local or not, and they are either paper or electronic. For Argentina, say, peso notes are a local paper instrument, and dollar-denominated bank deposits are a nonlocal electronic instrument. Consider the margin of substitution between a local paper currency and local electronic payment arrangements— for example, credit or debit cards. In the absence of bank interest rate restrictions, the profitability of implementing a substitute for currency includes the private benefit of reducing the incidence of the seigniorage tax on currency.[1]

---

[1] This characteristic is a hallmark of models in which currency competes with credit instruments as a means of payment (Lacker 1996).

An increase in inflation will make electronic payment instruments—credit cards, debit cards, and the like—more profitable. It is plausible that this is an empirically significant margin of substitution. Most governments probably earn far more seigniorage on paper currency than on electronic currency; for example, at the end of 2000, the amount of Federal Reserve notes outstanding was about 30 times the amount of deposits at Reserve Banks. Thus, changes in the demand for paper notes are likely to have a far greater fiscal impact than changes in the demand for bank reserves.

It is also plausible that changes in the margin of substitution between local paper and electronic currency are technologically driven, and so I think the author is right on target here. Payments arrangements are fundamentally little more than communications and record-keeping systems. We've seen dramatic reductions in the costs of communication and computing equipment in recent years. It stands to reason that such innovations pose a substantial threat to the demand for paper notes.

One might be able to find supporting evidence for Kroszner's conjecture in particular countries by looking at the time path of seigniorage revenues and checking for evidence that the revenue-maximizing rate of inflation fell. Did inflation cause the monetary base to decline? Did the use of other payment instruments increase? Which other payment instruments? Was the decrease in the monetary base large enough to offset the positive effect of inflation rates on seigniorage? In other words, on which side of the inflation–tax Laffer curve did the country find itself? Did reducing inflation lead to a recovery in seigniorage revenues?

One also should be able to document the spread of alternative payment instruments. For electronic instruments, there should be measures of transactions volume on the relevant clearing and settlement systems. These should show volume increases that match the inflation dynamics. Again, there should be evidence of significant variations in the inflation rate, at least for some countries. Indeed, one might find evidence of a "ratchet effect," in which successive bursts of inflation trigger long-lived investments in alternative payment arrangements—thus the persistent shifts in velocity.

Two observations are worth noting here. First, the author's conjecture is that the deployment of new payments technologies leads to a *decrease* in inflation. For this to occur, the implicit money-demand function must become *more* elastic as it shifts inward, so that the seigniorage-maximizing inflation rate is lower (assuming for a moment that the central bank maximizes seigniorage revenue). Conceivably, demand could shift inward in a way that results in an increase in the seigniorage-maximizing inflation rate. It is not immediately obvious how technological progress will affect the elasticity of money demand. Here, the author's thesis depends on the nature of the technological innovations taking place, as well as the regulatory regime hat constrains the substitution of private for public payment instruments.

My second observation is based on the U.S. experience: Payments arrangements generally change slowly. The rate at which the use of credit cards and ATM cards has spread, for example, is far slower than the rate at which other new consumer products have been adopted. One can speculate as to why this is so: Differences in the cost of alternative payment instruments could be quite small relative to the implicit value of other characteristics, which differ across instruments. Admittedly, American consumers have not seen the nominal interest rates associated with hyperinflation. Perhaps the adoption of new payments technologies has been more rapid in such economies. If so, this could be verified empirically with direct evidence on the volume of payments made with alternative instruments.

Now I want to consider the margin of substitution between local paper currency and foreign paper currency. The U.S. dollar and the deutschmark are both prominent, international reserve currencies. The pattern of trade relations of the these two countries, as well as the relative stability of their purchasing power, makes them promising candidates as substitutes for local currencies in countries with unstable monetary policy. It makes sense that the dollar and the deutschmark would be adopted in place of the local currency when the local currency is depreciating rapidly in real terms. However, the substitution of one paper currency for another is not likely to be directly related to innovations in payments technologies. Kroszner focuses heavily on technological innovations as contributors to the decline in worldwide inflation, yet the paper spends several pages documenting and discussing the rising international use of the dollar and the deutschmark. It seems to me there is a bit of a bait-and-switch going on. To the extent that the decline in inflation is the result of competition from the U.S. dollar or the deutschmark, it does not seem closely related to improvements in payments technologies.

The second question concerns political economy: Did many central banks and governments select lower inflation rates because they found it more difficult to raise seigniorage revenue through the inflation tax? First, I am not aware of evidence that seigniorage revenues have been an important consideration in postwar U.S. monetary policy. I recognize this is likely to have been different in other countries, particularly those experiencing hyperinflations. To make a really convincing case, however, it would be useful to see some direct evidence on the views of policymakers. Future research in this area might be directed at documenting what policymakers thought they were doing and why.

On this question, I think it would be useful if Kroszner could spell out more specifically what government behavior he is hypothesizing here. Is he saying that governments maximized seigniorage revenue? In other words, were they aiming for the top of the Laffer curve? Or did they back off maximizing seigniorage revenue because of concerns about the welfare cost of inflation? Were they equating the marginal deadweight cost of government revenue across various sources? These alternative models may have very different empirical implications.

What type of evidence would be useful here? Empirical evidence on the government's budget constraint is the obvious place to start, but I want to put in a plea for other evidence as well. There is a role here for monetary policy forensics: essentially, an answer to the question, "What were they thinking?" To make a really convincing case about the motives and perceptions of policymakers, we need the kind of history that diplomatic historians practice. We need to go beyond casual transcript reading, beyond finding dates to put names on. We need a close reading of primary sources: letters, memoranda, memoirs, interviews with participants, archival documents, and so on. The broader point is that to confirm Kroszner's conjecture about policymakers' intentions, we need to see more than circumstantial evidence—and circumstantial evidence is about all we have so far.

Let me mention two alternative hypotheses that might explain the empirical regularities that Kroszner has documented for us: one for those who think of policymakers as planners, and one for those who think of policymakers as agents. The first might be thought of as "spontaneous enlightenment." Policymakers and their constituents, tired of the costs of inflation, figure out how to stop it and muster the political will to do so. Marvin Goodfriend (1997) has written a narrative account of U.S. monetary policy from a similar point of view, wherein he terms this process "coming of age." It took time to learn that in the absence of the gold standard, the final vestiges of which were abandoned only in 1971, it is the central bank's responsibility to control inflation. It took time to learn how inflation works. It took time for the profession to learn, and then it took time for policymakers to absorb the lesson. It also took time for a political consensus to reduce inflation to emerge. And then, once the political will had been mustered, it took time to establish a credible commitment to low inflation. This is reminiscent of the experimental economies that Arifovic and Sargent display; in some of them, it took many "periods" to make it to the low-inflation Ramsey equilibrium.

A second alternative hypothesis is that inflation dynamics reflect the implications of the redistributive consequences of inflation. One redistributive flow is from the private sector to the government through seigniorage earnings—this is what Kroszner focuses on. But, in general, nominal debtors gain and nominal creditors lose, at least to the degree that inflation is unanticipated. Perhaps fluctuations in inflation have more to do with interest-group politics and the ebb and flow of the relative political power of debtors and creditors. In fact, we have good evidence suggesting that such considerations are plausible. Many recent large inflations have been associated with currency and banking crises, which are often followed by IMF lending programs. As many critics have pointed out, the way these crises play out results in large net transfers from middle-income taxpayers, who are called upon to repay the IMF indebtedness, to large debtors of the banking system, who benefit from the widespread forbearance. This suggests that in many countries, interest-group politics is capable of generating macroeconomic and regulatory policies that are wasteful, in the sense they result in fairly large extracontractual transfers.

REFERENCES

Goodfriend, Marvin S. 1997. Monetary Policy Comes of Age: A 20th Century Odyssey. *Federal Reserve Bank of Richmond Economic Quarterly* 83: 1–22.

Lacker, Jeffrey M. 1996. Stored Value Cards: Costly Private Substitutes for Government Currency. *Federal Reserve Bank of Richmond Economic Quarterly* 82: 1–25.

# Index